THE HEIRESS VS THE ESTABLISHMENT

THE HEIRESS
VS THE ESTABLISHMENT

MRS. CAMPBELL'S CAMPAIGN
FOR LEGAL JUSTCE

Constance Backhouse and Nancy L. Backhouse

UBC Press · Vancouver · Toronto

Published for The Osgoode Society for Canadian Legal History by UBC Press

15   14   13   12   11   10   09   08   07   06   05   04   5   4   3   2   1

Printed in Canada on acid-free paper

National Library of Canada Cataloguing in Publication

Backhouse, Constance, 1952-
    The heiress vs the establishment : Mrs. Campbell's campaign for legal justice / Constance Backhouse and Nancy L. Backhouse.

    (Law and society)
    Includes bibliographical references and index.
    ISBN 0-7748-1052-1

    1. Campbell, Elizabeth Louisa Bethune — Trials, litigation, etc. 2. Howland, Elizabeth Mary Rattray, Lady, 1840?-1924 — Will. 3. Inheritance and succession — Ontario. 4. Breach of trust — Ontario. I. Backhouse, Nancy II. Title. III. Series: Law and society series (Vancouver, BC)

KE237.C36B23 2004   346.71305'2'092   C2004-901749-7

UBC Press gratefully acknowledges the financial support for our publishing program of the Government of Canada through the Book Publishing Industry Development Program (BPIDP), and of the Canada Council for the Arts, and the British Columbia Arts Council.

This book has been published with the help of a grant from the Canadian Federation for the Humanities and Social Sciences, through the Aid to Scholarly Publications Programme, using funds provided by the Social Sciences and Humanities Research Council of Canada.

Printed and bound in Canada by Friesens
Designer: George Kirkpatrick
Copy editor: Judy Phillips
Proofreader: Sarah Wight
Indexer: Olga Backhouse

UBC Press
The University of British Columbia
2029 West Mall
Vancouver, BC V6T 1Z2
604-822-5959 / Fax: 604-822-6083
www.ubcpress.ca

CONTENTS

ILLUSTRATIONS

FOREWORD

The Osgoode Society for Canadian Legal History

FOR MORE than two centuries, lawyers and judges have been powerful and formidable members of the Ontario establishment. In 1826 Family Compact leader John Strachan asserted that lawyers "will gradually engross all the colonial offices of profit and honour." In some measure at least Strachan's prediction has been amply fulfilled.

In the 1920s one woman had the courage to challenge, almost single-handedly, leading members of the province's powerful legal establishment, and in 1940 she published a remarkable book about how some lawyers and judges used their power to defeat all her efforts and to discredit her. Hers is a story that richly deserves to be known to another generation.

We are therefore pleased to republish Mrs. Campbell's book with an extensive introduction, epilogue, and research notes by Constance and Nancy Backhouse that carefully scrutinize her account and explain and applaud her truly astounding victory. We believe Osgoode Society readers will be intrigued by this fascinating story.

The purpose of The Osgoode Society for Canadian Legal History is to encourage research and writing in the history of Canadian law. The Society, which was incorporated in 1979 and is registered as a charity, was founded at the initiative of the Honourable R. Roy McMurtry, a former attorney general for Ontario, now Chief Justice of Ontario, and officials of the Law Society of Upper Canada. Its efforts to stimulate the study of legal history in Canada include a research-support program, a graduate student research-assistance program, and work in the fields of oral history and legal archives. The Society publishes volumes of interest to its members that contribute to legal-historical scholarship in Canada, including studies of the courts, the judiciary, and the legal profession, biographies, collections of documents, studies in criminology and penology, accounts of significant trials, and work in the social and economic history of the law.

Current directors of The Osgoode Society for Canadian Legal History are Robert Armstrong, Kenneth Binks, Patrick Brode, Michael Bryant, Brian Bucknall, Archie Campbell, David Chernos, Kirby Chown, J. Douglas Ewart, Martin Friedland, Elizabeth Goldberg, John Honsberger, Horace Krever, Virginia MacLean, Frank

Marrocco, Roy McMurtry, Brendan O'Brien, Peter Oliver, Paul Reinhardt, Joel Richler, James Spence, and Richard Tinsley.

The annual report and information about membership may be obtained by writing to The Osgoode Society for Canadian Legal History, Osgoode Hall, 130 Queen Street West, Toronto, Ontario, M5H 2N6. Telephone: 416-947-3321. E-mail: mmacfarl@lsuc.on.ca. Website: www.osgoodesociety.ca.

R. Roy McMurtry
President

Peter N. Oliver
Editor-in-chief

PREFACE

THIS BOOK will be a revelation to persons concerned with the law, the court system, and, last but not least, the power and tenacity of a woman whose unquiet heart drives her actions. Professor Constance Backhouse and Madam Justice Nancy Backhouse's latest study did not come to me as a new revelation, however. In my early years at the bar, I had discovered in a used bookstore a card-backed book with a somewhat damaged dust cover carrying the compelling title *Where Angels Fear to Tread*. This was not fiction by E.M. Forster nor by any of the other five or six writers who had appropriated the same title. The phrase itself derives from Pope's "Essay on Criticism." The book I had found was one by Elizabeth Campbell; she was certainly no fool and she felt, reasonably enough, that the trustee of her late mother's estate had not dealt properly with its assets. She sought an accounting and thereby took her first steps into legal history.

As I was reading the Campbell book, with my then limited knowledge and understanding of the interstices of probate law and fiduciary accounting procedures, I did internally cheer Mrs. Campbell on with her campaign. As I read on, there arose in my mind the possibility that there might be more to the matter than the bare facts so compellingly related by Mrs. Campbell. I started to trace the path that Constance and Nancy Backhouse have outlined in their research. They entered the court archives. Professor Backhouse, as I had done, went to Boston and there found Mrs. Campbell's history — her marriage, her children, her siblings, her work at her husband's church. They followed Mrs. Campbell's investigations in Toronto leading to the citation requiring the trustee of her mother's estate to pass the accounts in the Surrogate Court. Constance and Nancy Backhouse have written the book that I felt was secreted in Mrs. Campbell's narrative. When they called me about my earlier researches, I opened my files to them with both alacrity and pleasure, knowing that at last the story that was hidden all along would now be revealed.

From the vantage point, then, of one who knows how tangled was the research, I commend the forthcoming exposition of the background and ultimate fruition of Mrs. Campbell's strong-willed prosecution of her rights. You will live with her and her ordeals and successes, with the lawyers who were her advocates, with judges who had the good fortune or misfortune of examining in (sometimes excruciating) detail the progress of Mrs. Campbell's journey, from the passing of accounts in the Carleton County Surrogate Court to her travels to and eventual personal appearance as a layperson advocating her own cause before the Law Lords who composed the panel of the Judicial Committee of the Privy Council—the metaphorical "foot of the Throne"—where indeed angels might fear to tread.

Mrs. Campbell's narrative is compelling, and Constance and Nancy Backhouse's research and exquisite rendition of Mrs. Campbell's saga is a paragon of legal exposition. Mrs. Campbell displayed tenacity in the face of many pressures—judicial, forensic, and financial—all of which are explored vividly in this volume. Mrs. Campbell concludes her account with the words "thank God, O, thank God for the Privy Council," and she goes on to "wonder what the state of affairs would be throughout Ontario should politicians ever succeed in abolishing the right of appeal to [Her] Majesty's Judicial Committee." As she wrote these words she no doubt pondered a comment by the young friend who said that only if she travelled to the Privy Council could she expect to achieve the satisfied heart—a heart at peace with itself, knowing that it had followed the judicial path to the end and had at last achieved the right.

The Hon. Sydney M. Harris,
retired judge, Ontario Court of Justice

ACKNOWLEDGMENTS

IN OCTOBER 2000, the Hon. Mr. Justice Maurice Cullity of the Ontario Superior Court forwarded to me a photocopy of a book titled *Where Angels Fear to Tread,* written by Elizabeth Bethune Campbell in 1935. In the accompanying letter, he noted that "some years ago," he had been "warned that there was some sort of injunction or interdict about it, and that the copy in the Great Library [at Osgoode Hall] was kept under lock and key in the Librarian's Desk." My interest was aroused immediately. Mr. Justice Cullity added that whatever interdict might once have existed appeared to have expired long since, and that "Mrs. Campbell's saga was obviously a cause célèbre that did not display the legal establishment in Ontario in a particularly good light." He asked me to read the book with a view to whether it might be worth republishing in Ontario these six decades later.

No one has so far been able to uncover any evidence of an official injunction on the distribution of the book, but the sense that it was circulated with stealth and read surreptitiously is certainly expressed by many lawyers and judges who recall hearing about it years ago. Knowing nothing of its context or of the circumstances that engendered the book, I sat down to read it at the end of my teaching semester, hoping to complete the task in between the seemingly infinite task of grading law school exams. I admit to initial skepticism about the project. *Where Angels Fear to Tread* did not bear the imprint of any recognizable publishing house. The title page stated simply that it was distributed from St. John's Rectory, 24 Alveston Street, Jamaica Plain, Boston. I was to learn later that this was Mrs. Campbell's marital residence. Self-published works from the early twentieth century are often cloying in style, and I began to read this one with some reluctance.

Before I had finished reading the Prologue, I knew I was hooked. I put aside all thoughts of grading papers and read the entire book in one sitting. What emerged from the pages was the extraordinary story of a remarkable character who challenged family members, elite lawyers, a host of judges, and a powerful trust company in a protracted legal battle to obtain redress for the improper dissipation of her mother's estate. The tale is told with grace and wit by a woman with acute powers of observation, a penchant for frankness, and an effervescent writing style. The author's strong personality permeates the text, charming and beguiling the reader with her spirited sense of mission.

I invited my sister, visiting in Ottawa, to give me her opinion. She too read the book in a single sitting. We sat up all evening talking about the case, about Mrs. Campbell, her lawyers, her claims of a pernicious and far-reaching conspiracy against her. We spontaneously decided to take on the project of republication together. From there, the trail widened. Mr. Justice Cullity advised us that there were people from St. John's Episcopal Church who remembered Mrs. Campbell. Through the assistance of George H. Kidder, counsel with Hemenway and Barnes in Boston, we met David A. Mittell. Mittell had taken tutoring sessions in Latin from Mrs. Campbell's husband, Thomas Clyman Campbell, when he was the rector at St. John's. Mittell, whose mother had preserved a signed copy of *Where Angels Fear to Tread* in her personal library, confessed to having spent more than ten years endeavouring to have the book republished. He was fascinated with the tale, and wondered why the book had not been made widely available in Canada. He passed along voluminous files on the Campbell family, along with his mother's precious signed copy of the book. David Mittell introduced us to the woman who had been the impetus behind his efforts to get Mrs. Campbell's book republished, Katharine G. Cipolla. Cipolla is the St. John's parish historian who had meticulously tracked down details of Mrs. Campbell's life for an article titled "The Privy Council's First Portia," published in the September 1992 edition of the church bulletin, *Eagle's Eye*. She too passed on her records.

To our surprise and delight, we discovered even more people who had begun to research the case before us. His Honour Judge Sydney Harris, retired from the Ontario Court of Justice, had read the book when he was still a law student in the early 1940s. It remained seared in his memory, but it took him until retirement in the early 1990s to begin further inquiry. He had been to Boston in 1992 to meet with those who remembered Mrs. Campbell, and had searched through the files at the Privy Council in London. It was he who had sparked Katharine Cipolla's interest in Mrs. Campbell in the first place. Judge Harris generously shared with us all the information he had compiled.

Brendan O'Brien, a senior Toronto lawyer and former treasurer of the Law Society of Upper Canada, remembered Mrs. Campbell and her case from his early days in practice. He had followed the litigation in the law reports, delved into the records of the Law Society of Upper Canada, and even located a used copy of *Where Angels Fear to Tread* via the Internet. (Subsequent Internet searches have turned up isolated copies tucked away in second-hand bookstores from Hamilton to Regina.) Brendan O'Brien lent all his notes and records to us—a researcher's dream. The Hon. Mr. Justice William J. Anderson of the Ontario Superior Court had tracked down many of the details of the litigation and published his superb article, "Where Angels Fear to Tread (*Campbell* v. *Hogg, et al.,* [1930] D.L.R. 673)," in the *Law Society of Upper Canada Gazette* in 1995. Eminent legal figures divulged their passing familiarity with Mrs. Campbell's travails. The Hon. Chief Justice William G.C. Howland, great-grandson of Mrs. Campbell's stepfather, Sir William Pearce Howland, noted that, as a young lawyer in the late 1930s, he "had heard about Mrs. Campbell's crusade." University of Toronto law professor Martin Friedland remembered reading the book in the Hart House Library, along with a number of his classmates, while still a law student in the mid-1950s. "We felt we were reading a manuscript that the legal establishment wanted to suppress," he reminisced, "an underground copy that the establishment couldn't do anything about." There were others who generously allowed us to interview them about the case and the people connected with it: Mr. Justice John D. Arnup, Ronald Graeme Slaght, Peter Newcombe, and Peter Campbell Brooks.

Nearly everyone we spoke with suggested that the Osgoode Society for Canadian Legal History was the perfect venue for republication. Situated in the heart of Osgoode Hall, its patrons and board members some of the most influential lawyers and judges in the country, this was surely the vehicle fate would have selected to reforge the public reception of Mrs. Campbell's monograph. Peter Oliver, editor-in-chief at the Osgoode Society, to whom we forwarded *Where Angels Fear to Tread,* began to read the volume and found that, like us, he could not put it down. He pronounced it "quite astounding." Members of his board, some of whom remembered the case first-hand, were equally intrigued by the book and the prospect of republication. History had come full circle.

The Osgoode Society suggested that we place the book in historical context, with an introduction and epilogue to provide background details and interpretive analysis. We decided as well to supplement Mrs. Campbell's writing with explanatory biographical and other research notes placed at the end of her manuscript. Emily Andrew, Jean Wilson, and Randy Schmidt of the University of British Columbia Press, all of whom read the book at the outset of this project, were enthusiastic and unremittingly supportive. Without Susan Lewthwaite's wonderful assistance at the Archives of the Law Society of Upper Canada, the legal biographies included in the notes would have been substantially impoverished. Paul Leatherdale and Elise Brunet at the Archives of the Law Society of Upper Canada also provided superb assistance in locating details about the Law Society connections, as well as photographs. Archivists Paul McIlroy and Christine Bourolias of the Archives of Ontario helped with the search for court records. Christopher Moore, well-known historian of the legal profession, offered generous assistance in tracking down biographical references. Belinda Peres, the University of Ottawa law student who began the background research on this book in 2001, was invariably encouraging and helpful. University of Ottawa law student Raquel Chisholm took over the task in 2002. Raquel tracked down endless references and offered creative ideas over months of painstaking work; she has been a full partner in the joys and tribulations of searching for remote sources and materials. Susan Lecorre at the Human Rights Research and Education Centre provided assistance with the reproduction of the manuscript. Camilla Jenkins and Judy Phillips offered very skilful editorial assistance at UBC Press. Olga H. Backhouse, who has been very supportive of this project from outset to end, completed the index for us. The Law Foundation of Ontario and the Social Sciences and Humanities Research Council of Canada provided ongoing financial support.

One can only wonder what Mrs. Campbell might have thought of this, in 1940, as she set about the daunting task of self-publishing and marketing her book. What might she have said had she known that her book would be republished by the prestigious Osgoode Society some sixty-four years later, launched from the very building in which she went down to ignominious defeat before the Court of Appeal, and distributed across the country to hundreds of Canadian lawyers and judges? Would she have felt it righted the balance of justice? This, as with the many other questions posed by her book, is worth considerable speculative reflection.

Constance Backhouse

★　　★　　★　　★

SHORTLY AFTER I was appointed to the bench, my sister asked me to read the self-published manuscript *Where Angels Fear to Tread.* I was affected by the eloquence with which Mrs. Campbell describes her long battle for justice.

I had recently read and loved A.B. McKillop's *The Spinster and the Prophet: Florence Deeks, H.G. Wells and the Mystery of the Purloined Past,* where it is suggested that Florence Deeks's claim, which she argued herself before the Privy Council, although unsuccessful, was legitimate. I was impressed by the courage of both the self-represented Mrs. Campbell and Ms Deeks to carry on with their fight in the face of defeat after courtroom defeat and, in the case of Mrs. Campbell, to be the first woman to appear before the highest court in the land.

It struck me that the stories of these two women had a lesson for a newly appointed judge. That lesson was to resist, at a time of ever increasing numbers of self-represented litigants, concluding too quickly that the claims of such litigants, seemingly obsessed with their cases, lacked merit, and to keep an open mind even where other judges had previously considered the matter and found it unmeritorious.

Mrs. Campbell's book highlights intriguing issues. As a former bencher of the Law Society of Upper Canada, I wondered whether the Law Society today would show similar reticence in disciplining a prominent member of the profession and bencher who had been proved guilty of grave breaches of trust. Mrs. Campbell's story reminded me of how uncomfortable I was when asked as a lawyer to sue or testify against other lawyers. Would someone in Mrs. Campbell's shoes today be able to attract leading counsel to take her case?

Even without the thorny issue of Mr. Hogg's prominence, given the relatively small amount of money involved, Mrs. Campbell's case raises interesting questions of access. Lawyers today would very likely show similar reluctance to that of Mr. Slaght and Mr. McCarthy to carry on with a case with such modest prospects. Mrs. Campbell, because of her background, social standing, and natural abilities, was able to overcome the access difficulties of that era and get her day in the highest court. Would someone today fare as well?

Finally, though, there is tragedy inherent in Mrs. Campbell's case. While she won a moral victory, there was no financial redress. In hindsight, if not from the start, this seems predictable given the costs of litigation and the fact that she was only ever going to get one-third of what was recovered. Given the high costs to her family, both financial and emotional, what lessons should be drawn?

These thoughts express some of the reasons why I feel a republication of *Where Angels Fear to Tread* will be of great interest to anyone engaged with the legal system.

Nancy L. Backhouse

CAST OF CHARACTERS

Charles James Rattray Bethune Mrs. Campbell's older brother, Toronto and Ottawa lawyer

Elizabeth Mary Rattray Bethune Mrs. Campbell's mother, Toronto socialite, 1843-1924

James Bethune Mrs. Campbell's father, Toronto barrister and solicitor, 1840-84

Lord Blanesburgh Law Lord of the Privy Council

Peter Campbell Brooks Mrs. Campbell's grandson

Edward Brown Clerk in the Judgment Office of the Ontario Supreme Court

Elizabeth Bethune Campbell Chief protagonist, 1880-1956

Elizabeth Thomasine Campbell Mrs. Campbell's daughter, librarian in the United States

James Bethune Campbell Mrs. Campbell's son, physician and surgeon in the United States

Thomas Clyman Campbell Mrs. Campbell's husband, minister of St. John's Episcopal Church, Jamaica Plain, Massachusetts, 1875-1943

Susan Revere Chapin Mrs. Campbell's friend and financial supporter, widow and parishioner of St. John's Episcopal Church

James Cowan Toronto lawyer, partner to Arthur Slaght

John Joseph Daley Chief Librarian of the Great Library of Osgoode Hall

Edward J. Daly Judge of the Carleton County Surrogate Court, who heard Mrs. Campbell's case

James Davey Ottawa manager of the Toronto General Trusts Corporation

Lyman Poore Duff Judge of the Supreme Court of Canada, who heard Mrs. Campbell's case

William James Elliott Toronto lawyer, who represented Annie McDougald in opposing Mrs. Campbell's claims

Robert Irvin Ferguson Toronto lawyer, partner to Arthur Slaght

William Nassau Ferguson Judge of the Ontario Court of Appeal, who heard Mrs. Campbell's case

Robert Grant Fisher Judge of the Ontario Court of Appeal, who heard Mrs. Campbell's case

Hector M. Forbes Assistant Manager of the Toronto General Trusts Corporation

Frank Gahan Counsel for the Toronto General Trusts Corporation at the Privy Council

Clarence Garrow Judge of the Ontario High Court, who heard Mrs. Campbell's case

David Inglis Grant Judge of the Ontario Court of Appeal, who heard Mrs. Campbell's case

Isidore Frederick Hellmuth Toronto lawyer, whom Mrs. Campbell was recommended to retain

Leonard D'Arcy Hinds Registrar of the Weekly Court

Frank Egerton Hodgins Judge of the Ontario Court of Appeal, who heard Mrs. Campbell's case

Agnes Louisa Rattray Hogg Mrs. Campbell's aunt, married to William Drummond Hogg

Frederick Drummond Hogg Mrs. Campbell's cousin, son of William Drummond Hogg, Ottawa lawyer and Toronto judge

William Drummond Hogg Mrs. Campbell's uncle, who managed Lady Howland's estate and opposed Mrs. Campbell's legal claims, 1848-1932

Lady Howland Mrs. Campbell's mother's name on her second marriage

Sir William Pearce Howland Mrs. Campbell's stepfather, Lieutenant-Governor of Ontario, 1811-1907

J. Hamilton Ingersoll St. Catharines lawyer, whose firm drew up Lady Howland's will

Nicol Jeffrey Judge of the Ontario High Court, who heard Mrs. Campbell's case

John Strachan Johnston Toronto lawyer, whose firm Mrs. Campbell engaged to prove the existence of her mother's will

Hugh Thomas Kelly Judge of the Supreme Court of Ontario, who rejected Mrs. Campbell's claim that her mother had left a valid will

William Lyon Mackenzie King Friend of the Bethune and Hogg families, prime minister of Canada

Arthur Courtney Kingstone St. Catharines lawyer, whose firm drew up Lady Howland's will

James Lang Toronto Estates Manager of the Toronto General Trusts Corporation

Archibald D. Langmuir General Manager of the Toronto General Trusts Corporation

William Lawrence Bishop of the Episcopal Church in Massachusetts, who supported Mrs. Campbell's case

O.E. Lennox Assistant Master of the Supreme Court of Ontario

Cora Ann Bethune Lindsey Mrs. Campbell's sister, who opposed her legal claims

Dudley George Lys Second Clerk of the Privy Council

D'Alton Lally McCarthy Mrs. Campbell's lawyer, Toronto barrister and solicitor

George McDonnell [Macdonnell] Ottawa lawyer, who refused to act as agent for Arthur Slaght on Mrs. Campbell's case

Annie Bethune McDougald Mrs. Campbell's sister, who opposed her legal claims

John Millar McEvoy Judge of the Ontario High Court, who heard Mrs. Campbell's case

A.J. McGillivray Taxing officer, who taxed the costs awarded in Mrs. Campbell's case

Ewart Victor McKague Toronto lawyer, who represented the Toronto General Trusts Corporation in opposing Mrs. Campbell's claims

James Magee Judge of the Ontario Court of Appeal, who heard Mrs. Campbell's case

Norman L. Martin Toronto chartered accountant, who acted for Mrs. Campbell in reviewing Hogg's books

Cornelius Arthur Masten Judge of the High Court of Ontario, who heard Mrs. Campbell's case

William Edward Middleton Judge of the Ontario Court of Appeal, who heard Mrs. Campbell's case

Enid M. Moore Assistant to the Privy Council

James Arthur Mulligan Judge of the Carleton County Surrogate Court, who heard Mrs. Campbell's case

Sir William Mulock Chief Justice of Ontario, founder of Toronto General Trusts Corporation and family friend of the Bethunes

Sir Charles Neish Registrar of the Privy Council

Peter Newcombe Ottawa lawyer, who saw Mrs. Campbell picketing

Brendan O'Brien Toronto lawyer and treasurer of the Law Society of Upper Canada, who saw Mrs. Campbell picketing

Reginald Holland Parmenter Toronto lawyer with the firm that Mrs. Campbell retained to prove the existence of her mother's will, brother-in-law of Arthur Courtney Kingstone

William Herbert Price Attorney General of Ontario

William Renwick Riddell Judge of the Ontario Court of Appeal, who heard Mrs. Campbell's case

Hugh Edward Rose Judge of the Ontario High Court, who heard Mrs. Campbell's case

Newton Wesley Rowell President of the Toronto General Trusts Corporation, Toronto lawyer and bencher, who presided over the disciplinary complaint against William Drummond Hogg

Lord Russell of Killowen Law Lord of the Privy Council

Henry W. Sherrill Bishop of the Episcopalian Church, who supported Mrs. Campbell

Robert Victor Sinclair Ottawa lawyer, who represented Cora Ann Lindsey and William Drummond Hogg in opposing Mrs. Campbell's claims

Arthur Graeme Slaght Mrs. Campbell's lawyer, Toronto barrister and solicitor

Robert Cooper Smith Judge of the Ontario Court of Appeal, who heard Mrs. Campbell's case

Ronald K. Smith London counsel for William Drummond Hogg at the Privy Council

William Norman Tilley Toronto lawyer, whose firm Mrs. Campbell retained to prove the existence of her mother's will

Lord Tomlin Law Lord of the Privy Council

John Tytler Judge of the York County Surrogate Court, who heard Mrs. Campbell's case

L.W.S. Upton Third Clerk of the Privy Council

William Ridout Wadsworth Toronto lawyer, who represented Cora Ann Lindsey and Mr. Hogg in opposing Mrs. Campbell's claims

Ada Wall Assistant to the Privy Council

W. Reeve Wallace Chief Clerk of the Privy Council

William G. Watson Assistant General Manager of the Toronto General Trusts Corporation

William Ralph West Toronto lawyer, partner to D'Alton Lally McCarthy

Leonard Wrinch Assistant Librarian at the Great Library of Osgoode Hall

James McGregor Young Toronto lawyer, who advised Mrs. Campbell informally on her case

THE HEIRESS VS THE ESTABLISHMENT

INTRODUCTION

YOU ARE about to meet Mrs. Elizabeth Bethune Campbell, a woman of formidable intellect, wit, and sarcasm, with the determination of steel. Her book, *Where Angels Fear to Tread*, written in 1935 and self-published in 1940 from her home in the rectory of St. John's Episcopalian Church in Jamaica Plain, Boston, raised considerable controversy when it first appeared.[1] Mrs. Campbell's fascinating entanglement with the law spanned fourteen years. It began in 1922, when she first came across an unsigned copy of her mother's will while sorting through musty family trunks. The saga peaked in 1930, when Mrs. Campbell appeared on her own behalf to argue her case in front of the Judicial Committee of the Privy Council in London. The legal battle finally ended in 1935, when the Ontario Court of Appeal issued its last decision on the matter of costs relating to the complex web of litigation spawned by Mrs. Campbell's inheritance.

The story that Mrs. Campbell tells is extraordinary, and not only because she appears to have been the first woman to argue in front of the Law Lords at the Privy Council. Mrs. Campbell's description of the barriers she surmounted before emerging victorious in England unveils the intricate, multilayered world of overlapping intrigue and influence that constituted the early-twentieth-century Ontario legal system. From her unique vantage point as both an insider and an outsider, she comments on the actions of lawyers and judges with acuity and perspicacity. Others might have thought as she did. None, so far as we have been able to find, spoke nearly so frankly. Mrs. Campbell's book charges some of the most powerful figures in Canadian legal history with unconscionably disreputable behaviour. *Where Angels Fear to Tread* must have been viewed as a ticking bomb when it first emerged in 1940. In many ways, it still is. A highly controversial character then and now, Mrs. Campbell and the story she tells evoke many different responses among readers. We hope not to influence readers before they have the opportunity to hear Mrs. Campbell's version in her own words. Consequently, this introduction will provide only the briefest contextual background and factual framework. Our analysis follows after the reproduction of Mrs. Campbell's book, in the Epilogue.

The author of *Where Angels Fear to Tread*, who was christened Elizabeth Louisa Bethune, was born at Stormont Lodge, her family residence at 238 Adelaide Street West in Toronto, on 23 September 1880.[2] Her father, James Bethune, Q.C., was a former politician, a Law Society bencher, and a prominent barrister. Widely acknowledged as a pillar of the social elite in Canada, Bethune was reputed to be "an outstanding counsel and leader of the Ontario Bar."[3]

Mrs. Campbell's mother was Elizabeth Mary Rattray Bethune, a "vivacious and intellectual" society woman, who was described as the "popular and hospitable hostess of Stormont Lodge, for many years a landmark of old Toronto at John and Adelaide Streets."[4] Mrs. Campbell was the youngest by far of a family of five siblings, two of whom had died by the time she began writing her book.[5] Cora Ann, sixteen years older than Mrs. Campbell, and Annie, thirteen years older, figure prominently in it.[6] In 1884, when Mrs. Campbell was only four years old, her father was stricken with typhoid, dying at the height of his career, at age forty-four.[7] James Bethune's will bestowed guardianship of the children, and bequeathed his entire estate, estimated at between $40,000 and $60,000, to his widow.[8] Mrs. Campbell's mother relied on her brother-in-law, Ottawa lawyer William Drummond Hogg, to manage the estate, and she and her children, although tragically bereft of husband and father, lived very comfortably.[9] As befit Mrs. Campbell's social status within an upper-class professional family, her childhood included a stint in convent school in Paris, along with extensive European travel, but no university education.[10]

In 1895, when Mrs. Campbell was fifteen, her mother remarried, to Sir William Pearce Howland, Ontario's former lieutenant governor.[11] Upon the marriage, Mrs. Campbell's mother automatically received the title "Lady Howland," along with the pomp and circumstance associated with the illustrious match. Sir William Howland was eighty-four years old and twice widowed by the time of this, his third marriage, and his new wife was some thirty years his junior. The relationship was not to be a permanent one, and the couple separated some years before Sir William's death in 1907.[12] Lady Howland and her youngest daughter remained financially secure, despite the unfavourable legal regime during this era that generally dispossessed married women from full control of their property, since she had had the foresight to protect her property by way of marriage settlement prior to her wedding to Sir William Howland.[13]

Elizabeth Louisa Bethune was "introduced" to society as a debutante in her late teens, with all the social whirl such an event entailed.

James Bethune

Lady Howland

Sir William Howland

Apparently one of her suitors was William Lyon Mackenzie King. The future prime minister of Canada had a penchant for "women who were handsome, vital, and intelligent," particularly if they were from "wealthy," "important" "society families." According to family lore, the two were almost engaged, but the match never came to fruition.[14] Prime Minister King went on to lifelong bachelorhood, while, at the relatively mature age of twenty-seven, Elizabeth Louise Bethune became engaged to an American Episcopalian cleric, whom she married in Toronto in 1907. Reverend Thomas Clyman Campbell was not particularly well-to-do, but he was well educated, having graduated from Princeton University, taught as a master at the upper-class Groton School in Massachusetts, and obtained a Bachelor of Divinity from the Episcopal Theological School in Cambridge, Massachusetts. Described as a serious man of "quiet demeanour," he stood over six feet tall and was reputed to have been a "great Princeton baseball catcher."[15] The wedding at St. Paul's Church on Bloor Street East, on 14 November, was one of the social events of the season. The elite guests included three Ontario chief justices, the Ontario premier, and many well-known judges and lawyers. The Mulocks, Falconbridges, Mosses, Mowats, Blaikies, Whitneys, and Lashes were out in full force.[16]

After their marriage, Reverend Campbell moved his bride to Boston, having been appointed the new rector of St. John's Episcopal Church in Jamaica Plain. The neighbourhood had been settled in the eighteenth and nineteenth centuries by the elite from Boston's Back Bay and Beacon Hill, who built grand country estates and summer homes beside Jamaica Pond. St. John's Episcopal Church, a commanding stone structure emanating majestic elegance, was built on the corner of Revere Street and Roanoke Avenue in 1882. By the time the Campbells moved to Jamaica Plain, it had become predominantly mercantile. The residents still lived in grandly rambling homes inspired by Greek revival and Italianate architecture, but their incomes issued from haberdashery, shoe manufacturing, crockery importing, banking, and publishing. A growing middle class commuted to the city on the new streetcars. The First World War brought further change. Swedish and German immigrants began to settle into the neighbourhood, transforming the single-family houses into multi-family dwellings and selling off portions of the front yards to construct new three-storey dwellings cheek by jowl with the original structures.[17]

Mrs. Campbell as a debutante

Mrs. Campbell's wedding photograph

Shortly after the Campbells moved to Jamaica Plain, the congregation built a rectory down the road from the church, at 24 Alveston
Street. The rectory was by no means the grandest residence in the
neighbourhood, but it was a substantial three-storey, four-bedroom
house with bay windows, gables, and a wide front porch. It would be
the Campbell family home for the next thirty years.[18] There the couple raised two children: James Bethune Campbell, born on 27 July
1909, and Elizabeth Thomasine (known as Thomasine), born on 6
May 1913.[19]

When the children were just nine and five years old, Reverend
Campbell left for military duties in England, where he served with
the American Red Cross as chaplain for American troops in English
hospitals from 1918 to 1919.[20] This seems to have been the last stint
during which Mrs. Campbell carried sole responsibility for daily child
care. Both children were subsequently sent to exclusive boarding
schools in Massachusetts: James to the Episcopal prep-college of St.
Mark's in Southborough, and Thomasine to Winsor, an elite girls'
school in Boston. In 1927 James enrolled at Harvard, where he board-
ed until he obtained his B.A. in 1931. He obtained a Harvard medical
degree in 1935. Thomasine studied at Columbia University (Barnard)
and in Vienna. The expense associated with such prestigious education was well beyond the financial means of Reverend Campbell,
although it is possible that the educational institutions reduced the
tuition for the children of an Episcopal minister. A wealthy parishioner, Susan Revere Chapin, apparently contributed generously
toward the cost.[21]

Those from the parish who remembered Mrs. Campbell during
these years described her as a striking figure. She stood five feet ten
inches tall, trim and absolutely erect. She was "very dignified," "beautiful," "well-spoken," and "always very beautifully dressed."[22] Some particularly recalled her majestic arrival at church on Sundays, when she
would make a "grand entrance" with her children, take her place at
the front pew, and sit "ram-rod straight" throughout Reverend
Campbell's long sermons, something that other parishioners maintained was "really hard to do in those pews."[23] They also recalled that
she was not actively involved in the affairs of the parish, or in any of
the local women's literary or drama clubs, and that she was absent for
long stretches of time, pursuing her "case" in Toronto and London,
England.[24]

St. John's Episcopal Church

The Rectory, Jamaica Plain

The Reverend Thomas Campbell in military uniform

The case was spawned by a series of disputes over Mrs. Campbell's mother's estate. Some years after her daughter moved to Jamaica Plain, Lady Howland retired to St. Catharines, Ontario. There she took up permanent residence in a large suite of rooms at the elite Welland Hotel, renowned for its access to mineral springs, and its solarium and spa facilities.[25]

By 1915, when she was seventy-five, Lady Howland's mind was beginning to fail.[26] Private nurses were retained to attend to her needs. On 6 October 1922, at the age of eighty-two, Lady Howland's faculties had deteriorated to the point that her daughter, Cora Ann Lindsey, obtained a court order declaring her mother incapable of managing her own affairs. Over the objections of Mrs. Campbell, the Toronto General Trusts Corporation was appointed "committee" of Lady Howland's estate, and the two elder daughters were appointed "committee" of her person.[27] Lady Howland died on 14 August 1924, at the age of eighty-four, without having recovered her mental capability.[28] Her estate was valued at $17,450, an amount that seemed to Mrs. Campbell to be substantially lower than it should have been.[29]

The disposition of Lady Howland's estate serves as the focal point for *Where Angels Fear to Tread*. In it, Mrs. Campbell puts forth her own perspective on the long and difficult struggle to obtain answers to questions about what had happened to her mother's money. She also writes frankly about her opinion of various counsel. During the tenacious legal journey, Mrs. Campbell was represented by a number of distinguished lawyers. Two stand out as central to the case. Arthur Graeme Slaght is singled out by Mrs. Campbell for his diligent initial efforts on her behalf. Born in Simcoe, Ontario, in 1877, Slaght developed a successful mining law practice in Haileybury before moving to Toronto. Noted as a flamboyant bon vivant and a specialist in mining law, Slaght became a prominent barrister who conducted a wide range of civil and criminal trials with great distinction. A man with political aspirations, Slaght was unsuccessful as a Liberal candidate for Temiskaming in the 1919 by-election. He would subsequently become the head of the Toronto and York Regional Liberal Association in 1932, and organize the successful election campaign of Premier Mitchell Hepburn in 1934. Slaght was elected federally in 1935, when he was sent to the House of Commons to represent Parry Sound, a seat he held until 1945.[30]

Elizabeth Thomasine Campbell and James Bethune Campbell

D'Alton Lally McCarthy is the second lawyer whose representation of Mrs. Campbell plays a major role in *Where Angels Fear to Tread*. Born in Barrie, Ontario, in 1870, McCarthy was the son of the famous lawyer D'Alton McCarthy and his wife, Emily Lally. After his call to the bar in 1895, Lally McCarthy began practice with his father's Toronto firm of McCarthy, Osler, Hoskin and Creelman. In 1916 he and his cousins founded McCarthy and McCarthy, with Lally McCarthy, Leighton McCarthy, and Frank McCarthy at the helm. In 1929 Lally McCarthy left the firm to practise as a solo litigation barrister. Widely regarded as one of the leading courtroom lawyers of the era, McCarthy sailed regularly on the Atlantic liners to plead Privy Council cases in London. He was renowned for his stature and gregariousness.[31]

One of Mrs. Campbell's chief opponents during her lengthy battle was William Drummond Hogg, the uncle who managed Lady Howland's estate from 1884, when her first husband died, until 1922, when the trust company he chaired took over the administration of the estate. Born in Perth, Ontario, in 1848 and called to the Ontario

Welland Hotel, St. Catharines, c. 1900

Welland Hotel interior, St. Catharines, 1907

17

bar in 1874, Hogg initially set up practice in Ottawa.[32] He was one of the leaders of the St. Andrew's Society of Ottawa, a Scottish benevolent and social organization.[33] Hogg married into Lady Howland's family when he wed her younger sister, Agnes Louisa Rattray, in a ceremony held in the Bethune family home. Agnes and Lady Howland were particularly close sisters, visiting each other often. The bonds between the two families were apparent at Mrs. Campbell's wedding, when William and Agnes came down from Ottawa to attend the nuptials, and Mrs. Hogg presided with Lady Howland over the bridal reception at the Queen's Hotel. Apart from the children, William and Agnes were the only two beneficiaries named in Lady Howland's will.[34]

Hogg established a successful Ottawa law practice, with specialties in Crown litigation before the Exchequer and Supreme Courts of Canada, and in banking and insurance law. In 1890 he was appointed Queen's Counsel (Q.C.). By the time Mrs. Campbell commenced litigation against him, Hogg was practising in partnership with his son Frederick Drummond Hogg.[35] William Hogg was first elected by his peers to help govern the legal profession as a bencher in 1896, and again in 1901 and 1906. He lost the 1911 election but was re-elected in 1916 and became an honorary life bencher from 1916 to 1940.[36] By the time Mrs. Campbell's case reached the Ontario Court of Appeal in 1928, Hogg was eighty years old, a well-known, highly respected legal figure. Judges from the Ontario Court of Appeal extolled him to be a "prominent" member of the legal profession.[37]

Mrs. Campbell's other nemesis was the Toronto General Trusts Corporation, launched as Canada's first trust company when it opened for business in 1882. The founders were a star-studded throng. The Hon. Edward Blake, former Ontario premier, was the first president. William Mulock (subsequently the chief justice of Ontario), Sir Aemilius Irving (long-time treasurer of the Law Society of Upper Canada), and Senator James Kirkpatrick Kerr all sat on the original board of directors. Blake was succeeded in the presidency by such powerful lawyers as Featherston Osler and Newton Wesley Rowell. Colonel Reuben Wells Leonard, the philanthropist who founded the Leonard Foundation scholarship trust, also served as a director. Assets rose from $9 million in 1892 to $124 million by 1921, and $248 million by 1942.[38] Trust companies were emerging as competitors for the traditionally legal work of estate management, provoking substantial

Toronto General Trusts Corporation advertisement,
Toronto *Globe*, 23 April 1930

Toronto General Trusts Corporation building

resentment among lawyers, as well as declarations from the Law Society of Upper Canada that it was incapable of stemming the tide.[39] In its prodigious advertising, the Toronto General Trusts Corporation touted itself as "Canada's oldest trust company," an "absolutely genuine trust company" that possessed the "confidence of the community throughout the country."[40] Mrs. Campbell's litigation against the company, which would ultimately inspire one reporter to brand it as "contemptible" and "chiselling," must have rankled more than its corporate officers cared to admit.[41]

Mrs. Campbell's protracted legal battle took place primarily in Toronto, a city that had expanded its population and industrial base so substantially in the 1910s that it began to rival Montreal as the premier city in Canada. A pronounced Anglo-Celtic cultural heritage and the infamous blue laws contributed to its self-satisfied reputation as "Toronto the Good," a phrase first coined in tribute to the moral purity campaign waged by Sir William Howland's son during the latter's term as Toronto's mayor.[42] Some referred to the city as "more British" than the monarch.[43] The lives of the elite had changed somewhat from the late nineteenth century, when Mrs. Campbell would have become accustomed to socializing with the upper crust at dinner-party dances, theatre and the opera, cricket and croquet matches, and balls at Government House.[44] Although upper-class women were still largely restricted to supervising stately homes, engaging in charitable works, and assuring worthy marriages, the female suffrage movement flowered into full strength after the turn of the nineteenth century, heralding an expansion of educational, business, and professional opportunities for women.[45] The opening decades of the twentieth century witnessed a series of other momentous changes. The First World War involved military mobilization and government expansion, financed by the new personal income tax, on a scale unprecedented in Canadian history. The Roaring Twenties ushered in years of prosperity and spectacular extravagance. Financial and industrial interests achieved greater and greater concentration in central Canada, until the stock market crash in October 1929 and the ensuing Great Depression unmasked the economic vulnerability of the country.[46]

The Ontario legal profession was known throughout the 1920s and 1930s for its aversion to reform, its conservatism, and its claims to "patrician" status. Building upon nineteenth-century traditions, when almost a third of Ontario lawyers were sons of professional men, most lawyers continued to emerge from professional, managerial, and business families. Few law firms hired solely on merit, and considerable barriers faced working-class aspirants, racialized and ethnic minorities, and all the women who sought admission.[47] The thirty benchers, who were elected every five years by the practising members of the bar to govern the legal monopoly, were primarily drawn from the "most

prominent, wealthy ... establishment law firms," "barons of the regional bar, and litigation stars." This was an era in which elite lawyers,
benchers, and judges moved in very small circles, intermingled their
families by marriage, and prided themselves on their unchallenged
invulnerability.[48] The ghosts of the fabled Family Compact, described
in Lord Durham's report of 1839 on the British North American
colonies as an entrenched, propertied, familial clique that despised
"republicanism and mob rule" and governed politics, the bench, and a
great part of the legal profession of Upper Canada, had been dislodged
only minimally.[49]

Knowledgeable observers of Mrs. Campbell's case would have been
struck by the intricate web of professional and familial connections
that contributed to Mrs. Campbell's reputation and stature in legal and
judicial circles. Her father's legal career overflowed with linkages to
powerful and important men. The principal for whom James Bethune
articled was Edward Blake, the son of Chancery Judge William Hume
Blake. Edward Blake became the premier of Ontario, the federal minister of justice, a bencher, and, finally, treasurer of the Law Society of
Upper Canada. When James Bethune joined the Blake firm, his partners were Samuel Hume Blake (Edward's brother, who became a
bencher and then a judge in Chancery Court) and James Kirkpatrick
Kerr (a bencher, corporate director, senator, and brother-in-law to
Edward and Samuel). The firm expanded to bring in Zebulon Aiton
Lash, the famous corporation lawyer who became vice-president of
Canadian National Railways. Bethune's partners would later include
other illustrious lawyers. Newman Wright Hoyles was the son of the
chief justice of Newfoundland and would become the principal of
Osgoode Hall Law School from 1894 to 1923. Sir Featherston Osler
was a bencher as well as a judge of the Court of Common Pleas and
the Court of Appeal who declined appointment to the Supreme
Court of Canada. Sir Charles Moss would become chief justice of
Ontario. His brother-in-law, Sir William Glenholme Falconbridge,
who was married to the stepdaughter of Sir Francis Hincks (the
English leader of the Reform party in Canada West in the mid-
nineteenth century), would serve in turn as chief justice of Ontario.
Sir Allen Bristol Aylesworth, who was married to the granddaughter of Chief Justice Sir G.W. Burton, would become a bencher,
postmaster-general, and minister of justice.[50] Mrs. Campbell's father's

professional connections meant that she could scarcely go anywhere without being recognized and reminded of her father's professional and social stature.

The riddles arising from Mrs. Campbell's litigation pose a host of difficult questions, some of which may be answerable, others open only to informed speculation. What underlay the dispute between the three surviving daughters of Lady Howland over the will and the distribution of the estate? Did William Hogg misappropriate funds from Lady Howland's estate? Was the treatment of Mrs. Campbell by her many lawyers unusual for the time? Was Mrs. Campbell an unreasonable, even querulous client, dangerously obsessed by the case? Did the senior lawyers and judges in Ontario conspire to protect Hogg from an embarrassing disclosure? Did Mrs. Campbell's status as a woman from a white, upper-middle-class, prominent legal family affect her treatment? What does it tell us about the efficacy of legal education, offered exclusively to the few admitted to the monopolistic, self-governing legal profession, that a woman without formal education and completely untrained in law could master the intricacies of legal procedure and substantive legal argument, to emerge victorious at the Privy Council? Was the Privy Council decision, in fact, a victory? In the end, who actually won when the protracted litigation finally came to a close? These are some of the complicated and fascinating questions that hover over Mrs. Campbell's case, and her remarkable opus, *Where Angels Fear to Tread*.

Where Angels Fear to Tread

ELIZABETH BETHUNE CAMPBELL

ELIZABETH BETHUNE CAMPBELL

Where Angels Fear To Tread

BY

ELIZABETH BETHUNE CAMPBELL

ST. JOHN'S RECTORY
24 ALVESTON STREET, BOSTON, U. S. A.
(JAMAICA PLAIN)

To
HIS MAJESTY'S
JUDICIAL COMMITTEE
of the
PRIVY COUNCIL
with respect and gratitude

PROLOGUE

LONDON, LOVELY on a May morning, Russell Square and Bedford Place![1][†] The strains of a hand organ, rivaling the voices of the street singers, mingle oddly with the cockney cry of the donkey cart man as he passes below, his cart laden with dewy white lilies. The soft west wind steals across the narrow iron balcony and flutters the curtains at the window of a room in one of those innumerable boarding places which, to a great degree, compose that Bloomsbury beloved by student and Bohemian alike. In the sunlight before the mirror a woman is dressing, her heart throbbing with a tremendous thrill. Softly she hums the "Spring Song," a joyous smile on her lips.

Once before life had brought a similar thrill, but that was long ago. Hours and hours of torture, then a blessed oblivion from which she had emerged, spent and shaken to be sure, but to a quite heavenly consciousness that at last the pain had ceased, and had seen a very tall white-faced husband anxiously bending over her — who had had this baby anyway? — and had heard a voice, which she vaguely remembered as somehow belonging to the family doctor, exclaim "Beautiful boy, my dear; beautiful boy!"

Never the same thrill until today; of course not, it is the thrill of achievement. For the past five years this woman, in her homeland across the sea, had struggled for justice, struggled valiantly but in vain. Aligned against her had been that foremost of fraternities, the legal fraternity, and a most powerful and aristocratic trust company, the first, and for some time the only trust company of Canada. In short her struggle had been that of a woman untrained in business or the law against "the powers that be." Though American by marriage with a wonderful American boy and girl and consequently, very devoted to her adopted country, she was at heart intensely British, indeed she realized now after this year in London, now with victory at hand, what it was that had enabled her to pick herself up time and again and go on against the many obstacles placed

---

[†]All notes have been newly added to Mrs. Campbell's original book to clarify and elaborate on various points.

31

in her path. Her pertinacity in the face of defeat seemed to be the wonder of both friend and foe, not to mention the astonishment of the reporters. It had been just her unspeakable and fervent faith in England and all that England stands for which had led her on. This faith had given her courage, and supported her too during those days in February when, defying tradition, she had appeared in Downing Street, quite alone, with neither Solicitor nor Counsel, nor even a friend beside her to plead her case in person before the final Court of the Empire, "King George's Court."[2] It was thus the gentleman of the press on the other side of the Atlantic had in their best journalese christened the Judicial Committee of His Majesty's Privy Council. What a fuss the press in general had made over her! It was very amusing, she reflected, when one had always been such a quiet little person, to see oneself starred in big headlines, "Privy Council's First Portia," "Woman Makes Legal History."[3] One headliner did really give her tremendous satisfaction though, perhaps because of the legal ancestry behind her. "Woman Turns Fresh Page in the Annals of the Privy Council." And now, propped against the mirror, stood the unstamped franked envelope bearing the insignia, grown strangely familiar during the past year, "On His Majesty's Service," and below, "Privy Council Office, Downing Street." Their Lordships were about to give judgment in her case; soon she and all the world would know what was written on the "fresh page" which she had dared to turn. She had somehow sensed success on leaving the Privy Council chamber at the conclusion of her hearing nearly two months before, and had awaited with eager anticipation the coming of the summons to appear again before the Law Lords. The silvery bells of Old St. Pancras chiming the quarter hour startle the woman. No more soliloquizing, she must not be late. Snapping a small watch on her wrist, with a final glance in the mirror as she pulls a tight fitting hat over the wavy hair, she is on the steep staircase and in another moment has started towards Downing Street. Turning at Russell Square down past the British Museum—how at home she feels there, most of the study and preparation of her case has been done in that great reading room—she stoops to put some pennies in the cap of the pavement artist busily at work this brilliant morning, making hay while the sun shines, no doubt. His dog, guarding his master's cap and his crayons, regards her gravely but gratefully; she has never been able to resist that dog, he lends a certain dignity even to the gaudy work of the artist.

Swiftly she threads her way through Charing Cross Road with its rows of old bookstores and songshops, the windows of the latter displaying the popular song hits of the moment, London's version of "Tin Pan Alley." The traffic tide of Trafalgar brings her to a sudden halt on the refuge; the lurching, swaying sea of buses, so skillfully guided by the nonchalant but extremely expert drivers, surges past. Then the "bobby" holds out his arm to stem the tide, and she crosses. The wonder of Whitehall; the never-failing fascination of the Life Guard, steel and scarlet set in mellow stone; and in the distance the exquisite towers and spires of the House of Commons and Westminster as they rise towards the pale soft sky. Before the Cenotaph the woman pauses reverently; Downing Street lies on the opposite corner, and how often during these arduous, anxious months, while handling the details of her case at the Privy Council Office, has she passed this way, and always she has wished that she might do visible homage, as is the custom of the men, who rarely, even in the buses, omit to bare their heads as they near this sacred shrine.[4]

The door of No. 2 Downing Street stands open, plain and unassuming it is, yet the gateway to such power. "Privy Council Office" on a brass plate and "Judicial Committee" inscribed above the entrance, white letters on a black ground, clear cut, typical of British justice, thinks the woman. Here black is black and white is white; no obscurity, no shading of the Law; the great inviolate Court of the Empire.

Friendly smiles greet her as, running up the steps, she enters the large square hallway. The attendants and messengers smile, the reporters smile — they are here in numbers this morning — and promptly gather around eager to know her exact feelings at this, the climax of her case — as though one could tabulate one's feelings at such a moment. Yes, certainly, they may "snap" her again and let us hope that the result may be better than their former efforts. One of the Law Lords passes through the hallway, a distinguished, white-haired man, with a keen, interesting face. He is not one of those who heard her case, but she had noticed him more than once in the days when she was arguing, standing at the back of the Privy Council Chamber, arms folded, listening intently. He raises his silk hat and bows in a courtly manner as he ascends their Lordships' stairway. But hark, "Big Ben" is telling London that it is half past ten. Knowing that she is quite alone one of the officials kindly comes to escort her to the Privy Council Chamber.

In the ante-chamber are assembled the Barristers and Solicitors for the opposing firms. There is also a sprinkling of Colonial Counsel; Barristers wear curly, lamb-like wigs and black gowns, the K.C.'s are resplendent in shining silk gowns, with a few additional curls to distinguish them from their less exalted brethren. Several Indian Counsel have strayed across from their Court; how curiously their brown faces contrast with the white wigs framing them! One of them approaches her with congratulations couched in splendid, though somewhat stilted English. India, it seems, is greatly interested in her fighting her way to the "foot of the Throne."

And now the court messenger is reversing a sign hanging on the panelled wall; it says, "Judicial Committee Sitting. Enter by Side Doors." There is an expectant rustle and a picking up of briefs as most of the gathering proceeds to the right, the respondent side of the Chamber. The kind official beckons her and holds open the door to the left. "Dear God, give me courage and keep me steady," the prayer that has been in her heart all through the pleading of her case. She enters, seats herself on the low, leather-covered seat to the left, directly in front of their Lordships. The bewigged Barristers on the opposite benches regard her wonderingly. With surprise she notices the number of Law Lords about the table — she had expected only the three who had heard her case, but here is an imposing gathering, eight to be exact.[5] The Senior Lord of Appeal, a well-known viscount, presides in the centre of the table. They all look very grave, they are assembled to do honor to the memory of a member of the Quebec Bar, a brilliant and distinguished gentleman indeed, who has passed away a few weeks since.[6] He had appeared before their Lordships many times, and they seem genuinely distressed by his sudden death. The woman realizes that someone else is seated on the bench beside her, turns and finds there, strangely enough, one of the most influential members of that legal fraternity of Ontario which has so opposed her.[7] A fine figure in wig and gown, he rises to thank the Judicial Committee on behalf of Canada and refers to the deceased

Counsel as "the flower of the Canadian Bar," although there is, she suspects, not too great an affection between the Bar of Quebec and that of Ontario. The Canadian accent falls very flat after the exquisite English of the Law Lords.

The rather touching little ceremony is over and the viscount relinquishes his chair to that member of the Committee who presided in her own case, the other Law Lords who comprised her Board take the chairs to the right and left. The Registrar, from the back of the Chamber, announces the name of her case, and that judgment will be given therein. Scarcely conscious of getting to her feet the woman finds herself standing at the small rostrum facing their Lordships. The presiding Law Lord is holding in his hands a long printed document, is reading from it. She sees him through a mist, his voice comes to her from afar. "In their Lordships' judgment it would accordingly be right that this appeal be allowed." The voice seems somewhat closer now, the mist is receding; once more the three elderly black-coated figures seated at the horse-shoe table become distinct. Does she hear aright? They are giving judgment in her favor, and are reversing the Order of the three Canadian Courts, a thing, she is well aware, not often done by the Judicial Committee. And what is this his Lordship is reading now about costs? Three quarters of her costs in all the Canadian Courts and of this Appeal to the Privy Council are being granted her; audible, above the beating of her heart, the voice continues "And their Lordships will humbly advise His Majesty accordingly."

The great gentleman lays down the reasons for judgment; he and his noble brothers have completed their task with regard to the woman, they have awarded her justice, that thing for which she has struggled so long. The "Appeal unto Caesar" is ended;

Victory, Victory, and the "Spring Song."[8]

35

BOOK ONE

THE LOST WILL

I BELONG to the old Canada, that Canada which is rapidly passing away.

My own father, James Bethune, Q.C., was one of the leading Counsel at the Ontario Bar, and my step-father, Sir William Howland, K.C.M.G., C.B., was the second Lieutenant Governor of Ontario, for whom the old Government House in Toronto was built.[1] Sir William's portrait in Windsor uniform has a place of honor on the walls of the new and palatial Government House of today. When we were in Toronto a year or two ago, my thoroughly American young daughter obliged me one very hot afternoon to make a special visit to Government House to inspect "Grandfather Howland's" portrait; she was much impressed by the old-world uniform, the sideburns, the sword.[2]

I should like to say just here that I feel quite sure that in my father's and stepfather's day the legal profession of Ontario and the trust companies, if any existed, were of the highest repute. My reading public will no doubt, as my story proceeds, form their own opinion as to whether these traditions of honor still hold good in high places throughout Ontario today.

My dear mother was a charming little woman, an old-fashioned gentlewoman, but with a certain brilliancy.[3] She had led a very full life as the wife of two rather noted men, had brought up a number of children and borne a good deal of responsibility. Toward the latter years of her life her mind began to fail, as do the minds of so many brilliant persons. Finally two years before her death it became necessary to have a guardian appointed, so the Toronto General Trusts Corporation was made committee of her estate by the Canadian Courts, and my two sisters—who are a generation older than I, and who live in Canada—were made guardians of her person.[4] In straightening out my mother's trunks, preparatory to the Trust Company's taking over her affairs, my second sister and I found a document which appeared to be a copy of a will made by my mother in my favor; there were bequests to my sisters and to others, but I was made her residuary legatee, and she named the Toronto General Trusts Corporation as her executor.[5]

I wrote at once to the Trust Company telling them of the copy and asked them to locate Lady Howland's will. In a few weeks I received a reply from their General Manager saying that they had communicated with the prominent firm upon whose paper the copy was made, and that the leading Counsel of that firm had written to say that they had no records in their office of drawing a will for Lady Howland, and that he thought no will had ever been signed.[6] My sisters also took this attitude, that no will had ever been signed.

Just at this time I was a very busy person, living away from Canada, in none too vigorous health, much taken up with the care of a large rectory and bringing up my children; and I had little leisure to bother about anything outside the daily routine.[7] Therefore, I accepted this theory of an unsigned will, though it did strike me as peculiar.

About two years later my dear mother died at the age of eighty-four, her mind completely clouded. Death at times can be a beautiful thing; my mother, though old, was still handsome, and the look of serenity and composure so long absent had returned to her face. One felt that she had won through to a great repose. After my mother's funeral, in thinking over my early life with her before my marriage — I was the child of her old age and never away from her except for a visit, the tie between us being singularly close — it came to my mind that it was very unlike her indeed to have left a will unsigned in her trunk for so many years; the document bore the date of 1915. I determined to visit the Trust Company before returning to my summer home in Nova Scotia and again ask them about the will.[8]

I presented myself at the Trust Company offices and demanded to see Mr. Langmuir, the General Manager. I was told that he had died very suddenly some months before and that Mr. Watson, who had taken his place, was very ill; but that Mr. Forbes, the Assistant Manager, would be happy to see me.[9]

I told Mr. Forbes who I was and then asked him what he was going to do about the copy of Lady Howland's will. He seemed greatly surprised and said, "Copy of a will? I didn't know there was ever any question of a will, she didn't leave a will."

I said, "Perhaps not, Mr. Forbes, but she left something quite like a will." And in my naive and inexperienced way I described the legal document which my sister and I had found in my mother's trunk.

Mr. Forbes became more and more interested and wanted to know where the document was.

I said, "Why I suppose you have it here among my mother's papers, haven't you?"

Upon this the Estate Department was instructed to make an immediate search, but in a few minutes reported back that no such document as we described could be found among Lady Howland's papers, and that, furthermore, it was not listed as ever having been received by the Trust Company.

Mr. Forbes appeared rather agitated at this information and said, "Mrs. Campbell, where do you think that document is? Where did Lady Howland die?"

I told him that my mother had died at my sister's residence, and that I presumed that the document was there, since the Trust Company hadn't taken possession of it.

Mr. Forbes then asked me to go to Mrs. Lindsey and obtain the paper and bring it to him. I jumped into a taxi and drove to my sister's residence in Parkdale, but was refused the object of my quest.[10] My sister said that although she had the document in question, it was of no value as it had never been signed, and that she would not give it to me.

When I returned to Mr. Forbes with this message, he became perturbed and declared it was most important and necessary for them to have the "will" in the Trust Company at once; and he despatched a messenger with a requisition to Mrs. Lindsey, telling me to sit and await the man's return. After some little time the messenger came in bearing in his hand the long envelope; but just then Mr. Forbes had been called away to attend a board meeting, so I was taken to the room of a Mr. Jones. With a few words of explanation the bearer handed him the envelope. Mr. Jones drew out the document, scanned both it and the envelope very carefully; and I leaned across the table towards him and said, "Mr. Jones, what do you think that is? Do you think it is an unsigned will?"

Mr. Jones was sitting sideways at his desk, and though this episode is a thing of the past, and I have lived through many dramatic and exciting incidents since then, I can still remember how he wheeled around and looking me straight in the eye, replied in a rather boyish way, "Unsigned nothing, Mrs. Campbell; this" (pointing to the document) "is a carbon copy of a will."

"But, Mr. Jones, your General Manager has written me that the Trust Company is unable to find any will. See these letters," said I, "and that Mr. Kingstone of Ingersoll, Kingstone, & Seymour writes they have no records in their office of any will having been drawn for Lady Howland, and that he thinks none was ever signed and, furthermore, my two sisters, who are both much older than I, write that no will was ever signed. Mr. Jones, what would you do if you were in my place?"[11]

Then Fate, in the guise of Mr. Jones, looked at me very intently. I wonder if perhaps this young man had for a moment a flash of second sight and foresaw the long dramatic struggle upon which I was entering. He paused, then replied, "Mrs. Campbell, if I were in your shoes, I should take the first train to St. Catharine's" — St. Catharine's is about three hours from Toronto, and for some ten years before her death my mother had made her home in this city[12] — "and I should make some enquiries myself from that firm," continued Mr. Jones. "You may never get the will," said he, "but you will certainly find some records. Behind that document" he emphasized his remark with his fist "there must certainly have been a will of which this is a copy."

Still a bit doubtful, I asked him how he knew all this.

He answered, "Good Lord, Mrs. Campbell, it's my job to know a carbon copy. Hundreds pass through our hands each year. How would I not know one!"

For a moment I gazed at Mr. Jones and the more I gazed the more impressed I became. He looked intelligent, as though his head was firmly fastened on his young shoulders. Notwithstanding the letter from the General Manager, I determined to take his advice.

Returning to the hotel, I gave the porter the word to call me for the fast early train to St. Catharine's. It was a sunny August morning, and still rather early when I arrived, but I went at once to the office of Ingersoll, Kingstone, & Seymour.[13]

40

I asked for Mr. Ingersoll, my mother's lifelong friend, a charming gentleman of the old school.[14] Learning that he was attending the Bar Association in England I enquired for Mr. Kingstone. He was a great friend of my brother and was solicitor for my sister, Mrs. Lindsey.[15] He was the gentleman who wrote that no record of Lady Howland's will could be found in their office. I was told that he was away playing golf somewhere, and just then a young Englishman stepped out of his room and asked if there was anything he could do for me. I told him that I was Lady Howland's youngest daughter and that I desired to locate her will.

He replied that he had been sorry to read in the papers of my mother's death and then said, much to my surprise, "You know, Mrs. Campbell, my name is Cummings. I drew that will for Lady Howland at Mr. Ingersoll's request and he and I witnessed it. Pray, just be seated a moment, I shall get the will for you." With this he left the room.[16]

Never shall I forget my feelings as I sat there that sunny August day awaiting his return; it was all I could do to control myself because it came to me with great suddenness that I was on the brink of a most interesting discovery, that the truth was coming to light notwithstanding the apparent effort to conceal it.

I cannot say how long Mr. Cummings was gone, because time stopped for me just then; but he came back, apologizing for his absence, a bit dusty and bearing open in his hands a very large book which he placed before me.

He said, "It is odd, Mrs. Campbell, I cannot find the will. It was with us for many years, but it seems to have disappeared, and there is no covering letter from Lady Howland asking for it, nor do I see any receipt; but here are the records of the drawing and execution of the will;" and he pointed to the large volume on the table, "and if you will excuse me a moment, I shall bring you further records."

He again left the room, returning this time with two books, one a large ledger and the second a small diary which proved to be Mr. Ingersoll's personal diary of 1915 in his own meticulous handwriting. There was the detailed account of the drawing and the execution of the will, and the record of the payment of the fee for the document itself and for the copy. As I looked at the books and listened to Mr. Cummings recalling the circumstances of my mother's coming to Mr. Ingersoll to have the will drawn, I realized that there was something very peculiar about those letters from Mr. Kingstone and the Trust Company regarding the unsigned will. I asked Mr. Cummings to have copies of the records made for me, which he did, and, thanking him for his courtesy, I drove to the station just in time to board my train for Toronto.

The next morning I saw Mr. Forbes and told him of my visit to St. Catharine's, laying before him the copy of the records which I had found.

Then I said, "Mr. Forbes, something tells me that there is crooked work here. Although I am a lawyer's daughter, I don't know enough about the law to put my finger on the trouble, but I intend to consult the best firm I can find in Toronto. Do you know of a Mr. Tilley? I hear he is very eminent."[17]

Mr. Forbes replied that Tilley, Johnston & Co. was one of the outstanding firms in Toronto, and that strangely enough their offices were in the Trust Company's building. So up I went in search of them.

Once more the Bar Association crossed my path; Mr. Tilley, like Mr. Ingersoll, was in London; but I was ushered into Mr. Strachan Johnston's room, the next senior partner.[18] He told me he had known my family for years, and recalled the many delightful occasions when my sisters were young girls, and he had been entertained at Stormont Lodge, my father's residence and my birthplace.

He listened very intently to my story of finding the records and said that it was quite possible in certain cases to offer a certified copy of a will for probate and that I might return to my summer home and safely leave the affair in his hands, and that he would write me as soon as he had looked into the matter. Not long after my return to Nova Scotia I received a lengthy letter from Mr. Johnston stating that he had been reading various authorities and that he thought it quite possible to offer the copy of the will for probate, and he cited one or two cases where such a thing had been done.[19] The letter concluded by telling me that he would communicate with me further in a few days.

I closed my summer cottage, returned to Boston, got the boy and girl started once more at their respective schools, and then I began to wonder why I heard nothing from Mr. Johnston. When I voiced this wonder to my husband, he, being very sensible and matter-of-fact, told me not to bother, that no doubt the man was busy, and that my affairs must surely be quite safe in the hands of so fine a firm. But I did worry. There was a certain something brought to my attention by the notepaper of Tilley, Johnston, & Co.: I noticed that one of the junior members of the firm was a Mr. Parmenter, and I remembered he happened to be a brother-in-law and very dear friend of Mr. Kingstone, the gentleman who had denied all records of the will.[20]

Another week went by with no letter from Mr. Johnston, and I decided to write him, but no reply came. I wrote again and waited in vain for some news. Then I telegraphed, and when no answer came to my wire, I decided to write the Trust Company. It may be interesting to my readers to know that trust companies always answer one's letters — one may not get a satisfactory answer but one will always get some answer. This time the answer almost took my breath away. They wrote that my sisters had taken out administration papers and that the Toronto General Trusts Corporation had signed them, that the Courts of Canada had granted them the right of administration, and that they were about to administer the estate and were sending me some final papers in connection therewith. This meant that the estate would be equally distributed between my sisters and myself, a substantial loss for me.

The letter came by the eleven o'clock mail. I threw some things in a dress suit case, telephoned for a reservation on the Toronto car, got my daughter to dancing school, and made the five o'clock train.[21] The next morning I walked into Mr. Johnston's office.

He looked somewhat confused and said, "You have come all the way back. Why did you do that?"

"Because of this, Mr. Johnston," and I handed him the Trust Company's answer. "Why did you not notify me as to what was being done about my mother's will? I am your client and you should not have allowed my sisters and the Trust Company to take out those papers."

"I made up my mind to act as I thought best," said the gentleman, getting rather red. "What do you want me to do now?"

"I want you to offer the copy of my mother's will for probate as you said you would."

So Mr. Johnston stopped the administration of the estate by some legal order, and then he wrote the Trust Company asking them if they would not offer the copy of Lady Howland's will for probate. They answered promptly that they would on no account accede to this request. Then Mr. Johnston turned his attention to discouraging me. At first he was very kindly and sympathetic, and appeared genuinely surprised when my attitude towards the probate of the will remained unchanged. He cited obstacle after obstacle while I sat quietly listening, then he looked at me and said, "You are a determined little lady, aren't you? It is just beginning to get to me. I should never have thought it to look at you."

"Why, Mr. Johnston," said I, "didn't you realize that determination is my middle name?"

After several days of this futile argument, Mr. Johnston began to be cross and peevish and finally lost his temper with me completely. He pounded his desk with his fists and said, his black eyes flashing, "I beg of you to go home, Mrs. Campbell. You are making a great deal of trouble for everyone. Don't you know you are?"

My reply to this was that I refused to go home, and that I was doing nothing wrong in seeking to establish my mother's will, and I quietly left Mr. Johnston's office. To this day the gentleman has never rendered me a bill, and appears rather uncomfortable whenever he meets me.

Next my search for a firm to push my case began. I was for some months with a very fine large firm, but nothing definite seemed to be done, although many consultations took place. I grew rather desperate, not being used to "the law's delay and the insolence of office," and one day, meeting an old friend and classmate of my brother, I said, after telling him of my case, "Casey, I want to break away from the rotten old family compact. Is there no able young man at the Bar, outside the compact, who will take my case? I'm sick and tired of these influential big firms."

"Yes," said my brother's friend, "I think A.G. Slaght would take your case. He is young and not a member of a big firm."

"But is he able, Casey?" I asked.

"Oh Lord, yes, Slaght's able," was the reply, "he is just a mind and a gown."

"The very person I'm after," thought I, and immediately began making plans to get to this man of the mind and the gown.

A few days after this something very strange happened. Another friend who has known me since my girlhood came home from a hunting expedition, and upon hearing all the trouble I was in, this elderly kind-hearted gentleman, himself a Counsel and K.C., set forth to place me and my case in safe hands. He did not find his task an easy one, and after several large firms refused him, he wrote me a letter telling me to present it at the office of one A.G. Slaght, K.C.; that in his estimation Mr. Slaght was one of the ablest of the younger men at the Bar, and that he thought he would be interested in taking my case.[22]

As the elevator whizzed me up to Mr. Slaght's office, I made a mental resolve that somehow I must induce him to act for me. When Mr. Slaght himself appeared, I knew at once that this was the fearless able Counsel I had been seeking. I presented the letter from the elderly K.C., but not without some difficulty did I gain his interest and his consent to take the case, but after an interview of considerable length—in which I told him the strange story of my finding the records of the will, but not the will itself, and that administration papers had been taken out over my head—he accepted me as his client, stating that he felt pretty confident of winning the case.

After months of delay, when we were just ready for trial, the Ingersoll, Kingstone firm gave Mr. Cummings a holiday, and he sailed very suddenly and quietly for England. Mr. Cummings, together with Mr. Ingersoll, was of course, necessary to establish the will, so the hearing was postponed. I could never make my readers understand, unless they themselves have gone through a similar experience, the suspense of those two months. After all Cummings was only a solicitor's clerk, in the employ of the Ingersoll Kingstone firm. Would he come back? He did, I am glad to say, was subpoenaed twenty-four hours after his return, and we came finally to court before Mr. Justice Kelly.[23]

Both my sisters opposed me bitterly. The Trust Company was made a party to the trial by the Court, but did not assist me in any way. Mr. Ingersoll was called. No one could doubt his word. He and Mr. Cummings proved beyond question that the will was duly executed by my mother, they being the witnesses, and that the copy offered for probate was the certified copy for which she paid. Mr. Ingersoll's evidence was that after executing the will, Lady Howland instructed him to place it in his vaults, which he did, and she left his office bearing the copy away with her, and that he never afterwards heard or thought of the will until I appeared asking for it.

The trial lasted six days; it was intensely warm weather. Mr. Justice Kelly, who seemed to me a rather ordinary old man for the Supreme Court Bench, was very brusque, and often quite rude to me.

I was for hours and hours in the witness box, a most trying experience. My sisters each had Counsel, which made my cross-examination doubly long.[24] During the giving of my evidence I was questioned about Mr. Strachan Johnston, and naturally told the story of his allowing the administration papers to go through with no notification to me. I was also questioned about Mr. Kingstone and was asked to retract the statement I made that the gentleman in question had denied all records of my mother's will; this statement I refused to retract, and I added that if his Lordship were willing, I thought Mr. Kingstone ought to come to court and tell why he made those statements.[25] No one would call Mr. Kingstone!★

Before I was released from the witness stand the opposition questioned me about one more gentleman of the legal profession; this time it was W.D. Hogg, K.C., of Ottawa, my mother's brother-in-law and my uncle by marriage.[26] He was my mother's Trustee, having managed her business affairs since my father's death in 1885 when she placed them in his hands.[27] When the Trust Company was made guardian of my mother's estate, Mr. Hogg—who was the chairman of the Trust Company's branch in Ottawa—turned over her estate to them. He made no statement of his long management, and the Trust Company did not ask him for one—a thing which I have since learned they should have done. My husband and I thought it strange that Mr. Hogg should not make any statement as to the disposition and management of my mother's property, and we wrote something of this to my sister,

★ Since writing this Mr. Kingstone has been made a Judge; his personable figure adorns the Supreme Court of Ontario. Occasionally I have seen him swinging through Osgoode Hall, and it has occurred to me how invaluable to Counsel must be his sagacity when trying a lost will case.

Mrs. McDougald. When the case came to court she was opposing me, and her Counsel read out this letter and cross-examined me upon it.

My husband, who was writing for me, had said in the letter, "Even the best of men have been known to do strange things with other people's money; we think, therefore, that Mr. Hogg should be asked for an accounting." This attitude of my husband's has since seemed to me prophetic.

Mr. Justice Kelly appeared very angry at this letter of my husband's and said he had been a great friend of Mr. Hogg for forty years, and that he was much shocked at seeing such a statement appearing about him.

The trial concluded. Mr. Slaght was brilliant throughout. His main points were that all records of the will had been kept from me until I myself discovered them, and that I had been told that the copy now offered for probate was an unsigned will, that there was no proof that the will ever reached my mother, the only evidence upon this point being that of a young fellow named Byrne, who was once a clerk in the office of Ingersoll, Kingstone, & Seymour. He stated in the witness box that during the year 1921 Mr. Kingstone told him that Lady Howland wanted her will and directed Byrne to take it over to the Welland Hotel where my mother made her home. He took what he supposed was a will across to the hotel and asked for Lady Howland, but was told that she was confined to her apartments. So he went up in the elevator, the elevator man stopping to let him out at Lady Howland's floor. He said a woman in the corridor advanced towards him saying, "Are you from Ingersoll, Kingstone, & Seymour, and have you Lady Howland's will?" whereupon he handed her the document. When questioned as to whether he could identify this person — my Counsel referred to her as "the lady of the corridor" — Byrne's reply was that he couldn't, but he knew it was not Lady Howland because the person was not an elderly lady.

The Judge asked Mr. Byrne why he received no receipt for the will and he said, "I was not told to do so, my Lord." That was the last time that anyone apparently ever saw the will; it was never at any time seen in my mother's possession.

Mr. Slaght's last point was that did my mother receive it and destroy it, she was of unsound mind, and therefore, according to

British law, the certified copy held good. Mr. Slaght cited the seven affidavits which were sworn to at the time the Toronto General Trusts Corporation were made guardians of my mother's estate. They showed beyond the peradventure of a doubt my mother's mental condition. My sister, Mrs. Lindsey, and Mr. Kingstone attended to the swearing of these affidavits: two were by physicians, one by my mother's constant attendant, one by each of her daughters, the others by friends who knew my mother. Mr. Justice Middleton made the order appointing the Trust Company committee; he did so because he was convinced that my mother's mind had completely failed.

Notwithstanding these affidavits, Counsel for my sisters, especially Mrs. Lindsey's Counsel, sought to show that my mother was of sound mind and that she had revoked her will.

About four months after our hearing, Mr. Justice Kelly rendered a decision of eighteen pages dismissing my case and ordering me to pay all the costs.[28] He found that my mother had received and revoked her will and that she was of sound mind. He said that because of my extreme demeanor and manner in the witness box — I have often wondered what he meant by that remark — and because of the aspersions which I had cast upon members of the legal fraternity, one of whom, a relative, performed useful and kindly offices for Lady Howland and visited her upon her deathbed, also because of my unwarranted suspicions with regard to those managing my mother's business affairs, he found me an incredible witness — in plain everyday parlance, the learned gentleman found that I had perjured myself, and therefore, he dismissed my case and ordered me to pay all costs.

Mr. Slaght broke the news to me by a long telegram and followed it by a letter saying that he felt the Judgment to be very erroneous and asked if I intended to appeal. He said he would not advise me either way; he had no need to, for from the moment my husband brought me the telegram, I decided to appeal, and at once, and wired Mr. Slaght to this effect.

We were kept from the Appelate Court for months because Mr. Elliott, my sister's Counsel, was taken ill with pneumonia and the Chief Justice of Ontario, Sir William Mulock, stayed the case until such time as Mr. Elliott could argue it, although there are, I think, quite five hundred other Counsel at the Ontario Bar, many of whom might have taken Mr. Elliott's place.

Mr. Slaght took the case before the First Appelate Division: the Chief Justice of Ontario, Mr. Justice Hodgins, Mr. Justice Magee, Mr. Justice Ferguson, and Mr. Justice Smith—who later was appointed to the Supreme Court of Canada.[29] For a day and a half Mr. Slaght argued and pled; he was wonderful and was, as it were, going down the line with the ball in his arms, the prospect growing worse and worse for the opposition every instant.[30] He was just taking up the affidavits as to my mother's mental condition and about to close his case—the Justices wrapped in their gowns were listening as if spellbound—when the Chief Justice electrified the entire Court by saying, "It is a shameful thing, Mr. Slaght, that this case should be settled by force of law; I halt the case and recommend that the parties get together and settle this affair. We shall proceed to the next case on the list."

Mr. Slaght bowed to the Bench and endeavored to pick up his brief and papers. He was ashen grey and his long thin hands shook. I made my way to him; together we left the Court. Arthur Slaght has the reputation, well deserved, of being the most imperturbable Counsel at the Bar—his friends refer laughingly to his "poker-face"—but for once I saw him shaken.

He said, as we walked down those long dim corridors of Osgoode Hall lined on either side by the portraits of dead and gone legal lights and Justices, "What do you make of that, Mrs. Campbell?"

I replied, "Arthur Slaght, you are up against something too big for even you to tackle; you will never be allowed into Court again with this case." And he never was.

"They cannot take my case from me, Mrs. Campbell. I have it in the hollow of my hand," said he.

Early the next morning I received word from Mr. Slaght's office, and upon going down he told me that the Chief Justice had ordered us, my sisters and myself, to appear, in the interests of a settlement, at Osgoode Hall at four o'clock, when the Bench would rise.

We were told on our arrival at Osgoode Hall that the Justices would confer with us in the Conference Chamber adjoining the

Appellate Court.[31] Mr. Slaght told me to sit in the Court Room, which was empty, and wait for him. I waited, what seemed to me an eternity. There was no sound except the ticking of the large clock.

Eternity ended and my Counsel stood in the doorway, very slim and white, but with a light on his face. He said, "I want you to come in with me now, Mrs. Campbell; I have obtained a settlement from the Judges for you such as you can take."

"I have no desire to settle, Mr. Slaght. I want you to go back and win your case," said I.

"No, Mrs. Campbell, it is wiser for you to accept this settlement. You need the money for your little family. I have taken the responsibility for you once, don't ask me to take it again," and he held out his hand and I followed him to the conference room.

The Judges were seated at a long table, the Chief Justice at the head. Magnificent in gown and flowing white beard, Ontario's

Osgoode Hall, c. 1900–5

50

"Grand Old Man of the Bench" is a most stately and imposing figure. The other Justices, looking very grave, were seated at either side of the table. My sisters did not appear, one sister sending her son, and the other her husband. These gentlemen were seated together with their Counsel beside the Judges; the place at the end facing the Chief Justice was evidently reserved for Mr. Slaght and myself.

The Chief Justice told me that their Lordships and himself were anxious for a settlement and asked me if I would be content to accept one half of my mother's estate, allowing each sister a quarter. I arose and said that I would acquiesce in their Lordship's settlement, but only if my summer home were safeguarded, because word had come to me that my second sister was making enquiries and strenuous endeavors to have it included in my mother's estate. This request was granted me, my sister's Counsel denying vehemently that any such intention had been in her mind.

Mr. Slaght was asked to draw up the settlement. We were each of us to pay our own costs, and the Trust Company's costs were to be taken out of the estate. My costs of course were very heavy, but there seemed nothing else for me to do.

Then came the astonishing climax to the whole dramatic scene. We were about, as I supposed, to sign the settlement when the Chief Justice said in a commanding voice, "You will write, Mr. Slaght, that to the day of her death Lady Howland was of sound mind and testamentary capacity."

I was aghast and sprang halfway to my feet when my Counsel said in a very low voice, "it will make no difference to you, Mrs. Campbell, it is wiser to sign it and accept the settlement," but his hand was unsteady as he wrote the sentence which took his case from him and ratified Mr. Justice Kelly's decision, and for a moment a deep flush spread over his pale face. I thought of my mother's mental condition at the time of her death and for some years before, all of which was brought out at the trial, and I remembered the affidavits filed in the Court and the order made by Mr. Justice Middleton under the Lunacy Act.[32]

After we had all signed this remarkable document, the Chief Justice arose, complimenting Mr. Slaght on his wisdom and sagacity in advising his client to settle. Everyone shook hands with everyone else and congratulated me, I do not know why. I have always considered the terms of the settlement a shocking thing and feel the sting of it today as keenly as I did then. No answer has ever been vouchsafed to me as to what happened to my mother's will or who received it. It just vanished from the vaults of Ingersoll, Kingstone, & Seymour.

There is an incident which I must not forget to relate, one which will always be linked in my mind with this dramatic and unprecedented settlement. The Benchers of the Law Society of Upper Canada are a very sacred and important Society, their number being only about fifty; to be a member is a much prized and coveted honor among the legal fraternity.

The Benchers are the governing body of the Law Society and make the laws for the behavior of Counsel, discipline them and, when necessary, take their gowns from them. At the time my case was before the Appelate Court, Mr. Slaght told me the Benchers were holding their quinquennial elections and that for the first time his name was up. He said, "Of course, Mrs. Campbell, I shall not make it this first time. One never does, you know. I'm about thirty votes behind, but it is an honor and next time I may be elected." When a day or two after the settlement of my case, I called at Mr Slaght's office, his partner, Mr. Cowan, walked out of his room and told me delightedly that the previous evening he had wired Mr. Slaght — who was on a case in Ottawa, I think — that he had been elected Junior Bencher of the Law Society of Upper Canada.[33]

Had my eagle's wings been clipped?

BOOK TWO

THE PLUNDERED ESTATE

THE TRUST Company now began to administer the estate. I was dissatisfied with the fact that Mr. Hogg made a return of only $8,200.00—he said that was all that remained of my mother's estate—and dissatisfied, too, that he made no statement as to how he had handled her money.[1] Furthermore, a small book had come into my hands; it was in an old trunk of my mother's; it had evidently been kept by her and was marked "Stocks, Bonds, and Mortgages." Together with the book were several letters in Mr. Hogg's own handwriting—the dates went back to 1905. I looked at the number of mortgages listed in the book and then I studied the letters. They all began, "My dear Bessie"—my mother's name—and were signed, "Yours affectionately, Will." Putting the two together, the letters and the book, and remembering the utter confidence my dear mother had always had in Mr. Hogg, I became convinced that an investigation ought to be made. So I went to Mr. Rowell, President of the Toronto General Trusts Corporation, and begged him to make some enquiries of his chairman, Mr. Hogg.[2]

Mr. Rowell gave directions that this should be done. A letter was despatched to Mr. Hogg at Ottawa. The reply confirmed my already aroused suspicions, and I requested Mr. Jack Langmuir, who was attending to the affair, to write once more. After a good deal of urging on my part, he did so, telling me all the while what a wonderful gentleman Mr. Hogg was and how unreasonable the desire on my part for a statement appeared, especially since Mr. Hogg had handled my mother's money for such a length of years. I remember my rejoinder to this, "I know all that, Mr. Langmuir; he has handled the estate since before the Flood, one might say, but just the same, he ought, I think, to make a statement."

When the answer to the second letter came, I saw that it was fictitious; but the Trust Company appeared completely satisfied, and I realized that Mr. Hogg was their chairman at Ottawa and that it was useless to ask them to make any further investigation.

It was then the end of May and in those days my life in summer was particularly busy looking after my young people and their friends, but I determined in the autumn to make some enquiries myself.

Early in October I slipped up to Ottawa.[3] As I had not visited there for some years no one recognized me. I went first to the Registry Office and then to the office of the Capital Real Estate Co. — or rather to what had been their office. The Capital Real Estate transaction which I unearthed was unusually interesting.

Listed in my mother's book was a mortgage to the Capital Real Estate Co., interest upon it had evidently been paid regularly to her for many years, and one of Mr. Hogg's letters read like this; "Your stock when sold produced $2,000.00; of this I sent you $200.00, the remainder, $1,800.00 was lent upon a mortgage to the Capital Real Estate Co., which is as good as gold." This was away back in January of 1905. I found that the Capital Real Estate Co. had been dissolved in 1922; but there was a note in my mother's book, "Mortgage made in 1905; Nelson Porter, Treasurer; W.D. Hogg, President of the Company."

I found Mr. Nelson Porter was now head of a large insurance and real estate office. He was very pleasant, and when I asked him about the $1,800.00 Capital Real Estate mortgage of Lady Howland he appeared at first surprised; and then, when I produced Mr. Hogg's letter, rather shocked. His face flushing, he assured me that she had never held an $1,800.00 mortgage with them; but one for $1,700.00 and another for $800.00. He begged me to return after luncheon and said he would have all the books of the Capital Real Estate Co. out for my perusal and that I should go over them with one of his young men in order to satisfy myself that no such investment as that referred to in Mr. Hogg's letter had ever existed, but that the Capital Real Estate Company paid interest regularly upon a mortgage for $1,700.00 until such time as it was released. There was a letter of Mr. Hogg's telling of this $1,700.00 mortgage and mentioning the $1,800.00 mortgage as well.

I spent the afternoon with Mr. Porter's books and his young clerk; and when I left his office it was with the shocking certainty that one W.D. Hogg, K.C., Senior Bencher of the Law Society of

Ontario and Chairman of the Toronto General Trusts Corporation at Ottawa, was a dishonest old man ...

The night seemed ages long, comfortable though my room was at the Château Laurier. In the morning I continued my research work at the Registry Office. There I made friends with one of the officials, an elderly man who had known my brother. This gentleman greatly assisted me in my search. By noon I had complete proof that both Mr. Hogg's letters to the Trust Company regarding the disposition of certain mortgages were quite untrue and that he had in no way accounted for these large sums of money. One of the sums in question Mr. Hogg wrote he had given to my brother, Charles Bethune, to hand to my mother upon the last visit my brother made to see Lady Howland. This mortgage was not discharged nor did Mr. Hogg receive the money until several months after my brother's death.[4]

To say that I was shocked at these revelations would be to put it mildly. My foundations rocked under me. It is true, I had had nothing to do with Mr. Hogg for many years; but my mind harked back to my girlhood days and I could hear my dear mother's voice, "Well, I will ask your Uncle Will"; it was almost her slogan when we thought, perhaps of taking a little trip or of doing anything not included in the "even tenor of our way." What was I to do! I wrote Mr. Slaght and then telephoned his office, but found he was out of Toronto, away at some assizes.

I decided to have an interview with Mr. Davey, the Manager of the Trust Company in Ottawa; so the next day I made my way to him.[5] Mr. Davey is a long nosed, very astute-looking man of my own generation. His looks, I have since reflected, do not belie him. As I sat there opposite him, recounting across his mahogany table the awful information about Mr. Hogg, turning hot and cold as I did so, it comes to me now that he was not as shocked as one might have expected; in fact he scarcely seemed shocked at all. Did he perhaps know the chairman of his advisory board better than I? But the one thing that Mr. Davey did appear anxious about was that I should get in touch with Mr. Hogg and at once. He said, "I felt sure, Mrs. Campbell, when those first letters were written Mr. Hogg from Toronto this spring that sooner or later you would come to Ottawa yourself; and now that you are here, we shall go right to Mr. Hogg. He, no doubt, will be able to explain all these things to you," and with that he got to his feet and, picking up what someone in Bloomsbury has called the hideous emblem of respectability, his "bowler" and his cane and gloves, he began politely but firmly ushering me through the door of his office. I protested that I did not care to call on Mr. Hogg, that I had not seen him for years, and that in my estimation he was a wicked man;—all of which Mr. Davey suavely disregarded.

He surprised me by stepping into a small lift, saying that the offices of Hogg & Hogg were just above those of the Trust Company.[6] So convenient to have the chairman of one's advisory board on the premises.

Upon reaching Mr. Hogg's floor, Mr. Davey preceded me and I followed him, my knees shaking. There at his desk sat Mr. Hogg, pompous and worthy-looking, exceedingly well dressed, and so bland and bald it took great courage to face him; but there was no escape. Mr. Davey stood beside me, so I managed a "Good morning, sir," to which Mr. Hogg growled, "What the devil are you doing here?" and I noticed that the blandness had disappeared and that the high bald forehead and the face above the rim of white whiskers were dyed crimson. If ever I have seen a guilty man caught in his tracks, it was W.D. Hogg at that moment.

Mr. Davey, noticing how terrified I was at this spectacle, hastened to explain that I had come to Ottawa to make some investigations with regard to Lady Howland's estate which no doubt Mr. Hogg would be happy to give me. Then Mr. Hogg turned on me with so much hatred in his look, and so much abuse on his tongue that even Mr. Davey, his suavity somewhat shaken, looked alarmed and endeavored to stop the estimable gentleman's tirade by asking whether he didn't think it would be a good thing to have an accountant in to look over his books and help him get them and his accounts in order; at which Mr. Hogg vehemently protested saying, "An accountant wouldn't be able to make anything of my books at present."

At this Mr. Davey, rather chagrined, practically took me by the hand. Bidding Mr. Hogg good-morning, the only response to which being a glare, we left the office. I recall Mr. Davey's saying on the way down in the lift, "That old gentleman seems very hostile to you, Mrs. Campbell." When we reached the Trust Company's offices, he seated me there, called in his typist, and had me make out a questionnaire of the points upon which I desired information from Mr. Hogg; and then he asked me what I intended to do. Astute Mr. Davey! His front line, upon which he had relied, the hope of a quiet settlement with Mr. Hogg, knocked sky high by our interview with that stormy old gentleman, he fell back on his second line of defence and begged me to proceed at once to Toronto for a conference with Mr. Rowell who is an eminent King's Counsel, and President of the Toronto General.[7] He is also one of Mr. Hogg's fellow Benchers, his special office just then being head of the Committee on Discipline of that august body.★

Mr. Davey assured me that Mr. Rowell would know just what to do, would in fact look after the whole matter for me and take it off my hands. Strange as it seems to me now, viewed in the light of what has since transpired, I believed him; nevertheless, I wanted to return to Boston to talk the matter over with my husband before getting in touch with Mr. Rowell and the Trust Company in Toronto. Within the next day or two I wrote Mr. Rowell telling him that I had conclusive evidence that large sums of money were owing Lady Howland's estate and begged for an interview with him.

Mr. Rowell's secretary responded immediately by night letter setting an early date for our conference. Once more I threw some things into my suit case and started for Toronto.

My appointment with Mr. Rowell was set for the afternoon, so this gave me time to dash to Mr. Slaght's office. Fortunately he had returned to the city, and although there was the usual line of worried looking persons waiting their turn, he very kindly sent out word to admit me at once. In case it should occur to any of my readers to wonder why I designate Mr. Slaght's "waiting line" or "queue" as worried looking, I hasten to explain that he is probably the last word in criminal law at the Ontario Bar. No doubt often these unfortunates as they await his advice so anxiously have visions passing before their mind's eye of the penitentiary for life, or at least for a long number of years, or, even more terrible still, visions of some loved one, some relative or husband, paying the

---

★ Mr. Rowell has since resigned the Presidency of The Toronto General Trusts. He is Chief Justice of the Supreme Court of Ontario.

supreme penalty with life itself, unless this clever Counsel, Arthur Slaght, can by his wits and skill save them. I might add he usually manages to do so. He once said to me in speaking of the large fees he commands, "I am a luxury, Mrs. Campbell, people only come to me when they are *in extremis*."

I have often reflected upon that oddly assorted waiting line: the weird yellow "Chink" up for trafficking in dope[8] next to a respectable little woman, her eyes red with weeping, probably for a husband in the cells, perhaps a case of manslaughter; then one or two big brokers in purple and fine linen caught red handed in a nefarious deal, and out on enormous bail trying to bluff it and look nonchalant, but showing in their eyes the terrible anxiety and strain; occasionally a young dashing looking woman seeking divorce or defending herself against it; and then myself. What chance had brought me there! Only in one or two other cases besides mine had Mr. Slaght ever attacked, almost invariably he had been on the defensive side.

But I have digressed.

My letter from Ottawa lay open on my Counsel's desk, so that he knew in a way what my visit was all about; and I hastened to lay my mother's book with the incriminating evidence against Mr. Hogg before him. It is an interesting fact that, hardened criminal lawyer though he is, it was Arthur Slaght who next to myself seemed most shocked by the information which had come to me; and he explained, the long index finger pointing to the Capital Real Estate page of the book, how serious and criminal a thing was the transaction. "It is horrible, Mrs. Campbell, for a man of Mr. Hogg's position and prominence to be doing this sort of thing; it's the old, old game of a fictitious mortgage, for which men are constantly going to the penitentiary," said he. "Hogg, instead of buying a security for Lady Howland, simply paid her interest on that money all down those years, and then pocketed the principal."

The term was new to me, I, of course, never having heard of a fictitious mortgage. Then after a few more words of explanation he told me that I was doing the wise thing in presenting my evidence to Mr. Rowell, that this was most serious for the Trust Company, and that in his estimation they would bring pressure to bear upon Mr. Hogg to at once make restitution, he being chairman of their advisory board.

He cautioned me not to leave any of my original evidence against Mr. Hogg, the mortgage book and the letters in Mr. Hogg's own writing, with the Trust Company, but to tell them they should have exact copies of them,— with this he rang his bell, and placing my papers in the hands of one of his typists directed her to make these copies for me at once.[9] Just as I was leaving the room, he looked up at me from his desk and said, "Mrs. Campbell, just in case Mr. Rowell does not attend to this for you, we shall push the Trust Company if you desire us to." I, not grasping the import of his words, said lightly, "Oh, no, Mr. Slaght, thank you just the same, but this time I shan't have to bother you, I hope. I'm sure Mr. Rowell will attend to it for me."

His only answer was an inscrutable, sphinx-like smile, if one can call this expression of his a smile; I have learned that when his face assumes it, the gentleman is peering into the future, and is already seeing events which to the rest of us who are not so highly endowed seem veiled in obscurity.

Promptly at 2:30 that afternoon, armed with my original evidence and my copies, I was shown into Mr. Rowell's private room at the Trust Company and there found my friend Mr. Davey, who had come up from Ottawa bringing with him another long rambling letter of explanation from Mr. Hogg, and some answers to my questionnaire which, the moment I read them, made me realize that with each false excuse Mr. Hogg was getting in deeper and deeper.[10]

Mr. Rowell was very polite, very attentive; I could feel that he saw Mr. Hogg's dishonesty at once. He listened most carefully to my story, discussing the various points with me for about an hour. Then he concluded the interview by saying that I might leave the book and papers with him, that he would bring the matter to the attention of his board immediately, and would advise me within a short time what steps would be taken by the Trust Company to recover the money.

I told him that I had copies of the book and papers for the Trust Company, but that I preferred to retain the original book and letters myself; then I made the suggestion that an accountant be put on Mr. Hogg's books. This is the one and only time I have seen Mr. Rowell look annoyed;—he is what is known as a very "Christian man," with a soft smooth voice and a somewhat sedative smile; but the soft voice lost its smoothness, and for a few moments the sedative smile faded as he replied, "No, Mrs. Campbell, you have placed this affair in my hands and I shall handle it the way I think best."

I thanked him; and politely holding my coat and handing me my umbrella he ushered me out of his office.

Perhaps some of my readers are asking, as the Justices of the Appellate Court, and later their Lordships in England asked me, what Mr. Rowell did after I went to him. I can only answer as I answered the Courts; in so far as I know, he did nothing—that is, nothing for me. In fact, although I've had the honor of a number of interviews with the gentleman since then, the result has always been the same. I have been treated with courtesy, have been smiled upon, have with great care been assisted into my coat, my umbrella and other impedimenta have been retrieved, and finally the door held open; but no help has ever been vouchsafed me by Mr. Rowell;—in fact, his personality has rather put me off the proverbial "Christian man."[11]

Frequently people in Toronto have said, "Don't you think Mr. Rowell, the President of the Trust Company, is wonderful?" to which I have unhesitatingly replied, "Yes, wonderful." He is wonderful from the standpoint of the Toronto General itself. In fact it would seem to me that all trust companies should lose no time in furnishing themselves with presidents such as Mr. Rowell. One sometimes hears of a skillful society surgeon's "beautiful bedside manner"; now I think Mr. Rowell is possessed of a perfect trust company manner. It must be remembered that to a great extent trust companies are dealing with widows and orphans, and quite generally with newly bereaved and deeply distressed people, and that soothing sedative smile and soft voice of the President of the Toronto General Trusts would have great weight and a generally soporific effect upon women in particular; it is calculated to allay their fears and suspicions for a time at least, and there is always the chance that when the patient does come to, the danger may be over. I came to quite quickly, for some reason, perhaps, because of my "suspicious nature" so greatly deplored by my friend, Mr. Justice Kelly. At any rate in a week or two Mr. Slaght and I were pushing the Trust Company pretty hard. The upshot of this was that in about six weeks' time they waited upon my Counsel with a cheque for the magnificent sum of $580.00 from Mr. Hogg, and said that in the Trust Company's estimation this investigation of his affairs had gone far enough and that they proposed to accept the $580.00 as a settlement and proceed to wind up the estate.[12]

Mr. Slaght stood firm and told them they could do no such thing and sent them back again to demand some proper accounting from their chairman.

Finally in January 1927, we received word that Mr. Hogg was about to pass his accounts in the Surrogate Court at Ottawa.[13]

By now Mr. Hogg admitted that when he had turned over Lady Howland's affairs to the Trust Company in 1922, he had quietly retained a substantial sum for the purpose of paying his bill, so he said; but no bill had ever been rendered and, as the Privy Council pointed out later on, when he was found with this money in his hands he seems to have felt that only by a general accounting could he endeavor to clear himself.[14]

I, being entirely ignorant at this time of both accounts and Surrogate Courts, hastened to Toronto once more, but stopped at Ottawa on the way up to secure a copy of Mr. Hogg's accounts filed in the Court. While in Ottawa I wanted to cash a cheque and needed some identification at the bank. So bethinking myself of Mr. Davey I strayed into the Trust Company's office; while seated at his table as he was telephoning, I noticed a letter from the Trust Company at Toronto. It interested me. They had discovered that the accounts filed by Mr. Hogg contained some grave errors and omissions and they forwarded a memorandum telling him that "our Mr. Mulkins will call upon you, no doubt you will rectify these mistakes." As a consequence, Mr. Hogg, assisted no doubt by Mr. Mulkins, submitted another set of accounts ten days later with about eighteen changes.[15]

If my Counsel's wings had been clipped, evidently the operation had not been entirely successful, because once more he went into battle for me on the side of justice. When I reached my boarding place in Toronto, I found a letter of explanation awaiting me. The letter made it clear that if Mr. Hogg succeeded in passing this fictitious and dishonest set of accounts, he would obtain a discharge from the Court and it would be almost impossible to collect the money which he owed the estate. Mr. Slaght went on to say that he was very busy at the moment, and he was not anxious to go to Ottawa. Furthermore, he mentioned a fee which for my circumstances in life was a pretty high one; he also mentioned that the Trust Company would not allow me anything towards this fee out of the estate, and then last of all he recommended several high standing Counsel at Ottawa who in his estimation were better fitted to undertake the job than himself. I was terrified because I had no confidence in these Ottawa Counsel— no confidence in anyone but Mr. Slaght. As far as the money went I knew I could borrow that, from a kind generous friend in our parish, but I could read in between the lines of my Counsel's letter that he was most loath to take on the job.[16]

As I dressed to go down to his office, I prayed very hard for courage for him, and for myself, that I might influence him to fight for me once more. When Mr. Slaght returned from his luncheon there sat I at his desk.

Face to face with me the excuses dropped away one by one; he said, "Mrs. Campbell, do not ask me to do this thing for you. To attack Mr. Hogg is most distasteful to me. He is a senior Bencher and a man of high standing, and I assure you the affair is a nasty one, unsavory to a degree; anyway it is going to cost you a lot of money,—money which you and your husband can ill afford. Get some other Counsel."

The one thing I was conscious of was that he didn't say, "I won't do it." My reply was, "Arthur Slaght,"—and I went across to his side of the desk and laid my hand on his shoulder for an instant— "you are going to fight for me and my children."

He said, "Come back at five o'clock, Mrs. Campbell; I shall give you a definite answer then."

The thing which encouraged me greatly was that never did my Counsel say, "It is foolish for you to attempt to dispute these accounts." In fact, I sensed that he realized only too well that my position in the eyes of the law was a strong one.

While waiting for this answer, so momentous to me, I saw Mr. Lang at the Trust Company—he is Estates Manager—and he informed me that the Trust Company had retained Mr. McKague, a young rather inexperienced Counsel, to appear presumably for the estate.[17] I questioned him as to what attitude my sisters had taken—I felt that it ought to be their affair too. I gathered that my sister, Mrs. McDougald was quite willing to allow Mr. Slaght and myself to do the fighting but that she would be glad to take her share of the money. As for Mrs. Lindsey, he was not prepared to say what she would do, but whatever it was, he looked very uncomfortable about it.

Five o'clock saw me once more in Mr. Slaght's office. I can remember so well how my heart beat as I waited for that door of his to open. It did at last, and I was shown in.

"I have decided to go to Ottawa for you, Mrs. Campbell," said he, and then added, "but I hope you won't want me to be too bitter or hard with Mr. Hogg; and now if you will wait for a few minutes while I sign these letters, we shall get to work at once. We shall have to prepare our case this evening, you know, because I am leaving on the 'midnight' for the North Country on a matter which will engage me until Wednesday; but I shall get into Ottawa early Thursday morning. Your appointment is for ten o'clock."[18]

I waited and in a few moments out came Mr. Slaght and walking towards Mr. Cowan, his partner, said, looking up at him, "Jim, I'm going to Ottawa for her."

The picture they made is stamped on my mind: my Counsel, himself quite tall, very slim, his thumbs locked in the armhole of his vest, with his fine fair head thrown back looking up at this huge stout Scotsman who towered inches above him. Evidently, I and my case had been a matter of some discussion between them; and was it my fancy, or did Mr. Cowan's rather Semitic looking face fall as his senior partner issued his ultimatum?[19]

"Now, all of you clear out. I shall need Jean for a while, perhaps, then she can go too. Mrs. Campbell and I have some tall work before us this evening."

Soon the busy office was quiet. Lighting a very large very black cigar and telling me to draw up my chair, my Counsel and I began to brief our case. I had all my notes on the discoveries made in Ottawa and also some ideas of my own. Whenever they were helpful ideas, Mr. Slaght would say, "That's a good point, Mrs. Campbell."

I was not conscious of it at the time, but on looking back I can see that it was during these hours that evening on the fourteenth story of the Royal Bank Building that my training for the Privy Council began. With A.G. Slaght, K.C., beside me in the Surrogate Court I was scoring heavily against my opponents.

Hour after hour passed, the little typist was dismissed, and still we worked on. Finally at about nine o'clock, my Counsel announced that he thought we had pretty well exhausted our case; "and ourselves, too, Mr. Slaght," I remember adding.

Placing all our material with a note of instructions for his able junior partner, Mr. Ferguson, to get the brief in shape for me to take to Ottawa on Wednesday, we put out the lights and left the office going across the street to a "Child's" for a much needed supper.[20]

The weather at this time throughout Ontario was shockingly cold, the thermometer hovering around fifteen to twenty below, and Mr. Slaght, knowing his North Country, was afraid of a blizzard snowing him up from Timmins to Ottawa; so he wrote to his agent, George McDonnell, K.C., in Ottawa that he was appearing for me against Mr. Hogg on Thursday at 10 o'clock in the Surrogate Court at Ottawa.[21] He told him that I was taking a leading part in the investigations, in fact that it was due to my efforts that this failure on Mr. Hogg's part to account for my mother's estate had been unearthed, and he begged Mr. McDonnell, in case

Childs restaurant, Toronto

64

he should be delayed by a storm, to go with me to the Surrogate Court and ask that the audit be adjourned until his arrival.

Before leaving for Ottawa on the noon train on Wednesday I called at Slaght and Cowan's office to obtain Mr. Slaght's brief, and was shown an answer from George McDonnell to the effect that he begged to be excused from assisting me in any way. The letter was rather a curt one. It was the first blow. The legal fraternity was rising to protect its own.

With what anxiety I watched the weather. The cold, severe enough in Toronto, became simply bitter as we rushed along towards Ottawa. Nevertheless, when the train drew in, the stars and a lovely young moon were shining brightly over the Château Laurier and the Parliament Buildings, and it didn't look like a storm after all. So I took heart!

Several times during the night I remember waking, notwithstanding the absolute comfort of my surroundings—the Château is one of the most delightfully appointed hotels to be found.[22] I remember, too, getting up and going to the windows to assure myself that the stars were still shining.

Chateau Laurier, Ottawa, 1931

I was awake when at about half past seven the telephone beside my bed tinkled and Mr. Slaght at the other end announced his safe arrival and said he would meet me for breakfast at a quarter to nine. He said the temperature had been forty below in the North Country when he had left the previous day, and that his arriving on time was entirely due to the railway's putting on a special train for a number of them,—gentlemen who like himself, were obliged to be in Ottawa early that morning. My gratitude went out to the Canadian National.

My Counsel was in good fighting shape. He mentioned while we breakfasted in the lovely dining room at the Château that he had won his case at Timmins, and we again discussed the main points in my case, and then he told me two most interesting things: He said that while he was shaving and dressing for breakfast the Estates Manager for the Trust Company—he and the young Counsel were also putting up at the Château—was in his room telling him what a pity the whole affair was and just an unfortunate mistake on Mr. Hogg's part. The second item was even more interesting: Mr. Slaght went on to say that his Honor Judge Mulligan, before whom the audit was to be held, had been a great friend of his father's and had known him since he was quite a young lad. "You know, Mrs. Campbell, I received a pleasant surprise just now when I opened my mail. There was a cheque from the Judge paying me money I lent him several years ago. The old chap is always hard up, he has an expensive family, and I certainly never expected he would pay the money back," said my Counsel, slapping his breast pocket in an appreciative manner.

I do not think I made any comment other than the conventional, "How splendid, Mr. Slaght!" Nor did my Counsel but as we rose from the breakfast table it seemed to me that for an instant there was a flash in his usually quiet eyes. The far-seeing A.G. Slaght, K.C., was on guard!

His Honor, Judge Mulligan, to whom I was introduced upon our arrival at the Surrogate Court, proved to be an exceedingly frail meek-looking elderly man.[23] I felt from the first that he was going to be totally inadequate to my case, a feeling which was justified. The Court stenographer was an elderly woman with blonde hair. My Counsel referred to her always as "this young lady" in a most pointed manner and paid her great deference. I felt that much depended upon how the "young lady" took down our evidence, though I little knew to what an august tribunal I was to present that evidence finally.

Soon Mr. Hogg himself came into the Court room quite jauntily, greeted his Honor graciously and in a somewhat patronizing manner, glared at me, and, taking no notice whatever of my Counsel, seated himself at one end of the long table in the Court room with the Trust Company's Estates Manager beside him. Mr. Hogg was sworn and the audit commenced.

My sister, Mrs. Lindsey, had as usual done the strange incomprehensible thing and was represented by an elderly individual whom Mr. Slaght greeted as "Sinclair."[24] She was appearing against the estate, to my astonishment. Mr. Sinclair said he wished to say that Mrs. Lindsey desired to express her gratitude for the careful way Mr. Hogg had looked after Lady Howland's estate.

It soon became evident that Mr. Hogg intended to brazen out his position. This was a pity,—for Mr. Hogg. I think he must often have regretted it since; but of course, he did not know my Counsel. At all times a master on cross-examination, Mr. Slaght becomes, if the witness proves brazen or untruthful, almost merciless. He once said to me, speaking of a lady witness guilty of the aforesaid errors, "The brazen old woman! People do not often lie to me, Mrs. Campbell, and never with impunity. I gave her just what she deserved." And he gave Mr. Hogg just what he deserved.

Before submitting his accounts at all to the Surrogate Court, Mr. Hogg swore that all his books which recorded his dealings with my mother's affairs had been destroyed. He said that when his firm moved their offices they had most unfortunately been thrown out or burned; he therefore was unable to say of what the original estate consisted.[25]

After about twenty-five minutes of brisk cross-examination on Mr. Slaght's part, the first book appeared and from then on during the day they kept appearing under pressure from my Counsel until finally we had a large pile of dusty ledgers; but nothing prior to 1905 could be secured except some letter books containing copies of letters which Mr. Hogg had written my mother covering a long period of years.

Curiously however, before leaving Toronto, Mr. Slaght's partner, Mr. Ferguson, had suggested to me that since Mr. Hogg could not say how much money he had received from my mother, I should obtain a copy of my father's will to go in as evidence of how much money she had been left.[26] This I did. It was a touching thing to me to read that yellowed paper in the Surrogate Court at Toronto where I finally found it: "I leave all that I die possessed of to my dear wife, Elizabeth Mary, and appoint her sole executor and guardian of my infant children," and then my father's rather bold flowing signature, "JAMES BETHUNE."

This will, together with these letters, proved most valuable, and with them my Counsel was able to gain an admission from Mr. Hogg that the money which he had received for investment was considerably in excess of what was shown by his accounts, he also admitted that he was a trustee, not merely an agent. This is the point upon which my whole case has turned, the point upon which I won in England, the fact that my mother had entrusted him with her money to invest and reinvest and that he had never made an accounting. Mr. Slaght led him on to tell of the intimate affectionate relationship which existed between my mother and himself;—he was her young brother-in-law, married from my father's house, befriended by my father in every way, and, as he himself said, "Naturally she turned to me." My father's death was terribly sudden, my mother was young and stricken with grief, and she knew little or nothing of business, and furthermore she trusted Mr. Hogg utterly. The evidence adduced by my Counsel upon the fictitious mortgage was terrible. With the money gained from the coal stock Mr. Hogg admitted buying a security for $800.00 only, presumably he used the remaining $1,000.00 for himself, but for twelve years, every six months when the cheque for the interest on $800.00 came to him he wrote my mother an affectionate letter in his own handwriting, never employing one of his several typists, and augmented the interest, thus leading her to believe that her money was safely invested.[27] His book showed the receipt of the small sum of interest, but his letters enclosing the cheques and the vouchers which my mother signed showed the augmented sum. Then years later when my mother's mind began to fail, he discontinued the interest and pocketed the principal. It was, as my Counsel stated, premeditated and diabolical, carried on over a long period of years. Mr. Hogg's only answer to this was that it was a complete mistake from beginning to end, and that he was at a loss to account for it. My Counsel very rightly rejoined that it could not be a mistake!

The old Judge looked most shocked during the examination; indeed, several times he seemed to me to be just ready to fly from his seat on the Bench above us. There below him sat the pompous and lordly W.D. Hogg, K.C., Senior Bencher of the Law Society, Chairman of the Ottawa Board of the Toronto General Trusts, being examined upon most nefarious transactions, producing falsified books and admitting that he had entirely failed to keep a trust account, that his money was all mixed up with that of his cestui que trust, submitting accounts which it was plain to be seen were false accounts which did not in any way comply with the Trustee Act.[28] What was he, the Judge, to do about it?

He tried once or twice very politely to stem the tide, but that first day in Ottawa it would have been just about as easy to stop Niagara as to have stopped my Counsel. I have always felt that the damage was done that first day. Determined and dignified, with his horn rimmed glasses poised in his long slim fingers, Arthur Slaght literally stood over Mr. Hogg pressing home point after point and never once, in spite of the fact that his witness was upon several occasions very rude and insolent, did he lose his temper; but steadily he made headway and steadily the blonde typist took down the damning evidence.

I kept Mr. Slaght's notes for him, not very well I am afraid, being then new to that sort of thing. Also more than once as I happened to look up I found Mr. Hogg's gaze riveted upon me with a look of positive hatred,—it was rather terrifying, and I think the notes suffered in consequence.

Just as we were finishing the morning session, both the Judge and Mr. Slaght advised Mr. Hogg to have Counsel beside him. By this time a good bit of the brazen manner had dropped away and he said he would consider the question of Counsel at the recess.

When we were "speeding" back to the Court House after our hurried luncheon my Counsel said, "Watch 'Sinclair,' Mrs. Campbell; in my estimation his appearing for your sister is just a blind, he is there to help Hogg." Mr. Hogg had already arrived when we entered the Court room, and sure enough, by his side sat "Sinclair," whose name and title I had by this time gathered was R.V. Sinclair, K.C. Were I permitted I should like to describe Mr.

Sinclair to you, because from now on he is constantly with us, from Court to Court, defending Mr. Hogg—a most unpleasant task I fancy—being at times most rudely treated by the Judges. As I once told him one could not but respect his loyalty to his client, at which tribute he grew very red. Indeed, I have often speculated upon the tie that binds these two men together.[29] There was one Court, however, that Mr. Sinclair didn't venture into and that was the Privy Council,—but of this anon.

The gentleman arose and informed his Honor that Mr. Hogg had accepted him as his Counsel so now he would have the honor to appear for him as well as for Mrs. Lindsey. It did strike me as Gilbertian; here were Mr. Hogg, who quite evidently had robbed my mother's estate; and my sister, who was entitled to one quarter of that estate, both of them represented by the same Counsel.

Mr. Slaght lost no time in resuming the examination, and the case grew worse and worse. I shall not weary you with what my Counsel so elegantly referred to as Mr. Hogg's depredations; sufficient to say that from the time my dear mother entrusted him with the care of her money, amounts—some large, some small—began to disappear, never to be heard of again. But one item I must tell you about because it stands out as an example of duplicity. Away back in 1885, Mr. Hogg lent a sum of my mother's money to two men by the names of Thomas Martin and James McAmmond.[30] He said these men were market gardeners. They brought him bonds as security and for years they appeared regularly every six months and paid their interest which Mr. Hogg in turn sent on to my mother;—she had it neatly noted in her little book. Suddenly, after about thirty-two years, these gentlemen, Messrs. McAmmond and Martin, desired to pay off their mortgage and get their bonds back. What kind of bonds these were was one of the things upon which Mr. Hogg's memory was hazy, but anyway they came bringing him two bank drafts, and he returned them their bonds, so he said. How delighted they must have been to get them back after thirty-two years! As he was about to make a visit to St. Catharine's on business just at that time, he took the drafts and gave them to my mother, but he unfortunately omitted to get any receipt from her, but there was no doubt whatever, oh none, but that he had handed them to her. Through about seventy

pages of examination and cross-examination the excellent gentleman stuck to the story, though at times it wavered somewhat suspi-
ciously; still the burden of it remained unchanged—he had handed Lady Howland the drafts.

My mother banked with the Bank of Commerce and we had
her account most carefully searched only to find that two small
sums of interest which Mr. Hogg had sent her at that time, and for
which he had receipts, were duly deposited; but no cheque or
drafts or anything else for the McAmmond and Martin sums could
be discovered. Then we had a search made to see if by any chance
she had kept a second account in any other bank, but this also
proved fruitless.

Under further cross-examination the tale became more lurid.
The Messrs. McAmmond and Martin had sold their belongings, it
seemed, at this date—March 1917—and had disappeared to the
States,—just vanished, leaving no traces in Ottawa. One of the
most remarkable things about the whole affair was that though
these men had come to Mr. Hogg's office so often during all these
thirty-two years, and he had had their bonds presumably in his safe
all that time, yet he had never known where they lived in Ottawa
nor where their place of business was.*

The poor old Judge's face was a study during this particular
stage of the audit. Then my Counsel got at the books on the
McAmmond and Martin transactions. They were, as he showed
the Judge, altered and tampered with. He called for the court magnifying glass. After some searching, a very grimy one was produced
and my Counsel pointed out to the Court that subsequent to my
visit to Ottawa and the discoveries resulting therefrom, the books
had been altered and fresh entries made by Mr. Hogg's own hand,
although he endeavored to say it was the work of his bookkeeper;
but Mr. Slaght firmly continued his cross-examination and finally
gained the truth: An admission that the books had been altered
some time after that October visit of mine.[31]

The Court adjourned until the next morning. The work of the
day over, my Counsel invited me to dine with him that evening

---

* It is interesting to note that three Canadian Courts accepted this
story.

and to go on to a hockey game afterwards. Arthur Slaght is a man who works hard, and he likes to play hard.[32] He was in a gala humor that night. The large dining room was filled, and a fine orchestra was playing and the dinner was delicious. He told me that the case was infinitely more serious than he had thought, but that it looked as though the old Judge was at last beginning to "take things in" as he put it. I did not dispute that; indeed, it would have been impossible for anyone not to have taken in such evidence as we had heard adduced that day, but the question in my mind, which I thought it wiser not to voice, was "what was the old Judge going to do with the evidence?" Would he give a verdict against the Senior Bencher, or would he endeavor to decently inter what he had "taken in," difficult of accomplishment as this might be?

After the hockey game — an exciting one — and a good supper to follow in the grill room, I decided to call it a day and retire to bed. My Counsel, so he told me, was going to "look in" at a large ball being given at the Château by some society of engineers, but he said he would be "on deck" for breakfast at a quarter to nine in the morning.

Mr. Slaght was already seated at the table with his morning paper when I got down. He said that I looked very fit indeed, and then he warned me that he himself was in a bad humour and that he had some hard fighting to do in the Surrogate Court that day.

The two "Trust Company boys" as Mr. Slaght dubbed them, Mr. Lang the Estates Manager and young McKague, their Counsel, were breakfasting near us, and as I sipped my orange juice and tried to jolly my Counsel into a better humour, I caught several times what my son calls a "dirty look" from Mr. McKague. He is pretty bright and was evidently beginning to realize the funda-mental mistake the Trust Company had made in ever allowing Arthur Slaght into the Surrogate Court with such serious evidence against their esteemed chairman.

My Counsel, hands in pockets, resumed his examination in a grimly determined manner, and by the mid-day recess he had made further important headway and his Honor was looking more and more uncomfortable. While I was assisting Mr. Slaght to gather together the many papers and to put them in his brief case before leaving for luncheon, I saw Mr. McKague look at him across the table. Mr. Slaght, turning to me, said, "You run along now and have your lunch. I'm going out for a bite with McKague." I was rather surprised, but told him not to bother about me, that I could manage quite nicely for myself, and I left the Court room. A little later, at the hotel, after a sandwich and some coffee, I had just stepped out of the lift and was walking towards my room when I saw my Counsel and young McKague coming down the long corridor almost arm in arm, evidently on most friendly terms. Mr. Slaght looked at me rather oddly, I thought, but asked politely if I had got some lunch, to which I replied in the affirmative. He said he would be at the Court House at two o'clock. I was alarmed and rightly so, because although he continued with the case for many days as will be seen, I think he never again fought with quite the same dash or élan as he did on that first day and a half. But fortunately, as I have said before, the damage of that first day's cross-examination was irremediable, it could never afterwards be undone. The Trust Company had been a bit slow on their job!

At five o'clock his Honor informed us that he would be unable to continue the next morning but could give us two days in about three weeks' time. The weather had moderated, so Mr. Slaght and I walked along to the Château. He told me that Mr. Hogg's books were in a shocking condition and that he thought it advisable to have an accountant put on them. He said it would cost something, but in his estimation the Trust Company ought to pay for it out of the estate. He also asked me to order him a copy of the evidence, saying that the typist had been quite speedy and more efficient than he had anticipated. He again invited me to dine with him, but I could see he was not in the gala humour of the evening before. He was not leaving for Toronto until eleven o'clock. I was return-ing home by the Montreal train sometime after midnight.

He said he would be greatly obliged if I would bring him the cheque for his services as he had just received word that the Trust Company would not allow him anything from the estate. Fortunately I had the money in my account at the bank, so I wrote out the cheque. It was a large one for the two days' work, but Mr. Slaght had told me what the fee was to be; and after all, if one retains a good Counsel one expects to pay him. What did surprise me rather was that the cheque didn't have a better effect on him.

The dinner, the orchestra, the gay throng of diners was just the same as the previous evening, and as for me I tried to be more than agreeable because I felt that something was wrong, but my Counsel would scarcely look at me, and a gloom seemed to hang over our little table. My host wasn't actually cross to me, but he was very close to it, and I was thankful when he arose and announced that he was going to join some friends in a game of bridge or poker, but that he would see me for a moment or two before his train went out at eleven. After interviewing the porter about my accommodation on the Montreal-Boston train, and packing my bag, I sat alone reading. A few minutes before eleven Mr. Slaght came up to the lounge to say good-bye. He was still very strange in his manner, but told me to let him know as soon as I decided what I intended to do about securing a chartered accountant for Mr. Hogg's books, and that he had ordered the copy of our evidence. I returned home feeling rather anxious about the case, and after talking it over with my husband I decided to borrow the money to retain an accountant, also to pay for the evidence. Court evidence is very expensive—having paid for many copies of it, I know whereof I speak. I was soon on my way to Toronto once more, to arrange for the accountant.

I called upon two of the best known chartered accountants in the city and told them what I desired them to do. The gentlemen, though most polite to me personally, were firm in their refusal to assist me with such an affair; indeed, they appeared quite shocked at the suggestion. In despair I reported this to my Counsel. He was in a bad humour anyway as he said some of his legal friends had that week reproached him bitterly for attacking Mr. Hogg, and had told him that he was not the sort of man to be associated with a nasty case like this. I remember his adding, "Had I known, Mrs. Campbell, how bad this case was going to turn out, nothing under heaven would have induced me to act for you."

I listened to all this patiently because I felt that no matter what Mr. Slaght said to me personally I must put up with it in the interests of justice—never could I replace him—but it was not easy; in fact, it was very dreadful. Only once or twice did I answer back during that whole awful winter; once, when my Counsel said,

"Your dirty rotten case is like a sewer, Mrs. Campbell, and I have to go poking my nose around in it."

I rejoined, "It probably is, Mr. Slaght, but I am not in the sewer."

And another time a few weeks later when he had been very angry and I said, "Mr. Slaght, please do not speak to me that way. Remember that after all I am a gentlewoman."

He looked at me across his desk white with anger, and said, "If you do not like the way I speak to you, why don't you retain some other Counsel? There are many others at the Bar. You are not obliged to remain my client."

I knew I was taking a chance in answering him as I did, indeed in answering him at all, but I was desperate. I said, "Arthur Slaght," and I looked him steadily in the eye, "since you ask me for the truth I shall tell you; I put up with your insolence and lack of good manners because of your brains and brilliancy."

It worked; the gentleman got very red, and for a few minutes devoted his attention to making marks on his blotter; and I do not think he was ever again so unbearably rude to me.

After a third firm of accountants refused to act for us, Mr. Slaght sent me to a Mr. N.L. Martin, an intimate friend of his.[33] I found Mr. Martin a genial little fellow,—the head, evidently, of a large business. He said he would act for us; and after a good deal of difficulty and writing back and forth my Counsel managed to get the books sent up from Ottawa to the Toronto General Trusts Corporation offices. Mr. Hogg didn't want those books to leave Ottawa, but Mr. Slaght assured Mr. Sinclair that all the work would be done at the Trust Company's office in Toronto. Finally, seeing there was no help for it, he and his Counsel had to consent and the books and vouchers came up.

Mr. Slaght told me he wanted me to work with the accountant because by reading the letter books I could materially assist him. Then he warned me that never was I to be alone with Mr. Hogg's books or vouchers; always the accountant must be in the room with me, or else the books were to be brought right out into the large public office of the Trust Company and I was to look them over there, sitting at one of the little desks surrounded by the young men who sat at similar little desks working for the Trust Company. My readers will see that though my Counsel was cross to me, yet he was going on with the case and furthermore, was protecting me against my opponents. But his crossness did very nearly break my heart; however, my pride saved me. I would have died rather than let him see that it hurt me.

There was too, something that always came to my mind when my Counsel was most cross. It was the memory of those six awful days in the Supreme Court before Mr. Justice Kelly; the memory of how this man, Arthur Slaght, had fought for me with every inch of himself mentally and physically; the memory too, of how, through that trying week he had in his quiet rather awkward way sought to look out for my comfort; messengers sent for glasses of water and fresh towels; had I taken some lunch; hadn't I better come down to the office with him and wait there; did I think I could go through another day of it in the witness box? I must indeed have been a sad nuisance to him. Never before or since has he ever had to look out for a client as he did for me, I feel sure of that, because I was so completely alone. And then the rare times when he had praised me. "By George, but you are a wonderful witness, Mrs. Campbell," and again, "My God, I was proud of you when you wouldn't retract your statements about Kingstone this morning." So perhaps these memories helped me through that winter.

The Trust Company refused to pay for an accountant out of the estate, or to advance me a cent of my money for that purpose, so I borrowed the money necessary from a dear kind friend. Day after day, I worked in the little room at the Trust Company beside the accountant, reading letter after letter in Mr. Hogg's marvellous copperplate writing, getting from these letters a clearer and clearer idea of the case and making notes on them for Mr. Slaght. This ended, my Counsel said he wished me to make him a copy of a certain little book of Mr. Hogg's. His contention was when the book had come to light that first day in Ottawa that Mr. Hogg had compiled the whole book at one time in his own hand, after another little book which was evidently the key to my mother's estate had been destroyed. I sat at one of the small desks I have told you about, copying, copying, for hours at a time. I have often thought how embarrassing and humiliating it must have been for the high-up officials of the Trust Company to have had me doing this work, sitting in their public office with their chairman's falsified and altered books beside me, and to have had all their young employees in the office witnessing this. The young chaps were very polite and interested, and often waited on me rather shyly, sharpening pencils and producing erasers and blotters, etc. I have no doubt that my Counsel really wanted a perfect copy of the little book—it was a help to him—but I have sometimes thought that perhaps, also, he wished to show the Trust Company just what a scandal the affair was, and perhaps, too, with that uncanny foresight of his, sensing that I might sometime have to go on alone, he desired me to be very familiar with the case.

When our audit was resumed, Mr. Martin was present to make his report upon the books. His task was necessarily a difficult one: there was no starting point, the books being destroyed down to 1905, and those that were produced having very little in them relating to my mother's business. I think perhaps it was the things he didn't find in the books that made the strongest point of his evidence; certainly, it was these that helped me win in England. He established beyond a doubt that Mr. Hogg had not kept a proper trust account and had mixed his money all together with my mother's. This, as most of my readers will realize, is very serious on the part of a trustee. Then he would find evidence of certain mortgage investments, but the books failed to disclose what had happened to them. His statement showing that the ledgers scarcely agreed at all with the accounts Mr. Hogg was endeavoring to pass, I found very helpful, too, later on. Also the small man's genial rubicund presence was a decided assistance to me personally, because my Counsel's bad humor seemed to reach its peak during those three days, and I had need of some encouragement. I remember not long after this, when I was again in Toronto doing some research work on the case, that I happened to meet Mr. Justice Ferguson of the Appellate Court.[34] He had known me since my girlhood days and was always most friendly. He asked me what I was doing again in Toronto, and I told him about my case. Then I said, "My Lord, what do you suppose makes Mr. Slaght so terrible to me? It is awfully hard to fight one's own Counsel as well as one's opponents."

He replied, "Why Mrs. Campbell, Slaght doesn't want to go against Mr. Hogg; this affair is a nasty business, it gives us all a black eye, don't you see? I've never known of a similar case since I've been on the Bench."

His Lordship never doubted my story for a moment; in fact, in looking back I can see that what I told him of my Counsel's behavior was the surest proof of the strength of my case.

Mr. Martin made one or two slips, but I was able to rectify these and later on retrieved the sums before the Privy Council.

But during this period what was the Trust Company doing to assist in the audit? I can only answer that they were keeping very quiet indeed and doing very little. Once or twice at the beginning, Mr. McKague endeavored to alter the course of things and to curb Mr. Slaght, but his Honor refused and told my Counsel to continue. Then as Mr. Justice Magee said later on when the case came before the Appellate Court, "They counted the vouchers," and I added, "Yes, my Lord, and they counted them wrong." Mr. McKague and Mr. Lang counted and handled all the vouchers. It was an interesting fact, which I noticed when the case came into my hands, that though there were, of course, a number of vouchers for sums of principal, yet mostly the vouchers were for interest, and, what was even more noteworthy, that in one or two instances where principal was said to have been paid over at a certain date there would be vouchers for sums of interest about then, but no vouchers for the missing sums of principal. But on the fourth day of our hearing the Trust Company evidently came to and sat up and took notice. Mr. Sinclair produced a most peculiar document which purported to be a complete list of all the mortgages held in Lady Howland's name, culled from the Registry Office at Ottawa. Mr. Slaght, before admitting this document as evidence, demanded that Mr. Sinclair be sworn and be cross-examined upon it. His evidence was that he had made a thorough search at the Registry Office and that these were the only mortgages he could find in my mother's name, and that he, assisted by the Toronto General Trusts Corporation's Estates Manager, had prepared this little document the previous evening to show that when one mortgage investment was discharged and Mr. Hogg had received the money, he had immediately bought another with the sum. So it went, to and fro, back and forth, from year to year, all down the years since 1885, until in 1922 just $8,200.00 remained of the estate, which was the sum turned in by Mr. Hogg at the end of his long management of it,—an estate which in 1885 must have amounted to at least $60,000.00. The document was indeed an illuminating one. Again the audit was adjourned, much to my disgust, as it meant our all returning once more to Ottawa, but I was powerless to prevent this.

In the long run this delay, so hard at the moment, proved very helpful, because it gave me an opportunity to look up some mortgages, the interest upon which I had noticed in the accounts, and of which no mention whatsoever was made in Mr. Sinclair's document. I found these two quite large mortgages in trust, and at the close of our hearing we called the Deputy Registrar to prove them. At first, Mr. Hogg attempted to deny that they were investments made for my mother, but in the end Mr. Slaght forced the truth from him, and later on I won upon these investments in England.

Nearly three months or more after the conclusion of the audit, when I was every day expecting the decision, Judge Mulligan having reserved it, Mr. Hogg produced my mother's old mortgage book and desired it to be given to his Honor.[35] He offered no explanation of how he came to have this book in his possession when all other papers belonging to my mother seem to have been destroyed, and, unfortunately, my Counsel did not summon him for cross-examination. He merely went to Ottawa, a consent was filed and the book was presented to the Surrogate Judge by the two Counsel, Mr. Slaght and Mr. Sinclair. The Trust Company's Counsel was not present at this important moment, nor did they seek to have their chairman questioned regarding this book, which, as their Lordships of the Judicial Committee subsequently pointed out, was the one very important document in the case. Because Mr. Hogg was not cross-examined, because the Trust Company failed to make known what was the result of their enquiry regarding the mortgages entered in this book—entered in Mr. Hogg's own hand—many of them not brought into his account which he was seeking to have audited, the estate was unable to recover these very substantial sums. It was only when I arrived at the Privy Council that I realized what a serious mistake had been made.

Having from the outset been duly impressed by Judge Mulligan's total inadequacy to our case, his decision when at last he rendered it—which, by the way was a few weeks prior to his death—was not the shock it might have been.[36] But it was an almost unbelievable decision in the face of the evidence adduced by Mr. Slaght. Taking no notice of the fictitious mortgage, no notice of the falsified books, making no mention of the absence of a proper trust account, nor of the large sums of principal and interest for which there were no vouchers — it completely exonerated Mr. Hogg! Nay, it whitewashed him and finished by finding that he owed the estate $201.60 — the sixty cents seemed to me the last straw! So much for all my research work in and out of the Registry Office, so much for our many trips to Ottawa, so much for Mr. Slaght's masterly cross-examination!

Indeed, as I scanned the document, I was for a moment inclined to agree with a remark my Counsel had made, when, after the settlement of my will case, I had asked him if he believed in British justice, and he had replied very bitterly, "Justice? Justice is what you get, Mrs. Campbell."

But this loss of faith on my part was only momentary; my telegram to him read, "Surprised but not discouraged. Appealing immediately. Shall be in Toronto Sunday."

BOOK THREE

COUNSEL LAY DOWN THEIR BRIEF

"MY USEFULNESS to you is over, Mrs. Campbell," announced my Counsel as, placing his teacup on the table, he drew from his breast pocket Judge Mulligan's decision. He had come to my hotel Sunday afternoon to have tea with me and, as I thought, to discuss our appeal.

"What do you mean, Mr. Slaght?" I questioned in surprise.

"I mean just this," said he rising, "that this matter is a serious one and I can go no further for you. If you intend to appeal—remember I do not encourage an appeal—you must have someone else, some Counsel with prestige. I lack that, look at this Judgment," giving the paper a scornful toss.

"But, Mr. Slaght," exclaimed I, now cold with fear, "you don't lack brains and ability, and that is what I need. I've sufficient prestige for two; in fact, I suffer from prestige, that has been one of the great hindrances in my case all the way through. I am mixed up with this miserable old family compact, belong to it unhappily, with its prejudices, with its friendships—worse than Galsworthy's 'Loyalties.'[1] How can I go on without you? I should never have confidence in anyone else. You will win your case on appeal before another type of Judge, you know you will, and besides I've paid you all the money I have, and now you say you won't go on! Arthur Slaght, you can't do this thing to me," out of breath, I paused.

"This case," indicating the wretched decision, "is over and a new case is starting," said my Counsel showing signs of agitation. "I am fully and amply repaid for my services, Mrs. Campbell,"—as indeed he was—"you must retain someone else now, you must no longer be associated with me or my firm," and it seemed to me that into those eyes usually so quiet and thoughtful there shot a strange flash—was it of fear?—fear of what? "As you know there are more than five hundred Counsel at our Bar, any one of whom you may choose. I should, however, recommend one of the 'Big Three,' the 'Three who do no wrong,' Tilley, Hellmuth, or McCarthy.[2] In my estimation, Mr. Hellmuth is the very man for you."

The Big Three didn't interest me; I wanted to keep Arthur Slaght. In vain did I beg and plead and coax, in vain did I entreat. "If it is money you want, Mr. Slaght, I have well-off friends behind me, I can get it for you."

To which he gravely replied, "It is not money, Mrs. Campbell," and I noticed that, as he paced the floor, great beads of perspiration stood out on his brow, also that he seemed terribly white. At all costs I and my case must be got rid of, that was very clear. My pleading was of no avail. This time the man was adamant. Realizing it, I bowed to the inevitable, but the blow was a bitter one. I was acquiring steadiness and endurance in a stern school, surely.

The upshot of this upheaval was that I elected D.L. McCarthy, K.C., son of one of my father's dearest friends, as my choice; he had the desired prestige (obnoxious word). It is a generally recognized fact, I think, in legal circles that "Lally McCarthy" has every gift the gods have to bestow, birth and breeding, training and personality, with any amount of ability thrown in. One hears it said that, able Counsel though Dalton McCarthy was, his son is even more gifted.

No sooner was the choice made than Mr. Slaght metaphorically speaking, picked me up, together with my many papers, and placed me with McCarthy and McCarthy. His relief as he did this was manifest.

Mr. McCarthy received me as his client in a manner both courteous and kind, referring to the close friendship which had always existed between "my governor and your father, Mrs. Campbell"; also he seemed to understand and sympathize with my desire to appeal. This all touched me greatly and I felt myself becoming somewhat resigned to the change of Counsel. A few days later Mr. Slaght came over to McCarthy and McCarthy's office to draw up my notice of appeal which my new firm was to publish. As he took his departure that afternoon, his task completed, I remember him saying, "I've had over twenty-five years' experience at the Bar, and this," placing his hand on my evidence, "is one of the worst cases that has ever come to my notice — a case of the most pre-meditated wrongdoing."

Thus I ceased to be Arthur Slaght's client, for although after that he sometimes advised me, it was always as a friend. Two things this man taught me that have stood me in good stead in the struggle which I have waged from Court to Court; the first is never to be bitter, because one cannot win if one is bitter; the second, equally valuable to one of my ardent temperament, is to do one thing at a time.

The Trust Company informed me that they were quite satisfied with Judge Mulligan's Judgment in regard to their chairman's accounts. Though guardians of my mother's estate appointed by the Courts of Ontario, they declined to assist me in any way with the appeal, declined even to allow me any of my own money to pay for copies of the Court evidence. Incredible as this seems inscribed in black and white, it nevertheless remains a fact that they deliberately sat by while my Counsel and I fought for the safety of the estate. "Oh, put your loved ones in our hands!"

Again a delay in getting to Court! Some Judges, Mr. McCarthy did not care to come before, it seemed, while others, so I gathered from him, were not anxious to hear the case. The weeks wore wearily away, finally my Counsel decided upon Mr. Justice Masten.[3]

For several days I worked with Mr. McCarthy and Mr. West as they got up their brief.[4] I must even then have known the case pretty thoroughly, because I was told long afterwards that Lally McCarthy expressed his surprise at my being able to do this. But during these days something, which at first had been only a suspicion to be immediately dismissed, took shape, and forcing itself upon my consciousness would no longer be denied. My Counsel's attitude towards my case was certainly changing; he was not so keen, not so sympathetic; the climax came when on my drawing his attention to a shocking spot in Mr. Hogg's testimony before the Surrogate Court he said, his face puckered and perturbed, "The Judge won't be at all interested in that, Mrs. Campbell." It was the same with the falsified books; and seeing him push them across the table I felt that he would have been very happy indeed could they be spirited away. So far as the legal fraternity was concerned, the dice were undoubtedly loaded against me, "but there is always the

Judge," thought I hopefully, little knowing the subtle bond between Bench and Bar, or is it perhaps Bench and Benchers, which exists in Ontario. This was brought home to me shortly, however.

The name Masten was new to me, but it had a rather more congenial sound than Kelly or Mulligan, and Mr. Justice Masten was one of the Appellate Judges. At the last moment I decided to ring up Mr. Slaght to ask him if he would be present in Court as a friend, and to my surprise and satisfaction he consented to do so.

Our case headed the morning's list.[5] As he took his seat on the Bench, Mr. Justice Masten said, "Mr. McCarthy, perhaps you had better tell your client that I am a great friend of Mr. Hogg's. I formerly had dealings with him, and though I think that despite this I can do justice to the case, Mrs. Campbell may not care under these circumstances to have me hear it." Looking somewhat disconcerted, McCarthy arose and left the Court room, beckoning me to follow. In the corridor we were joined by Mr. Slaght. "You have heard his Lordship, Mrs. Campbell, what are you going to do?" said my Counsel. "It's going to be mighty difficult to get any judge to hear this case of yours, you know." Sagely Mr. Slaght nodded in assent.

Completely taken aback by the situation I hesitated, and in that moment proved anew the truth of the trite old saying, "He who hesitates is lost." The Christmas holidays began next week, and having been detained in Toronto most of the autumn I was greatly needed at home; also trips back and forth were becoming expensive. Then, too, remnants of that faith to which I had been bred — faith in a Judge on the Bench — still clung to me. Had his Lordship not said that he could do justice to the case despite his friendship for Mr. Hogg? I decided to allow him to do so, and found myself promptly propelled into the Court room again by Mr. McCarthy, while behind us slowly and silently sauntered Mr. Slaght. Only after the whole heart-breaking interlude was over, when on the front sheets of the newspapers there appeared in large print, "Judge states he is great friend of W.D. Hogg, K.C.," did I begin to have misgivings with regard to the strange reluctance mentioned by Mr. McCarthy on the part of the Judiciary of Ontario to hear my case. I asked myself; could the whole affair have been skillfully staged? And Mr. Justice Masten had spoken of having had dealings with Mr. Hogg; what was the nature of these "dealings"?[26] I have never ceased to wonder about that; somehow the word as used by his Lordship had an unfortunate sound.

Back in the Court things went badly from the start. Several caustic remarks from the Bench caused Mr. McCarthy to become somewhat nervous in his pleading, and a bit hesitant about presenting the damaging evidence, especially the altered ledgers. Time and again I was forced to put documents and exhibits in his hands and point to certain important passages in the evidence, urging him to bring them to the attention of the Judge. As I listened to the Judge's remarks and noted the steely glance accompanying them, I was filled with anxiety and could not help feeling that perhaps his Lordship and myself had been over-sanguine as to his ability to do justice to my case. Indeed, looking closely at the learned gentleman it occurred to me that his appearance was rather suggestive of a handsome elderly Mephisto who, his scarlet cape for the moment flung aside, had wrapped himself in robes of office and deserted the Brocken for the Bench.[7] Across the Court room sat Mr. Slaght, erect, motionless, a sphinx in gown and bands, cynically watching now McCarthy, now his Lordship. Late afternoon found us with every point save one lost; Judgment being given orally as the case proceeded and the defense having been scarcely called upon to reply. My Counsel was concluding his argument upon the fictitious mortgage and the Court was preparing to rise, when the Judge said tauntingly, "You had better argue that question before the Appellate Court, Mr. McCarthy," and with this adjourned the case until the following morning.

Mr. McCarthy resumed his argument with an attack against the fantastic tale of McAmmond and Martin. Surely a Supreme Court Judge could not accept such a story! For a time, hope flickered within me, only to be dashed again when at noon, his Lordship surrounded now by the altered ledgers announced that he would reserve Judgment for a few days and added, "But, Mr. McCarthy, were I to disbelieve Mr. Hogg's words upon this branch of the case, I should be accusing him of perjury; and I couldn't do that, Mr. McCarthy, could I?"

Out in the corridor my Counsel and I once more faced each other. Mr. Slaght had vanished. Lally McCarthy, though of undeniable charm is rather short of stature and a bit short of temper as well; his face always high-colored was scarlet as he passed the finely monogrammed handkerchief across it. My legal censor forbids my giving you the conversation in detail, sufficient to say that I gathered from the eminent gentleman's remarks that he felt that he had been wasting his time in the Court room and that no Judge in Canada would give me a decision against Mr. Hogg. Indeed, my impression was that somehow a concerted action of the Benchers and the Judges was in progress to white-wash that worthy King's Counsel, who I, furthermore, gathered would "jolly well" be in jail right at that moment had he been an ordinary mortal—say the fellow on the street, or you, or I—instead of being what he unfortunately was: a chairman of the foremost Trust Company of Canada and senior Bencher to boot. It was appalling, what was to be done?

Now my nearest and dearest often say smilingly that they consider me a perfect exponent of that line in the old hymn, "Let courage rise with danger." Perhaps they are right; be that as it may, I can still see the curious glance with which Mr. McCarthy greeted my question as to whether there was an appeal to any further Court. "There is," said he, "to the Appellate Court, but you may argue the appeal yourself, for I certainly shall not do so. But I tell you what I will do, Mrs. Campbell, if you go on. I will draw up your notice of appeal and my firm will publish it for you and perhaps I can help you in getting up your argument." Then he added very earnestly, "But I assure you, never short of the Privy Council, never on this side of the water, can you win this case."

"What about the Privy Council, Mr. McCarthy, should I win it there?"

To which came the reply, "Ah, the Privy Council, that is different; wrongs are righted in the Privy Council. But, you aren't there, you see." "No," said I, "but I shall be. I am going on, Mr. McCarthy." Unconsciously I had made the momentous decision, a decision which I have never regretted. Shaking hands with my Counsel I thanked him; but as I left the old Hall, my mind was already filled with thoughts of how I should ever manage to argue a case before the Appellate Court, and I am fain to confess that at the moment it looked like rather a tall order.

Mr. Slaght seemed to approve of my decision, for upon hearing that I was going to find it difficult to pay for the requisite six copies of Court evidence for my appeal because the Trust Company had given me to understand that they were more than satisfied with my second defeat and had again refused me any funds from the estate, he kindly sent me to Mr. Newall, the Police Court reporter at City Hall, who, when he learned I had been a client of Arthur Slaght's, made me a most advantageous price and promised to rush the order through; one could see that he admired my former Counsel. Then Mr. McCarthy and I drew up our notice of appeal.

When the learned Judge's written reasons were handed down, we found that the point granted us was an important gain, not from a monetary point of view — it was scarcely over eleven hundred dollars — but because a Judge and a Court found that Mr. Hogg had been guilty of retaining trust funds.[8] This bucked me up tremendously, notwithstanding the fact that as we worked, Mr. McCarthy once more recited the legal and judicial obstacles in my pathway. The notice of appeal was to be ready shortly, and it was arranged that I should come down to look it over before its publication.

Early next morning I was aroused by a message from Mr. West to say that Mr. McCarthy desired to see me at once. Now Lally McCarthy is so eminent a Counsel and altogether the atmosphere of McCarthy and McCarthy was one of such dignified quiet, almost gloom, with the women typists in their "decent black," offset by collars and cuffs of white — so striking a contrast to the "young ladies," kindly note the distinction, of the other offices, who, clad in clothing of the most cheering variety and latest style, appeared quite chipper — that I felt almost as though a Royal Command had issued; and racing through my bath and breakfast was soon on my way.

"Good-morning, Mrs. Campbell," said Mr. McCarthy courteously rising as I was shown into his private room. "Mr. Justice Masten has withdrawn his Judgment.[9] He wants to reopen the case, you see, and desires us all to go before him again, so I'm afraid you won't be able to appeal after all."

"I most certainly shall appeal and immediately, Mr. McCarthy. I was a fool once to have allowed that old man to try my case. I shall not be one again. You or Mr. Sinclair or Mr. West or anyone else who so desires may go before Mr. Justice Masten, but I've ordered and partially paid for my copies of evidence, and I'm taking the case before the Appellate Court. What silly business is this, anyway," I added, now thoroughly incensed, "a Judge withdrawing his Judgment? Neither you nor Mr. Justice Masten nor any one else can force me to go back again."

Mr. McCarthy peered at me over his glasses, his face was very nearly purple, one could see the muscles twitching, he didn't relish his task. "Very well, Mrs. Campbell, you may go on alone. You are no longer our client and you will have to leave our office and file and serve your notice of appeal yourself. I doubt if you can do that."

"Perhaps not, sir," said I, "but I shall endeavor to do so; and I should like to remind you of what was always said of my father: that he won most of his cases because he didn't know when he was beaten."

"I rather think you're his daughter, aren't you?" parried the gentleman, then sharply ringing his bell turned to Mr. West, who answered the summons, "Bring Mrs. Campbell her papers now. She is no longer our client and is leaving the office. She will serve and file the notice herself." Mr. West wore a curious expression as he returned carrying my portfolio of papers. Taking them from him, I shook hands with Mr. McCarthy, at the same time wishing him a "Merry Christmas,"—it was the day before Christmas Eve—and walking through the great mahogany doorway of McCarthy and McCarthy I found myself out on the steps of the Canada Life Building.

It had all been so terribly sudden. Dazed, I stood there on the steps with death in my heart, and in my arms the heavy papers. After a time the steadily falling snow brought me to my senses. They shouldn't stop my appeal; no one should stop me. But how did one serve and file papers for an appeal, anyway? I should have to beg the Registrars at Osgoode Hall for help; perhaps they would show me. Then I remembered reading a notice somewhere to the effect that on Christmas Eve the Hall would close at noon. Christmas Eve—why that was tomorrow! There was little time to lose, so clasping the portfolio more tightly I hurried down the steps. Just around the corner I met, or rather "barged into" Mr. McGregor Young, an old friend of our family.[10] "Merry Christmas, Mrs. Campbell," said the jovial K.C., "where are you off to in such a hurry?" I must, I suppose, have looked rather stricken because, the festive greeting dying on his lips, he kindly steered me into a sheltering doorway and demanded to know what was the matter. When he heard that I had been put out of McCarthy and McCarthy's office and why, he seemed very disturbed and implored me to return to Arthur Slaght. I explained, of course, that this was impossible. "But how on earth can you serve and file these papers yourself, Mrs. Campbell, you don't know anything about it."

"Now, Mr. Young," I interrupted, "stop being so sympathetic, I can't stand sympathy. Just tell me the steps I have to take, I'll manage it somehow."

So producing an envelope and pencil from his pocket he wrote down the necessary directions, explaining them to me the while. I recall so clearly this little episode because it was the first assistance rendered me along the path of "Appellant in Person."

The Registrar of the Appellate Court approved of Mr. Young's directions and added a few of his own.[11] He also expressed his opinion of the way I had been treated, but this was not inscribed upon the envelope. At the King Edward Hotel I found a typist who, upon hearing my plight, laid aside all other work to take on my job. All afternoon we worked, I dictating and directing. By evening things were pretty well completed.

The next morning I managed to serve my two opponents, Mr. Hogg's Solicitors and the Trust Company, and finally to file, after affixing some enormous stamps, my notice of appeal. Almost twenty minutes to twelve; I had just made it and no more!

When after the holidays I went in search of the withdrawn Judgment, it had been returned quite unaltered. Edward Brown, K.C., Clerk in charge of the Judgment Office, refused to allow me to pay for the copy. He said with old time courtesy, "We here who remember James Bethune have always revered his memory. I couldn't possibly take money from one of his daughters."

May I pause here for a moment to tell of the many kindnesses shown me by those whose lives are lived within these venerable Law Courts of Ontario? — some of them Justices, some merely officials, who with wise advice and patient direction so often sought to protect me against my skilled opponents. The use, too, of the stately law library, where Mr. Daley together with his young assistant Mr. Wrinch, have never once in all these years been too busy to bring me the book I desired and have many times helped me to look up the law.[12] My heart goes out to them all in gratitude. True, there has upon occasion been great injustice, hardest of all to bear, and unkindness and even rudeness; but I had always the feeling after those encounters with the Registrars of which I shall tell later on, that some pressure had been brought to bear upon these men and that in their hearts they were really with me.

Before setting down the appeal the order had to be settled. Thinking naturally that as Mr. McCarthy had won the case, he would take out the order, I wrote him. His reply was surprising, explaining as it did, that I had never at any time been his client, but always Mr. Slaght's and that he had been called in only as Counsel; but that undoubtedly Mr. Slaght would be happy to draw up the order and attend upon the settling of it. Reading this, I rubbed my eyes and felt rather like "Alice in Wonderland," because McCarthy and McCarthy had just rendered me a lengthy bill for their services. Mr. Slaght smiled when I showed him the letter and the bill, and I gathered that were this really the case, Mr. McCarthy would have to collect his fees from Mr. Slaght instead of from me.

"As you know I have had nothing whatsoever to do with this appeal, nor can I help you now, Mrs. Campbell," said he firmly. So Mr. Hinds, Registrar of the Weekly Court, drew up and settled the order for me.[13] As a client, I was not greatly in demand. My opponents could scarcely conceal their elation over the way things were going and, especially, over the fact of my being forced to argue the appeal myself. I remember one of the Trust Company's officers saying, "You don't seem to have much luck with your Counsel, do you, Mrs. Campbell?"

The copies of the evidence arrived shortly bound in flaming red. Lying on the Registrar's table they stood out noticeably from the evidence in all the other cases, which seemed to be done up modestly in blue. As one young disciple of Blackstone remarked rather wittily, "That is evident evidence, all right." Mr. Slaght's comment was amusing, when one day he strolled into the Appellate Office, but it also gave one food for thought: "Nice cheerful color that fellow Newall has chosen for your evidence," then a bit drily, "Oh well, it won't be mislaid easily."

Some Frenchman has said, "C'est le premier pas qui coûte." It is borne in upon me how true this is, as, turning to gaze down that long vista of legalities on this side of the Atlantic and in England, I catch, across the years, a glimpse of myself preparing the argument for my appeal, alone amidst an awful confusion of papers. So appallingly difficult it all seemed, yet child's play to what was to follow. Once when I had asked Mr. Slaght if he thought I had a strong case, he replied, "You have too damned much case, Mrs. Campbell." Wrestling with those papers I rather thought I had.

My hearing was set down for the First Appellate Division.[14] With the exception of Mr. Justice Grant the Judges would know me personally. I told myself, whenever I panicked at the thought of the Court that after all they were only elderly men and would be obliged to listen to me even though I was arraigning the senior Bencher of the Law Society. Nevertheless, it was a somewhat terrified appellant in person who, on that January morning, stood beneath their Lordships.

Never before had I spoken in public, and my voice, always rather low, gave out completely at first; so the Chief Justice commanded me to come before the K.C. bar that I might be heard.[15] But once started the nervousness abated, and it soon became apparent that the whole Bench was interested in the case. Indeed, Mr. Justice Magee and Mr. Justice Ferguson were both fighting for me tooth and nail, and even Mr. Justice Hodgins was coming through now and then with helpful questions, in spite of his feelings, it seemed to me, because he had been so against me in the will case. Mr. Sinclair, though admitting that Mr. Hogg was seeking to pass his accounts as trustee under the Trustee Act, submitted a document on behalf of my sister, Mrs. Lindsey, who had appeared against the estate in the Surrogate Court. Mr. Sinclair said he still represented the lady, and this document set forth that Mr. Hogg had never at any time been a trustee for Lady Howland but always an agent. It looked as though the old childish slogan of "heads I win, tails you lose," was about to be adopted. Not, however, by the Judges. They fell upon Mr. Sinclair, and the document, which Mr. Justice Ferguson aptly characterized as a "smoke screen" was withdrawn.

My books and papers lay on the K.C.'s desk behind me and in picking them up from time to time, I noticed that the Court was crowded: Counsel from the big firms, law students, many officials of the Hall, and several Judges even seemed to be following the argument; and on the very end row whom should I see but Mr. Slaght,—he was in his gown and was listening intently.

I pled for a day and a half, in spite of the fact that more than once the Chief Justice and Mr. Justice Hodgins did their best to stop me.[16] They were quick to notice that I had a carefully prepared typed argument and asked me whether I would not rather submit it instead of pleading, but thanking them, I declined and continued to argue. Again while I was reading some of the most shocking evidence—there was page after page of it—the Chief Justice said it was not necessary for me to continue as they could all read it for themselves. Hugging the large scarlet volume to my breast, I replied, "My Lords, with your pleasure, I shall proceed," and succeeded in getting the whole seventy pages across to the Court room.

There was no doubt but that the seriousness of the case struck home. "Why had no trust account been kept," the Judges questioned. Why indeed! The falsified books created consternation, Mr. Justice Ferguson rising frequently to peer at them over the shoulder of the Chief Justice. Later on an irreverent Junior remarked, "Those books were a hot shot for the old boys, weren't they?"

Mr. Sinclair, though he argued at great length, made little headway and was not treated too politely, I thought. Mr. Hogg was cross-appealing on the sum granted us by Mr. Justice Masten.

By now Mr. Slaght had moved forward to the K.C. row, and Lally McCarthy was from time to time beside him. During my rebuttal of a point or two which Mr. Sinclair had endeavored to make, Mr. Slaght was actually passing me little notes across the K.C. bar. Indeed, my former Counsel were among the first to congratulate me at the conclusion of the case. They were loud in their praise of the way in which I had presented it. "You argued splendidly, Mrs. Campbell," said Mr. McCarthy, "and have won your case right from the Bench."

My reply to these felicitations was, "Thank you, gentlemen, perhaps I have, as you say, won from the Bench, but I'm not getting excited about that. Remember I've not received the Judgment yet. You notice it was reserved."

For months I waited. Spring came and went, summer merged into autumn, and still no Judgment. The long delay was terribly hard to bear. At times I felt very anxious, more especially as I received word of the illness of my good friend, Mr. Justice Ferguson. He was not expected to recover. Yet as I reviewed those days before the Appellate Court and ran over in my mind their Lordships' remarks, it was difficult to see how under the law they could escape giving a favorable Judgment — and that for a substantial sum. Either this, or refer the crooked accounts back to the Surrogate Court at Ottawa. Then in November, only a few days after Mr. Justice Ferguson's untimely death — he was the young virile man of the First Division — came a telegram from the Registrar: "Judgment delivered today one thousand dollars in your favor."[17] Just nine months since my hearing!

The train, in reality racing along, seemed almost slow, but so eager was I that night to reach my destination that I doubt if even the "Scotsman" on a non-stop trip would have been fast enough for me.[18]

"Never on this side of the water. Never short of the Privy Council can you win this case." Yes, Mr. McCarthy knew his Canada well — knew his Judges, I reflected. One thousand dollars in the face of such evidence as had been presented to the Court — it was unbelievable! And was the way open now to the Privy Council? I wondered. Much would depend upon their Lordships' reasons for Judgment. These, however, had not been handed down, so the Registrar informed me when I dashed into the Appellate Office the following morning; then covered with confusion, for he was a gentle timorous soul, he intimated that the "Chief" would like to see me when the Bench rose at four o'clock. Ontario's Grand Old Man greeted me most affably.[19] What a picturesque figure he was, tall and erect with a wealth of snow-white whisker which, falling over the heavy black gown, almost concealed collar and bands. "Sit down here and tell me what you think of our Judgment," said he.

Truly, I was in a difficult position. His Lordship had me at a tremendous disadvantage; he had known me in those years long past — in those gay care-free years when I had been a frequent visitor at his residence, and I thought of the beautiful wedding-gift from Lady Mulock and himself which was still one of our household treasures. How then tell him that I considered his Judgment a shocking one. I hesitated.

"Come, come, why won't you tell me?" he demanded.

"I'd rather not, my Lord — because — well, because I have always had the greatest respect for your Lordship and a good deal of affection for you because of the old days. I'd much rather not," I faltered, now thoroughly distressed.

It was evident that my answer hit hard. "That means, then that you are not satisfied with our Judgment?"

"No, my Lord, not at all satisfied, and," plucking up courage, "might I have the reasons for your Judgment, please?"

"Oh, the reasons. Why, I can just tell you the reasons," answered his Lordship airily.

"But," I protested, "in the event of an appeal it would be better to have written reasons, I think."

"An appeal, better not appeal," was the rejoinder, "better take this thousand dollars we are offering you. You have had a lot of litigation already, you know; rather like the famous 'Jarndyce vs. Jarndyce,' aren't you? But come," said he, rising, "we shall go to see my brother Judges."[20]

I wanted awfully to ask why, but thought better of it and obediently followed his Lordship through the doorway. We must, I think, have been an unusual sight, the magnificent old man clad in his flowing robes with me in tow, and we must have occasioned some surprise because I seem to recall that several officials whom we passed turned to regard us curiously, as we traversed the Hall and toiled up the steps to "Brother Grant's" chambers. That gentleman sat beside his fire, and, unless his looks belied him, wasn't so awfully glad to see us.

"Ah, Brother Grant," quoth the Chief Justice genially, "this is Mrs. Campbell, she is James Bethune's daughter, you know; you must remember what a distinguished Counsel he was." Silently I asked myself what this last had to do with the case. "She is not satisfied with our Judgment allowing her one thousand dollars, but I've just been telling her she ought to think it over and accept it."

Mr. Justice Grant's rather sour but exceedingly able face changed color for a moment. I had not liked him during those days before the Appellate Court but had at once recognized his ability. "Well, my advice," said he, "is to take the thousand; it's much better than nothing, you know, and Mrs. Campbell may lose everything if she appeals. After all a thousand dollars is a thousand dollars." Having uttered this eternal verity, to which I made no reply, his Lordship continued with some polite and complimentary comments about my father, obviously in response to the remark of the Chief Justice, and to my relief the interview was at an end.

"Brother Hodgins," it seemed, was next on our visiting list. His chambers lay away across the Hall, and when we arrived, his door was locked and he had departed for the day.

But Mr. Justice Magee's door stood open and the dear old gentleman—it is thus I always think of him—was at his desk. My heart had warmed to him during my will case, he had looked so sympathetic and had spoken so charmingly of my father and mother. He greeted me with his usual gentle courtesy. Though he has lived his life in Canada, there still clings to him in speech and manner and even in dress something of the Old Land. He told us that his reasons for Judgment were ready and that I might have them at noon tomorrow. "Litigation is very expensive, as you know, Mrs. Campbell; perhaps it might be wiser were you to accept this offer as the Chief Justice suggests. The law's delays are very great, I am afraid," quavered his Lordship; but though the voice quavered and the straight spare form trembled slightly, I divined that the shrewd old Irish eyes were sending me a definite and unmistakable message. His Lordship with his wealth of experience gleaned from a lifetime on the Bench was on my side; the rugged North of Irelander and I were allies in the cause of Justice. It was a heartening thought, so much so indeed that when the Chief Justice once more advised me to think over his offer, I found myself looking up at him quite calmly—awe-inspiring though he is—with an answer in which was neither doubt nor hesitation. "It's not worth talking over, much less thinking over, my Lord. I'm going to take the case to England."

Mr. Justice Magee's twenty-one pages of considered Judgment were fine.[21] He had dissented from his brother Judges and refusing to accept Mr. Hogg's erroneous accounts, desired them to be sent back to the Surrogate Court for a further and proper accounting. He said the whole enquiry was nugatory and that the finding was contrary to the evidence, pointing out as it did that large sums had come into Mr. Hogg's hands for which he had entirely failed to account. Reading over those reasons I realized that on appeal they would prove a formidable weapon.

Having seen the report of the Judgment under the Osgoode Hall section of the daily papers and having looked it up in the large Judgment book I drew up the order and sought an early appointment for the settling of it. The Registrar announced, looking most unhappy as he did so, that the reasons for Judgment of the Court would be handed down shortly and that until that time, no order could issue. Why on earth should everyone look so uncomfortable over this case of mine? I waited for ten days — what interminable days they were; then the Bench handed down not only reasons for Judgment but a second Judgment, apparently to the utter amazement of the Bar.[22] "What next?" said those members of the legal fraternity who gathered around me at the Hall or stopped me on the street to question. "Yes, there were two Judgments; one on page 305 of the Judgment book, the second a bit further on at page 321." Certainly Mr. Justice Hodgins had written a Judgment dismissing my appeal unless I took the thousand dollars offered me as a settlement in full, and the Chief Justice and Mr. Justice Grant had concurred. "Was it true that their Lordships had stated that this second Judgment superseded the former? Surely not!" Upon receiving confirmation of this last, these gentlemen said nothing more, but their faces registered the consternation they felt. They were not Benchers, nor yet the distinguished advocates, rather were they from the ranks, younger Barristers, and what might be termed the more humble Counsel.

And truly, Mr. Justice Hodgins had gone the limit in his endeavor to whitewash Mr. Hogg. Accepting the crooked accounts he allowed the cross-appeal on the sum granted me by Mr. Justice Masten and offered me one thousand dollars as a settlement in full of my claim. If I declined this singular offer, which seemed to me to savor of a bribe, my appeal was to be dismissed. This meant that whether I accepted or declined, Mr. Hogg would receive a discharge or clean sheet from the Courts and that thousands of dollars of my mother's estate would remain in his hands. "Unbelievable," you say. All that and more.

Yet strangely enough my heart sang within me and I almost welcomed the Judgment, because with the dismissal of my appeal the way was clear to the Privy Council and also because its very unfairness would lay the Judgment open to reversal in England. The learned Judge held that Mr. Hogg had not been a trustee for my mother, but only an agent and backed this up by quoting the memorandum submitted by my sister, Mrs. Lindsey, which the Court had obliged Mr. Sinclair to withdraw before the hearing. Quite apart from the impropriety of using withdrawn evidence, the Judgment was illogical and contradictory. Were Mr. Hogg not a trustee but an agent, then the Appellate Court had had no right to entertain my appeal, much less to dismiss it. Only because the accounts were being passed under the Trustee Act was the case before them at all; otherwise they would have had no jurisdiction. This point had been fully discussed before the Court previous to my argument.

It was very clear to me that I must immediately decline that offer of settlement. What did the Judgment say? Hastily I leafed over the typed pages — yes, here it was:

"I think the Appellant should have a month wherein to signify in writing to the Registrar of this Court either her acceptance or declination of this additional amount. If she accepts, Judgment may be entered for the amount found due by the Surrogate Court Judge plus one thousand dollars. If she declines, or does not accept within one month, her appeal should be dismissed and Mr. Justice Masten's Judgment with the variation I have indicated above affirmed, both without costs."

The Judgment had been handed to me in the morning; at about four o'clock of the same day I presented the following answer to the Registrar, in my own handwriting,— which, so my family assures me, is as illegible as it is stylish:

> Iverholme,
> 74 St. George St.
> Toronto
> Nov. 29, 1928.

My dear Mr. Harley,

Will you please thank their Lordships for giving me their final Judgment in my appeal.

It is most kind and gracious of them to suggest my taking a month in which to consider their Judgment, but while grateful for this suggestion I shall be unable to do so as it is some time now since my hearing in February.

On no account could I accept the $1,000 so kindly offered me by their Lordships as a settlement in full by Mr. Hogg and I herewith refuse it and I judge therefore, my appeal from Mr. Justice Masten's decision is dismissed by the First Divisional Court or Court of Appeal and that they further order Mr. Hogg to retain the $1,155 which Mr. Justice Masten ordered him to pay over.

With my regards and many thanks to yourself for your courtesy and kindness which I shall never forget,

Sincerely yours,

ELIZABETH BETHUNE CAMPBELL.

Evidently the press was undaunted by my chirography, as the following day the letter confronted me from all the evening editions, thereby creating somewhat of a sensation.[23]

BOOK FOUR

MY STRUGGLE FOR ENGLAND

WHAT STEPS did one take in an appeal to the Privy Council? Vainly I cudgelled my brain. But all I seemed to have heard was that when the Appellate Court dismissed one's case, one might go on to the Supreme Court of Canada, or, if the matter were of sufficient moment and if one had sufficient money—and this last "if" was always greatly stressed—on to the Privy Council; apparently one was given a choice of Courts. Beyond this my ideas were of the vaguest; indeed, it would have been surprising had they been otherwise, because to even the average lawyer throughout Canada the Privy Council is more or less remote, more or less of a closed book, and only a few of the larger firms are in any way conversant with the procedure governing this final Court of the Empire. But as luck would have it there was staying at my pension a young university instructor; interested in my case, he referred me to an authority entitled "Bentwich" — this gentleman, it appeared, had written a book which, so my informant hopefully assured me, "would jolly well get me to the Privy Council."[1] My readers will, I think, agree that this was no idle boast but that in the ensuing struggle "Bentwich" fully justified the young professor's faith in him. The volume, though inexpensively and plainly bound, was found, not upon the open shelves of the library at Osgoode Hall, but in a small select case behind doors, the key of which was in the librarian's custody. "Privy Council Practice," and on the title-leaf:

The
THE PRACTICE OF THE PRIVY COUNCIL
IN JUDICIAL MATTERS
in
Appeals from Courts of Civil, Criminal, and
Admiralty Jurisdictions

and in
Appeals from Ecclesiastical and Prize Courts
with the
Statutes, Rules, and Forms of Procedure
by
Norman Bentwich
of Lincoln's Inn, Barrister-at-Law

Glancing through the index I found, "Appeals from the Self-Governing Dominions," with the Dominion of Canada heading the list. I must furnish myself with one of these books, so returning Mr. Daley his copy, which was at once restored to its accustomed niche in what I irreverently dubbed "the little cupboard behind the Throne," I hastened away to a law publisher's. "That will cost you eleven dollars and seventy-five cents, madam," bowed the salesman handing me my purchase. It was a blow, eleven seventy-five for a book; however, it was probably worth it, I reflected, as I made out the cheque. Recalling this I smile, but am honest enough to confess that it was only after my papers were safe on the high seas *en route* to the Privy Council and when some wit of a reporter wrote an amusing story underneath the caption, "Cheap Law Book and Woman's Will Bests Red Tape," that it came to me that perhaps my attitude towards the price of the book had been a bit humorous; but that was many months hence.[2]

Now I was warned by a literary gentleman when first the subject was broached of my writing — what a quaint old farmer in our lovely Nova Scotia is pleased to call my "meemoirs" — that the all important thing for me was sequence, never must I lose that. Therefore, I beg of you to return with me to our rectory where during those Christmas holidays, snuggled in the corner of the old mahogany davenport before the fireplace, I studied Bentwich earnestly whenever I had a few quiet moments. As I studied, the haziness surrounding the Privy Council cleared away and my appeal began to take shape.

I had been right, one was given a choice of the Privy Council or the Supreme Court of Canada but it was very clear that if one lost in the Supreme Court it would be pretty difficult to go on to the Privy Council. This was the rule:

"Their Lordships are not prepared to advise His Majesty to

exercise his prerogative by admitting an appeal to His Majesty in Council from the Supreme Court of the Dominion save where the case is of gravity involving a matter of public interest or some important question of law, or affecting property of considerable amount, or where the case is otherwise of some public importance, or of a very substantial character."[3] And then further on: "It has been said that where a person has elected to go to the Supreme Court it is not the practice to allow him to come to the Board except in a very strong case. It is different where a man is taken to the Supreme Court because he cannot help it. But where a man elects to go to the Supreme Court, having his chance whether he goes there or not, this Board will not give him assistance except under special circumstances."[4]

In the Province of Ontario one was privileged, if the matter in controversy exceeded the sum of $4,000.00 to deposit a bond for $4,000.00 or $2,000.00 in cash with the Registrar of the Appellate Court and go on to the Privy Council by right of grant.[5] No special leave was necessary apparently.[6] So far so good, but this was a large sum of money. Then there was the printing of the record which was also a heavy expense as, it seemed, sixty copies must be deposited with the Registrar at Downing Street; in addition there would be the Privy Council Office fees, and I should have to get myself to England to argue the case.[7] Reading further in Bentwich something most interesting cropped up: if one were very poor and could take an oath that one was not worth more than $125.00 in the world apart from wearing apparel and the subject matter involved in the appeal, and could procure a letter signed by Counsel to the effect that there were "reasonable grounds for appeal," a petition could then be sent to His Majesty in Council begging for leave to appeal in "forma pauperis."[8] I discovered that this leave was often granted by the Privy Council. The pauper appellant was absolved from depositing any security, or from paying any Privy Council Office fees; and he borrowed the money to pay for the printing of the record and frequently some young Counsel was found eager and anxious to argue the case. I yearned to be a pauper. But alas, there was no such luck for me! I was obliged to sell the few shares of good stock which I held and this amount together with some savings of my husband enabled me to deposit my $2,000.00 security with the Appellate Court. I did this on the day before the New Year. Then the struggle began. The Trust Company appeared as respondent, refusing not only to assist me in any way with the appeal, but refusing to give me any of my own money in their hands. "Nothing can be paid out while the estate is in litigation" was their convenient excuse. Unwilling to accept the approval of my security by a single judge my opponents forced me to go before the full Court.[9] Strenuous efforts were on foot to block my way to England; no doubt about that.

There would be five Judges, perhaps four, on the Bench; there was a probability that two might be with me, but I needed a third—three Judges I must have. When I had noticed that Mr. Justice Hodgins in his Judgment had used evidence against me which had been withdrawn before the hearing of the case, I pointed the fact out to the Chief Justice who immediately sent me to "Brother Hodgins'" chambers to direct his attention to this oversight. Mr. Justice Hodgins was unbelievably rude, refusing either to listen to me or to read his Judgment, he rose angrily, almost shaking a fist at me, and said in shrill tones, "Leave my chambers at once and never dare to appear before me again, do you hear?" Judges must not show bias; Judges must not show bias!—the phrase ran through my head. Where had I heard it? Yes, I remembered now; once when browsing about in the library at Osgoode Hall I had come across it under an article or perhaps it was a statute entitled "Judges Act." Suddenly it came to me that were I to accuse Mr. Justice Hodgins in Court of showing bias by citing the aforesaid episode, he might have to retire and allow some other Judge to take his place. On the other hand, if he remained and heard the case he might well prove the third Judge whom I needed; this in order to "save his face" and to demonstrate to the Canadian public his good faith and his judicial attitude. Indeed, in thinking the matter over I could see no other course open to his Lordship. Courage and plenty of it would be needed to expose Mr. Justice Hodgins' peculiar behavior, nevertheless I decided to do so if it became necessary. The following morning to my surprise three Judges took their places on the Bench, the Chief Justice, Mr. Justice Middleton, recently appointed to the First Appellate Division, and Mr. Justice Magee.[10] They heard several motions but just as I arose to speak, in came Mr.

Justice Hodgins and took his accustomed seat. I should have to make a fight for it!

"With great respect, my Lord, I should like to say that Mr. Justice Hodgins told me never to dare appear before him again. He has shown bias in this case and I ask that he be retired from it."

For a moment there was a ghastly silence in the big Court room. Mr. Justice Hodgins seemed to shrink within his gown as from a blow.

"Perhaps you had better sit down, Mrs. Campbell. We shall hear from Mr. Sinclair whether he has any objections to your going to the Privy Council," quoth the Chief Justice suavely. My scheme was about to succeed! From then on Mr. Justice Hodgins fought for me to go to the Privy Council, because he did not dare do anything else; to be sure his fighting was somewhat in "reverse." Mr. Sinclair and the Trust Company did not desire me to appeal. Naturally not, thought I.

"Mr. Sinclair," said Mr. Justice Hodgins, "if Mrs. Campbell, with the decision of three Courts against her, wishes to go on to the Privy Council, and wishes to lose her money and waste her time and energy, is it for you to stop her? Many cases with no more merit than this one, have gone to the Privy Council. I'd like to know what business it is of yours, Mr. Sinclair." His Lordship was most amusing. The Chief Justice endeavored to silence Mr. Sinclair by asking him if perchance he had become Mrs. Campbell's Counsel instead of Mr. Hogg's. Was the Chief Justice also "saving his face"? I wondered.

But Mr. Justice Middleton spoke his mind in no uncertain terms as to my unquestionable right of appeal to the final Court of the Empire. And it was he who, some weeks later, handed down the Judgment which allowed me to go to England, and which censured Mr. Hogg for bringing me before the full Court. This Judgment was signed by all four Judges. My arraignment of Mr. Justice Hodgins had gained me another point because not long after this the Registrar received instructions that the Judges of the First Divisional Court desired a memorandum to be appended to their reasons for Judgment to the effect that certain evidence used therein had been withdrawn before the argument of the case. It was somewhat of a triumph! I was going before the Privy Council with two and a half Judgments from the Appellate Court. Surely a unique position. "Functus Officio," whispered the officials about the Hall; "Functus Officio," said the Barristers and wagged their heads.[11]

The next step according to Bentwich which by now had become my Bible, was to obtain the papers of the case; this was known as the "record." The printing of the record might be done either in Canada, or the record, certified by the Registrar of the Court from which the Appeal came, transmitted to the Registrar of the Privy Council for printing in England.[12] I noticed among my papers filed in the Court a transcript of our argument during my appeal; I have never discovered who placed it there. I read it over more than once and made some notes. It was helpful to me because it showed how forcibly the Judges had expressed themselves in my favor while on the Bench as contrasted with the strange decision they had ultimately rendered. Also it showed how strongly the late Mr. Justice Ferguson had felt with regard to the justice of my case. No one seemed to know what had become of Mr. Justice Ferguson's papers. The Chief Justice when I applied to him merely told me that he had left no decision on my case.

I engaged a typist to come up to Osgoode Hall to type the papers for the record. On the morning upon which she was to begin her work the transcript, to my surprise, was missing from my bundle of papers.[13] I informed the Appellate Registrar of its disappearance. Looking flustered he produced from his vaults an envelope sealed with a large amount of sealing wax and stamped with the Court Seal; underneath this was written "not to be opened except by the instructions of the full Court." To my highly indignant enquiries came the response that Mr. Justice Hodgins had descended from his chambers and, demanding to see my papers, had removed the transcript and ordered that it be sealed up, which order had been obeyed. I sought the Chief Justice, begging him to restore the document, but he replied that Mr. Justice Hodgins having dealt with the matter he could do nothing. I obtained an interview with Attorney General Price.[14] He also, it appeared, was powerless. He was, however, sympathetic and proffered some advice, the shrewdness of which I did not wholly appreciate until months later when I stood before the Law Lords in the Privy Council Chamber and his words came to my mind. The Attorney

General had said, "Don't worry about the transcript of evidence being withheld, Mrs. Campbell. Sometimes one is just as well off without a thing as with it, better in fact." But at the time my heart burned within me. I needed that transcript to facilitate the settling of the record because it showed that certain letters and documents had been discussed before the Appellate Court which my opponents were now refusing to have included in the record. I ought perhaps to explain that in order to settle the record, i.e., to decide what documents are necessary, one must meet with one's opponents at the office of the Registrar because it is he who, in addition to certifying the papers, rules upon any disputed items; everything is submitted to him subject of course to a final ruling by a Judge if either party so desires. Those meetings were terrible. I can never forget what I went through at the hands of my opponents and the Registrar. Frequently for two hours at a stretch I would stand my ground against three Solicitors with no assistance from anyone, that is no one except Bentwich. I kept the volume open on the table between us all and by dint of the information and the rules and regulations therein fought my way inch by inch.

The sudden change in the Registrar's attitude was very disconcerting, because hitherto he had been rather friendly and always most courteous. However "I gave as good as I got" and slowly I made headway but it was very exhausting. Furthermore, I was conscious that my enemies sought frequently to trap me. That anyone so inexperienced and unversed in the law as I was should have escaped these pitfalls seems to me now little short of miraculous. Counsel for Mr. Hogg and Mrs. Lindsey desired that her name might be left out of the style of cause, or title of the case. Naturally, I was not anxious to have a third respondent against me, and during one of the meetings before the Registrar, it was suggested to me that I should just drop Mrs. Lindsey's name from the matter, as she did not wish to have it included or to be represented in England, but I had learned by now to move warily and to think things over carefully. Reading about in Bentwich I came upon a paragraph to the effect that unless the proper parties to an appeal are before them, the Judgment of the Judicial Committee will not be binding. I might so easily have assented to the suggestion put to me that very afternoon. I determined to ask the full Court to decide whether Mrs. Lindsey were a party to the Appeal, and at the same time to ask the Court for the transcript of evidence. The transcript was refused me; my opponents stated that they did not need it, that they were getting along very nicely without it, which last was only too true. The Chief Justice said these "notes" had been made for the convenience of the Judges. I replied that some leading members of the Bar had assured me that in a Privy Council case the parties were often allowed to have the "notes" and I added that it looked very much as though someone wished to conceal something or the transcript would not have been sealed up. "A very unwarranted expression of suspicion," this from the Chief Justice; but the transcript was never handed back to me and is still, so far as I know, reposing in the Osgoode Hall vaults with its weighty seal unbroken, and I feel that my suspicion was very well founded.[15] As to Mrs. Lindsey's status, things went better on this point. The full Court declared she was not a party to the case.[16] I had shifted the responsibility to the Judges, and I resolved to have a copy of their decision beside me in England in case it should be needed.

My typist worked at the Hall under my supervision from ten to four each day.[17] One morning several of the typed sheets, which she had piled in the corner the previous evening, were mislaid. No one knew anything about them and the Appellate Registrar, who treated me more kindly than his superiors, due perhaps to the fact that he unlike the other two, did not belong to the legal fraternity, was distressed. At noon he and I chanced to be alone in the office; he said, as he gazed steadily out of the window his back turned to me, "Mrs. Campbell, have you ever thought of getting your printing done in England? They know so much about it over there. It would be pretty bad if mistakes were made and you had to have your printing all redone; it would be very expensive, I mean." From that moment I determined to get myself and the record to England as speedily as possible, and to have all the printing done over there. I notified my husband to book a passage for me in April. I also rented a safety deposit box in the Dominion Bank vaults, at first a small box then a large one. Five o'clock each evening saw me tucking a pile of refractory papers into the box assisted by the Superintendent of the vaults who had become interested in me and my case. As the work on the record progressed, it was found that the first document necessary to it, Mr. Hogg's Statutory

Declaration upon which he had based his accounts, was missing. We wrote to the Surrogate Court at Ottawa as to why it had not been sent up with the other original papers, only to receive the reply that apparently it had never been filed with them though mentioned in our evidence and that they knew nothing about it. When I had decided to appeal to the Privy Council, Mr. Slaght turned a great file of papers over to me, saying, "Mrs. Campbell, I am doing rather an unusual thing. I am handing you all the papers on the case, even my own brief and notes; you will find among the papers some most valuable to you. I should take the utmost care of them, you know." A word from the wise was sufficient. I bought me a stout attaché case with a fine Yale lock, and everywhere that I went the attaché case went too. In Mr. Slaght's brief was a carbon copy of the missing declaration. It had been discussed before the Appellate Court and was, I knew, extremely important because Mr. Hogg had sworn therein to the "investment and reinvestment" of my mother's money; this showed that he had been a trustee rather than an agent, which Mr. Justice Hodgins' Judgment held him to be, a vital distinction. It was Mr. Justice Magee who finally steered me in the right direction by advising me to go look for the original declaration at the Trust Company. I had already telephoned the Estates Manager but had received a negative reply; the paper I desired could not be found. But after the shrewd old gentleman's tip, I went down to the Trust Company's offices and asked Mr. Lang to look again through Lady Howland's papers. When he got up, I adroitly followed him and walked into the vaults beside him. Of course, I had no right to do this, but he was so dumbfounded that, though he protested the "thing" couldn't be there, he got out my mother's bundle of papers and hastily ran through them. I watched carefully and to my joy spied the document I sought tucked in amongst the other papers. "Look, Mr. Lang, there it is," shouted I, "it's just like my copy." Quickly unlocking my case I produced Mr. Slaght's brief with the carbon copy. "I can have these two copies certified to now by the Judge who is going to settle my record. I've been told it's to be Mr. Justice Middleton; and as the original seems to be lost, the copy will be admitted; two copies will be as good as the original." Even in my excitement I noticed a strange look flit across Mr. Lang's face. Ushering me out of the vaults into his office, he said, "Sit down, Mrs. Campbell, I want to 'phone our Solicitors." From what I could gather Mr. McKague, the young Solicitor, had had the original statutory declaration in his possession all the time, through some omission it had not been filed in the Surrogate Court and he had apparently just picked it up. He brought it to Osgoode Hall the next day. The Registrar took us all before Mr. Justice Middleton who ordered it at once to be included in my record.

It is but fitting that in this story of my struggle I should pay tribute to the sterling qualities and ability of that Judge without whose assistance I should not, I think, have succeeded in obtaining my record for England.

William Middleton, gentleman and Jurist! With his keen sense of justice, with his mind steeped in the law! The door of his book-lined chambers is always open; the carpeting worn away is repaired and worn away again by the feet of the Registrars, by Counsel young and old, and by his brother Judges who come constantly seeking direction and advice. That direction and advice are freely given by his Lordship. His patience is inexhaustible, this together with his impartiality and never-failing humor has greatly endeared him to both Bench and Bar.

But to return to my record. The weeks were passing. February and March had blustered themselves out and April was just blowing herself in, still the record was not ready for transmission to Downing Street.[18] A second very important paper, the transcript of my mother's bank account, had not been filed in the Court. I held a copy, but this time the Trust Company had neither the original, which had been sent them by the Bank of Commerce at St. Catharine's, nor had they a copy. My opponents said the paper was not necessary to the case; I said it was. A heated argument took place which Mr. Justice Middleton finally settled by ordering the Trust Company to at once secure another certified transcript from the bank. "This lady's record shall not go to England without this necessary document," said his Lordship firmly.

When, following this episode, Mr. Hogg's Solicitors began objecting to his ledgers and letter books being sent with the other original papers to the Privy Council, I decided to appeal to the Attorney General for assistance. Complaining of the conduct of his Registrars, I also pointed out that more than three months had been consumed by wrangling and by the loss of documents, that my record was still far from ready, and that my passage to England had of necessity been cancelled because it was my intention to remain in Canada until the despatch of my papers.

Evidently the Attorney General looked into the affair. The Registrars are under his control, and things began to speed up a bit. Towards the end of April the record, in pretty good condition, thanks to Bentwich, was completed. The carbon duplicate of the record which was safe in my deposit box at the bank I proposed taking with me to England where it would be got ready for printing.

Following the advice of Mr. Justice Magee I made a trip to Ottawa to ascertain whether any trace could be found of those missing gentlemen, Messrs. McAmmond and Martin. His Lordship had told me that the Judicial Committee would be very apt to question me as to whether I myself had endeavored to locate these men, and that my position, he thought, would be greatly strengthened were I able to answer in the affirmative. For several days I fine-combed Ottawa, which though Canada's capital is still a small city. No one apparently had ever heard of the persons I sought. In the Carnegie Library I found the old directories of the City of Ottawa and the telephone books for years past. I went carefully through these volumes line by line but was unable to locate either McAmmond or Martin. Mr. Hogg had stated that these men were market gardeners. After some difficulty I got in touch with the old Market Inspector, but neither he nor the present incumbent who had succeeded him knew anything about Messrs. McAmmond and Martin. They looked mystified as I questioned them, but of one thing they seemed quite certain; no such firm as I mentioned had ever done business on the Market. Making notes on the futility of my search, I returned to Toronto.

Mr. Hogg's ledgers and letter books had now to be packed. The Appellate Registrar suggested that one of the carpenters who worked about the Hall would bring up a packing case from the basement, and that he would help us pack. The man lined the case carefully with brown paper and the Registrar and I packed all the ledgers and original papers, checking them off on a list to be transmitted together with the record. The carpenter was proceeding to screw on the lid. While he was doing this something prompted me to lift one end of the box. As I did so I noticed that a wide board in the bottom was quite loose, in fact, was giving away; the brown paper was visible and it would not be long before the contents would sag through. Everything had to be unpacked and the workman disappeared rather shamefacedly, I thought, taking his box with him. I insisted upon ordering a proper box from a nearby factory and when it was delivered the Registrar and I repacked it.

The taxi stood at the side door of the Hall. The Registrar with the record under his arm marvellously wrapped and sealed, and I in my hat and coat were on our way to despatch it, together with the box of exhibits to England. But no one could be found to move the heavy box; all the attendants seemed to have vanished. I was leaving in a few hours for Boston; every moment counted. I managed to drag the case out of the office but could get it no further. Down the corridor I sped, and dashing out to the taxi driver pressed a dollar bill or two upon him, and almost pulled him in to give me a hand. Between us we succeeded in stowing the box away in the taxi. I hopped in after it, the Registrar with the record reluctantly bringing up the rear.

Back to Osgoode Hall from the Express Office raced my taxi. There remained one last thing for me to attend to before boarding the Boston train. I had desired a copy certified to by the Registrar of the first Judgment given me by the Appellate Division. I had asked the Chief Justice if he would allow this to be made from the Judgment book. Angrily he had refused, adding: "What a pertinacious woman you are to be sure, Mrs. Campbell." Immediately after this interview I had sworn to an affidavit to the effect that a copy of the Judgment had been denied me by the Chief Justice of Ontario. I wanted this affidavit together with the Judgment dealing with Mrs. Lindsey's status in the appeal, as well as the Judgment refusing to return me the transcript of evidence, to be included though not printed in the record. My opponents, backed up by the Registrar, had flatly refused to allow this. I was determined however, that somehow these documents should reach England; I might need them, I reflected. I begged the Registrar for certified copies of the documents I desired. Rudely he refused me although I placed Bentwich in front of him and pointed to a paragraph which to me seemed to more than provide for the carrying out of my request. It read: "but the documents omitted to be printed or copied shall be enumerated on a typewritten list to be transmitted with the record."[19]

Perhaps if I were to show Bentwich to his Lordship, Mr. Justice Middleton, I might be allowed the papers. Along the corridor and across the rotunda, up the stairway and down more corridors, I hurried with Bentwich in my hand. Breathless I reached Mr. Justice Middleton's chambers.

"It is my opinion, Mrs. Campbell, that once you are before the Privy Council those documents will not be needed," said his Lordship, "but I do not see why I should not grant you your perfectly reasonable request." Taking up his telephone he gave instructions to the Registrar to at once have copies of the documents I had requested prepared and placed in an envelope and sealed with the Court seal. Upon the envelope there was to be a direction written by the Registrar to the effect that I should present the same at the Privy Council Office. Smiling and handing me my Bentwich his Lordship escorted me to the glass doorway which shut off the northeast wing from the rest of the Hall. For a moment he looked at me, then, placing his hand on my shoulder, said, "You are very like your father, aren't you? Good-bye, and God speed to you, Mrs. Campbell. I wish you the best of luck and don't forget the Trustee Act."

BOOK FIVE

DOWNING STREET: THE PRIVY COUNCIL

MY RECORD and the exhibits sailed on the Mauretania early in May, heavily insured with a British company and directed to the Registrar of the Privy Council, 2 Downing Street, London, S.W.1. I followed them very shortly on a much more modest ship of the same line after hastily setting my house in order and bidding my family and intimate friends good-bye. What a hectic few weeks it was, to be sure; reservations and passports, visas and letters of credit, some slight sartorial preparations on my part, intermingled with the farewells and the incessant ringing of the telephone.

It is interesting to look back and recall what I saw in those eyes that bade me farewell. My children and husband—especially the latter, I think—felt that "Mother would win her case;" but in most instances, though the lips uttered the usual "good luck" phrases, the eyes said only too plainly, "Poor dear, she certainly has courage, but what a crazy thing to be doing, dashing off this way to England and to be trying to argue her own case over there too," and then nearly everyone asked, "but what on earth is the Privy Council?"

Two there were, however, in whose eyes I read other things; to them I owe much. One is a very gracious lovely lady, affectionately spoken of by her large circle of friends as "Susan Chapin."[1] From the very beginning of my struggle she had stood beside me, assisting me not only financially but also with an understanding and warm-hearted encouragement such as only rare personalities possess. A great-grand-daughter of Paul Revere, I have sometimes thought that her patriotic inheritance caused her to be particularly incensed by the flagrant injustice of my case and the tremendous odds against which I was fighting. Furthermore, having lived much in England she did not have to ask, "What is the Privy Council?"

Never once during those strenuous years of which you have read did her loyalty fail me nor her interest flag.

One of the many questions which the Canadian press put to me in the interview which I granted them after my victory in London was, "Did you have American finance behind you?"[2] My reply was, "Gentlemen, if you mean by finance, dear wonderful friends who, when I needed money, sat down and wrote a cheque saying the while how happy they were to help, I most certainly did." The chief among these friends of justice was Susan Chapin.

William Lawrence, "first gentleman of Massachusetts," the great Bishop of our Church, was the other friend who never doubted but that ultimately I should win and seemed to understand, even without my telling him, that it was faith in British justice which was taking me across the seas.[3] I so well remember his paying me the honor of coming out to Jamaica Plain upon a very hot day eager to "know all about it," and more than once through the months of work in London, of which I am going to tell you, he managed, though so busy a person, to send encouraging little notes and occasionally a cable.

Notwithstanding the fact that I intended to handle and plead my case myself I thought it advisable to have some assistance, especially in the matter of reading the law and in hunting up cases bearing on the Trustee Act. Through a mutual friend I had been put in touch with a young Counsel in London, said to be very brilliant. Indeed, because of this ability he had recently won a Scholarship and had spent a year at the Harvard Law School.

This young man's answer, when I wrote him after finally winning my leave to appeal, showed me that he was keenly interested in my case and he assured me that he would be happy to give me the desired assistance. Immediately upon my arrival in London, therefore, even before unpacking, I presented myself at his chambers, New Square, Lincoln's Inn. I found him very like the description which the friend who had placed me in his care had given of him; we smoked a cigarette or two and discussed the situation and the astonishing things I had been through at the hands of the Canadian Courts. He then said that his wife would call on me and that he hoped I would come to their home, which, strangely enough, was in a neighboring square just around the corner from my hotel; so we arranged that I should leave my papers and make a little table of dates showing the various happenings in the case, and that when he had looked them over, he would communicate with me.

I was not in when Mrs. Prine called, but the day after I accepted her invitation to tea, taking with me all my precious papers and a note for her husband. We two women, when me met, did not like each other, and I could feel instinctively that Mrs. Prine was most unsympathetic towards my case and the fact that I was venturing to argue it myself; however, she was polite, and said, as she poured out tea, that she would give her husband the papers that evening. This was on Thursday; on Sunday night — I had just had my bath and was putting out the light in my tiny bed-room on the top floor of the quaint Bloomsbury boarding-place where I had "dug myself in" — when the porter knocked with a "parcel for you, madam." I opened the door and to my utter amazement was handed my papers together with a note. Mr. Prine, although knowing how carefully I had guarded those papers, had not even returned them to me personally, but had evidently just sent them. His letter, which rambled through several pages, was composed of insincere apologies and threadbare excuses as to why he could have nothing to do with my case; his health, he went on to say, was poor, and at present he was quite exhausted. (He had seemed to me a very good-looking, very well set-up young man indeed.) Then he advised me to at once place myself in the hands of one of the following firms of Solicitors; he mentioned several, they were firms that manage the Canadian appeals which come across to the Privy Council. More especially did he recommend the firm of Blake and Redden as being particularly desirable. Now this was curious because it happens to be the remains of my father's former firm.[4] The Blakes have a London office, and though for many years no Blake has been in the firm, yet because of the name and connection, Blake and Redden are still in very close touch with Canada, and I was aware that they were going to handle the case for the Toronto General Trusts Corporation. The letter was a terrible blow. Almost stunned I sat on the edge of my narrow iron bed with my papers beside me; I had counted on Mr. Prine's advice and help — I had no money to engage a Solicitor, I knew that their fees were high in England and I had barely enough money to pay for the printing of my record—the appellant bears all the cost of printing, and the Privy Council Office fees. The sense of being quite alone in this vast London was overpowering and great waves of desolation swept over me. However, the night wore away at last, the big moon which had been gazing in my window sank down behind the forest of chimney-pots; dawn came and the sunrise, which seemed to be followed almost immediately by my early morning tea. I must of course have fallen asleep in between. To me nothing is ever so bad by daylight, so I pulled myself together and wrote Mr. Prine a note, not a long note, not an impolite note, but one which I fancy that gentleman will not easily forget.

Then I wandered about London endeavoring to decide what to do, endeavoring also, not always successfully, to choke back the tears. But finally my Highland ancestry asserted itself. I remembered what had been told me about my father, "that he won most of his cases by not knowing when he was beaten"; remembered, too, that the last case which he argued before the Privy Council—

Doorway of the Privy Council Office, no. 2 Downing Street

the case which cost him his life at so early an age—he had won against almost insurmountable obstacles. The case is still quoted in international law.[5] Was I not my father's daughter? I would go in and win!

Therefore, the next day I started forth to the Privy Council Office to ascertain whether my record had arrived safely and somehow to get it in shape for the printer, guided by my trusty Bentwich.

The uniformed messenger on the other side of the swinging doorway of No. 2 Downing Street, when I told him what I had come about said, "You want Mr. Lys' office, madam," and proceeded to direct me to a room on the left of the square stone hallway. The Second Clerk of the Privy Council, Dudley George Lys, proved to be a strikingly alert wide-a-wake looking gentleman. He had need of these attributes, because through his hands passed all the appeals, and he was in constant touch with a host of Solicitors and Barristers in London and from the various parts of the Empire who come to the Privy Council to prosecute appeals. Mr. Lys looked at me with interest and also, I thought, with surprise; in fact, I had the feeling that he had expected someone more militant looking than I, someone with horn rimmed glasses and perhaps greater avoirdupois to her credit. "Yes, Mrs. Campbell, we have been expecting you. Your record and the box of exhibits have arrived safely. We know all about you over here, you see." With this he crossed to his desk and unlocking a drawer to my surprise drew from it column after column of clippings, some pink, some yellow, from the Canadian press—clippings dealing with my recent struggle to obtain my record from the Canadian Courts.[6] The accounts of my clash with the Registrars at Osgoode Hall were highly amusing and Mr. Lys "twinkled." He had, as I was to discover, a delightful sense of humor, so an amicable relationship was established between us at once. I have never found out whether friend or foe sent those clippings, but I have always felt they were very helpful to me. He then enquired who was appearing for me. Never shall I forget the flash in his eyes—they were expressive eyes—when I informed him my intention was to handle the case entirely alone, having neither Solicitor nor Counsel. He said, "I suppose you realize, Mrs. Campbell, that you are doing a most unusual, rather daring, thing?" My reply was, "No doubt I am, but there doesn't seem to be any other course open to me, because I have no money to engage either Solicitor or Counsel."

Here I should perhaps explain for the benefit of my readers who are not familiar with the English Bar, that if one has a Counsel, one must first have a Solicitor who appoints that Counsel, the Solicitor attending to all the technicalities of the case and the preparation of it, the Counsel coming in at the end to argue it; and if one "briefs a Silk,"—that is: retains a King's Counsel—he is known as a Leader and he in turn must have his Junior, and this Junior receives two thirds of the fee which the King's Counsel is privileged to charge. This makes litigation in England an exceedingly expensive business.

"Have you thought," continued Mr. Lys, "what will happen if their Lordships do not find in your favor? Remember you have the order of three Canadian Courts to reverse; have you considered what it will be to lose with all the costs against you; have you thought of the risk?"

"I have, Mr. Lys, indeed I have. I've thought of all that, but you see I'm going to win my case, not lose," said I.

Privy Council Chamber with the historic "Horseshoe Table"

Again the flash in those eyes. "That's the British spirit, Mrs. Campbell," and rising from his seat on the edge of the table he pulled forward a huge book and opening it said, "I take it, then, that you wish to enter an appearance, you see your opponents have already done so." There underneath Privy Council Appeal No. 56 of 1929, Campbell vs. Hogg and Others, on appeal from the Supreme Court of Ontario, was entered the name of Bischoff, Coxe, Bischoff, and Thompson, for the first respondent, W.D. Hogg.[7]

Mr. Lys then produced a form which I signed, at the same time paying the Privy Council Office fee of one pound for entering an appearance. I think I may safely say that never before or since have I signed a document with greater elation nor paid over money more gladly. What though I was quite alone in London, what though I knew not where to turn to read the law, what though I was more than puzzled as to how to get a record of my case in shape for a printer; I was at long last before the Privy Council, "the place where wrongs are righted!"

Two interesting incidents occur to me in connection with my entering an appearance: the first is that the form used in the Privy Council had to be altered by striking out "Solicitor for the Appellant" and substituting "in person" underneath my signature; the other occurrence is that two days after my appearance the Blake and Redden firm registered for the Toronto General Trusts Corporation, the second respondent. I have often speculated as to what would have occurred had I followed Mr. Prine's ardent advice.

The record and box of exhibits we found safe in Mr. Upton's room—he was the Third Clerk of the Privy Council and in charge of the Record Office.[8] I had with me the duplicate of my record and Mr. Lys endeavored to explain and show me how to arrange it in acceptable Privy Council form, and sent me home to accomplish my task rather like a child with so many lines to write in her copy-book. In their quiet impartial manner the Privy Council had accepted their female appellant in person, and as I went back and forth to Downing Street for many months busy with the arduous details of my case, no one betrayed any surprise, no one caused me to feel that I was doing anything unusual; I was treated throughout with gracious kindness and exquisite English courtesy.

The preparation of the record was to me terribly confusing. Of course, this is scarcely surprising, because the London Solicitors get big fees for doing this work. Again I read my Bentwich assiduously and tried to follow Mr. Lys' instructions; but when I said, "See, Mr. Lys, is this all right?" he very often had to answer, "No, Mrs. Campbell, I'm afraid it's all wrong; look, this is the way." His kindness and patience were inexhaustible. It would, I realized, have been so much easier to have taken the record and prepared it himself, but this he was not privileged to do; he could only show me and correct me. Some of the work I did over four times and the paper was in places almost worn through from frequent erasures when finally it was ready for the printer.

There are only certain printers who are entrusted with Privy Council printing; they are picked out by the Registrar. My evidence was placed with Messrs. Eyre & Spottiswoode.

Towards the end of the month it became necessary to deposit the money to cover the cost of printing, and to my sorrow I discovered that I needed another $1,000.00. Mr. Lys, who could estimate almost to a fraction the cost of printing, announced that we should need three hundred pounds. We decided, therefore, to send part of the record; the cost of this was covered by my letter of credit for $700.00. I had just a month in which to obtain the further $1,000.00, if I was to be heard at the Hilary Sessions in January.

In response to my S.O.S. came a lovely letter from Mrs. Chapin together with a cheque, then we mortgaged our little summer home and managed to secure the money just in time to prevent a delay in our hearing.

This first month in London was an exciting and dramatic one.[9] I had great need of courage and steadiness. Although I was quite a woman of the world and had travelled much, especially before my marriage, life had been a very sheltered thing, and for the first time I found myself in surroundings utterly foreign to me. Indeed, I have since thought that almost the only familiar thing in my environment was the sound of the English language. Of necessity I was forced to live cheaply, and Bloomsbury had been recommended as being reasonable and highly accessible.[10] The small hotel which I happened upon was in Russell Square and, like most of its neighbors, was composed of house after house identically alike. This property belongs, I believe, to a Ducal Estate, and our hotel had the distinction of having one bedroom which differed from the others — a large room with exquisite ceiling and a still lovelier white marble mantle with fairy-like carvings. Legend has it that this was once the boudoir of a mistress of one of the former Dukes of this House.

I used to amuse myself by fancying that the hotel had been fashioned by someone taking a huge hammer and with a blow or two knocking the houses all together, and then doing comic things with the plumbing and telephone, such as inserting bathrooms where they could only be reached by parading through a well-filled lounge clad in one's bathrobe, or installing the sole telephone of the establishment right on the wall in the front hall of the centre house, which frequently meant crossing the dining room, perhaps in negligee, to answer a telephone call, and always meant being overheard by the guests passing in and out of the hallway.

But stranger than all this were my fellow-guests: men and women whose ages ranged from the quite elderly to the middle aged with a sprinkling of young people, some married, some single, some just quietly living together "without benefit of clergy," the woman having donned a wedding ring as a "sop to Cerberus" and lastly a few unfortunate children whose parents must, I feel sure, have bitterly regretted their growing up in such an atmosphere.[11] Someone has called Bloomsbury the home of the social outcast; I think to a great extent this is true. One was conscious that with few exceptions these people had slipped from their own world; in some instances one actually felt their past looking over their shoulders as they sat in those deep-seated comfortable chairs indigenous to English lounges, and occasionally when in repose one saw stamped on their faces stark tragedy, and felt somehow so ashamed and hot all over to have witnessed it. Then the bitter gossip and worst of all the cruel hardness and lack of mercy or pity for someone of the group who had perhaps unfortunate habits. It is generally conceded I think that the "Passing of the Third Floor Back," the play which Sir Johnston Forbes-Robertson immortalized, is a great play; but one must sojourn for a time in a Bloomsbury boarding place to realize just how great it is.[12] I am not, as our New England friends say, much of a "mixer," also being busy, kept to myself. I made just one friend, he was a young ex-officer with a gallant career behind him, his life, poor chap, pretty much shattered. I at once recognized him as belonging to exactly my world; we had much in common, notwithstanding the gap in our ages and our different upbringing, and were singularly congenial. An omnivorous reader himself, he assisted me in obtaining a card of admission to the reading room of the British Museum and showed me how to find the law books which I needed.

I have spoken of the almost overpowering vastness of London, but I was to be brought face to face with its astonishing smallness, one might say. Two or three days after my entering an appearance at the Privy Council, while hurrying along—my friends always accuse me of walking like the wind—whom should I run across, or rather run into, in Regent Street, but Mr. Justice Hodgins, impeccably dressed in the full regalia of the London season then at its height, and wearing his morning coat, gardenia, white spats, not of course like a Londoner—no other man can quite do that—but nevertheless I am bound to admit making a rather fine appearance. He turned very red indeed, and I passed on, needless to say, without bowing. When I reached my hotel the porter handed me a cable. I opened it and read, "Hodgins in London. Be wise. H—." My dear friends in Toronto had sent it. I relate this because it seems to me such an amusing coincidence.

The engaging of my room at the hotel was done through the clerk in the office, and I had practically no conversation with Mr. G—, the Manager, beyond bidding him good-morning and good-evening, but I remember thinking him an unprepossessing little man and recall that I did not like his face. The wife was rather a sweet-looking woman, much engaged in caring for her ménage. On the morning of which I write I was hurrying along to the Privy Council Office when down the steps of one of the large hotels in Southampton Row walked Mr. G—, and coming towards me took me most familiarly by the arm, saying, "You don't mind my putting my arm in yours, do you?" I was terrified; my heart, I am sure, stopped beating just for an instant, and my speech forsook me entirely. Still holding my arm he continued, "It's G— of the 'Dayton.' Don't you know me?" My presence of mind returning, I pulled myself away and, heedless of the traffic, dashed across to the square. I remember hearing a screeching of brakes as some cars pulled up sharply; but I reached the curb in safety, and as swiftly as my shaking knees would allow made my way around the corner to the hotel. Mrs. G— was in her sitting room and I related what had happened. She seemed both shocked and apologetic. In fact, the conversation, short as it was, ended in tears on both sides. I dried mine quickly, however, no time for tears now! My passport lay locked in my small travelling case. I secured it and hailing a taxi told the driver, "Scotland Yard as fast as you can." The traffic in Trafalgar and Whitehall was heavy so that by the time we drew up in front of the Yard my composure had somewhat returned, though I was still pretty frightened.

The huge officer at the top of the steps, in response to my, "I want a policeman at once," replied with British calm and courtesy, "Oh, no, madam, I don't think so; you want one of our inspectors." In a moment I found myself in a large, high-vaulted room which even though the day was warm seemed dim and cool, rather like a frigidaire. The coolness and dimness took effect, and when the inspector appeared, I was quite coherent again. He was an unassuming young man wearing a lounge suit, the last person one would ever suspect of being an official of the famous Scotland Yard. I produced my passport which he took and after looking it over handed it to a uniformed messenger who bore it away. Gravely and attentively he listened to my story of coming to England to argue my own case before the Privy Council, betraying no surprise when I told him that I felt I was fighting powerful opponents, and that I was entirely alone in London. He remarked when I related the incident which had just occurred, "You have acted wisely in coming to us, Mrs. Campbell; and now what do you intend doing? Shall you leave that hotel or shall you stay on?" I explained that it was only now after much cabling that my mail was coming to me directly from home, furthermore that I was in the midst of preparing my record for printing, and that I did not feel that I could hunt another abode at present, but I begged that Scotland Yard would look out for me. He said that the police in Russell Square would be notified and, my passport being returned just then, he handed it to me with a slip of paper upon which was written the address of the nearest police station, Hunter Street. "If anything untoward or suspicious should occur and you need assistance, communicate with this address at once, and in the event of your moving away from the vicinity of Russell Square, kindly inform us," said he, then with an amused smile, "I rather think that fresh gentleman's wife will attend to him, don't you?"

With what a feeling of relief I ran down those steps which a short time before I had so anxiously ascended! It gave me a sense of great security to know that behind me was Scotland Yard.

Before dinner that evening Mr. G— sent word to ask if he might speak to me in the drawing-room. He was waiting when I entered; the gentleman was abject, he apologized, nay he grovelled, and nearly wept. I said, "Sir, I accept your apology and shall remain under your roof until such time as it is convenient for me to move." Just as I was about to pass through the door he wailed, "But why, oh why did you go to my wife?" Apparently the inspector had predicted rightly!

I had not forgotten what those wise gentlemen, Mr. Justice Magee and Mr. Justice Middleton, had bade me do, "Hear the Judicial Committee in session," "Get the aura of the Privy Council." Therefore, that July, in between working on my record, I would often slip up the winding stone stairs through the swinging door of the ante-chamber and into the Privy Council Chamber itself, where sat five great Law Lords engrossed just then in Dominion Appeals, as it is during June and July that many of the Canadian Counsel seek to have their appeals heard. In the second Court, which is smaller, Indian appeals were in progress.

Were I to be asked what had impressed me most forcibly about their Lordships as they listened to the Canadian Counsel and those native Indian Barristers pleading, my reply would be: the utter informality, the impartiality, the charm and grace of bearing, and the kindly humor of these "specialists in the law." Also their patience and the painstaking care with which they examined and discussed even the most minute point of the case—one felt how anxious they were to arrive at the truth of the situation no matter how much time was consumed in accomplishing this purpose. Conversant only with Canadian Courts, where frequently I had heard a most able Counsel scarcely allowed to take up a point, had heard him, in fact, admonished with, "Now, Mr. B—, we can't give you any more time," this leisurely atmosphere of the great tribunal was a revelation.

In August my search for the law began in earnest, because nothing further could be done on the record until the return of the proof from the printer. W. Reeve Wallace, O.B.E., Chief Clerk of the Privy Council, suggested that I might like to use the Privy Council library, and the messengers, Mr. Polly and Mr. Jennings, delightful Dickens-like persons who always appear in full dress suits, were placed at my disposal to bring me the law books I desired. I sat in a small room next to Mr. Wallace's, and often this charming, kindly gentleman would look in to ask how I was getting on, and occasionally he helped me to find cases and explained what some of the queer legal abbreviations in the ponderous volumes meant. I grew very friendly with Mr. Wallace and with Miss Wall that August and found myself feeling strangely at home at No. 2 Downing Street. Miss E.M. Moore and Miss Ada Wall are the two women connected with the Privy Council Office. They are not officially known as their Lordships' secretaries, but really act as such. Not only are they exceedingly efficient but are women of charm and refinement. Miss Enid Moore, tall, slim and fair; Miss Ada Wall a piquante little brunette. Like everyone else at No. 2 Downing Street, they have taken the oath of secrecy and are discretion itself.

One day while being shown about the Privy Council Office I had a curious experience. Mr. Lys asked me if I should like to take a look at the Counsels' Robing Room. It seemed that the eminent advocates from the various overseas Dominions and Colonies as well as from India who are in the habit of appearing before the Judicial Committee frequently keep a gown and wig in this room rather than bring these articles back and forth.

"The K.C.'s wigs are kept in here," said Mr. Lys, opening a large cupboard, and displaying row after row of quaint Victorian tins, resembling large old-fashioned biscuit tins — they were black and bore in golden letters the names of their respective owners. Here was Mr. Tilley's and next to it I spied Mr. McCarthy's, "D.L. McCarthy, K.C." Even as Mr. Lys was explaining that Mr. McCarthy's father had used that same receptacle for his wig, a strange feeling crept over me. Somewhere a long, long time ago I had seen a similar tin with "James Bethune, Q.C." inscribed in those same golden letters. I was a small girl again, in pinafore and long braids, standing beside my mother in our attic store-room; I could almost hear the rustle of her heavy black silk, could almost catch the pungent odor of camphor which had always pervaded the attic. My father's wig and gown must after his death have been sent home from the Privy Council.

With September our examination and proof reading commenced. What a business it was! I look back on it now as a sort of nightmare. Miss Moore was the examiner and had before her the record and original exhibits, the opposing firms each sent a solicitor's clerk, and I held the copy of the record which would be returned to the printer for reprinting; and every word, every comma, each semi-colon and interrogation mark, was compared with the original. As I knew absolutely nothing of proof reading or the weird cabalistic signs used therein, it was a pretty trying time, but the solicitor's clerk for Bischoff, Coxe, Bischoff, and Thompson — the firm acting for Mr. Hogg — was a nice lad, who evidently thought my carrying on alone "rather sporting," so he and Miss Moore assisted me with these puzzling signs, and then Mr. Lys often wandered in and lent a hand as well.

Having gone through three Courts, the record was naturally a heavy one, and we decided to separate it and have it bound in two volumes, making it easier for their Lordships to handle.

For each day of examination I paid two pounds. The record was examined twice, and then Sir Charles Neish, the Registrar, because of the "nature" of my case, ordered a revise; so this really meant that we went over it all three times.[13] Finally Messrs. Eyre and Spottiswoode delivered the sixty copies. How marvellous they looked! Only a certain fine paper and pica type are allowed and the Privy Council printers' work is meticulous. I think I must have experienced the same satisfaction as does a young author when he sees lying before him one of his works particularly well turned out, and as I reflected upon my ignorance and relived the past laborious weeks, I felt that those completed records were somewhat of a miracle. As a matter of fact their perfection was largely due to Dudley George Lys' vigilant guiding hand, and he, too, I think, was pleased.

A day or two after this, the Trust Company hurled a bomb, and only the fact that behind me were the Privy Council officials seeing to it that I had fair play prevented serious damage to my appeal. In a Privy Council record each page of evidence is earmarked in the margin, "plaintiff's evidence" or "defendant's evidence," as the case may be, and the Toronto General Trusts Corporation, though having a most expert Solicitor on the case who was constantly handling appeals, had allowed the Trust Company's name to be joined as plaintiff with Mr. Hogg's. I, not knowing it was incorrect, had not altered it, so there it appeared all through the record. Messrs. Blake and Redden were in an awful funk. They said instructions had come across from Canada that my record had been wrongly printed and that it would all have to be re-done; that it was a most serious mistake for the Trust Company — as indeed it was — could it not be rectified, because were they plaintiffs they would in all probability be made liable for costs together with Mr. Hogg in the event of his losing.

Mr. Lys telephoned me to come down at once to Downing Street, that something serious had cropped up. Hurrying out I caught my 177 bus and was soon there. Apparently it seemed quite unfair to Mr. Lys that the Trust Company's Solicitors having sat there all through our lengthy examination should now come forward to lay the blame on me, especially as I was handling my case entirely alone. But there was another angle quite as serious; even if I was not ordered to bear the cost of reprinting, there was the question of delay. Blake and Redden's clerk and one of the Bischoff, Coxe men had come in, so Mr. Lys took us all to Mr. Wallace's room. Evidently he was the person with authority to settle the matter.

He did settle it promptly, very politely, very icily. I had not noticed before that those eyes which I had thought so kindly could be like steel, nor that mellow English voice of his so cold. There would be no alteration of the record; it was, he said, a mistake, "but no doubt, Mrs. Campbell," turning to me with an encouraging smile, "when presenting her appeal will draw their Lordships' attention to the fact that an error was made, but that the Trust Company's Solicitor became aware of it only after the final printing." The style of cause would be altered in any future papers relating to the appeal, and especially with regard to our printed cases, which we would now begin to prepare. With this the Chief Clerk of the Privy Council bade us all good-morning. I breathed a sigh of relief, as you may imagine, and Mr. Lys and Miss Moore rejoiced with me.

I had intended to leave the Dayton as soon as my Petition of Appeal was safely launched, but my departure was hastened by a happening which I feel sure the Scotland Yard inspector would have classified as "untoward," a delightful phrase. The Sunday morning upon which it occurred, the last one in September, the Feast of St. Michael and All Angels, was a golden day such as September sometimes brings to London; and I, dressed for church, sat smoking in the lounge. I ought perhaps to explain that I created somewhat of a sensation by being the sole person in the hotel—with the exception of one or two Roman Catholics— who took the slightest interest in church. One of the group in the lounge asked to what church Mrs. Campbell was going that morning, to which I replied, "St. Martin-in-the-Fields." Now the main service at St. Martin's, unlike those at most other London churches, does not begin until eleven thirty, so I smoked another cigarette before starting out. The inspiring service and the sermon by Canon Elliott of St. Paul's, who instead of preaching leant quietly on the pulpit and talked from the fulness of his heart, will ever be a beautiful memory. The Canon's theme was "Guardian Angels." This has always been one of my favorite themes, and he quoted the passage which in all the Prayer Book I love the best, "For He shall give His angels charge over thee, to keep thee in all thy ways. They shall bear thee in their hands, that thou hurt not thy foot against a stone." My mind was soaring as I came out of church, and I stood for a moment to allow the crowd to move on—people had been standing in the aisles—when I noticed a man ascending the steps. He had in his hand a lighted cigarette, and this struck me as strange. Coming straight towards me he lifted his hat and said with a bow, "I think we know each other, do we not?" My eye took in at a glance his good-looking clothing and that he was a singularly handsome youth, tall and golden-haired. Had I ever met him, I should most certainly have remembered— rarely do I forget a face—so looking up at him I replied, "Sorry, but I'm afraid you have made a mistake," and started to descend the steps. Nothing daunted he followed me and turning sharply I said, "I assure you I don't know you at all."

"But won't you let me walk home with you anyway?" said he, by now quite close beside me in the street.

Just ahead of us stood the "bobby" who is always stationed at the junction of Charing Cross Road and St. Martin's Lane, and I crossed to him quickly. I must, I suppose, have trembled, because looking down at me he said, "You're all upset, madam."

"Do you see that man?" said I, pointing to my would-be companion, who was making off up St. Martin's Lane as fast as his long legs and gold-headed cane would carry him, "He tried to stop me and talk to me just now on the steps of St. Martin's."

"Oh, he did, did he?" smiled the bobby reassuringly. "Well, don't you mind, we'll look after him," and then, quickly looking me over and glancing at my rings, "Do you often attend the service there, madam?"

"I've never before been to a service, but have often stopped in when I've passed on my way to Downing Street." said I.

"I see," nodded the bobby, "well, we'll keep a lookout, madam."

I thanked him and turned away in search of some strong black coffee at the nearest Lyons Corner House. The thing had upset me, because I knew that in London handsome golden-haired young men are not stopping women of my age, not seeking to escort them home, rather is it the other way about; a large army of women, golden-haired and gray-haired alike, are seeking not only young men but men of almost any age — this is, of course, an aftermath of the Great War. No, my common sense told me that the man had been sent to St. Martin's that morning to get into conversation with me. The winning of my appeal depended very largely upon myself, upon my personality. I had, it is true, a strong case; but I knew that even with Counsel, personality and reputation are a factor in his winning of a case; and could my reputation be in any way discredited, I might just about as well throw my papers over London Bridge and sail for home. I decided to say nothing to anyone of the episode, but to at once give the usual week's notice at the hotel and install myself elsewhere.

The Petition of Appeal is an important document in a Privy Council case; it is directed to His Majesty in Council and sets forth the grievance against which one is appealing. If Counsel for the Appellant wins, it is incorporated in the "King's Order," of which you shall hear later on. Having received my "legal training" at the hands of so fearless a fighter as A.G. Slaght, and perhaps because of a strain inherited from my father, it was natural in framing my petition I should strike straight from the shoulder; then again, I had grievous wrongs to be righted and knew that only by laying them very clearly, very concisely, before the Judicial Committee could I hope to succeed. When I took the draft to Mr. Lys, he read it point by point, and then said with one of his "twinkling" looks, "I'm afraid, Mrs. Campbell, it will be necessary to show this to Sir Charles, because sometimes a Registrar refuses to accept a Petition of Appeal if he considers that it contains scandalous matter," and then he pointed to the last paragraph in which I prayed that if any further accounting be done, it be done in England by British or American accountants and not in Canada. I was conscious of the fact that he thought my whole petition rather scandalous, the more so because the evidence in the case showed it to be true.

When he returned, it was with a broad smile. He reported that Sir Charles felt that as the lady was handling her own appeal, it was not for him to proffer advice as to how she should conduct her case, and that her Petition of Appeal might therefore be accepted. After some correction in wording and form it was typed on the largest most important looking paper which I had ever seen — it has, I think, some special name — and upon my paying the usual Privy Council fee, it was published and took its place among the other documents relating to the appeal.

One's printed case, which is bound together with one's record, takes up the points upon which one is appealing or defending an appeal, states a short history of the matter, the various Courts through which it has gone, the Judgments received, ending with one's reasons for appeal. The Counsel having completed their case sign it, then it is lodged with the Registrar of the Privy Council. After all cases have been lodged, the parties exchange cases and then each side becomes aware of the points upon which the other intends to attack. The most interesting point I learned was that though Mr. Sinclair had evidently prepared Mr. Hogg's case and signed it, his signature was struck out and underneath was the signature of one R.K. Smith.[14] Upon enquiry I gathered that Mr. Sinclair "preferred English Counsel to handle the case."

Mr. Lys in his kindly helpful way made a small schedule giving me the latest possible date upon which I could send the case for printing and also the latest date for setting down the appeal in order to be heard at the Hilary Sessions. This was December 31, the last day of the year. There was no time to waste, my case had to be in the printer's hands in a little over a month.

October and November are not pleasant in London; it rained incessantly, day and night, and blew regular hurricanes. Then, though the hotel to which I had moved was supposed to be more modern than the Dayton and to be centrally heated, I must say I was never conscious of the fact and really suffered from the awful penetrating damp and chill, so different from Canada's snow and sunshine, different even from our winter in Boston where, to quote Mark Twain, we have "lots of weather but no climate."

During the day I betook me to the British Museum and there in the reading room, itself an inspiration, with Lewin and Underhill on Trusts on one side of me, with Bentwich and Bowstead on Agency together with the information I had gleaned from my reading of the law at the Privy Council Office on the other side, I worked steadily day after day.[15] This great room is a world—a catholic cosmopolitan world, composed of all nationalities, creeds and colors. Here at those perfectly appointed desks which offer every comfort and facility one sees seated students from the four corners of the earth, interesting personalities, absorbed it may be in their work, or perhaps in some literary treasure which the reading room has in its keeping.

It has always struck me that this reading room of the British Museum is the most efficient, noiseless, and smoothest running place I have ever been in; like the comfortable chairs at the desks it appears to move literally on wheels, greased wheels, one might say. All this London bestows upon the readers of the world free of charge; one is not even permitted to give gratuities to the attendants in the cloak room.

The guests at my present hotel had slipped even further from their world than had those at the Dayton, but they wore a braver disguise; some of them were charmingly educated and cultivated, and each evening there was music. Close to the grate fire I would listen for a time to the playing and singing and then taking my papers would seat myself at one of the small cubicles in the writing room, there to work for an hour or so, always knocking off for that cosy English custom, midnight tea, about eleven o'clock. I thought of the little writing room as the "morgue," it was a slice taken off the hallway and devoid of heat. I usually slipped on my satin over-shoes and fur coat to ward off the chill.

Bit by bit the case took shape, but it was hard work. I knew, of course, the points which I desired to stress, but the arrangement was difficult, although Mr. Lys had lent me the cases in two Canadian appeals to follow. However, the first draft was almost completed when a quite wonderful thing happened,— "For He shall give His angels charge over thee, to keep thee in all thy ways." — My dear friends in Toronto have for a son-in-law the finest type of Englishman. A rising young Barrister in London, when the War broke out he enlisted in the Flying Corps, gaining before the end of the War all kinds of distinction. The War ended, he accepted an appointment in the Egyptian Legation, where again he is gaining honors. That autumn there was, as he expressed it, a "spot of bother" in Egypt, consequently he was dashed across to England. His mother-in-law, dear person, anxious about me alone in London, had begged him to hunt me up. He sympathized deeply with my struggle for justice and told me I showed tremendous courage to be handling and arguing my case alone.

It seemed that he had an intimate friend, somewhat older than himself, a Barrister, who he felt sure would assist and encourage me. He was leaving London in a day or two but said he would write. I heard nothing from him for three weeks or more, then came a letter. He was sailing for Egypt, but had lunched with his friend, Mr. E— before leaving London and had arranged that I should call upon him; the eminent gentleman had promised to befriend me. The promise was more than fulfilled. Mr. E— proved to be the same wonderful type of Englishman as the friend who sent me to him, with so kind a heart that he could not see anyone in distress without going to his assistance. I took him a copy of my record, and he was aghast at the "shocking nature of my evidence," and more especially at the two strange Judgments given me by the Appellate Court. When I read him the draft of my case, he pronounced it excellent, but suggested that I should change the arrangement of it and lent me one of his own cases before the House of Lords to follow.

I had borne such heavy responsibility for months and been so utterly alone that it was really like heaven to feel that right behind me was Mr. E. Naturally the first copy of my case, after it was lodged with the Privy Council, went to him; and in return came a letter of congratulation; "Your case would do credit to any Counsel," ran the letter. You may imagine with what courage this imbued me.

I myself believe in Fate, for this perhaps my Highland ancestry is responsible. Many of my readers will probably not agree that Fate had anything to do with my finding myself in Mr. E's chambers that rainy November day — "clearly coincidence" I can hear them say — yet they will, I think, admit that it was a curious coincidence. When I obtained my passport a few days before sailing for England and the officials queried "What address," I could not seem to remember any other than Mr. Prine's, who was the one person in London with whom I was then in touch; consequently his address No. —, New Square, Lincoln's Inn, stands today on that passport. Imagine my surprise when my friend in the Egyptian Legation wrote, "You will find Mr. E. a wonderful man and I have made arrangements for you to call upon him at his chambers, No. —, New Square, Lincoln's Inn." The same address as Mr. Prine's in the same building on the floor below! Even Mr. E., when I showed him his address on the front page of my passport, admitted, with true British caution, that it was "a bit odd!"

The preparation of my argument came next, as I desired to have it not only firmly fixed in my mind but typed before me as had been the case in the Appellate Court in Canada. I still worked at the British Museum but more often now at the Privy Council Office. There I pored over Halisbury on the Trustee Act and hunted for and sought to comprehend the cases referred to, going back and forth frequently to Mr. Wallace and Mr. Lys for an explanation of some particularly puzzling reference.[16] During these seven months of work at Downing Street, I witnessed an interesting procession pass; advocates bringing appeals from the far flung corners of the British Empire, I saw all shades of complexion, heard the English language spoken in varying accents, and not infrequently caught sight of some turbaned Indian or full blooded African negro, or again it might be an Australian or Rhodesian, who, while not conducting his own appeal, had nevertheless come to England to hear his Counsel do so. We children of the Empire had all sought and found sanctuary with the Privy Council; indeed, I have often thought that a sanctuary ring such as one finds on the massive doors of the ancient cathedrals might fittingly be affixed to the door of the Privy Council Office. Once before this great tribunal no harm can come to us and we all receive the same impartial treatment; and justice, in search of which we have travelled far, is administered, as nearly as it can be in a human world. Herbert Bentwich, editor of the English Law Journal, wrote in the English Review, "The King, the Navy, and the Judicial Committee (of the Privy Council) are the three solid and apparent bonds of Empire; for the rest the Union depends upon sentiment."[17] With this opinion I heartily agree.

My American public may be interested to hear something of the ancient origin and wide scope of the Judicial Committee of His Majesty's Privy Council, highest Court of Appeal for the whole of the Empire with the exception of England, Scotland, and Northern Ireland, whose cases go to the House of Lords.★ This powerful tribunal, the Privy Council, which has jurisdiction over 450,000,000, just about one third of the world population and over millions of miles of territory, makes all other Courts seem negligible; even that great Court at Washington, the Supreme Court of the United States of America, is the final Court of Appeal for a mere 125,000,000 or so.

According to Dicey, who seems to be the leading authority, the Judicial Committee dates back to antiquity and arises in the King's Permanent or Continual Council. This is what he says:

> The importance attached in the Middle Ages to communication between a king and his nobles as between a baron and his vassals bears distinctly on the history of the Council. That the king might have advisers, he at times convened as many of his great men, "magnates" or "notables," as could attend, and at all times kept about his person a body of officials, themselves nobles, such as his Marshall, his Justiciary, and his Chancellor, and in fact had at his palace, on a large scale, just such a court as each baron kept up within smaller limits in his castle. The nobles assembled on special occasions

---

★ The Privy Council has jurisdiction in England in ecclesiastical and certain maritime appeals.

by special writs, formed in combination with the officers of the court the "great council" or "common council" of the realm. The chief advisers of the Crown who were permanently about the King constituted the "Permanent" or "Continual" Council, whence in later years arose the Privy Council. The difference of names is important since it shows that in the earliest period of its history the small council was generally contrasted with the greater councils not as being private while they were public, but as being permanent or continual, whereas they were of their nature temporary. The three centuries intervening between the Norman Conquest and the reign of Richard II (1066-1376) are the period during which English institutions assumed a form from which they have never essentially varied. At the end of this period there is found in existence a Parliament of Two Houses, distinct Law Courts, and a Council with peculiar powers distinguishable from the Law Courts and from Parliament.

Professor Dicey then speaks of the "Curia Regis" or "King's Court."

Long after the erection of the Law Courts the Council exercised though peculiar, judicial authority. This anomaly is easy to explain. The exercise of judicial power is a royal prerogative. ... This more direct exertion of the King's power was naturally and of necessity called into action when for any reason the Law Courts were unable to give justice. They might fail to grant redress either because, to use the expressive words of various ordinances, "there was too great might on the one side and too great unmight on the other," or because the grievance referred to them was one which the technical rules of the Law did not meet. In each case the person aggrieved would naturally apply for aid to the King and his Council.

History repeats itself! After these many centuries I was doing just what those people of the Middle Ages had done and for exactly the same reason, "because there was too great might on one side," — the might of the legal fraternity, the might of the Toronto General Trusts Corporation — "and too great unmight on the other," surely this last, though written in medieval days, described perfectly my plight.

One sometimes hears it said that the Privy Council is an over-hang of the old Star Chamber—the "Camera Stellata." I again take the liberty of quoting Professor Dicey:

> If any institutions can claim a sympathy more generally accorded to human beings than to their works, the Council of the English monarchy may demand our especial interest. Its history stretches back to remote antiquity. Its powers arose amidst all the dangers of a barbarous age. The benefits it con-ferred in periods when it was the real protection of the weak, the true "poor man's court," more than counterbalance the evils which it produced when in later years it rose as the Star Chamber, to be the most oppressive power which ever threat-ened the liberties of England.[18]

Interesting it is to reflect that though the Star Chamber has fallen, yet the Council continues, perhaps because it once more

Garden of the Privy Council Office

fulfills much of its original purpose, and "confers benefits," the inestimable benefit of justice, and is again the "protector of the weak." In 1833, Lord Brougham framed the constitution of the Judicial Committee as it now stands. The Lord President of the Privy Council is the head of the Committee, though unless he happens to be a lawyer he does not sit with the Court. Although there are several ex-Chancellors and many leading Judges, whose time is occupied in various other positions, who are technically members of the Committee, the panel of Judges is usually drawn from the following: the Lord Chancellor, the Lords of Appeal— who also sit in the House of Lords—seven in number, some Judges with Indian experience and one Hindu Judge. These latter together with the Lords of Appeal hear the Indian cases. Then there are nine Dominion Judges, honorary members of the Committee, who are privileged to sit.[19] Occasionally one does so, his expenses being paid by his government. One must have been a Judge of a superior court or have had fifteen years' standing at the Bar before one is made a Lord of Appeal; it is a life office and there is no retiring age. Sometimes three Judges form the Court but more frequently five.

The scope of the Judicial Committee is wide indeed; it is called upon to hear civil, constitutional, and criminal cases, and to administer most varying laws, a situation easily understood when one considers the extent of the British Empire. It hears also maritime and ecclesiastical appeals, in these last Bishops of the Church sit as ecclesiastical assessors. One such interesting appeal was that of the Reverend John Wakeford in 1921, where, in addition to four of the Law Lords, the Bishops of London, Gloucester, Rochester, and Ely sat.[20] Upon this case the thirty-five page Judgment delivered by the Lord Chancellor concludes with the following:

> Their Lordships have applied their minds to this case with great care and much solicitude. But the conclusions which they have reached seem to them inevitable. Reluctant as they were to believe such a charge against a man in the position and with the history of the appellant, they scanned vigilantly every circumstance and every argument which could possibly be urged in his favor. They have reached the conclusion that the Judgment of the Consistory Court must be upheld. It is a

source of satisfaction to them to find that the views which they entertain are shared by the Right Reverend Prelates who have been good enough to give them their assistance upon this occasion. The result, therefore, is that their Lordships will humbly advise His Majesty to dismiss the appeal. Costs must follow the event. The appellant's action has involved the Bishop of Lincoln (he was the respondent) in heavy expenses; and their Lordships see no reason why he should not, so far as may be, be recouped for the expenditure which he has incurred in the execution of a public duty.

The Reverend Gentleman, a married man, was charged with improper conduct with an unknown woman at the Bull Hotel, Peterborough.

Some of the odd cases which their Lordships have heard during recent years are: whether a god, an Indian god, I think he was, should be draped; whether women are eligible to sit in the Canadian Senate[21]; whether the marriage of a French-Canadian in Paris was subject to French or Canadian law and whether it was null because of the omission of the civil ceremony[22]; a most bitterly contested dispute between Hindus as to who owned the family elephant; and in 1931 the famous Devil's Island case. The appellant, Gregoire Kossekechatko and his companions after escaping from the French penal settlement Cayenne in French Guiana landed in a small boat at Trinidad. Here the authorities detained them under the Extradition Act. Their Lordships, while not minimizing the fact that the men were criminals, quashed the sentence because the French authorities did not prove that the crimes were committed on French territory, thus failing to meet the requirements of the Extradition Act under a special treaty existing between French Guiana and Trinidad.

I have been told that the Harvard Law School hands the decisions of the Judicial Committee to their advanced students as models of what decisions should be.

Occasionally, though very rarely, the Judicial Committee grants special leave for a criminal case to come before them; it cannot otherwise come and this is done only in cases where there is reason to believe that the principles of natural justice have been violated, or the rules of evidence or of procedure disregarded. It is thus that a widely scattered Empire safeguards her subjects from a miscarriage of justice.

The case of Dr. Benjamin Knowles vs. the King, heard in 1929, aroused wide interest.[23] Tried in Ashanti without a jury, and without being allowed either Solicitor or Counsel to defend him, he was sentenced by the Circuit Judge for the murder of his wife. The chief evidence appeared to be her death-bed confession that the revolver had accidentally gone off, which was disbelieved by the trial Judge. Dr. Knowles was ill and poor, but with the help of relatives and friends managed to make his way home to England and was granted special leave to appeal. After many days of fine-combing the evidence the Law Lords were satisfied that Dr. Knowles had been wrongfully convicted of murder. The question of manslaughter not having been raised by the trial Judge, the appeal was consequently allowed and the conviction quashed. Dr. Knowles was present in the Privy Council Chamber when the decision was announced and walked down the steps of No. 2 Downing Street a free man. Their Lordships' reasons for Judgment were not given until some months later.

Very important are the abstract cases which more and more in recent years are being referred to the Judicial Committee. The following are some of the references: what were the rights of the British South Africa Company in the lands of Southern Rhodesia[24]; questions frequently arising regarding boundaries such as that in 1921 between Northern Ireland and the Irish Free State; and more recently the question between Canada and Newfoundland as to who owned Labrador, which the Judicial Committee decided in favor of Newfoundland.[25] The following article entitled "War Inventions" taken from the London Times of August 3, 1932, shows that a link exists between the United States and the Privy Council:

UNITED STATES AND BRITISH CLAIMS. The United States Commission investigating claims of British subjects upon the United States' Government in respect of War inventions began its sittings yesterday at the Offices of the Privy Council. The steel helmet is among the inventions in respect of which claims are being made. The basis of all the claims is that the inventions were utilized by the United States in the

Great War, either directly or through the medium of the British Government. The Commission consists of Lieutenant Colonel McMullen (presiding), Mr. Charles Rugg (Assistant Attorney General of the United States), Mr. Harvey H. Bundy (Assistant Secretary of State), and Commander Robert A. Lavender, U.S. Navy. The Commissioners sat in the Court where the judicial Committee of the Privy Council hold their deliberations.

Then there are instances of misconduct on the part of Judges in the Colonies, which are often a matter of reference, and although the decision of the Privy Council in these cases has no force of law, yet it is invariably acted upon by the parties concerned. These references are argued by Counsel as would be an ordinary appeal.

Amidst the work and responsibility of these past months I had lost sight of time, and it was really with surprise that I awakened one morning to the fact that it was the middle of December; so I locked up my papers and began looking about for some means of forgetting that Christmas was at hand and that for the first time I should be far from family and home.[26] Christmas Eve, therefore, found me, after a terrific scramble at Victoria — was everyone, like myself, leaving London and from the same station? — having tea before one of the numerous grate fires in the lounge of an attractive hotel on the sea front at Eastbourne. Many gay parties had already assembled; the weather was shocking, and every few minutes more guests, dripping with rain and laden with dressing bags, would blow in and, after being divested of their wet wraps, would join these groups about the fireplaces. The doors and mantles were festooned with great garlands of green and holly with the reddest berries, while sprays of ivy, unbelievable ivy, trailed their graceful way across the walls. At dinner, for which everyone was in gala attire, I was surprised to see seated at the tables about me whole families, father and mother and perhaps two or three growing boys and girls with here and there a bachelor uncle tucked in; and I gathered from the conversation that they were in the habit of coming each Christmas. I had always thought that in England, Christmas would be essentially a home festival. With the dessert, crackers and balloons appeared, all donning their paper caps and blowing deafening blasts from toy whistles as they tossed the balloons from table to table. The scene resembled the captain's dinner on a large liner, and had somewhat the same air of forced merriment, except as regards the young people. I have been told that this custom of spending one's Christmas at a hotel has grown up in England since the Great War because it is less hard than to remain at home and remember.

After dinner everyone played bridge or danced; there was a Paul Jones so that the few strangers like myself might become acquainted. On Christmas morning I was among the few guests who sought a church, such an adorable little old church exactly like a Christmas card, even to the fat robin on the grass. Once inside, the garlands, the poinsettias, and the candles on the altar, the cherubic choir boys carolling, also the dear quaint people kneeling beside me assured me that after all the old England had not passed away. Some cables awaited me on my return from church, but they made me feel more than ever lonely; and that afternoon, with the rain pouring down, and the strains of a dance orchestra floating up from the ball room, seemed endless. Dinner was marvellous, everyone enjoyed the best of champagne and other wine, no one in the

Garden of the Privy Council Office, looking toward the Treasury Arch

whole hotel apparently taking too much. I could not help con-
trasting this with what I knew the situation would have been on
our side of the world. There was again dancing for young and old
until the wee sma' hours. In England Christmas does not end with
Christmas Day, the twenty-sixth is known as Boxing Day; it is the
servants' festival when they receive their gifts, presumably in boxes,
hence the strange name which had puzzled me at first, seeming to
savor of Mr. Dempsey and Mr. Tunney.[27] In the hotels there is on
this night a fancy dress ball and a collection is taken up for the
staff. The guests, both men and women, had gone to what must
have been a great deal of trouble to construct costumes. The lady
who won the first prize—elderly and very stout—represented a
basket of flowers and was an amusing sight!

On the twenty-eighth, I returned to London because I wished
to settle myself and my belongings in a smaller pension to which I
had been recommended; my friends told me I should find it very
congenial. Also my appeal had to be set down for a hearing on the
last day of the year. It was exciting when, after New Year's, I was
given one of the Hilary Lists of Business of the Judicial Committee
and I saw "No. 56 of 1929, Campbell vs. Hogg and Others" set
down with "Appellant in Person" figuring opposite in the list of
Solicitors. Mr. Lys then told me that Sir Charles desired to speak
with me; now, I had seen this lordly looking gentleman only in the
Privy Council Chamber, where usually he was standing behind
their Lordships, on guard as it seemed to me, or sometimes when
he had passed me in the corridor. I was terribly frightened but
decided to make the best of it; and I noticed that Mr. Lys, as he
took me up their Lordships' stairway and opened Sir Charles' door,
seemed quite pleased. In a room, the walls lined with books and
old engravings with windows which overlook a delightful small
garden that seems as though it might belong jointly to No. 10
Downing Street and the Privy Council Office, at his mahogany
desk sat Sir Charles Neish, K.B.E., C.B., Barrister-at-Law and
Registrar of the Privy Council.★ He rose and came forward, greeting me with great courtesy, and I suddenly lost all fear and found
myself looking up into kindly sympathetic eyes set in a fine old
face with its frame of snow-white hair, and heard a beautifully

---

★ Sir Charles Neish, K.B.E., C.B., has since passed away.

141

modulated voice stating that "they" all considered I had shown great courage in crossing the sea to plead my own case. "And now, Mrs. Campbell," he added, "I judge you would like your appeal heard as soon as possible; so I am going to write the Lord Chancellor to ask, since you are quite alone in London, if he will give it precedence over the other Dominion appeals. You will notice," pointing to the list, "that there are several." I was so touched that although I cannot now remember whether I actually took his hand in both of mine, I know I wanted to as I stammered my thanks; and when I passed through the door, which Mr. Lys again held open, I felt that I had made another friend at Downing Street.

Not long after this I was seated in the Privy Council Chamber — the Court had not yet convened for the Hilary Session — looking up some final point of the law, when seeing Sir Charles come in, I rose. He wanted to assure himself that I was aware on which side of the Council Chamber, I, as appellant, was to enter, and also whether I knew where to stand to present my argument.

Lord Sankey, the Lord Chancellor, gave his sanction to my appeal being put ahead of everything on the Hilary List with the exception of an Irish case which had been unduly delayed. This meant that my hearing would in all probability be the last week in January.

I had my argument pretty well prepared; dear Mr. E. very kindly took two Saturday afternoons to go over it with me, making some suggestions and polishing it off. He stressed the danger, which I feared, of a reference back, the thing which Mr. Slaght had warned me of. I resolved that it would be over my dead body, metaphorically speaking, that Mr. Hogg's accounts would be referred back to Canada; above all things this must not happen.

Among the guests at Miss Ropes' little establishment, mostly students, professors, and teachers, my case became the absorbing topic of interest. I was working one evening at the desk in the smoke room when someone asked what Mrs. Campbell intended wearing in Court. I replied that Mrs. Campbell hadn't given the matter of apparel much thought as she was too busy working on what she should say. A young Dane, studying the book business with Bumpus — I had christened him Baron Hirschsprung because of his good looks and polished Continental manner—spoke up, "Many women have I known but never one like this; she say not first, 'what shall I wear, how shall I look, but what shall I say'; the lady is an astonishment." Nevertheless as the time drew near I had the pleats in my suit—an old one which had been dyed a deep plum color—carefully pressed and bought a tight fitting little English hat to match. This was due to a generation of Counsel behind me who no doubt were most careful to make a good appearance in Court. I should, however, have taken even more care had I known that the details of my costume and appearance were to be blazoned over England and America by the press.[28] I lately took out my box of press notices and was struck by the fact that in nearly every one my "neat plum-colored costume," my soft voice, my slenderness, and my determination are mentioned; it is quite amusing to get side lights on one's make-up.

That last week or so while waiting for my hearing was a tremendous strain. I suffered from sleeplessness, always my enemy, yet did not dare take a sleeping draught because I needed a steady head with all my wits about me; also I was haunted by a fear of something happening, something nameless, which at the last moment would prevent my arguing the case. When I voiced this to Mr. Lys he seemed to understand and said, "Mrs. Campbell, if we should telephone at any time now and should fail to get you, we shall at once send a messenger." He then produced some large square envelopes or cases; printed on them was "On His Majesty's Service" in big letters, and below in the corner, "Privy Council Office."

"Better carry your papers and record in this when you come back and forth," said he. The envelopes were most noticeable and they gave me a sense of protection.

"The Day," February 3, dawned beautifully bright; I had my case well in hand, and as for my argument, every "i" was dotted and every "t" crossed.[29] I experienced a peculiar elation when after breakfast I jumped into the waiting taxi, my fellow guests waving me good luck from the doorway.

"I'm sure, if you will allow us, madam, we all wish you great success," smiled the messenger as I entered the Privy Council Office. It came to me that many years ago my father must have been a familiar figure about these corridors, and I felt this morning that in wig and gown he walked by my side. Mr. Upton greeted me with a cheerful, "Good morning, Mrs. Campbell, we are sure you will feel very satisfied with your Board"; naturally, I was anxious to know who composed the Board, but was told this is a thing never divulged beforehand, and that I should learn the Judges' names only in the Ante-Chamber.

Before I could hang up my coat reporters were prowling around already seeking interviews; they were shooed away by Mr. Lys. Just then Miss Moore arrived bearing a bunch of the loveliest white heather "for luck"; together we fastened a spray in one of the blank pages of my record and a tiny sprig underneath the lapel of my coat. Mr. Lys made arrangements for luncheon. "You know we can't have our female appellant fainting on our hands; you can order anything you want from the caterer who looks after their Lordships, and the waiter will bring it to you," said he. "And now, Mrs. Campbell, if you are ready we had better go up. Have you all your papers?"

The anteroom was filled with Barristers, Solicitors, and reporters. On the table lay a slip of paper bearing the names of the Judges: Lord Blanesburgh, Lord Tomlin, and Lord Russell of Killowen, a brilliant Board; a Scotsman, an Englishman, and an Irishman! The opposing firms having signed the paper, I was instructed to do likewise. Then seating myself I had a pleasant conversation with some of the members of the opposition, and of course the "press" crowded around wanting to know how I felt. My answer was, "Gentlemen, I'm thrilled to be here!" and I was.[30] The thrill even overcame the nervousness and accounted perhaps for my "composure" and "coolness" which was reported to the world. Mr. Polly, busy about his duties, stepped up to say, "As how he and Mr. Jennings hoped I would accept their best wishes for success in the case, Madam." Just then Mr. Jennings reversed the card hanging on the wall. Their Lordships awaited us, and I found myself on the appellant side of the Privy Council Chamber, Miss Moore and Mr. Lys following.

I took my stand, my record and papers before me, at the rostrum, confronted by three keen-faced elderly gentlemen seated about the horseshoe table; behind them were standing Sir Charles and Mr. Wallace. My prayer for courage and a clear head was answered, apparently, because I learned afterwards that my voice, almost inaudible at first, grew gradually stronger, also that my hands ceased to tremble. Personally, after my opening speech, one of gratitude for the kind assistance which had been rendered me by the Privy Council officials in the preparation of my record, I was conscious only of my case and of the Judges to whom I was presenting it.

Let me describe my "Board" to you: Lord Blanesburgh presiding in the centre, urbane, able, man of the world, although not so massive very like the late Chief Justice Taft of the Supreme Court of the United States. When he smiled, and the smile deepened into much the same sort of laugh to which Mr. Taft was wont to give vent, I readily understood why I had heard him spoken of as the most beloved member of the Judicial Committee. On the right Lord Tomlin—dark, high-colored, with keen hawklike face—said to be one of the most brilliant Judges in the House of Lords; one could understand that also. He had, to me, a very fascinating way of speaking; someone has described it as "educated Cockney"— rather more aloof than Lord Blanesburgh, yet at a good point in the case the hawklike face became irresistible. Lord Russell of Killowen, son of the great Earl Russell—small, alert, intensely interested in the case, with a delicious sense of humor, the invariable accompaniment to the three-cornered Irish smile that is his— a very astute yet human personality.

Although the Barristers were in wig and gown their Lordships wore good-looking lounge or morning suits, because technically the Privy Council is not a Court but His Majesty's Judicial Committee.

I cited the rule of the Ontario Surrogate Court under which Mr. Hogg as trustee of my mother's estate asked for an audit of his accounts. "Very good, Mrs. Campbell, now we have our jurisdiction; please proceed," said Lord Blanesburgh.

Mr. Hogg, as you have read, had gone from Court to Court in Canada as a trustee, but in his printed case before the Privy Council he changed his plea saying he was merely an agent—a serious point for me. This no doubt was what had been in Mr. Justice Middleton's mind when he had said, on bidding me good-bye, "Don't forget the Trustee Act." I, therefore, started my argument by showing that Mr. Hogg was a trustee, but Lord Blanesburgh interrupted me. "We assume, Mrs. Campbell," said he, "that Mr. Hogg was a trustee; he presented his accounts as such and we shall not trouble you at this time to pursue the question further."

Bowing to his Lordship I turned over the pages of my argument; I saw the writing on the wall for Mr. Hogg, my first great point was gained, the case would be fought out on the Trustee Act.

In the three Canadian Courts when it was stated by my Counsel or myself that Mr. Hogg's behavior as trustee was, to say the least of it, highly irregular and improper, the rejoinder had been, "But surely Mr. Hogg was Lady Howland's brother-in-law, and would naturally look after her affairs in a very different manner from those of a stranger. You wouldn't expect the same accounting from a relative, would you?" This attitude had always annoyed me, first because of its injustice and secondly, because in this kind of case it imposed a barrier which the Trustee Act was powerless to break down. Therefore, I sought from the outset to show their Lordships that for the very reason that Mr. Hogg was my mother's brother-in-law and on affectionate terms with her he had been enabled to "get away with the goods," as it were. She would have demanded an accounting from a stranger and would not have trusted him so implicitly. To my tremendous satisfaction as I was putting forth this argument Lord Blanesburgh again stopped me. "It will not be necessary for you to argue this, Mrs. Campbell; my noble brothers and myself quite understand; this Board has made it an invariable practice to demand the strictest of accounting from a relative acting in the capacity of trustee." Things were coming along very well indeed!

It was interesting to note how deeply shocked their Lordships appeared to be as the case with its damning evidence was unfolded before them — the two Judgments ten days apart rendered by the First Appellate Division, the refusal to grant me a copy of the first Judgment, and then the withholding of the transcript of what had taken place before the Appellate Court. "Well, Mrs. Campbell," said Lord Blanesburgh upon hearing this, "there seems to be no other course but for you to inform my noble brothers and myself of anything that arose during the argument before the Appellate Court which you may think it important that we should know." When later I proceeded to do this, Mr. Hogg's Counsel arose and

Mrs. Campbell conducts her case, from the *Scotsman*, Edinburgh

objected, saying that my word was being taken on the point in question. Lord Tomlin answered the objection in his delightful way, "But, Mr. Smith, had Counsel come from Canada to argue the case, we should accept his word, should we not, about what happened in a previous Court? It seems to me that the lady stands in exactly the same relation to her case as a Counsel." Mr. Smith sat down hurriedly. The using of withdrawn evidence against me by Mr. Justice Hodgins in his Judgment was also in my favor.

Point by point I was showing that "manifest error and irregularity hath intervened"; in other words, that there had been a gross miscarriage of justice — only so could I hope to reverse the orders of three Courts. The opposition was relying on my inability to do this, and it was, as I well knew, no easy task.

One o'clock! Their Lordships closed their records and adjourned the Court for an hour. No stopping the press now; the hallway was filled with them. Some carried weird concertina-like affairs — their cameras. They begged to photograph me outside in Downing Street, and then, not satisfied, took several flashlights in the hall. The representative of the leading Edinburgh paper, the "Scotsman," said as he got ready his flashlight, "Would you mind taking your papers under your arm and looking more legal, madam?" On the ... [previous] page will be seen the result of my endeavor to comply with the gentleman's request. Then the questions, all kinds of questions, as to my age, my home, my husband and children; indeed, my whole past, apparently, had become of absorbing interest to the public. One amusing phase of this questionnaire comes to my mind: no one asked, "Are you a university woman?" They one and all said, "Which is your university, Mrs. Campbell?" Or, "Are you a graduate of a Canadian or an American University?" And when in shame and confusion I plead not guilty to ever having attended, much less to being a graduate of a university, their faces were a study. The man from Edinburgh took it particularly hard, but seemed somewhat consoled by the fact that my grandfather — himself a Scotsman — had graduated from the Edinburgh Medical School, and that I hoped some day my son might likewise take a degree there.[31]

The appearance of the waiter bringing luncheon released me. I told myself, as I rested and enjoyed my sandwiches and coffee before Miss Moore's cosy grate fire, that I was making progress, but the greatest danger in my case — a reference back to Canada — lay before me, in all probability to be reached that afternoon when I should begin to attack Mr. Hogg's accounts. It was impossible that these accounts could be accepted by the Privy Council. Towards the end of the afternoon I was reading from Mr. Justice Magee's favorable Judgment when Lord Blanesburgh looked up and said, "Mrs. Campbell, these are not accounts at all. What do you want us to do? Send them back to the Surrogate Court for a further accounting?" My heart skipped a beat. There was nothing for me now but to throw myself on the mercy of the Privy Council. "Anything but Canada, my Lords. I have fought my way to you against untold obstacles. Might it not be settled in England?"

Their Lordships seemed touched by my plea, especially Lord Tomlin. "Pray be seated, Mrs. Campbell, and rest; we wish to confer upon this matter," said Lord Blanesburgh. Very informally the Law Lords turned their chairs; before my mind's eye now rises a picture of the three heads bent close together; there was a breathless stillness in the Council Chamber, and in my heart the prayer of the Psalmist of old, "that I might be delivered from the hand of mine enemies."

The bent heads were raised, I stood once more. "My noble brothers and myself are much impressed by what you say, Mrs. Campbell; and although we are of the opinion that this account should be referred again to the Surrogate Court at Ottawa because it does not in any way comply with the requirements of the Trustee Act, nevertheless, we are willing to allow it to stand, if you so desire; and if you can pick out items and prove that they have been erroneously charged against the estate, we may be able to grant you those items," said Lord Blanesburgh, "but the account may not be reopened in England."

This was quite a blow, but I recognized it was wiser for me to salvage what I could in England rather than be sent back to Canada. Mr. Smith arose and said he was not at all sure that his client would consent to this course being adopted—it was evident that Mr. Hogg counted upon a reopening of the whole thing at Ottawa beneath the sheltering wing of the Surrogate Court. For a moment or two the Presiding Law Lord's urbanity deserted him; very sternly did he silence Mr. Smith by directing his attention to Mr. Hogg's position with regard to costs did his accounts go back. Mr. Smith acquiesced, but not too gracefully, I thought.

"Mrs. Campbell, you have a difficult task before you," said Lord Blanesburgh. "Can you prepare a list of the items you intend taking up and have it ready for my noble brothers and myself by tomorrow morning? We realize that it does not give you much time." My reply, which seemed to please them, was, "My Lords, I have done worse things than this in a shorter time."

"You have no typist, no one to assist you, Mrs. Campbell?" continued Lord Blanesburgh, then beckoning Sir Charles, "Will you be good enough to place Miss Moore and Miss Wall at Mrs. Campbell's disposal tomorrow morning, Sir Charles, and would it be possible to have the Privy Council Office open before ten o'clock in order that the typing may be done for the lady?" Sir Charles signified his assent with a bow, and the Court was adjourned until the following morning.

That evening, dinner over, I lit my gas fire, took down my hair, and putting on a warm wrapper set to work. It was indeed a difficult task which confronted me; not only did it mean picking out the items upon which I was going to attack and gathering the material for this from my record, but it necessitated to a certain extent the revamping of my whole argument. Only by being very familiar with the case was I enabled to do this in the time at my disposal. I remember that I stopped my labors more than once during the night to make myself strong tea and eat some sandwiches. The hours simply flew by. St. Pancras was chiming five o'clock and the comparative hush which falls over London after midnight was giving way once more to the roar of traffic when I decided to "call it a night," snap off the light, and get some rest. I had my argument ready for their Lordships.

When some four hours later my taxi drew up before the Privy Council Office I found the great doorway just being opened with much clanking and creaking of hinges. Within, off the long corridor, a delightful old "char" was making her rounds, dusting up the rooms and kindling the fires in the grates. "Ow, ye're ever so brive a lidy now, aren't ye?" she said as with a poke she caused the coals to leap into cheerful flame. "We's been reading abaht ye in the pipers last night. We does wish yer the best of luck, dearie. Hi sez to Mrs. Guffins, lidy opposite ye know, hits a shime, sez I, that there pore woman 'avin' 'er money took from 'er." These sympathetic utterances were cut short by the entrance of Miss Moore, who upon being given my notes, prepared at once with Miss Wall to type them for the "Board." I was attacking upon twelve items.

That was a hard day for everyone concerned. For nearly five hours, with a short recess for luncheon, I argued and pled and answered questions put to me by the Law Lords, endeavoring not to lose my place in my argument while so doing. I was filled with the case, had it so at my finger tips that at times I went too quickly. It was a heavy case and, as was later said, a complex one. Lord Blanesburgh had occasion to stop me more than once: "Now, Mrs. Campbell, not so fast, if you please. You see, my noble brothers and I have not had the privilege of dwelling with this case as you have. Will you be kind enough to repeat that point for us." Again when he wished to clarify my argument: "As we Scots say, Mrs. Campbell, the warp and woof of it is this, you desire to convey this to us, do you not?" stressing the point I had been trying to make.

The Council Chamber was filled with persons apparently interested in the case, among whom were several women. I heard later these were lady Barristers.[32] The Privy Council officials kept coming back and forth during the day and Sir Charles Neish, seated at his table behind their Lordships, followed my argument closely. I remember Lord Russell, at one stage when the Judgments were being referred to which commented upon the fact that no question had ever been raised against Mr. Hogg in Lady Howland's lifetime, saying in a most human, kindly way, "You do understand, Mrs. Campbell, don't you that you stand here before us in your dear mother's shoes; I mean that you have her rights precisely." I thanked his Lordship as I replied in the affirmative.

It is rather interesting to view that day from the standpoint of the press. The following is copied from the "Scotsman," Edinburgh:

Highest Tribunal
Woman's Appeal before Judicial Committee

In a quiet but quick manner a woman continued her argument yesterday in the course of her appeal to the Judicial Committee of the Privy Council from a decision of the Supreme Court of Ontario, Canada.

The appellant, Mrs. Elizabeth Bethune Campbell of Boston, United States, often spoke so rapidly that the Law Lords had to appeal to her to go a little more slowly. She is the first woman to appear in person to conduct an appeal before the Tribunal, and the legal fight is over the estate of her mother, Lady (Elizabeth) Howland, who died in Canada in August 1924.

Mrs. Campbell, who wore a mauve coat, frock, and hat, argued her case with the confidence of an experienced Counsel.

I had not forgotten Mr. Slaght's injunction to "get Hogg's original books into their Lordships' hands," a thing easier said than done as any Counsel who is in the habit of appearing before the Judicial Committee will tell you, because everything lies printed in one's record in front of the "Board." However, Lord Tomlin, I believe, called for the first ledger; a massive magnifying glass bound in silver (I had never seen such a large one) was presented and those keen eyes of the Law Lords peered through it as they investigated the altered accounts, their faces flushing in consternation. From then on all the original books were scrutinized. When, in their Judgment, their Lordships called attention to the interpolated entries made by Mr. Hogg's own hand, and stated that they were much affected by his altering and tampering with books of entry, I had cause to realize anew my former Counsel's prescience. The flagrancy of the case was winning Lord Tomlin, no doubt about it. As I have said, he was more aloof, more impersonal than either Lord Blanesburgh or Lord Russell; he did not question me directly as did they, but from the moment his Lordship saw those books he became exceedingly alert, exceedingly vigilant. The day had been an exhausting one, and the announcement of an adjournment until Thursday, as Wednesday it seemed was "House of Lords," was most acceptable.

Mr. E. had made me promise to run up to Lincoln's Inn each day after we were dismissed so that he might know "how things were going." He would draw the heavy chairs closer to the fire, take the cigarette box from the mantle, and listen attentively to the day's happenings. My arguing the appeal myself evidently intrigued him. "How were their Lordships taking it?" He was delighted that Lord Tomlin was showing interest; and, "was such and such a point going well," and always this kindly gentleman sent me forth again with renewed courage.

The adjournment gave me the opportunity to look over the avalanche of news clippings which descended from the press-cutting agencies.[33] With every post fat envelopes were handed in from Messrs. Woolgar and Roberts and Messrs. Romeike and

Curtice, and other firms whose names escape me. This went on for days. Where on earth, I wondered, had they found out so much about myself and my family in so short a time; they published many details of my father's life of which I had been only vaguely aware. It was curious, too, to see oneself in the news sheets. When I was confronted by a particularly unsightly picture of myself from the *Paris Daily Mail* I was reminded of what Disraeli is supposed to have said about a likeness of his; "That may look like me but thank God I don't look like that."

The American press was naturally very much on the job and the Boston Herald endeavored to speak with me over the telephone. In the night, about twelve o'clock, I was awakened by Miss Ropes who had run up the flights of stairs to get me, "Sorry to rouse you, Mrs. Campbell, but America is calling." Throwing on my coat I followed her hastily to the 'phone. Alas, neither America nor I had any luck. All I could hear was an awful roar and buzzing, and the operator said they would put through the call later. Towards three A.M. I was roused again; this time I could hear, very indistinctly to be sure, "Hello, hello, Mrs. Campbell, this is America …," then no more. Finally the London operator announced that because of unfavorable weather conditions America had abandoned the call. "Time Marches On!" The whole establishment in Russell Square was thrilled by this episode. It is only a few short years and a transatlantic call is all in the day's work and arouses no comment, and is of no interest, except to the parties concerned.

Lord Blanesburgh having contracted a severe cold, there was a further adjournment of our hearing but the following Thursday, I resumed my argument, finishing on Friday.[34] The Law Lords had listened to me for just four days and had called upon my opponents to begin their defense on Monday.

"Woman Speaks Twenty Hours," wrote the reporters. How much of that work would Mr. Ronald Smith, Counsel for the first respondent, be able to undo? I asked this of myself rather anxiously as I watched, from my seat on the appellant's bench, the tall, striking-looking Barrister arrange his papers at the rostrum, and noted across the Council Chamber the Solicitors for the Trust Company lean close to the Solicitors representing Mr. Hogg. The British Solicitor, by the way, is not clad in wig and gown; he usually wears morning coat and striped trousers.

Mr. Smith had a rotten case, no one knew this better than he, unless it was myself, but one is not a Counsel for nothing, and just at that moment I felt keenly the defenselessness of my position. However, this was no time for feelings. What was the funny Cockney expression—something about a ticket?—that was it; courage and a steady head "was the ticket." Already my opponent was quoting some law which I could not understand very well; rising, I begged that he might be allowed to repeat the passage.

"Certainly, Mrs. Campbell, but have no anxiety about the law. Upon points of law this Board will protect you." said Lord Blanesburgh.

It was difficult to sit still and listen to Mr. Smith. He had never had the case before and made what seemed to me rather outrageous misstatements; my anxiety to correct these earned me a well-deserved rebuke from their Lordships.

"Please do not interrupt, Mrs. Campbell. You must not disturb Mr. Smith's argument. You can make a memorandum of anything you wish to correct and you will be given the opportunity to speak later on." With an apology I subsided.

It has been said that one of the best attributes of the British Bench is the fact that the British Judges condescend to argue the case with the Counsel appearing before them. Certainly their Lordships were arguing with Mr. Smith. I thought as I listened to him battling every point, that he was arguing a bit too vehemently, especially with regard to the concurrent findings of the three Canadian Courts, and it struck me that at times he almost clashed with their Lordships. Indeed, at the close of the day's hearing I felt that I was completely satisfied with Mr. Smith as a Counsel for Mr. Hogg.

The following day, after Mr. Smith had concluded, Mr. Gahan arose for the second respondent, the Toronto General Trusts Corporation.[35] He looked very bright indeed and talked and quoted the law at length. I have since been asked by the Canadian Judges what exactly he did talk about, but I have never been able to remember. He handled things very sagaciously indeed for his client, the Toronto General Trusts. I was to learn this later when, in their Lordships' reasons for judgment they set forth my losses and my gains. My greatest loss had not come through Mr. Smith's determined fight to uphold Mr. Hogg's honor and the concurrent findings of the three Canadian Courts, a fight which had proved utterly unsuccessful, but through the failure of the Trust Company to make known what they had learned about a most important document in the case. I have told you of this old mortgage book belonging to my mother which Mr. Hogg only produced two months after the Surrogate Court Judge had examined his accounts at Ottawa. It was evident that this book gave their Lordships great concern; many times throughout the long hearing did they knit their brows over it. I recall Lord Blanesburgh, the book in hand, saying, "But, Mr. Smith, this exhibit, 44-A, why did Mr. Hogg not submit himself to cross-examination upon these Toronto Mortgages?" The following extract from their Lordships' Judgment will, I think, make it clear to my readers why I was defeated upon this one branch of the case:

"And, first, as to those items with respect to which the appellant has in their Lordships' Judgment failed in her contention. 1. Ten mortgages on properties in or near Toronto of $12,750.00 in amount entered by Mr. Hogg in Lady Howland's book, 44-A, with the receipt also in his handwriting for the first payment of interest." Then, after expressing their regret and dissatisfaction with the fact that Mr. Hogg made no explanation either by affidavit or otherwise when tendering 44-A as evidence in the Surrogate Court, their Lordships continue: "The Trustee Corporation on behalf of the Estate presumably inquired into the matter at Toronto. It would have been satisfactory if they had stated the result of their inquiry. They have not done so; the whole question therefore remains in some obscurity. In these proceedings however that obscurity is fatal to the appellant," and in conclusion, "the appellant's claim on this head fails."[36]

Silence is golden, the silence of the Toronto General Trusts Corporation had saved their chairman, W.D. Hogg, many thousand dollars and caused a financial loss to an estate committed to their care by the Courts of Canada. The Toronto General has an active publicity department and I always smile, a bit cynically I confess, when I see the literature it issues for the edification of the public. Their insignia is an old pilot at his wheel and beneath this touching picture appear advertisements such as this:

You Obtain the Services of Outstanding Business Men

The practical effect of making this Corporation your Executor and Trustee is to secure the services of experienced business men to manage your affairs. Investments and important matters of policy, affecting the welfare of your estate are decided upon by its Directors, all of them men who have achieved outstanding success in the fields of Law and Business.

Our long hearing was almost at an end. The presiding Law Lord called me to the rostrum, and going over the items upon which I had attacked, asked me what further I had to say regarding certain of these; he then signified that the Board would be able to allow six or seven other items. This was followed by a spirited plea for costs on the part of Mr. Smith and Mr. Gahan. I remember Lord Blanesburgh saying, "My noble brothers and I comprehend you completely, Mr. Gahan, and do you not think it might be well to draw this argument to a close?" I was then given the opportunity to address the Board as to costs. I said their Lordships would understand that the costs incurred in going from Court to Court were very heavy, but that I desired to leave the matter entirely in their hands, also I desired to thank their Lordships for their patience and courtesy in listening to me for so long. Then Lord Blanesburgh speaking for the Board complimented me upon my handling of a "case of so much complexity," and with a bow and gracious smile dismissed us. Everyone at the Privy Council Office appeared greatly pleased at the favorable outcome; there was, it seemed, nothing for me to do now but to "rest up" and await their Lordships' reasons for Judgment.

The strain of the past months had been heavy and the feeling of relief was wonderful. A great burden had slipped from my shoulders. Glad news travels fast and my good friend at Lincoln's Inn was awaiting me all smiles and congratulations. Happily I made my way home to Bedford Place. My hitherto carefully guarded papers, with the exception of my argument which had been requested by the Court Reporter for their Lordships' perusal, were thrown into the wardrobe and that night I went to Noel Coward's "Bitter

Sweet"; since then whenever I hear this hauntingly beautiful music it takes me back to London and I live over again that eventful day.

For the next few weeks I slept, the sleep of utter exhaustion, hour after hour, right through until twelve or one o'clock. Nature was reasserting herself and making up for the nights when lying in the darkness I had wrestled with some important point of the case. In looking back I realize that much of my best work was accomplished during those wakeful nights.

I went to Paris for Easter. I had not been in France for many years, not since my school-days when, as "La petite Canadienne," I was a pupil at the Couvent de l'Assomption. It was interesting to return, but also rather sad, and there were moments when, wandering about Paris, I was reminded of DuMaurier's "Peter Ibbetson."[37]

On returning to London an envelope from Downing Street greeted me, announcing that Judgment in Campbell vs. Hogg and Others would be delivered on the first of May. May Day, how lovely thought I, because May has always been my lucky month; our little daughter was a May baby. "Utterly irrelevant," I can hear many of my readers grumble; perhaps, but that is the way the feminine mind works. How quickly the "Master Jurists" had given Judgment! Contrasted with the suspense and months of waiting which the Canadian Courts had occasioned me, it seemed too good to be true.

The Judgment was twenty-seven pages long. Lord Blanesburgh read only the conclusion. It was a glorious moment. Mr. Hogg's concurrent findings were in ruins.[38] Their Lordships found that Mr. Hogg was trustee for my mother and that he had retained trust funds.[39] They had reversed the order of the three Canadian Courts. I had won! I had won! "Fools rush in where angels fear to tread!" I remembered what had been said of me in legal circles and at the dinner tables of my acquaintances and erstwhile friends in Toronto and Ottawa. Mr. Hogg was also held responsible for the "heavy cost of these proceedings throughout." "It would be wrong," continued the Judgment, "that any of these costs should fall upon the Trust Estate." Mr. Hogg was ordered to pay the Trust Company the costs incurred in all the Courts of Ontario and of this appeal to the Privy Council, and three quarters of my own costs in all Courts, including the Privy Council appeal.[40]

"Wrongs are righted in the Privy Council," Mr. McCarthy had

spoken the truth! Outside the Council Chamber I was showered with congratulations and literally besieged by reporters and the photo-press men who desired an appointment to photograph me at my boarding place. I sought the privacy of Miss Moore's room. Mr. Lys brought me a number of the Judgments. I noticed that these original documents bore the word "confidential" at the top. This had been blue pencilled and was omitted from those given me later, and from those sent by Sir Charles Neish to the Chief Justice of Ontario to "file with the archives of your Court." The Judgment was politely scathing, reversing, as it did, the order of the three Canadian Courts except as to the disallowance of any remuneration to Mr. Hogg; this was the one point that Canada had handed to me.[41] The Judicial Committee drew attention to the fact that, upon his being questioned as to his handling of the estate, Mr. Hogg wrote statements which were "quite incorrect," and that when he was found to have sums of money in his hands belonging to my mother "he seems to have realized that he could seek his discharge therefrom as a result of a general account and in no other way."[42] In sharp contrast to Canada was their Lordships' comment on the absence of any trust account. Dealing with the account itself their Lordships, after pointing out the unusual, improper nature of the same, commented upon it in a way that was going to give Mr. Justice Masten and the First Appellate Division, with the exception of Mr. Justice Magee, "un mauvais quart d'heure." I could imagine their faces as they read it. Their Lordships also made it quite clear that Mr. Hogg's account had been allowed to stand not because they approved of it, but solely because I had been "content" to accept the position to which the Canadian Courts had "relegated me."[43] I had been wise indeed to cast myself in my "too great unmight" upon the mercy of the Privy Council. The "Scylla and Charybdis" of concurrent findings of the three Canadian Courts which for months had darkened my horizon, had been overcome because their Lordships decided that these "so-called findings" had been based upon "an erroneous proposition of law," and that "within the Board's rule there has been no finding at all; they therefore were compelled to investigate her case afresh."[44]

I wondered how the old Judges in Canada would take the polite but none the less severe reprimand meted out to them in more than one place of the Judgment, especially where their Lordships referred to the $1,000.00 offered me by the Appellate Division as a "settlement in full."[45]

The Capital Real Estate transaction had not gone over.[46] Their Lordships found that Mr. Hogg had paid interest regularly upon an investment which "never existed" and had failed to account for the principal, liquidating it only in this general account, which Lord Blanesburgh had intimated was not an account at all. Similarly the McAmmond and Martin item which, like the Capital Real Estate transaction, was accepted by the Canadian Courts had failed to pass the Privy Council. Mr. Hogg was held answerable for the money.

In conclusion the Judgment drew attention to the fact that Mr. Hogg had left my mother's money, especially during the latter years, in his own hands or in the hands of his firm,* uninvested and carrying no interest for periods of indefinite duration.[47] I had won seven of the items upon which I had attacked.

One phase of the Judgment was very surprising to me; their Lordships held that under the Surrogate Court Statute, which Mr. Hogg had invoked in order to obtain his discharge as trustee, "no interest on uninvested balances or any sum in the nature of damages could be charged against him."[48] The interest would apparently have to be collected in Canada. For years the Surrogate Courts in Canada had been awarding interest and damages against a trustee who was found to have retained trust funds; it appeared now that the Surrogate Judge had no power to do this. The practice could no longer continue after this decision in my case. Therefore, the Judges of the Court of Appeal for Ontario were forced to take a Bill to the Legislature to amend Section 65 of the Surrogate Court Act because of "a recent case, Campbell vs. Hogg."[49] The Bill received the Royal Assent in April 1933 and became the law.

I have always considered it a strange trick on the part of Fate which left it to a woman, untrained in business or the law, to cross

---

* For years this firm has been Hogg and Hogg. Not long after this decision it was dissolved, and recently the other half of Hogg and Hogg, F.D. Hogg K.C., has been appointed a Judge of the Supreme Court of Ontario.

the sea "with her little blue bag," as my former Counsel put it, and cast the stone which amended the Surrogate Court Act of Ontario.

The interest upon the principal which I had won in England amounted to nearly $18,000.00.[50] This was granted the estate first by Mr. Justice Jeffrey, then, as Mr. Hogg appealed, by the Court of Appeal for Ontario, and finally by the Supreme Court of Canada, Sir Lyman Poore Duff presiding. The Courts of Canada were unable to go against the Privy Council decision even in this detail. It is interesting to note that Mr. Justice Masten differed from his brother Judges of the Court of Appeal for Ontario on the question of interest and, true to my estimate of him, wrote a lengthy and dissenting Judgment in a last desperate effort to save his friend, W.D. Hogg, K.C., a large sum of money.

The following weeks in London proved pleasurably exciting. I was awaiting the Order of the Sovereign in Council. Upon my return to Canada I should file this Order in the Appellate Court of Ontario. Also my costs were to be taxed.[51] There were innumerable cables, telegrams, and messages of congratulation. These last accompanied by flowers made me feel like a debutante once more, despite the span of years. My friends in London gave me a wonderful time. At a dinner dance at the home of Mr. E. I met a number of the leading Barristers and Solicitors all of whom seemed delighted by my success. In the restaurants and even in the shops I was addressed in the most friendly and congratulatory terms. One morning at Downing Street, while I was waiting for some paper in connection with the taxation of costs, a gentleman came into Mr. Lys' office. I later learned that he was one of the Solicitors from India House. Bowing, he said, "Pardon me, but this is Mrs. Campbell, I presume." Then as he gazed down at me, I was seated in the corner by the big desk, he said, "I suppose you realize, Mrs. Campbell, what a remarkable thing you have accomplished in pleading this case alone before the Judicial Committee and winning it? I've never heard of anything like it, really you know, I consider you and Amy Johnson the two most amazing women in the world." Miss Johnson had just then electrified London by her famous flight.[52] Laughingly, I told him I was greatly flattered, as Miss Johnson was a very daring young person indeed. When not long after this the following editorial under the title of "A Good

Woman," appeared in the "London Law Journal," I wondered if the gentleman from India House had perhaps collaborated with the editor.[53]

> The palm for the greatest forensic achievement by a woman in this country since women have been called to the Bar goes to Mrs. Bethune Campbell of Boston, U.S.A. She is neither Barrister nor Solicitor nor any other kind of legal practitioner, but during a twenty hour speech, packed with legal citations and sound legal argument, she persuaded the Judicial Committee of the Privy Council to advise His Majesty to set aside the Judgment of a Supreme Court of Canada.
>
> It is not surprising that my Lords paid her the handsome tribute of a sincere and well-turned compliment.
>
> Never so far as I can find, has a women on her own by forensic skill combined with serene endurance evoked or earned such high approval.

The costs of the work done on a Privy Council Appeal are taxed before the Registrar at Downing Street. I should have to render a bill of costs on the taxation. It puzzled me to know how to do this as I was not privileged to charge up my time as a Solicitor, nor charge a Counsel fee for the six days in Court. I, therefore, made out a bill for my board and expenses all these weeks in London and my ocean trip coming over and returning, and added to this the regular cost of printing and binding the records, and the Privy Council Office fees. It was necessary to serve my opponents with the notice of appointment of taxation. After much hunting about and getting lost in the City, I toiled up a dark, dingy stairway and located the firm of Bischoff, Coxe and Co. Their offices were grim and redolent of age. I told one of the several solicitors' clerks that I desired to serve some member of the firm with a notice. To this day I am not sure of the identity of the gentleman to whom I was escorted with much swinging open of baize doors. He may have been a Bischoff, or perhaps Coxe, or he may even have been Co. At any rate the seals on his watch chain jingled importantly as he rose from a brief-covered table, and I felt very new and insignificant indeed. He took my notice and adjusting his pince-nez said, looking at me severely, "I suppose you are aware, Mrs. Campbell, that Mr. Hogg has only you to thank for this mess he is in. All the costs against him. He's an old client of ours and this will not be pleasant news. If you had had Counsel or anyone but yourself handling your case, in my estimation, it would never have been opened up. Their Lordships rarely consider a case where there have been concurrent findings of fact in the Courts below. You know this, I suppose." His annoyance was most amusing; it was the perfect tribute, and I smiled radiantly, I imagine, and as he proffered his hand in good-bye he smiled just a trifle himself.

I had, it appeared, created a precedent in the annals of the Privy Council. Never before had it been necessary for them to tax the costs of a winning appellant in person, therefore, the High Court had been consulted as to its method of procedure. Sir Charles said that he felt sure that before beginning the taxation my opponents would not object to his expressing his congratulations to Mrs. Campbell and the satisfaction that he felt in the lady's courage in pleading her own case. I was automatically granted three quarters of the cost of printing the record and binding ten copies and the Privy Council Office fees. When it came to my personal bill there was of course some discussion.[54] I remember Sir Charles saying, "Gentlemen, this lady has been most successful with this case; were she the winning Counsel, Mr. Hogg would have a large bill to pay. I think you will agree with me that it is only fair she should be compensated for her labors." One item of my bill seemed to amuse everyone concerned. In connection with my ocean crossing I had put down "Deck chair and tipping." "Deck chair and tipping?" read Sir Charles, a smile wreathing his face. However, after some explanation on my part it was granted together with the other items, and three quarters of the whole sum, a substantial one, was certified by Sir Charles. I learned that it would be incorporated in the "King's Order" as would be the costs payable by Mr. Hogg to the Trust Company. I also learned that my $2,000.00 deposit would be released from the Appellate Court upon my return to Canada. Realizing the heavy costs with which Mr. Hogg was faced, I remembered Mr. Lys' warning issued to me on that day in July nearly a year ago, that to lose a case in the Privy Council was an expensive business.

Towards the end of May His Majesty's Order in Council or the King's Order was delivered to me by Sir Charles. Printed on palest grey-blue paper it bore the Royal Seal in the upper left hand corner and across the top:

"At the Court of Buckingham Palace"
Present
The King's Most Excellent Majesty
Lord President   Master of the Horse
Lord Privy Seal   Dr. Addison

Then followed my Petition of Appeal and the report of the Judicial Committee. The document concluded with:

His Majesty having taken the said report into consideration was pleased by and with the advice of His Privy Council to approve thereof and to order as it is hereby ordered that the same be punctually observed, obeyed, and carried into execution.

Whereof the Lieutenant Governor of the Province of Ontario for the time being and all other persons whom it may concern are to take notice and govern themselves accordingly.

It was signed by the Clerk of the Council,

M.P.A. Hankey.★

With my work in England at an end my thoughts turned homewards, and a June evening a few weeks later found me aboard an American-bound steamer. In my cabin secure in my dressing bag lay the King's Order. We glided down to the sea. The banks of the Clyde were bathed in almost unearthly beauty as the long twilight merged into moonlight. I sat in my sheltered corner of the deck reflecting upon the events of the past year. In spite of the happiness which I felt at returning to my home, the good-bye to my English friends and the farewell to London had been astonishingly hard. Why? I asked myself. Was it perhaps that in that brief space of time, scarcely twelve months, I had lived a life-time of responsibility and achievement. Then my mind drifted to an evening just

---

★ Sir Maurice Hankey.

before I had sailed for England, when some of my boy's classmates from Harvard had been dining with us.[55] They had frankly and openly questioned, "Why does Mrs. Campbell want to go across to the Privy Council?" But one, the son of an internationally famous family, had answered in the picturesque language of his people and with all the understanding of his race; "Because she will never have the satisfied heart unless she does." The "satisfied heart." That was it exactly. Thank God, O thank God for the Privy Council! And I wondered just what the state of affairs would be throughout Ontario should politicians ever succeed in abolishing the right of Appeal to His Majesty's Judicial Committee.[56]

St. John's Rectory
Jamaica Plain, Boston
January, 1935.

EPILOGUE

THE LITIGATION CONTINUES ... AND CONTINUES
... AND CONTINUES

DESPITE THE elation that overwhelms the end of Mrs. Campbell's book, the case was far from over. Legal proceedings back in Toronto would occupy most of Mrs. Campbell's efforts for the next five years. In all instances, she continued to appear in person without counsel. Mrs. Campbell fired the opening salvo in the fall of 1930, in an attempt to recover the Ontario costs awarded by the Privy Council. When the bills she submitted to Osgoode Hall for $2,000 were slashed to $800, she launched an appeal with the Surrogate Court. William Hogg cross-appealed, Mrs. Campbell appealed to the Ontario High Court, and then Hogg appealed to the Ontario Court of Appeal. The upshot was that Mrs. Campbell's claim for reimbursement of her accountant's fees was disallowed, and her claim for Slaght's legal fees was dismissed except for a paltry $100. The final sum recoverable from Hogg would have been approximately $200. The Law Lords, who had taken such care to ensure that Mrs. Campbell be reimbursed to the extent of "three-fourths of her costs in all courts," surely would have been dismayed.[1]

The next proceeding began innocently enough but soon spun out of control. Mrs. Campbell had been advised to file the order of the Privy Council in the Ontario courts in order to secure enforcement. Exhibiting a refreshing change of heart, the Toronto General Trusts Corporation this time took the lead and filed the documents on behalf of the estate.[2] William James Elliott, K.C., again acting as counsel for the trust company, had apparently rethought the matter. The company now acknowledged that Hogg had breached his trust to Lady Howland. Elliott admitted that Hogg had "appropriated" moneys "to his own use," "intermingled" Lady Howland's money with his own, failed to "pay the interest or income derived therefrom to the party entitled," and delivered an account "in which he did not account for the same."[3] The first snag occurred in October 1930, when High Court Judge Clarence Garrow dismissed the trust company's motion for leave to issue execution and advised that the parties would have to commence an action.[4]

Clarence Garrow

In response, Mrs. Campbell and the trust company joined forces to do just this, claiming judgment in the amount of $7,027.34, as the Privy Council had indicated. They also asked for compounded interest, which had not been included in the Privy Council decision. This would seem to be a bold move, but it was in accord with general legal practice in which judges customarily added interest to awards. Indeed, many of the members of the bench and bar seem to have been astonished that the Privy Council had intimated there might be some problem with such an approach.[5]

Not to be outdone, Hogg also went on the offensive. He refused both to pay into court and to admit liability for the $7,027.34. He filed a statement of defence in which he asked the Ontario court to reconsider the declaratory Privy Council judgment. He sought to adduce fresh evidence to show that the Law Lords had been mistaken about certain items. He argued the statute of limitations. He even questioned whether there had been a finding that he was a trustee. Chief Justice Hugh Edward Rose, who heard the arguments at first instance, seems to have been astonished by Hogg's intransigence.[6] He commented that Hogg was trying to go behind the Privy Council ruling and dismissed all his claims, adding that it was high time the "long and expensive law suit came to an end." On 13 November 1930, Chief Justice Rose ordered judgment for the plaintiffs on the principal of $7,027.34, with interest from the date of the Privy Council order. He also gave the plaintiffs the right to proceed to trial for the larger claim for back interest.[7]

On 9 June 1931, Mrs. Campbell took the very unusual step of bringing a motion before the Supreme Court of Ontario "for the removal of W.D. Hogg, K.C., from the Rolls of the Law Society of Upper Canada." Had this been a nineteenth-century action, it might have been more understandable. However, legislation passed in 1876 had given the Law Society the power to discipline members of the profession, and by the turn of the century, complaints were customarily made to the benchers, not to the courts.[8] Did Mrs. Campbell think she might get a fairer hearing from the court than from the Law Society? Mrs. Campbell's motion claimed that Hogg's conduct was "unbecoming to a Barrister and Solicitor," because he had "retained trust funds over a long period of years," "submitted false accounts," and "altered and tampered with books of business entry." Mrs. Campbell noted that he had in his hands trust moneys belonging to her, which

Hugh Edward Rose

he had been ordered to pay "pursuant to a finding by His Majesty's Judicial Committee, over a year ago." She had "repeatedly demanded" that he pay up, but Hogg had given "no attention to these demands." Hogg filed an affidavit in response, claiming that Mrs. Campbell was motivated by "vindictiveness and personal spite," and that she was "so obsessed with hatred" that she was "not of sound mind."⁹

Mrs. Campbell's response to Hogg's affidavit was incisive: "I am not actuated by any motives of hatred or malice," she asserted, "nor am I ... of unsound mind, unless it be a mark of unsoundness of mind to want one's money paid one." If anything, Mrs. Campbell thought her behaviour should be characterized as "quite kind and lenient," because she could, had she wished, have "pressed the criminal side of his conduct." She summed up:

> Fictitious mortgages, lying letters, altered and falsified business books, and retention of trust funds are serious offences in the eyes of the law and Mr Hogg has been shown to be guilty of all these offences. I have never sought revenge, but I do want my money. My situation between the Trust Company and their Chairman, Mr. Hogg, is a pitiable one. Surely such a man should not remain upon the rolls of the Law Society. Surely, if he wishes to retain his gown, he should make restitution and pay up his liability.¹⁰

Despite her spirited advocacy, the unusual motion to disbar must have been dismissed, as Hogg remained on the rolls.¹¹

Undaunted, in October 1931, Mrs. Campbell renewed her quest to have Hogg disbarred. This time she brought the complaint before the Law Society, which duly forwarded it to the discipline committee. Hogg himself had sat on the discipline committee for decades, although by 1930 he was no longer coming to bencher meetings and had been removed from the committee roster. As luck would have it, the current chairman of the discipline committee was none other than Newton Wesley Rowell, K.C., bencher and president of the Toronto General Trusts Corporation. Rowell marked the complaint down for investigation on 30 October 1931, and then stood it down "for further information." The matter rested there, without further incident, for the next two and a half years.¹²

Newton Wesley Rowell

Litigation over the remaining claim for interest began in earnest before Judge Nicol Jeffrey of the Ontario High Court in March 1932. Judge Jeffrey held that the Privy Council's statements regarding interest had not fully overruled the long practice of Canadian courts. He stated that Hogg had been "proved guilty of breaches of trust," and that the "gravity" of the breaches required that the trustee "should be penalized by awarding interest." He calculated the interest compounded half-yearly, resulting in a sum of $17,250.40. This must have seemed a staggering amount to Hogg, but heaven-sent to Mrs. Campbell.[13]

Hogg lost little time in appealing to the Court of Appeal. None of the judges agreed with the Privy Council suggestion that the court might lack jurisdiction to award interest.[14] Their decision noted that the money Hogg owed could undoubtedly have been invested "at even more than the half-yearly rate charged by the learned trial judge."[15] But this did not mean they were prepared to support Jeffrey's judgment in favour of Mrs. Campbell. The case was heard by five judges, including Mulock, Masten, and Magee, all of whom had sat on the earlier proceedings. Some observers have subsequently suggested that it might have served the appearance of justice better if Judges Mulock and Masten, both of whose decisions against Mrs. Campbell had been overruled by the Privy Council, had "elected not to be included."[16]

Judge Masten was the most outspoken, and his dissenting judgment fully endorsed Hogg's argument that the question of interest was *res judicata*: Mrs. Campbell had failed to ask for interest when she first launched her suit, the Privy Council had not awarded it, and it was now too late to ask.[17] Chief Justice Mulock, who wrote for the majority, was somewhat less harsh but also refused to endorse Judge Jeffrey's interest award. He noted that there was "no fixed rate of interest chargeable under all circumstances against a trustee," and declared that the matter should be sent back to the master, who would have to ascertain what sum was due based on further evidence.[18] Judge Magee wrote a concurring decision, in which he observed that interest should not have been compounded more frequently than yearly.[19] The final word would come from the Supreme Court of Canada, which dismissed an appeal in a short and confusing judgment in 1933.[20] The result was that Mrs. Campbell would be sent back to the master to have the interest considered afresh. On 26 October 1933, Assistant Master O.E. Lennox revisited the question, ruling that Mrs. Campbell was entitled to "interest at the rate of five per cent, compounded yearly."[21]

Even this decision did not end Mrs. Campbell's legal tribulations. When it came time to wind up the estate and pay out the balance to Mrs. Campbell and her two sisters, the Toronto General Trusts Corporation discovered that it had never been reimbursed for a portion of its legal expenses. The Privy Council had ordered Hogg responsible "for the heavy costs of these proceedings throughout," and stipulated that "it would be wrong if any of those costs should fall upon the trust estate." But, as always, the costs actually recovered from litigation opponents were substantially less than those expended. The amount of $3,502.25 was still outstanding. In 1934 the trust company brought a motion to obtain the legal costs from the remaining funds in the estate, along with a fee of $1,000 in compensation for its efforts of administration. One can only imagine Mrs. Campbell's reaction. Any forgiveness she might have had for the trust company officials when they took steps to enforce the Privy Council decision must have evaporated instantly. She must have been distraught when Judge John Tytler of the York County Surrogate Court sent the legal bills to be taxed, and ordered the trust company to relieve the estate of $1,249 in legal costs, along with $1,000 in administration fees.[22]

Mrs. Campbell appealed to the Ontario High Court of Justice in the fall of 1934. Her dismay was audible from her argument:

> I took all the risk and responsibility. There would have been no money in the estate today to pay the solicitors' bill had I not put it there. May I remind your lordship that had I not fought for the estate the trust company would, by their neglect and mismanagement, have allowed the estate to be robbed—and robbed by their own chairman, W.D. Hogg, K.C.[23]

She would undoubtedly have been elated with the decision, in which Judge John Millar McEvoy disallowed the payment of all the legal costs to the trust company.[24] He concluded that "in all equity and justice they ought not to be paid out of the very funds won by Mrs Campbell upon her appeal to the Privy Council." He also disallowed the $1,000 payment for the administration of the estate with a curt comment:

James Magee

The administrator did not assist the appellant in her fight for the $7,027.34, which the administrator now proposes to lay hold of wherewith to pay its own costs of an ill-advised losing battle and thus to deprive the appellant of the greater part of the fruits of her lone and successful fight with at best only a grudging assistance from the administrator.[25]

The praise for Mrs. Campbell's litigation talents, along with the open criticism of her adversary, must have seemed to Mrs. Campbell precious and long-overdue recognition from an Ontario judge.

The elation was not to last. The Toronto General Trusts Corporation appealed the order to the Ontario Court of Appeal in 1935. Judge William Renwick Riddell, who seems to have viewed Mrs. Campbell's actions with some distaste, completely reversed McEvoy's ruling. Riddell listed off all the times Mrs. Campbell had been "dissatisfied" with the administration of her mother's estate. She had "strenuously opposed" the appointment of the trust company in 1922. She had become "dissatisfied with Hogg" in 1923. Even after the resolution of the division of the estate in 1926, Mrs. Campbell was "still dissatisfied with Hogg," forcing Hogg to pass his accounts in the Surrogate Court. At the conclusion of this hearing, "Mrs. Campbell was not satisfied and she appealed to the Supreme Court of Ontario." At the conclusion of the appeal, "Mrs. Campbell, still dissatisfied, appealed to the Court of Appeal." When that ruling came down, "Mrs. Campbell, dissatisfied, urged the [trust company] to appeal to the Privy Council, or to furnish her with money out of the estate to pay for such appeal." When these requests were not complied with, "she took the appeal in person and at her own expense." Riddell also stressed how critical Mrs. Campbell had been of her adversaries. She had characterized the trust company personnel as "dangerous and skilful opponents," who had "opposed" her "bitterly."[26] It was not a pretty picture.

Riddell was at pains to emphasize that Mrs. Campbell's two other sisters were satisfied with both Hogg and the trust company throughout the long and acrimonious legal proceedings. He noted that Mrs. Lindsey and Mr. Hogg had even shared counsel at some points, "a fact that throws light on the relative views of the two sisters." Mrs. Campbell's sisters, who were "entitled to as much of the estate as Mrs. Campbell," thought that their younger sister "was persecuting her old

William Renwick Riddell

uncle." The elder sisters' position was a central factor in Riddell's decision to reverse McEvoy's ruling: "In view of the position taken by the beneficiaries, it was not incumbent upon the [trust company] to take an appeal." Furthermore, a trustee was "not required to foresee the result of any proceeding in Court, appeal or otherwise; whether any different view of the facts would be taken at Westminster no one could prophesy; the learned members of the Judicial Committee who passed upon the appeal would be the last persons in the world to say that their opinion was so clearly right that the trustee should have appealed to His Majesty in His Privy Council."[27] Judge Riddell seems to have been piqued at Mrs. Campbell's tenacity, and possibly with the ultimate Privy Council ruling.[28]

In the end, Riddell held that a trustee was "entitled as of right to full indemnity out of his trust estate against all his costs, charges and expenses properly incurred." The trust company's "great expense" had "greatly depleted the assets of the estate," but this could not be helped. It was entitled to recoup from the estate all the extra legal costs that had not been collected from Hogg. It was also entitled to be paid the $1,000 administration fee, which could "not be said to be unreason-

Meeting of judges of Ontario and benchers of the Law Society of Upper Canada, 18 February 1932

able."[29] At the end of this long, convoluted road, the estate left to be distributed to the three sisters had dwindled dramatically. The cash remaining after the trust company took its due totalled $2,201.02, supplemented by a few unrealized assets of "undetermined" value.[30]

By this point, Mrs. Campbell seems to have lost all patience. In June 1934, she renewed her efforts with the Law Society to have Hogg disbarred. The matter was resolved with despatch. The notation in the disciplinary committee records said simply: "Matter was before Com[mittee] on 15 Oct. 1931 when she was asked for particulars which have not been given and as matter is now before Courts we will not take any action." The issue was debated before the full convocation of all the benchers on 18 October 1934, when Mrs. Campbell's letter was read before the assembled throng. Then the secretary was instructed to write to Mrs. Campbell informing her that the action of the discipline committee had been approved, and "the matter so far as the Law Society is concerned is to be taken as concluded."[31]

At about the same time that she renewed the disciplinary complaint, Mrs. Campbell also launched criminal proceedings against Hogg. Apparently her earlier "kind and lenient" decision to keep the matter out of the criminal realm had given way to true anger. In February 1934, she personally laid criminal charges of forgery, false pretences, theft, and perjury in the Ottawa police court. The case was delayed for several weeks because of Hogg's claim that he was unable to appear "due to a serious and possibly a fatal illness." Ultimately, the criminal prosecution failed too. All charges were dismissed.[32]

At the end of the litigation trail, Mrs. Campbell seems to have been exhausted and at the end of her rope. In a dramatic gesture of public display, she began to picket, with a sandwich board strapped to her front and back, on Queen Street in front of Osgoode Hall and on Bay Street in front of the office of the Toronto General Trusts Corporation. Picketing seems quite out of keeping with Mrs. Campbell's stature and character, and may suggest that she had lost all hope of achieving her goals through traditional means. It may also suggest that the stress and pressures of the interminable legal proceedings had caused her, as it has occasionally caused other litigants, to unravel to some degree. At the end of the protracted lawsuits, she simply could not bring herself to stop.

Brendan O'Brien, who was a young lawyer at the time, remembers seeing Mrs. Campbell during the late 1930s: "She'd put in a full morning or afternoon picketing. She was rather pleasant-looking, middle-aged, of medium build. She went up and down Queen Street. She also picketed the trust company on Bay Street. She didn't try to stop people coming and going. But out of natural curiosity, people would ask her things. People all got to know her, and she would chat with people on the street. We had a nodding acquaintance."[33]

Peter Newcombe, an Ottawa resident who would begin his legal studies in the late 1930s, also recalls Mrs. Campbell picketing in Ottawa, in front of the Toronto General Trusts Corporation on Sparks Street. His father, a lawyer, would point out the lady with the sandwich board walking up and down in front of the trust building in the capital city, as they drove home in the afternoon.[34]

Mrs. Campbell's presence—indeed, the protracted case itself—attracted a great deal of attention within legal circles at the time. Brendan O'Brien, who would later become a treasurer of the Law Society, recalls that Mrs. Campbell's case was "widely discussed," and that the "legal profession was divided into two camps." Some apparently thought that "Mr. Hogg was very hard done by," and others "thought he was a crook."[35] Peter Newcombe, who would subsequently become a prominent Ottawa lawyer, says that "most people felt Mrs. Campbell was a crackpot who had succeeded."[36] All, however, were agreed that the case was "highly unusual." It was simply "unheard of" that a woman, who had lost every round of litigation in Ontario, who had been represented by some of the most outstanding counsel at the bar, had taken her own case alone to the Privy Council. And won.[37]

MRS. CAMPBELL: THE WOMAN BEHIND THE LITIGATION

What are we to make of the "Privy Council Portia," the remarkable woman behind the prolonged litigation? The author of *Where Angels Fear to Tread* was incontestably tenacious, highly intelligent, and possessed of an intriguing sense of humour. Although some might argue that the Prologue is overly laboured in style, Mrs. Campbell's book generally reveals a woman who wrote with ease and polish. Her book discloses an erudite individual, well versed in literature, drama, and history. Her tale is told by a true raconteur, one who makes lawyers, judges, and witnesses come alive on the page. The reader comes away from the text with a strong sense of the woman behind the prose. But what did her contemporaries think of her? Lawyers and judges were both impressed and frustrated with Mrs. Campbell. At points they would stand back in undisguised admiration, as she locked wits brilliantly with the leading counsel and judges of the day. At others, they were reduced to fury over her intransigence. A woman who had uncovered clear evidence of financial misdoing with her mother's estate, Mrs. Campbell seems to have begun her quest for rectification innocently enough, and then become gripped with the case to the exclusion of all else for over a decade of her life. What do we know about her that might enable us to understand her status and background, her motivation, her behaviour, and the ultimate result?

At the outset, it is important to recognize that Mrs. Campbell held an unusual position within these rarefied legal circles. She was an insider by class, race, and ethnicity, an outsider by gender. Mrs. Campbell's upper-class stature was central to her success. The prominence of her family preceded her at every stage. In both Toronto and London she found herself assisted, even indulged, by legions of law clerks, lawyers, and judges who had fond recollections of her father, mother, and brother. Her access to money, even if sometimes in short supply, was critical to her success. The press stressed how "refined looking" Mrs. Campbell was, a clear signal to readers of her class.[38] A sense of entitlement transfuses the book, leaving an indelible impression that the author possessed a class-privileged comprehension of herself and her place in the world. A comparison with Florence Deeks, a Canadian woman who followed in Mrs. Campbell's footsteps two years later, is instructive. Deeks had much in common with Mrs. Campbell but significantly fewer elite connections. Florence Deeks's efforts to argue her own case in front of the Ontario Court of Appeal and the Privy Council two years later, in a notorious lawsuit alleging plagiarism against the influential British author H.G. Wells, went down to spectacular defeat.[39]

Mrs. Campbell's race and ethnicity were equally central to her success. A white woman, she describes herself as "intensely British."[40] The "Britishness" that had been transplanted to colonial dominions in the nineteenth and early twentieth centuries encompassed a sense of British history, a eulogizing of the rule of law and constitutionalism, and social understandings about matters as diverse as table manners, child rearing, diet, dress, high culture, popular culture, war, and character. Public glorification of British heritage proved very useful in allowing members of the Canadian ruling elite to establish hierarchical boundaries between themselves and Aboriginal peoples, the French, and non-Anglo-Saxon immigrants.[41] Mrs. Campbell's identification with the race that founded the Empire was enormously helpful to her cause. "I am proud to belong to a race which has a Privy Council ... [the] only one ... in the world," was her ringing endorsement to the Toronto *Daily Star.*[42]

Mrs. Campbell's sense of distance from the Asian clients in Slaght's waiting room, whom she describes in the racist terminology of the day as "Chinks," is palpable. She thought it worthwhile to comment on the "Semitic looking" features of Arthur Slaght's law partner, James Cowan. She is patronizing in her description of the "full blooded African negro" and "Indian counsel" who were appearing side by side with her at the Privy Council, noting "how curiously the latter's brown faces contrast[ed] with the white wigs framing them," and remarking on their "splendid, though somewhat stilted English."[43] Her own accent, which her grandson recalls as "quite British" though she had lived all her life in Canada and the United States, was much preferable in her own mind.[44] There is a sense in which she felt she was sojourning in London, and appearing before the British Privy Council, by right of blood, unlike the racialized counsel, who struck her as so anomalous. Her pronounced pride in her British heritage may have struck the London legal officials as quaintly endearing and very probably enhanced her prospects for success.

It was only gender that marked Mrs. Campbell as an outsider in this world. Her description of her time in London indicates how keenly she felt the vulnerability of gender. Although she had travelled widely, Mrs. Campbell had apparently not done much without family, friends, or chaperones in tow. She found herself quite shocked by the "fresh" behaviour of the manager of her hotel, and the persistent attentions of the young man outside the church.[45] While some might view her responses as overreacting, her behaviour reveals her deep consciousness of the perils of a woman alone.

Everything about Mrs. Campbell's advocacy before the Privy Council was laced with gender. The buzz that greeted her entrance to the Downing Street courtroom was permeated with prurience over the spectacle of a woman out of her element. The frequent reference

James Cowan

to "Privy Council Portia" reminded everyone that, like the Shakespearean character, women in law were "exceptional curiosities, assuming borrowed robes and roles."[46] Lord Blanesburgh's solicitous treatment seems premised on his sense of feminine fragility. He instructed Mrs. Campbell to sit down whenever the judges were discussing something amongst themselves. "We don't want you to be more fatigued than is necessary," he told her, obviously anxious about the physical strain on a respectable woman who had to stand for any length of time.[47]

The press was equally cognizant of Mrs. Campbell's femininity. "Dressed simply in a mauve costume and hat, surrounded by voluminous law books, be-wigged lords and learned counsel, Mrs. Elizabeth Bethune Campbell, daughter of Lady Howland, a Canadian Portia, said to be the first woman privileged to appear before the empire's highest court, imparted a delightfully informal touch to the Privy Council to-day," was the way the Toronto *Star* put it.[48] The Yorkshire *Evening News* described Mrs. Campbell similarly:

A slim figure in plum-colored hat and costume, she stood outlining her case and discussing points of law with as much composure as if she were attending a social gathering with the three judges — Lord Blanesburgh, Lord Tomlin and Lord Russell of Killowen. She spoke in a soft, conversational voice which was scarcely audible in the public seats, and throughout the proceedings maintained complete self-possession.[49]

Mrs. Campbell was a woman who maintained a certain pride in her figure and wardrobe. In advance of the hearing at the Privy Council, she had her suit dyed and pleats pressed, and purchased a "tight fitting little English hat" to match the ensemble. She was a thoroughly fashionable woman of the stylish 1920s, one who took pleasure in the daring habit of smoking. If her comments in *Where Angels Fear to Tread* are indicative, Mrs. Campbell took the press focus on her appearance and dress with a mixture of bemusement and pleasure.[50]

Mrs. Campbell was not a woman who was tied in any identifiable way to the feminist movement. She did not belong to any of the elite women's organizations, such as the National Council of Women, which had been established in 1893 by Lady Aberdeen, the wife of the governor general.[51] She seemed curiously indifferent to the feminist legal victory in the "Persons Case," a decision confirming women's right to sit in the Canadian Senate. The Privy Council decision had been released in October 1929, while Mrs. Campbell was in London preparing her case, but she gives it the briefest of mention in *Where Angels Fear to Tread*. Perhaps Newton Wesley Rowell's having been counsel for the "famous five" female appellants had put her off.[52] Yet for all that, she seemed pleased that several of the British women lawyers were in the audience when she argued the case.[53]

Clara Brett Martin had become the first woman admitted to the profession of law in the British Empire when she was called to the bar in Toronto in 1897. She had much in common with Mrs. Campbell, having descended from a well-connected elite, Anglican-Irish, white family in Ontario. She too found her appearance, deportment, and office decor scrutinized at every turn for evidence of femininity. The profession was unremittingly self-conscious about its masculinity and tended to greet the entrance of women with a sense of horrified fascination.[54] Women trickled into law after Clara Brett Martin's historic breakthrough, though many married and subsequently withdrew from practice. Most gravitated toward, or were forced into, family law, real estate, and trust work. Few litigated. Vera Parsons, Helen Kinnear, and Margaret Hyndman, who developed sizeable litigation practices in Toronto, were notable exceptions. Not one woman ran for bencher in Ontario until 1946; the first would not be elected until 1975.[55] Within this masculine realm, Mrs. Campbell's decision to litigate her own case, and her unexpected success, were little short of revolutionary.

This raises some intriguing questions about Mrs. Campbell's education. It is tempting to ask what value formal legal education had, if a woman with no university or law school training could teach herself enough about the substance, procedure, and advocacy of law to succeed before the Privy Council. Mrs. Campbell describes her own education as "quite the old fashioned kind."[56] Apart from what she had learned under the guidance of governesses and her mother at home, Mrs. Campbell's period at convent school in Paris was her only claim to formal education. The latter most likely a form of "finishing school," historically popular among the British and American elites, who sent their daughters to Paris to learn French and German, music, drawing and painting, before negotiating the marriage market.[57] How does this compare with the training Ontario lawyers would have received?

In James Bethune's era, almost all legal study was done through private reading and apprenticeship during the articling term. Would-be lawyers boned up on Anson on Contracts, Taylor's Equity, Smith's Common Law, and Blackstone. The Law Society established its first lectures in law in 1854, but suspended them in 1868. Pressures for change mounted from south of the border, where Harvard University had established a three-year postgraduate law degree in 1870. Quebec, Nova Scotia, New Brunswick, Manitoba, Alberta, and Saskatchewan moved toward the model of university-based legal education, but the Law Society of Upper Canada stubbornly held out. The benchers eventually founded a law school at Osgoode Hall in 1889, which they jealously continued to run independently. Students with university degrees apprenticed under articles for three years, while attending part-time lectures and sitting examinations in doctrinal law and procedure at Osgoode Hall. Others were required to put in five years of articling.[58] It was not much, compared with today's standards, but it was certainly substantially more than Mrs. Campbell had.

Asked how she had amassed her knowledge of law, Mrs. Campbell told the press that she had "never studied law before this case," but volunteered how she had overcome her "primary handicap" of "ignorance of law":

Through the help of a friend I secured admission to the British Museum Library, where I swotted up court procedure and the law on agency and trusts. This was a severe ordeal, necessitating frequent adjournments for cocoa drinking, but the task was lightened by the kindness of officials. During the summer I had the library and librarian of the Privy Council placed at my disposal. The next obstacle was nervousness—I am highly strung—which made inroads on my sleep and health ... A strong dislike for speaking in public also embarrassed me. These difficulties were personal and inevitable.[59]

In what was clearly a brief encounter with what the articling experience might have entailed—watching senior counsel at work—Mrs. Campbell added that she had attended Privy Council hearings during her stay in London to hear "N.W. Rowell argue cases" in order to acquaint herself with procedure.[60] One can only imagine what Rowell must have thought of this acknowledgment of his unwitting tutelage.

The Toronto *Star* had its own opinions, suggesting that "the fact that her father was a lawyer may explain her familiarity with the law."[61] Whether this was in reference to some genetic transmission, or the presumption that the availability of law books and legal conversations in the home might filter knowledge from parent to daughter, was unclear.

Beyond the obvious indicia of class, race, ethnicity, gender, and education, what can we tell about Mrs. Campbell's psychological make-up? The evidence from *Where Angels Fear to Tread* suggests that Mrs. Campbell's primary emotional bonds lay with her parents. Mrs. Campbell writes effusively of James Bethune, attributing her personal success to his intellectual leadership. It is her "Highland ancestry" and James Bethune's professional example that she credits for her fortitude and determination. Yet virtually all that she knew of her father, who had died when she was just four years old, must have come from stories passed down by family and friends. In fact, it was most likely Lady Howland who acted as the formative influence on Mrs. Campbell's life. A woman widely acclaimed as a glittering socialite, fluent in languages and conversant with the depths and intricacies of the political realm until well into her seventies, Lady Howland would have been a formidable female mentor.[62]

The ties between mother and daughter were obviously powerful. Mrs. Campbell was often described as "Lady Howland's favourite daughter," the child of her mother's "old age."[63] It is true that when Lady Howland's ailing health forced her to leave the Welland Hotel, she did not move in with Mrs. Campbell, as one might have expected. The decision to move Lady Howland to Mrs. Campbell's older sister's home, however, may have reflected a preference to keep the elderly patient in southern Ontario rather than move her to the United States, or the greater spaciousness of Cora Ann Lindsey's Parkdale home.[64] The 1915 will, which left jewellery, personal effects, and specific sums of money to each of the children, discriminated substantially in favour of Mrs. Campbell.[65] Whether Lady Howland chose to make such unequal bequests for emotional reasons or because of economic motives is unclear. She may have thought that Mrs. Campbell, whose husband's ministerial stipend was not substantial, was in greater financial need than her other children, who had the benefit of legal and business incomes. There is some evidence that Mrs. Campbell called upon her mother for financial assistance from time to time.[66]

But Mrs. Campbell also seems to have taken the will and her mother's estate as symbolic of her special relationship, fighting to enshrine this visible tribute in the courts. Psychological and financial factors may have intertwined to create a deep-rooted need to win this lawsuit.

Whatever Mrs. Campbell's relationship with her parents, it is obvious that she was deeply estranged from her siblings. Her book mentions Charles only in passing, and the hostility toward her sisters, in particular Cora Ann, is palpable. Disagreements over the care of ailing relatives and the dispersal of inherited estates can complicate sibling relationships in many families, but the acrimony seems to have been acute in this case. The ages of the Bethune children were sufficiently spread out that they may have grown up quite distant from each other. Cora Ann Lindsey and Annie McDougald were a generation older than Mrs. Campbell. Even Charles, with whom Mrs. Campbell lived for years with her mother, was eight years older. The traumatic events of James Bethune's death, Lady Howland's remarriage and separation, Lady Howland's subsequent illness, and Charles Bethune's death could also have driven wedges between the remaining three sisters.

Wills had provoked estrangements between members of Mrs. Campbell's family for some years. Evidence that there had been "legal trouble" over James Bethune's will was given in testimony during the trial before Judge Kelly.[67] Charles Bethune's will, in which he left all his property in 1921 to his eldest sister, Cora Ann, created more difficulties.[68] Lady Howland's will seems to have ignited the conflagration beyond repair. Cora Ann Lindsey's position was that Lady Howland had deliberately revoked the will in 1921. Cora Ann testified at the trial before Judge Kelly that, shortly after the death of her husband in 1920, she had gone to tell her mother that her own financial situation had become quite troubled.[69] She swore that it was at that point that Lady Howland had decided to destroy the earlier will, exclaiming, "Nobody will ever quarrel over any will of mine so nobody will feel hurt. I have made a will but ... will destroy it."[70] It was Cora Ann, after all, who nursed Lady Howland through her final months. She, too, had an obvious emotional and economic interest in the outcome. Annie McDougald's role was less defined; at points she supported her elder sister, and at others, she stood back quiescent. Quite likely for a multitude of reasons, Mrs. Campbell refused to believe that her mother had revoked the will. Even had Lady Howland done so, Mrs. Campbell insisted, her mental faculties were so

Charles Bethune

confused by the early 1920s that any such gesture would have been meaningless. The litigation drew a rift between the three sisters that was never resolved. Once legal proceedings commenced over Lady Howland's will, they never spoke to each other again.[71]

Mrs. Campbell's widest circle of friends was in Toronto. She counted on their hospitality during her many days and weeks of legal preparation in that city, and they sent cables of congratulation and floral tributes upon her victory in London. Apart from Susan Revere Chapin and Bishop William Lawrence, whom she describes as financially and emotionally supportive of her case, Mrs. Campbell made few close friends in Boston, despite her more than thirty years' residence as the wife to the Episcopalian rector there. Mrs. Campbell's pronounced affections for Britain and its empire may have caused social distance from the Massachusetts community, where Loyalists were traditionally defined as traitors. That she travelled from home regularly, and for long stretches of time, frequently in connection with the case, also caused some resentment among her neighbours and the parishioners. Some felt that Mrs. Campbell did not take on her share of rummage sales, bazaars, and the other responsibilities that traditionally had fallen to the rector's wife. Others wondered that she left her children and husband alone for months at a time.[72] Some of the disaffected members of the Ladies' Auxiliary and several "irreverent" vestrymen were even known to have dubbed her "Lady Campbell." The nickname was probably a reaction to the widely shared sense that Mrs. Campbell thought the parishioners, with the exception of Susan Revere Chapin, beneath her social status.[73]

Something of a social recluse in Boston, Mrs. Campbell's main ties there were with her children and husband. Searching for words to describe her triumph before the Privy Council, Mrs. Campbell's memory seized upon her elation at the birth of her first child, James. "Once before life had brought a similar thrill," she recollects, "... the thrill of achievement."[74] Mrs. Campbell's second child, Thomasine, a "May baby," inspired her to count her good fortune that the Privy Council decision would be released in May, "my lucky month."[75] Mrs. Campbell's legal exploits took her away from home for long stretches, provoking some neighbours to speculate that the Campbell children "went to boarding school because there was nobody there to take care of them."[76] Such comments seem somewhat uncharitable, as well as indicative, perhaps, of a lack of familiarity with the upper-class British norms of child rearing. Other neighbours described her as a "devoted wife and mother."[77] Both children excelled scholastically. James Bethune Campbell graduated from Harvard University and Harvard Medical School, served with the US Army medical corps in the Second World War, and then conducted research in neurosurgery while holding prestigious academic appointments.[78] Thomasine graduated from Columbia, going on to study in Vienna. She eventually launched a career as a librarian at Princeton and Harvard Universities.[79]

Although Mrs. Campbell does not write openly about her relationship with her husband, her only grandson, Peter Campbell Brooks, recalls a certain degree of strain between his grandparents. "She was ambitious for him, and wanted him to position himself to be the bishop of Massachusetts," he explained. When this did not come to pass, the distance between the two grew.[80] Others who knew the couple suggested that the rector was "not a dominant person" but, rather, someone who allowed Mrs. Campbell to "run the show." Whatever the situation, it was obvious that Rev. Thomas Campbell gave his wife unwavering support during the litigation process. He used his savings to finance the litigation, he allowed her to mortgage the summer home in Chester, Nova Scotia, to cover the cost of printing the record at the Privy Council, and he expressed unguarded optimism about her prospects for success. As she became more and more engrossed with the litigation, she had to leave her husband and her children for long periods, even over traditional religious and family holidays such as Christmas and Easter. Reverend Campbell fended for himself for months — almost a year at one point — while she was in Toronto, Ottawa, and London preparing.[81]

What Reverend Campbell thought about the extended litigation in the 1930s to try to recover the money, and the picketing at the end of the decade, is unknown. As circumstances would reveal, the family could certainly have used the money and the interest on the award. Reverend Campbell took ill in the summer of 1942 and resigned his position with the church that November. Forced to vacate the rectory immediately, the family moved to 204 Commonwealth Avenue, an exclusive Boston apartment the Campbells could ill afford. Diagnosed with cancer shortly thereafter, Reverend Campbell wrote to his brother from Massachusetts General Hospital on 13 April 1943, noting that financial assistance for the hospital bills had been forthcoming from his daughter-in-law and a bishop of the Episcopalian Church, Henry W. Sherrill, but that his health was much in doubt. Characteristically, he added: "Betsy is well but very busy, naturally."[82] He would die fourteen days later, on 27 April 1943.

Peter Campbell Brooks, who visited his grandmother as a young boy, described her as "old-fashioned," "charming," and "energetic," as someone who had "a certain amount of sparkle." With the distance of time, he characterized Mrs. Campbell as "rather eccentric," a "Miss Marple type." Although Mrs. Campbell never spoke to her grandson about the case, he heard a great deal about it from other family members, who expressed some pride that Mrs. Campbell "had made legal history." He observed that the litigation provided his grandmother with an "opportunity to exercise creative talent in an age when there were few opportunities for women to do so."[83]

One can imagine that Freudian psychiatrists and feminist therapists might draw dissimilar conclusions from this evidence. The former would likely point to Mrs. Campbell's troubled family history, to wifely ambitions foiled, and speculate that her actions regarding the litigation exemplified a deep sense of inadequacy. The latter would probably describe Mrs. Campbell as a woman of great intelligence and ideals, restricted by gender discrimination from realizing career options in keeping with her obvious capabilities, and committed to demonstrating her competence as a female litigator within a masculinist legal system. Mrs. Campbell, although not a woman who would have claimed feminism, might have preferred the latter perspective. Interviewed by a reporter for the Toronto *Telegram* the morning after her victory at the Privy Council, she was asked for her "impressions of the Empire's highest court and her Portia-like encounter with the Empire's finest legal brains." Her reply was compelling: "Naturally I am proud to be the first woman ever to plead in person before the Privy Council, and especially at having won. Had I lost, a woman's ability to sustain a case before masculine talent would have been questioned. My victory has paved the way for more sensational victories by women better equipped than I was."[84]

WILLIAM DRUMMOND HOGG:
"HARD DONE BY" OR A "CROOK"?

Throughout the legal proceedings, observers seem to have been deeply divided over what to make of the case. Was Hogg an honest man persecuted by his niece, or was he a crook, as some said? The money trail was a complicated one, no matter how one tried to follow it. It may help to start at the beginning. What was the value of the estate Hogg was originally entrusted to manage?

Hogg's connection with the Bethune-Howland estate began in 1884. Upon the death of James Bethune, he assisted Mrs. Campbell's mother in processing the will before the Surrogate Court, and he undertook to manage the estate on an ongoing basis. The personal property amounted to $39,850, supplemented by real estate, the value of which appears never to have been recorded in any surviving document. Mrs. Campbell estimated the full value of her father's estate to be at least $60,000, a very substantial sum in the 1880s. The Privy Council noted that in 1885, Lady Howland handed "considerable sums" to Hogg for investment, adding that, "strangely enough," the precise particulars were neither supplied nor discoverable.[85] The needs of the family would have been considerable, with the estate having to bear the costs of living for the widow and her children, and the expense of educating the two younger children—Charles in law and Elizabeth in Europe. The Privy Council, relying on Hogg's testimony, noted that "the best use of all of it had to be made if Mrs Bethune's children were to be educated and she and they maintained."[86]

And what was the value of the estate Hogg finally turned over to the Toronto General Trusts Corporation in 1922? Initially Hogg reported holding only six mortgages for Lady Howland, valued at $8,200.[87] Pressed for more particulars, in 1926 Hogg admitted he had somehow failed to turn over to the trust company $1,161.42, an amount he claimed could be conveniently reduced by $1,155 in legal fees. That he had never charged the estate for fees before did not go unremarked by the Privy Council Law Lords. Queried again about the accounts, a month later Hogg conceded holding an additional $800, and after another elaborate calculation, remitted $581 to the trust company.[88]

In January 1927, Hogg presented two additional sets of figures

William Drummond Hogg

to the Surrogate Court. Initially he claimed to have receipts of $39,972.86, with $486 still due. The second version advised that the receipts actually totalled $46,567.61, with $573 still due.[89]

The Canadian courts, with only minimal tinkering, accepted Hogg's last version of the accounts.[90] The Privy Council did not. The Law Lords found Hogg had wrongly testified to paying sums to Lady Howland that had never been forthcoming. They concluded that some of the payments Hogg swore he had turned over to Charles Bethune had been for moneys not received until after Charles's death. The Law Lords found a balance of $600 owing under the Armstrong loan, $1,000 under the Lyon mortgage, $1,000 under the Patterson mortgage, $1,200 under the O'Toole mortgage, $1,100 under the Betts mortgage, $35.25 under the Larocque mortgage, and $1,600 under the McAmmond and Martin loans. Hogg had claimed that the value of Lady Howland's property for which he was responsible totalled $46,567.61, with disbursements of $45,994.64. The Privy Council found that the property actually totalled $51,660.36, and the disbursements stood at $44,633.02. It pronounced the sum owing to be $7,027.34.[91]

If we take the Privy Council ruling as the correct one, Hogg was wrongly holding money belonging to Lady Howland's estate. But that does not answer the important question of whether the errors were inadvertent or intentional. One interpretation might be that Hogg's intermingling of accounts reflected his sense of himself as a close member of Lady Howland's family. The substantial and long-standing connections between Lady Howland, her sister Agnes, and brother-in-law William Hogg may have caused Hogg to think of himself as serving in something other than an official trusteeship capacity, and to be relatively careless with record-keeping. The Canadian judges found Hogg to be an honest and creditable witness. They excused all the discrepancies and gaps in the accounts as due to the passage of time — "acts extending over forty years" — and a certain dulling of memory because of Hogg's advancing age.[92] At the time of the Privy Council decision, Hogg was eighty-two years old.[93]

The Privy Council expressly overruled the finding of credibility, although the Law Lords were extremely careful not to impugn the lawyer's intentions. Their judgment stated:

Their Lordships would be slow to conclude that any statement on oath by Mr. Hogg in this or any other case could be a statement he knew to be untrue. But they are much affected by his tampering with business books and his shifting statements on that subject, while in his evidence at the hearing, just as in his correspondence before it, he repeatedly made statements, in fact quite incorrect, with an assurance no less positive than that displayed when his statements were accurate. Without imputing any moral blame to Mr. Hogg, for they remember his years and his prepossessions, their Lordships are unable to profess themselves satisfied either with regard to the correctness of his testimony on any disputed item or generally in relation to this case.[94]

At other points in the judgment, the Law Lords stressed again that they "would be slow to impugn" Hogg's "*bona fides*." However, they harshly criticized Hogg, "professional man though he was," for "many indications of a failure on his part to treat seriously his undoubted responsibilities in this matter," for "neglect of ... elementary duty," for the failure to comply with the requirement to keep records of the transactions "even in the simplest form," for "completely defective" accounts, for accounting that was "to say the least unusual," for "off-hand and irrelevant" replies to questions about the estate, for "carelessness of assertion," for "strange" testimony, and for "his practice, increasing in the later years, of leaving [Lady Howland's] balances in his own hands or in those of his firm uninvested and carrying no interest for periods of indefinite duration."[95] Although never characterized as bad faith or deliberate misbehaviour, this was high censure of Hogg.

The item that gave the Privy Council, and indeed the parties themselves, the greatest difficulty was the McAmmond and Martin loan. McAmmond and Martin were the two Ottawa market gardeners who had allegedly borrowed $1,600 from the estate, offered their bonds as security, paid interest in person for thirty-two years, and then vanished right after they redeemed the bonds in 1917. Mrs. Campbell had described the story as a "lurid tale" and scoffed at Hogg's testimony that he had never taken down details about their residence or place of business. It was Mrs. Campbell's position that such a mortgage had never existed, or at best had existed only briefly, and that Hogg himself had used the $1,600, accounting for the interest as if the loans were legitimate.[96] This placed the issue squarely before the court. The impugned behaviour fell well beyond sloppy accounting and slipshod management. If the market gardeners' loan was fictitious, Hogg was indeed a crook.

And this was the item on which the Law Lords came closest to finding deliberate wrongdoing. Yet, at the final moment, the Privy Council shied away from drawing that conclusion. The Law Lords hinted at it, they implied that it was a distinct possibility, but they couldn't quite bring themselves to say it. It is worth reading the analysis in full:

Mr Hogg's evidence with regard both to McAmmond and Martin and their loan is very extraordinary. On his case it must be taken that they had been paying him interest regularly for 32 years; and he had held their bonds throughout as security. Yet he did not know the address of either. All he could say of them was that they were engaged in some kind of market business, and they looked like respectable men. Nor could he recall what the charged bonds were, although these were Lady Howland's only security. He thought they were municipal bonds. Nor did he explain whether he or the mortgagors collected interest on the bonds; nor how if they did, they were able to do so if he held the bonds, or why if they did not, they also paid him the half-yearly interest as, his evidence was, they did regularly. Then it is pointed out as a strange thing that as late as October 26, 1926, Mr Hogg apparently thought that — the loan — a joint loan, had been one for $1,700 and not $1,600. He said so in his letter of that date. It is strange, too, that in his account (ex.20), 1913-1918, the sum received and paid in 1917 is entered at $1,700 and not $1,600, and in the corresponding interpolated ledger entry the figure first entered and then erased is $1,700 also.

Now, if their Lordships had to determine whether there ever were loans to these individuals they would find in these facts no sufficient justification for saying that there were not. But whether these loans continued as loans after 1903 or whether they subsisted in 1905 their Lordships would hesitate to affirm. The vagueness of Mr Hogg's knowledge of the men and of their security is natural enough if he had ceased to have anything to do with either for over 20 years; it is more difficult to understand if he had been on close terms with them continuously for 32 years up to 1917.

This, however, is not the question which the Board is now called upon to answer. All it is required to decide is whether Mr Hogg has discharged himself of this sum of $1,600 by a payment of $1,600 which he claims to have made to Lady Howland in March, 1917.[97]

Mrs. Campbell's accusation that the loan had never existed was clearly rejected. But her fallback position, that the loan might have existed during the early years of Hogg's trusteeship and been maintained on the books subsequently as a sham, was not. Indeed, the Law Lords had said they "would hesitate to affirm" Hogg's claim that the loans had continued after 1905. It was a cautious statement, a finding that was not really a finding at all. And then it was gently swept aside with the conclusion that the validity of the loan was "not the question" that was before the Privy Council. "Upon the issue so raised in its broadest aspect," noted the Law Lords, "their Lordships are not required to pronounce." It was with a clear sense of relief that the Law Lords turned instead to the matter of whether the $1,600 had ever been paid back. They found unequivocally, after reviewing a host of data, that it had not.[98]

This tone is prevalent throughout the decision. The Law Lords were surprised and chagrined over Hogg's management of Lady Howland's estate. They rejected Hogg's testimony as lacking credibility. They rolled back the findings of the Canadian judges affirming Hogg's accounts. They delicately hinted, with adept turns of phrase, that at least a part of the misdoing might have amounted to something more sinister than mere negligence. And then they backed off, stressing that they would be "slow to impugn" Hogg's *bona fides*.

Hogg served as trustee of his sister-in-law's estate from 1885 to 1922, presumably out of a sense of obligation to a dear family member. Was it common for family trustees to mismanage estate funds? Ironically, the Toronto General Trusts Corporation emphasized just that point when it sought to attract clients. "Instances in which widows, orphans and others interested in trust funds have incurred ruinous losses through the dishonesty, culpable carelessness or incompetency of the trustee to whom their affairs were entrusted" were, warned company brochures, "unhappily, matters of common experience."[99] That its own chairman might be embraced by such dire predictions would most certainly have shaken up the company promoters. However, it is also worth noting that throughout the thirty-seven-year period, Hogg never sought financial reimbursement for his efforts. It is quite possible that the work eventually began to seem like a thankless task, something that rankled and caused him to feel put upon. For all her social accomplishments, Lady Howland appears to have been a woman who believed that she was entitled to rely upon male family members to look after her, whether they wanted the responsibility or not. There is a sense from the judges' decisions that they, too, recognized the time and labour involved in managing Lady Howland's affairs. Might it have seemed to Hogg only fair recompense to borrow from the estate?

It may have started out with a few faked mortgages, with interest duly paid on time. Perhaps Hogg thought he could use Lady Howland's money more effectively himself. And it would be easier to fudge the accounts if proper records were not kept. The absence of accounts over time may have caused even more errors, as Hogg got more and more mixed up about what was owed to whom and when, until many of the boundaries collapsed between his own funds and Lady Howland's. When he was called to account for the moneys, Hogg appeared angry and dismissive. Initially he went into the legal proceedings unrepresented by counsel. As he became more and more flustered with the inquiry, he borrowed his niece's lawyer, only much later retaining his own. He seems to have been astonished that anyone would question his management of the estate, especially since Lady Howland had never done so during her lifetime. His responses to Slaght's cross-examination were as ill-informed and off-handed as his management of the estate had been. Then he dug in, and attempted to justify every transaction, even those that seem inexplicable.

Readers will ultimately draw their own conclusions, but we have in the final analysis opted to side with Arthur Slaght, who was convinced that instead of buying securities for Lady Howland, Hogg had "simply paid her interest on that money all down those years, and then pocketed the principal." Indeed, Slaght's final verdict, which carried the authoritative imprimatur of his considerable criminal law expertise, caused him to think others had served time in "the penitentiary" for nothing worse.[100]

Was There a Conspiracy?

Mrs. Campbell charged that she was victimized by "a concerted action of the Benchers and the Judges" designed to "white-wash" William Drummond Hogg. She asserted that Hogg would "'jolly well' be in jail" had he been "an ordinary mortal—say the fellow on the street, or you, or I—instead of being what he unfortunately was: a chairman of the foremost Trust Company of Canada and senior Bencher to boot."[101] It seems somewhat ingenuous for Mrs. Campbell to suggest that *she* would have been jailed just like the fellow on the street. Mrs. Campbell came from the same elite circle as Hogg and would most likely have benefited from the same beneficence that she claimed cradled Hogg and his affairs.

Mrs. Campbell's allegation of "concerted action" was also possibly overreaching. It conjures up images of groups of lawyers, judges, and trust company officials meeting privately in cloistered rooms at the Toronto Club, plotting how they might collectively assist Hogg to

Chief justices and judges of the Ontario Supreme Court, c. 1936

defeat Mrs. Campbell. Although the case undoubtedly inspired conversations among like-minded benchers, lawyers, and judges, it is far
more probable that the individuals Mrs. Campbell accused of behav-
ing improperly acted separately, unreflectively, even instinctively, to
protect one of their own against what they perceived to be an unfair
attack.

But Mrs. Campbell's larger charge, that Hogg was sheltered from
professional disgrace and legal sanction because of his stature in law
and society, requires careful consideration. A parallel question is
whether the mantle of protection also descended in reaction to Mrs.
Campbell's assertiveness. The majority of lawyers and judges who
came in contact with her seem to have been astonished at the ways in
which she breached customary gender boundaries—refusing to
follow the advice of counsel, standing up to judges, encroaching upon
the male bastion of professional legal practice. Their hostility may have
been premised, in part, on what they viewed as outlandish female
behaviour.[102] That powerful Ontario lawyers and judges would with-
hold legal services and judicial remedies because they could not toler-
ate a woman who insisted on pursuing her rights is as problematic as
any protective motivation extended on Hogg's behalf.

So what does the record reveal in terms of misconduct? According
to the evidence, one of the chief villains was the Toronto General
Trusts Corporation. As even the most supportive judges admitted,
Hogg's accounts were in terrible disarray when he turned the estate
over to the trust company. In the early years, the trust company was
undeniably remiss in its obligations to check into this.[103] In the later
phases, it spent substantial sums to litigate against a beneficiary of the
estate who sought to correct the errors that had resulted from the
desultory care of the estate.[104] On the surface of things, this is surprising. If anything, one might have thought that Lady Howland's estate
would be guarded with vigilance. Her family connections within the
tangled web of elite corporate, legal, and judicial society were notorious. Many of James Bethune's former law partners had served as
founding directors of the trust company, and some of these officials
had been guests at Mrs. Campbell's wedding.[105] Did Hogg's involvement override all the other historic corporate and professional linkages? Certainly Mrs. Campbell believed that it was significant that the
company president, Newton Wesley Rowell, was "one of Mr. Hogg's
fellow Benchers."[106] Indeed, the two men overlapped in their terms

from 1916 to 1936.[107] No doubt it was also a ticklish matter to check up on the records submitted by the trust company chairman. It was probably even more unheard of to take an adversarial legal position against the corporate chair. And the Toronto General Trusts Corporation, under Rowell's presidency, avoided doing so until it was impossible to do otherwise. The involvement of William Drummond Hogg seems to have had a serious impact on the manner in which the trust company fell down on the job.

Mrs. Campbell's treatment at the hands of judges illustrates a range of judicial response. It is widely recognized, of course, that judicial personalities differ, and that their court personae can vary substantially. Ontario Court of Appeal Justices William Renwick Riddell and William Edward Middleton, for example, were at polar ends of the judicial spectrum. Riddell was famous for his "sharp tongue" and "bitter sarcasm."[108] Middleton was equally renowned for his invariably polite and gentlemanly manner.[109] But Mrs. Campbell's experience with the judiciary occasionally strayed into more complicated territory. Two of the judges who sat on this case professed great personal friendship with Hogg. In the midst of the trial over Lady Howland's will, Judge Hugh Thomas Kelly of the Ontario Supreme Court became angry over a letter written by the Campbells casting aspersions on Hogg's management of the estate. He announced that "he had been a great friend of Mr. Hogg for forty years," and was "much shocked at seeing such a statement appearing about him."[110] Before his elevation to the bench, Kelly had served as president of the York County Law Association and of the Toronto Bar Association. In these capacities, he would have fostered many links with the benchers of the Law Society. Hogg's administration of the estate was not yet under litigation, but it was injudicious to make assertions such as this from the bench. Judge Kelly's friendship with Hogg seems to have predisposed him to rule against Mrs. Campbell.

Judge Kelly also took a visceral dislike to the plaintiff before him, pronouncing her to be a woman who had made "unwarranted attacks in her correspondence and in her evidence on reputable members of the legal profession, one a relative of the family, who performed useful and kindly business services for Lady Howland." Declaring Mrs. Campbell to be an "extreme," "excitable," and ultimately incredible witness, Judge Kelly stated that such unwarranted suspicions were "not conducive to the authenticity of her statements generally."[111] Mrs.

Hugh Thomas Kelly

Campbell was equally unimpressed with Judge Kelly, whom she describes as "very brusque, and often quite rude."[112] Clearly, the two rubbed each other the wrong way, and this affected the outcome of the litigation. But the critique of Hogg, which Judge Kelly refused to countenance, also underlay the face-off.

The second judicial figure with admitted ties to Hogg was Court of Appeal Judge Cornelius Arthur Masten. Judge Masten was quite open about this, announcing at the outset of the hearing that he was "a great friend of Mr. Hogg's," and that he had "formerly had dealings with him." His comments were deemed worthy of newspaper headlines, with reporters revealing that Masten had a "close friendship" with Hogg, and "had acted for him in a good many things."[113] D'Alton Lally McCarthy, who was representing Mrs. Campbell at this point, would later divulge in his draft autobiography that Judge Masten had actually spoken with him prior to the hearing: "He sent for me to tell me that he thought he should not take [the case], or at least that I should know he had been a student in Mr. Hogg's office and that he had the highest regard for his honest [sic] and integrity and suggested that I should have the hearing postponed."[114] McCarthy probably would also have known that Masten and Hogg had served together as benchers of the Law Society of Upper Canada. Masten had been elected in 1908 and served for at least three years of overlap with Hogg, until his judicial appointment in 1915.[115]

McCarthy spoke with his client about his meeting with Judge Masten, divulging the judge's connections with Hogg. However, he counselled Mrs. Campbell to continue before Judge Masten, as he admits in his draft autobiography: "I said I felt sure if the matter comes before him he will lean in your direction rather than be subject to being criticized for giving a finding in favour of Mr. Hogg with whom he had been in such close connection."[116] This advice turned out to be quite miscalculated. Things seem to have gone off the rails right at the outset, as indicated by Mrs. Campbell's description of Judge Masten's "caustic remarks" and "steely glance." Judge Masten gave substantial berth to Hogg's testimony, despite recognizing the very serious problems it created. Reporters disclosed that Judge Masten accepted that Hogg had made "mistakes," that his book entries showing "discrepancies" were "unsatisfactory," and that he had given "somewhat confusing evidence ... on his cross-examination." But in the final result, Judge Masten pronounced himself to have "no doubt

Cornelius Arthur Masten

regarding the substantial value of the services rendered by Mr. Hogg nor regarding the complete honesty of all his actions." He added, "if I were to allow this appeal I would be obliged to do so on the ground that Mr. Hogg was perjuring himself by inventing out of whole cloth the statement, clearly and circumstantially asserted by him, that the drafts from McAmmond and Martin were made out directly to Lady Howland and were personally handed by him to her when he visited St. Catharines on professional business."[117]

These were the very assertions the Privy Council would later reject, and over which the Law Lords came closest to pronouncing Hogg's misconduct as intentional. Yet Judge Masten would have none of it. According to the press, he declared himself unprepared to make a finding of perjury, and dismissed the appeal. Mrs. Campbell recounts similar statements about perjury during the argument. She notes that Judge Masten had exclaimed at the close of the hearing: "But, Mr. McCarthy, were I to disbelieve Mr. Hogg's words upon this branch of the case, I should be accusing him of perjury; and I couldn't do that, Mr. McCarthy, could I?"[118] Such statements suggest a measure of pre-judgment that was quite unfair. As with Judge Kelly, this seems to be another instance where personal contacts between Hogg and the judiciary substantially influenced the outcome of the legal proceedings.

Chief Justice Sir William Mulock was also probably far too personally involved in the case for any semblance of judicial impartiality. He had fewer connections with Hogg's side, the only linkage being his much earlier term on the board of directors of the Toronto General Trusts Corporation, but he was tied very closely to the Bethune, Howland, and Campbell families, being a long-standing friend of James Bethune and Lady Howland. Indeed, many members of Chief Justice Mulock's family had been represented at Mrs. Campbell's wedding, where his granddaughter had served as the flower girl. Mrs. Campbell even writes about how she prized the wedding gift the Mulocks had presented to her at the time. During the hearing, Chief Justice Mulock mentioned in open court that he had last seen Lady Howland in the dining room at the Welland Hotel, when their paths had crossed during his court session in St. Catharines.[119] Those concerned about judicial neutrality might well have feared that Chief Justice Mulock's ties to Mrs. Campbell's family would have helped her case. Yet this was far from Mrs. Campbell's sense of it.

Sir William Mulock

She complains bitterly of Chief Justice Mulock's repeated efforts to pressure her to settle. He halted the first Court of Appeal hearing just as Arthur Slaght was in full flight, insisting that the parties shift to settlement discussions under the supervision of the full bench the next afternoon. Mrs. Campbell depicts Mulock as "imposing" and using a "commanding voice." At one point, she even describes some "pounding of the table." For his part, Chief Justice Mulock called Mrs. Campbell "a pertinacious woman."[120] Chief Justice Mulock intervened again, after the second Court of Appeal decision had been issued granting Mrs. Campbell an additional $1,000 for the estate. He took the unusual step of inviting Mrs. Campbell up to his chambers to discuss the decision before reasons had been issued. He brought her into the chambers of Judges Grant, Hodgins, and Magee, all of whom attempted to dissuade Mrs. Campbell from appealing.[121] Judge William J. Anderson, writing about the case years later, would characterize it as "a most unusual effort."[122] It was quite possible that Chief Justice Mulock was dismayed at what he thought was a family squabble between three sisters over his long-time friend's estate. During one hearing, he was quoted as saying: "Is it not a shameful thing that the daughters of such parents as these should be fighting over the estate?"[123] While the chief justice's discomfort was perhaps understandable, subsequent litigation would show only too clearly that Mrs. Campbell's claims were legitimate and well founded. The chief justice's obvious embarrassment over litigation that involved close family friends stood in the way of Mrs. Campbell's right to have her dispute resolved judicially.

Judge Frank Egerton Hodgins was another judicial figure who behaved in peculiar ways. He, too, would have been very familiar with Hogg through professional linkages. Before his appointment to the bench, Hodgins had acted as the legal agent for the federal government in Toronto. In his early years of practice, Hogg had been partnered with Daniel O'Connor, K.C., who served as the chief legal agent for the federal government. Hodgins's term as bencher from 1910 to 1912 had also overlapped with Hogg's. And Hodgins consistently favoured Hogg's side of the case — from the appellate ruling that would be reversed by the Privy Council to the subsequent ruling over interest that wiped out most of Mrs. Campbell's award. The outburst with which Judge Hodgins greeted Mrs. Campbell's presence in his chambers after the 1929 Court of Appeal hearing was remarkable.

William Herbert Price

Mrs. Campbell had, after all, been sent there by Chief Justice Mulock after she drew his attention to the fact that Judge Hodgins had used evidence that had been withdrawn before the conclusion of the case. Instead of advising Mrs. Campbell that protestations such as these should be directed to her appeal record, the chief justice simply sent her to "'Brother Hodgins'' chambers to direct his attention to this oversight." Judge Hodgins was distraught at Mrs. Campbell's appearance—whether over the substance of the message, or that she had dared brave his doorway in person. According to Mrs. Campbell, he lost his temper, and with a raised voice and almost shaking his fist announced: "Leave my chambers at once and never dare to appear before me again, do you hear?"[124]

The situation deteriorated still further when Mrs. Campbell discovered that the transcript of her legal argument before the Court of Appeal had been removed from the record and sealed on the orders of Judge Hodgins, not to be opened "except by the instructions of the full Court." It is quite unusual that such a transcript existed; most often it was the evidence that was produced in transcript form. This transcript had been prepared by one of the judges' stenographers and had "by inadvertence" found its way into the record.[125] What was more unusual was that Judge Hodgins would maintain such a personal interest in Mrs. Campbell's case that he would have "descended from his chambers," demanded to see Mrs. Campbell's papers, and, on discovering the transcript, ordered it sealed. Mrs. Campbell's remonstrations to the chief justice and to Attorney General Price were to no avail.[126] When Mrs. Campbell went back to the Court of Appeal with a motion for delivery of the transcript, Judge Hodgins wrote the decision refusing her access. He also ordered costs against her on the motion, regardless of outcome of the Privy Council decision.[127] Mrs. Campbell perceived the entire sequence of unusual events to indicate that "someone wished to conceal something." Chief Justice Mulock's comment that this was "a very unwarranted expression of suspicion" seems a bit off the mark.[128]

Mrs. Campbell's difficulties were not restricted solely to judges; they extended to lawyers as well. The Ingersoll, Kingstone, and Seymour firm in St. Catharines drew and executed Lady Howland's will, and then mislaid all copies, failed to keep records of how the documents had been removed from the law firm vaults, and denied ever having drawn such a will regardless of substantial evidence to the

Arthur Courtney Kingstone

contrary. This was surprisingly sloppy legal practice.[129] Strachan Johnston's legal representation of Mrs. Campbell was even more astonishing. He failed to file the copy of Lady Howland's will for probate, despite undertaking to do so. Then he ignored his client's inquiries about the estate, all the while allowing the sisters and the trust company to take out papers of administration as if no will existed. When Mrs. Campbell confronted him in person in Toronto, embarrassed and defensive he responded that he had acted as he "thought best."[130] Was this the type of service that prominent Ontario counsel customarily offered to the paying public in the early twentieth century? To clients of the stature and class of Lady Howland and Mrs. Campbell? One would be loath to accept such an assessment. Mrs. Campbell clearly suspected that the breaches of solicitor-client obligation had more to do with Arthur Courtney Kingstone's professional relationship with her sister, Cora Ann Lindsey, as well as the presence of Reginald Holland Parmenter, the brother-in-law and "very dear friend" of Kingstone's, on the Tilley, Johnston law firm roster.[131]

Determined to "break away from the rotten old family compact," Mrs. Campbell chose as her next lawyer Arthur Graeme Slaght, who was not related by birth or marriage to any of the grand old families of Ontario law. While everyone extolled Slaght's extraordinary courtroom skills, he was also viewed as "a bit of an upstart." Arthur Slaght had a reputation as a bon vivant, a hedonist, and a charming lady's man who was often depicted as "living on the edge of scandal." Elected to the federal Parliament in 1935 to represent Parry Sound, Slaght was soon dubbed "the Beau Brummel of the Commons."[132] This may explain some of Mrs. Campbell's apparent fascination with Slaght's mannerisms and personality. She seems to have been captivated by her magnetic counsel, and deeply devastated when he resigned the brief.

Of all the lawyers who represented Mrs. Campbell, Slaght seems to have done the best job. Mrs. Campbell writes glowingly about his mesmerizing litigation skills, and she considered his early efforts on her behalf to be outstanding. Of his failure to call Hogg back to the witness stand for cross-examination on Exhibit 44-A, an omission that ultimately cost Mrs. Campbell substantially before the Privy Council, she was uncharacteristically restrained in critique. Her main concern appears to have been the possibility that Slaght would be intimidated by the more powerful lawyers and judges who thought the case better abandoned. Mrs. Campbell's suspicion that her "eagle's wings" had

Reginald Holland Parmenter

Arthur Graeme Slaght

been "clipped" during the settlement discussions at the Court of Appeal was likely unfounded. Slaght was no stranger to rough-and-tumble negotiations, given his extensive background in the adversarial world of politics and his years at the litigation bar. He was not the sort of lawyer who would have been easily intimidated. Slaght may well have felt he had no alternative to settlement, given the clear message from the judges that, in their opinion, his client's case lacked merit.

That Slaght might have sold her out in return for more votes in the bencher election, which Mrs. Campbell intimates, seems highly unlikely. It is true that Slaght barely slipped past the cut-off; in the 1926 election he squeaked through in last place. However, it is improbable that Slaght's votes did not come as part of the ordinary electoral process. A barrister of Slaght's reputation would have been a strong candidate for bencher. Judges did not vote, and it is improbable that they would have been making calls to the lawyers who appeared before them soliciting votes for a particular candidate in an election they did not control. Thousands of lawyers voted in the election. That the results of the election were made known within a day or so after the settlement also suggests that the timing would not have allowed for any substantial vote-swaying.[133]

The most serious questions about Slaght's behaviour relate to his resignation from the case. One of the reasons he offered was that the litigation would cost money that Mrs. Campbell could not afford. Slaght's substantial fees were a matter of some repute, and he may simply have felt that the value of the case did not justify litigation. Lady Howland's estate was registered at $17,450 at her death. Since there is no way of ascertaining how much larger the estate would have been had Hogg dealt properly with the assets, it would have been difficult to evaluate the cost implications fully. The second reason Slaght offered was the status of Mr. Hogg. He advised Mrs. Campbell that it was "distasteful," "unsavory," and "nasty" to attack a "senior Bencher and a man of high standing." He told Mrs. Campbell that his legal friends had "reproached him bitterly for attacking Mr. Hogg."[134] Sentiments such as these would be echoed by other lawyers Mrs. Campbell approached, including Lally McCarthy, who also resigned from the file. Indeed, Hogg's counsel, William Ridout Wadsworth, expressed the opinion in open court that "no solicitor could make the charges against Mr. Hogg" that Mrs. Campbell sought to make.[135] Statements such as these suggest that Hogg's stature within the legal community did indeed wreak havoc on Mrs. Campbell's ability to pursue her legitimate estate claim.

D'Alton Lally McCarthy was the final lawyer to take on Mrs. Campbell's case. Slaght had advised her to retain "some counsel with prestige," and McCarthy was nothing if not prestigious. Born into a famous legal family, McCarthy found his early years filled with "wealth and prominence," debutante parties, riding to hounds, and trips to Europe. Margaret Mary Robinson, his wife, came from the same elite circles as Mrs. Campbell, for she was the daughter of Sir John Beverley Robinson, the former chief justice of Upper Canada. McCarthy began practice with McCarthy, Osler, Hoskin and Creelman, and then founded the elite firm of McCarthy and McCarthy with his cousins. A bencher from 1924 to 1941, McCarthy would also serve as the president of the Canadian Bar Association and the treasurer of the Law Society of Upper Canada, from 1939 to 1944. Mrs. Campbell had indeed returned to the "family compact."[136]

At the outset Mrs. Campbell found McCarthy to be "courteous and kind," a lawyer who "seemed to understand and sympathize." Mrs. Campbell noted the generous remarks McCarthy made about the close friendship between their two fathers, and almost resigned herself to having lost Slaght. Within short order, however, she found a change in McCarthy's attitude. "He was not so keen, not so sympathetic," and he seemed to lose patience with the level of direction that Mrs. Campbell wished to assume over the pleadings. Mrs. Campbell attributed this to loaded dice within "the legal fraternity."[137] Was this fair?

McCarthy seemed first to be surprised, and then to chafe, at Mrs. Campbell's command of her own case and her desire to be intimately involved in its progress. When she drew his attention to what she felt was a "shocking spot in Mr. Hogg's testimony before the Surrogate Court," he took umbrage, asserting that the judge wouldn't "be at all interested in that, Mrs. Campbell." When the hearing began, the relationship unravelled further. Concerned about the way the case was going, time and again Mrs. Campbell would stop McCarthy to put documents into his hands and point out certain important passages in the evidence.[138] One can imagine the consternation of a counsel as esteemed as McCarthy when repeatedly and publicly chastised and directed by his female client. These passages show Mrs. Campbell at her most difficult, even as the stereotypical querulous law client. It was certainly unseemly to behave like this in the courtroom, and it

D'Alton Lally McCarthy

was unlikely to have endeared her to the bench or improved her prospects legally.

On the other hand, Mrs. Campbell may have been right about her assessment of McCarthy's advocacy. The brilliant litigator John Robinette would later reminisce about McCarthy's hit-and-miss approach to cases. McCarthy was "full of wit, bright, but despised preparation," recalled Robinette. "He would pick up the case a day or so before it was coming on for hearing, and have [his juniors] tell him all about it, and he would be ready." One of his most famous faux pas came in a case where he began arguing the wrong side, and when alerted by a junior, continued right on, "saying imperturbably that that would be his opponent's argument and these were the reasons to reject it."[139]

Fortunately for posterity, McCarthy was one of the few people involved with Mrs. Campbell's case who recorded his perspectives on it.[140] The relevant passages of McCarthy's draft autobiography, housed with the Law Society Archives, began with accolades about James Bethune, whom he "recognized as one of the ablest lawyers at the Ontario Bar," and who was "on the very best of terms" with his own father. McCarthy reminisces about how Bethune and his father would travel together "on the same ship" to attend the sittings of the Privy Council. He claims that when Mrs. Campbell first came to ask him to argue the appeal, he had "no idea" that James Bethune's widow had married Sir William Howland, or that Hogg, "a well known solicitor in Ottawa," was Lady Howland's brother-in-law. When Mrs. Campbell asked him to take on the appeal, McCarthy advised her that it would be better for Slaght to continue, as "he knew all about the case, the facts and circumstances in connection with the matter." He also explained the "difficulty" he would have taking on the case, because he and Hogg were "fellow-Benchers," while "Mr. Slaght had not at that time been elected a Bencher." In this statement, of course, McCarthy is mistaken. Slaght had been elected in April 1926, and the appeal did not take place until December 1927. Nevertheless, McCarthy recounts that Mrs. Campbell "induced" him to "take the brief."

According to McCarthy, he had no particular problem with Mrs. Campbell until Judge Masten's decision was delivered. Mrs. Campbell was apparently quite "indignant" and expressed her regret that she had "allowed that old fool of a man to hear the case." McCarthy notes that

Judge Masten "happened to be a great personal friend," and that he "vehemently resented Mrs. Campbell's remarks." He told her right off that he would "prefer to be relieved of all responsibility." His autobiographical remarks continue:

> [Mrs. Campbell] describes the situation in the book which she wrote "Where Angels Fear to Tread" ... She describes my attitude as follows: "Mr. McCarthy peered at me over his glasses (at that time I did not wear glasses), his face was very nearly purple. One could see the muscles twitching. He did not relish his task." This picture is far from the truth, for never at any time had I any other attitude for Mrs. Campbell than pity and sorrow. I did everything in my power to help her, but in view of the remarks she made to me about Mr. Masten I told her very plainly that I would like to be relieved of the matter and she was free to get whatever Solicitor she might be advised.
>
> She further goes on to say that after this short controversy I sharply rang my bell (again I have to contradict Mrs. Campbell, because I had no bell in my room) and Mr. West answered the summons. It is certainly true I turned over her papers to her at the time and was much relieved to be rid of the case under the circumstances, which was not a pleasant one; besides which, Mrs. Campbell told me she was without funds to carry on the proceeding.[141]

McCarthy explains that Mrs. Campbell was helped to launch her own appeal, "through the kindness of the different officials at Osgoode Hall and some members of the Bar." He notes that he and Arthur Slaght "actually went in and sat behind her" during the argument at the Court of Appeal, "and helped her in every way we could." In fact, McCarthy credits himself with giving Mrs. Campbell the very idea of appealing to the Privy Council:

> On the very day judgment was given I happened to be walking in the Queen Street gates at Osgoode Hall when Mrs. Campbell was coming out. She was excited but greeted me pleasantly, and I then said to her: "I don't think you will ever win this case unless you get to the Privy Council." She then asked me how that could be accomplished. I told her the practice was

comparatively simple but it meant a very considerable outlay in cash, which she would have to face, because I did not think any Ontario Solicitor would be anxious to undertake her case even as a speculation, with concurrent findings of two Canadian courts against her on a comparatively simple question of fact.[142]

McCarthy is quite dismissive of Mrs. Campbell's efforts before the Privy Council. He notes that although he "was sorry to have missed the argument," his friend Tilley had heard it all:

The court was not a very strong one, but apparently Lord Blanesborough [sic], seeing Mrs. Campbell's embarrassment, almost took the argument out of her hands, with the result, as we all know, she succeeded in her appeal. Whether she gained anything as a matter of money, I do not know, but we all remember how for months she paraded up and down Bay Street with placards front and back, condemning the Toronto General Trusts Corporation for some alleged wrong-doing, I assume in carrying out the judgment of the Privy Council ... Lord Blanesborough ... will probably be remembered as being the Law Lord who took the famous Mrs. Campbell's brief ... Thanks to Lord Blanesborough's efforts she won her case in England, in which she had failed out here. I took the brief for her before Mr. Justice Masten in single court, but she could never afford to pay counsel. She took her own case. It was I who advised her to go direct to the Privy Council, and if any of you have had the luck to read the book which she wrote, you will observe I got full credit for that.[143]

Indeed, McCarthy underscores how "fortunate" he had been to get a copy of the book, which he "deeply prize[d]."

The factual discrepancies over glasses and bell suggest some sloppiness in Mrs. Campbell's recounting of events, but no more than McCarthy's faulty recollection of the date of Slaght's election as bencher, his mistaking Lord Blanesburgh for "Lord Blanesborough," and his incorrect notation about the publication details of *Where Angels Fear to Tread,* which he erroneously indicates was printed at "Alvinston Street" rather than "Alveston Street." Mrs. Campbell did indeed credit McCarthy with knowing his judges well when he told her: "Never short of the Privy Council, never on this side of the water, can you win this case." And although it was Slaght whom she recalled passing helpful notes to her during the argument, she did concede that McCarthy had congratulated her for arguing "splendidly."[144] She did not, however, recollect anything about McCarthy advising her as to the procedure or cost. These were matters she laboriously taught herself from Bentwich. McCarthy's comments about Mrs. Campbell's impecuniousness seem a trifle odd, given the sizeable bill she had settled with him for his professional services. McCarthy's dismissal of Mrs. Campbell's efforts at the Privy Council, his paternalistic assessment that she could never have won without the intercession of one of the Law Lords, and his sarcastic depiction of her "parad[ing] up and down" with "placards front and back," carry a discernible measure of defensiveness. Most important of all, however, is McCarthy's admission that Hogg's status as a bencher made him extremely reluctant to take the case. One of the fundamental premises behind a self-regulating, monopolistic legal profession is that clients in need of representation have access to legal services. That so many of those involved with this case spoke openly of their disapproval of Mrs. Campbell's legal actions is of grave concern. It adds further weight to the growing body of evidence that Hogg's stature insulated him from legal attack.

The manner in which the Law Society processed the disciplinary complaints about Hogg adds still further indicia of protectionist treatment. Mrs. Campbell lodged two separate complaints seeking to have Hogg disbarred for "conduct unbecoming." The 1931 complaint languished in committee for two and a half years, never to see the light of day. When Mrs. Campbell renewed her complaint in 1934, the Law Society's explanation for the stall was that she had been asked for "particulars" and had failed to provide them. Yet Mrs. Campbell had filed extensive material in 1931. She had produced the notice of motion filed earlier with the Ontario Supreme Court, itemizing Hogg's wrongdoing with respect to the estate, recording the Privy Council decision against him, and indicating that he had yet to pay the judgment ordered. She had also filed the documentation that was before Chief Justice Rose when he ordered the enforcement of the Privy Council judgment in 1930. The Law Society never stipulated what, if anything, further was required. Instead, the benchers finally dismissed the case in October 1934, because the matter was "before the courts." The explanation was confusing, since the criminal charges against

Hogg had been dismissed in February 1934 and the only outstanding litigation involved the trust company's claim against the estate for costs and fees. Hogg's misconduct was not before any other tribunal.

Historical research on the disciplinary practices of the legal profession is still in its infancy, but early indications suggest that one's race, class, and stature within the legal profession were critical variables. American studies illustrate that elite lawyers rarely believed that the ethics codes applied to them. They drafted rules against solicitation of clients and misappropriation of funds in order to "stamp out the practices of the new generation of immigrant lawyers." The leaders at the bar were almost never disciplined, protected by unspoken assumptions that exempted their "noble endeavours" from the rules they were enforcing against others.[145] In Ontario, disciplinary records show that lawyers were typically called to account for soliciting clients, advertising, and "ambulance chasing." Lawyers of Jewish, African, and other ethnic origins, who were thought to be "overly zealous," were frequently singled out.[146]

Disciplinary activity picked up substantially in the 1930s, in part because of the economic pressures of the Depression. That decade, the Law Society disbarred eighty-five members, four times the number in the previous decade. The majority were struck off the rolls for stealing from clients, often by dipping into their clients' trust funds.[147] Despite this, the Law Society opposed increasing calls that lawyers be bonded for the protection of the public. Benchers argued that bonding would give clients a false sense of security and impose a burden on honest solicitors to pay for the defaults of the dishonest. It was not until 1936 that the Law Society would finally require members to deposit moneys they held for clients into trust accounts separate from their own, and to keep records that could be audited in suspicious cases.[148]

The records filed by Mrs. Campbell proved Hogg to be in serious dereliction of professional duties regarding trust funds. Hogg was never called upon to produce a response to the complaints. Should he have been? There was no tradition of disciplining lawyers for negligence or incompetence, and the Law Society may have felt that, given the Privy Council's reluctance to find Hogg guilty of an advertent breach of trust, there was no disciplinary mandate. And although the disciplinary committee made no reference to this, it may also have been relevant that Hogg had taken on the administration of Lady Howland's estate as a relative, not as a practising lawyer. It does appear, however, that the Law Society's treatment of the complaints was affected by Hogg's status as a long-time bencher who had sat for years on the disciplinary committee. That Newton Wesley Rowell, K.C., was chair of the discipline committee that exonerated Hogg is also surprising. For the president of the trust company so implicated in the estate dispute to presume to sit as chair on a disciplinary complaint arising from the matter seems to be a clear violation of natural justice.

Are Mrs. Campbell's allegations of conspiracy borne out by the evidence? One could argue that certain of her criticisms are unwarranted or overstated.[149] And at points, she writes positively about the kindness and assistance extended to her by specific lawyers, clerks, and judges.[150] Yet, at the core, there is strong evidence that many of the powerful lawyers and judges who came into contact with Mrs. Campbell's case behaved in unethical and unconscionable ways. As Peter Newcombe sums it up: "the benchers used to protect their own."[151] Some of the lawyers and judges simply refused to believe that a man of William Drummond Hogg's stature could have behaved negligently or unscrupulously. Influenced by long-standing friendships and professional connections, they disregarded clear evidence of financial mismanagement and blocked Mrs. Campbell's efforts to seek legitimate redress. Some seem to have been motivated by desire to protect a member of the legal elite from public censure. As Judge William Nassau Ferguson put it: "This affair is a nasty business, it gives us all a black eye, don't you see?"[152] Others seem to have been motivated by blatant hostility toward Mrs. Campbell, a woman who refused to stay within the confines of respectable upper-class femininity.

What Price Victory?

By any account, Mrs. Campbell came out victorious at the Privy Council. The flurry of press coverage that greeted her foray into the upper echelon of this sanctified inner circle of law suggests how spectacular Mrs. Campbell's accomplishment was for the time. Front-page headlines acclaimed her the "first woman ever privileged to appear before the highest court in the empire to fight her own cause."[153] Mrs. Campbell was elated: "It is a glorious feeling to realize that there is no other court to go to," she told the London *Daily Herald*. "All must abide by a Privy Council decision. Mine was the appeal to Caesar."[154]

William Nassau Ferguson

Elation suffuses the opening and closing of *Where Angels Fear to Tread,* where the euphoria of victory simply leaps off the pages.

But one must assess the very real celebratory prescriptions against the price Mrs. Campbell paid to achieve success. Litigants occasionally become psychologically enveloped by their cases, to the exclusion of all else. Mrs. Campbell is an extreme example. Anything short of that level of obsession likely would not have launched her all the way through to the Privy Council. But in many ways and for quite some years, she appears to have taken on the aura of the "Privy Council Portia" as her primary persona. Mrs. Campbell's immersion in her case must have had a transformative effect on her personality, accentuating characteristics that were already there, as well as adding new ones. The qualities that assist one in litigation of this nature — relentlessness, single-mindedness, intensity, self-absorption — are not necessarily ones that are socially endearing.

Years away from home and family, estrangement from siblings, financial debt, and long periods of intense stress undoubtedly took a toll on Mrs. Campbell. The seemingly endless legal proceedings in the wake of the Privy Council ruling must have accentuated all these problems. Mrs. Campbell became increasingly embittered between 1930 and 1935. Her multiple efforts to have Hogg disbarred and prosecuted criminally suggest a level of recrimination that was absent earlier. At points after her return from England, Mrs. Campbell became so distraught over the prolonged litigation and the rulings of the Canadian courts that she threatened to return to the Privy Council to plead her case anew.[155] There were no avenues back to England at this point, but Mrs. Campbell's comments suggest a level of frustration that had begun to erode the rapture of the earlier victory. Interestingly, she says little about these problems in *Where Angels Fear to Tread.* Mrs. Campbell completed her manuscript in 1935 and published it in 1940. She could have written at some length about her ongoing tribulations but, apart from the briefest of remarks about the efforts to collect interest, she made little mention of the lengthy post-Privy Council litigation, and none about her picketing. Had these receded in her mind, dwarfed by the significance of the Privy Council victory? Or did she wish to record for posterity that the Privy Council litigation had always been the fundamental issue?

Then there was the question of monetary recompense. Hogg was eventually forced to pay the $7,027.34 awarded by the Privy Council.

From the perspective of the early twenty-first century, this is a relatively small amount for all the effort, although the judges at the time referred to it as "a very substantial sum," and efforts to adjust for inflation suggest that the award was closer to $52,000 in today's currency.[156] The amount was supplemented by 5 percent interest compounded annually.[157] The cold reality was that by the time the Toronto General Trusts Corporation came to distribute the estate, the money had dwindled to approximately $2,000.[158] Mrs. Campbell never fully recovered the costs incurred in the litigation, and although no surviving records quantify these, there must have been substantial losses here.[159] The Toronto *Star* confirmed that Mrs. Campbell was well aware of this, advising that she had been "fighting more for principle than profit."[160] Peter Campbell Brooks recalls his mother saying that there "was not much money left by the end of the case," and that the family characterized it as "really a moral victory" rather than a financial one.[161] Arthur Slaght's concern that the lawsuit did not warrant the cost was ultimately borne out, although no one could have predicted anything like the totality of the costs that attended the five years of litigation after 1930.

With the winding down of the legal jousting, the chief protagonists finally untangled themselves and went their separate ways. The Toronto General Trusts Corporation began to lose its prominence as "Canada's first trust company" when competitors such as Royal Trust, Montreal Trust, and National Trust opened their doors and intensified the competition. Its president, Newton Wesley Rowell, resigned in 1934. His involvement in Mrs. Campbell's case had done nothing to mar his future. He was elevated to the prestigious post of treasurer of the Law Society in 1935, and appointed chief justice of Ontario in 1936. He died shortly after Hogg, at the age of seventy-four, on 22 November 1941.[162] By 1961, the Toronto General Trusts Corporation merged with Canada Permanent Trust Company, a former bank that had taken on trust activities in 1913. In 1986 the merged corporation was purchased by Canada Trust, which was subsequently acquired by the Toronto Dominion Bank in 1999.[163]

William Drummond Hogg seems never to have recovered from the notoriety of the case. He must have been appalled at the unremitting press coverage of every stage of the proceedings, and at the effusive public celebration that surrounded his reversal at the Privy Council. He stopped attending bencher meetings and slowly withdrew from

Frederick Drummond Hogg

practice. The only respite came when his son Frederick Drummond Hogg was appointed to the Trial Division of the Supreme Court of Ontario in 1935.[164] The stain that had tarnished Hogg Senior's professional reputation had not dulled his son's judicial prospects. One wonders whether the appointment also reflected ongoing sympathy for Hogg Senior within powerful legal and political echelons.[165] With the appointment of his son to the bench, Hogg's law firm dissolved, and he retired.[166] It must have seemed an ignominious end to an illustrious career. His wife, Agnes, had died in 1932, in the middle of the protracted family litigation, and Hogg moved in with relatives until his death on 2 January 1940. He was impecunious at death, with an estate worth less than $4,000, of which more than $2,000 was in the form of life insurance.[167] Efforts to track down senior members of the Ottawa bar who knew Hogg personally have proven unsuccessful, as have attempts to locate any living descendants.[168] Hogg's obituary described him in glowing terms, at age ninety-two as "Ottawa's oldest lawyer" and "one of Canada's outstanding members of the legal profession."[169]

As for Mrs. Campbell, after the death of her husband in the spring of 1943, she moved to an apartment at 88 Exeter Street in Boston, where she lived for the rest of her life. She soon lost touch with everyone from St. John's Episcopal Church except Susan Revere Chapin, who remained a steadfast friend. She travelled occasionally to Europe, and visited with her grown children and only grandchild in New York and California. The ties between Mrs. Campbell and her son, daughter-in-law, and daughter became strained over the years, but she remained close to her grandson.[170] Peter Campbell Brooks recalls going to movies, museums, and restaurants with his grandmother, but found her passion for British heritage somewhat overwhelming: "Every Christmas she would give me a present, typically a book about the clans and tartans of Scotland, or biographies of illustrious figures of the British Empire."[171] Mrs. Campbell remained "hale and hearty" until her death in Boston at the age of seventy-five, in January 1956. To the end, she treasured the memories of her Privy Council victory. After she was deceased, her family discovered in her apartment carefully preserved copies of all the legal documents and all her press clippings about the case, as well as numerous copies of *Where Angels Fear to Tread*.[172]

APPENDIX:
SEQUENCE OF LEGAL PROCEEDINGS

The following list chronicles the majority of the legal matters heard in Mrs. Campbell's estate litigation.

Cause: Application by Mrs. Lindsey to declare Lady Howland incapable of managing her own affairs, and to appoint Toronto General Trusts Corporation committee of Lady Howland's estate and Mrs. Lindsey and Mrs. McDougald committee of her person.
Court: Supreme Court of Ontario, William Edward Middleton, J.
Date of decision: 6 October 1922, unreported.
Result: Order granted.

Cause: Trial on the revocation of Lady Howland's will.
Court: Supreme Court of Ontario, Hugh Thomas Kelly, J.
Date of decision: 20 October 1925, unreported.
Result: Decision that will was revoked.

Cause: Appeal of decision of Kelly, J., on the revocation of Lady Howland's will.
Court: First Appellate Division, Ontario Court of Appeal, Mulock, C.J.; Hodgins, Magee, Ferguson, Smith, JJ.A.
Date of decision: n/a.
Result: Settled, according to press coverage 7 May 1926.

Cause: W.D. Hogg seeks to pass accounts under the Trustee Act.
Court: Carleton County Surrogate Court, James Arthur Mulligan, J.
Date of decision: 21 October 1927, unreported.
Result: Decision largely accepting Hogg's accounts.

Cause: Appeal and cross-appeal from Mulligan, J.'s, passing of Hogg's accounts.
Court: Single judge sitting as ad hoc judge of High Court of Ontario, Cornelius Arthur Masten, J.
Date of decision: 19 December 1927, unreported.
Result: Decision to dismiss Mrs. Campbell's claims, except for the addition of $1,155. Dismissed Hogg's cross-appeal for costs. Subsequently tried to withdraw judgment to reopen case.

Cause: Appeal from Masten, J.'s, decision on Hogg's accounts.
Court: Ontario Court of Appeal, Mulock, C.J.; Magee, Hodgins, Ferguson, Grant, JJ.A.
Date of decision: 19 November 1928, unreported, details no longer survive.
29 November 1928, superseding 19 November 1928, summary of which is reported as *Re Howland* (1928), 35 O.W.N. 175 (C.A.).
18 March 1929, unreported.
Result: 29 November 1928: Majority decision written by Hodgins, J.A., affirmed Masten, J.'s, judgment but disallowed the $1,155 as an error and added $1,000 as "more satisfactory ending to the case." Magee, J.A., dissenting, would have allowed the appeal and sent the case back to the Surrogate Court for reconsideration upon further evidence.
18 March 1929: An order instructing that a memorandum be attached to reasons for judgment stating that Mrs. Cora Ann Lindsey had withdrawn her memorandum prior to argument.

Cause: Motion brought by Mrs. Campbell for allowance of security upon proposed appeal and for an order admitting the appeal.
Court: Ontario Court of Appeal, Mulock, C.J.; Magee, Hodgins, Middleton, JJ.A.
Date of decision: 1 February 1929, summary of decision reported as *Re Howland* (1929), 35 O.W.N. 319 (C.A.).
Result: Court admitted the appeal.

Cause: Motions brought by Mrs. Campbell for delivery of a transcript of the argument on appeal, and for an order declaring Cora A. Lindsey to be a party to the appeal to the Privy Council.
Court: Ontario Court of Appeal, Mulock, C.J.; Fisher, Hodgins, and Magee, JJ.A.
Date of decision: 18 March 1929, summary of decision regarding motion to make the sister a party was reported as *Re Howland* (1929), 36 O.W.N. 53 (C.A.).
Result: Decision refusing both motions written by Hodgins, J.A.

Cause: Appeal of Ontario Court of Appeal decision on Hogg's accounts.
Court: Judicial Committee of the Privy Council, Lord Blanesburgh, Lord Tomlin, Lord Russell of Killowen.

Date of decision: 1 May 1930, reported as *Campbell* v. *Hogg,* [1930] 3 D.L.R. 673 (P.C.).
Result: Decision found Hogg was a trustee who had retained trust funds in the amount of $7,027.34.

Cause: Motion by Toronto General Trusts Corporation for an order for leave to issue execution against Hogg for $7,027.34.
Court: Ontario High Court, Clarence Garrow, J.
Date of decision: 17 September 1930, reported as *Re Howland* (1930), 33 O.W.N. 78 (High Court).
Result: Dismissed motion, advising parties they would have to commence an action.

Cause: Appeal and cross-appeal brought by Mrs. Campbell and Mr. Hogg of costs awarded by taxing officer A.J. McGillivray regarding the previous litigation.
Court: Carleton County Surrogate Court, Edward J. Daly, J.
Date of decision: Unknown, unreported.
Result: Disallowed Mrs. Campbell accountants' fees and Arthur Slaght's legal fees.

Cause: Appeal by Mrs. Campbell of Daly, J.'s, decision on costs.
Court: Ontario High Court, Hugh Edward Rose, C.J.
Date of decision: 12 November 1930, reported as *Re Howland: Re Campbell and Hogg* (1930), 39 O.W.N. 292 (High Court).
Result: Upheld disallowance of accountants' fees but restored portion of legal fees.

Cause: Statement of claim by Toronto General Trusts Corporation asking for judgment against Mr. Hogg for $7,027.34 found by the certificate of the judgment of the Judicial Committee.
Court: Ontario High Court, Hugh Edward Rose, C.J.
Date of decision: 13 November 1930, reported as *Toronto General Trusts Corporation* v. *Hogg* (1930), 39 O.W.N. 296 (High Court).
Result: Judgment for the plaintiffs on the principal of $7,027.34 with interest from the date of the Privy Council order, and right to proceed to trial in respect of the larger claim for back interest.

Cause: Appeal by Mr. Hogg of Rose, C.J.'s, decision on costs.
Court: Ontario Court of Appeal, Latchford, C.J.; Riddell, Orde, and Fisher, JJ.A.
Date of decision: 6 March 1931, reported as *Re Howland, Re Campbell & Hogg,* [1932] 3 D.L.R. 623 (Ontario Court of Appeal).
Result: Decision that the Court of Appeal had no jurisdiction to overrule a Surrogate Court taxation of costs, setting aside Rose, C.J.'s, decision and restoring Daly, J.'s, order for costs.

Cause: Notice of motion by Mrs. Campbell for disbarment of Mr. Hogg for conduct unbecoming.
Court: Ontario Supreme Court.
Date of decision: Notice dated 9 June 1931, scheduled for hearing 17 June 1931, no further details regarding date of decision.
Result: Unknown, presumably dismissed.

Cause: Action taken by Toronto General Trusts Corporation to recover interest.
Court: Ontario High Court, Nicol Jeffrey, J.
Date of decision: 26 March 1932, reported as *Toronto General Trusts Co. v. Hogg* (1932), 41 O.W.N. 102 (High Court).
Result: Order that Mr. Hogg pay interest in the amount of $17,250.40.

Cause: Appeal by Mr. Hogg from the decision of Jeffrey, J., on interest.
Court: Ontario Court of Appeal, Mulock, C.J.; Magee, Riddell, Masten, and Orde, JJ.A.
Date of decision: 7 April 1932, reported as *Toronto General Trusts Co. v. Hogg,* [1932] 4 D.L.R. 465 (Ontario Court of Appeal).
Result: Decision vacating the order of Jeffrey, J., on interest, and ordering a reference to the master of the Supreme Court of Ontario to ascertain what sum was due based on further evidence.

Cause: Appeal by Mr. Hogg of the Ontario Court of Appeal decision on interest.
Court: Supreme Court of Canada, Duff, C.J.C.; Lamont, Smith, Crocket, and Hughes, JJ.
Date of decision: 28 June 1933, reported as *Hogg v. Toronto General Trusts Corp.,* [1933] 3 D.L.R. 721 (S.C.C.).

Result: Appeal dismissed, matter referred back to master of Supreme Court of Ontario.

Cause: Reference to the master to ascertain interest.
Court: Supreme Court of Ontario, assistant master O.E. Lennox.
Date of decision: 26 October 1933, unreported.
Result: Ruling that Mrs. Campbell was entitled to interest at the rate of 5 percent compounded yearly.

Cause: Presentation by Toronto General Trusts Corporation of bill of costs, requesting payment out of the estate of Lady Howland.
Court: York County Surrogate Court, John Tytler, J.
Date of decision: Unknown, but before end of September 1934, unreported.
Result: Order directing that costs be paid out of the estate.

Cause: Appeal by Mrs. Campbell of Tytler, J.'s, order directing costs be paid out of the estate.
Court: Ontario High Court of Justice, John Millar McEvoy, J.
Date of decision: 29 September 1934, reported as *Re Howland,* [1934] O.W.N. 555 (High Court).
Result: Decision allowing appeal, costs not to be paid out of the estate.

Cause: Criminal charges of forgery, false pretences, theft, and perjury brought by Mrs. Campbell against Mr. Hogg.
Court: Ottawa Police Court, Deputy Magistrate M.J. O'Connor.
Date of decision: Unknown, unreported, but covered in press on 13 October 1934.
Result: Charges dismissed.

Cause: Appeal by Toronto General Trusts Corporation of McEvoy, J's, decision disallowing costs to be paid out of the estate.
Court: Ontario Court of Appeal, William Renwick Riddell, J.A.
Date of decision: 18 June 1935, reported as *Re Howland,* [1935] O.W.N. 340 (Court of Appeal).
Result: Decision allowing appeal, reinstating decision to permit trust company to take its costs out of the estate.

NOTES

All page references to *Where Angels Fear to Tread* are to the pagination in this publication.

1 Even though all the copies of the book that we have been able to obtain show a publication date of 1940, there may be more than one edition. David A. Mittell recollected an earlier publication in 1935, the year he graduated from Roxbury Latin and entered Harvard University; see correspondence from Mittell to Rev. Henry W. Sherrill, 7 April 1997 (copy on file with authors). Brendan O'Brien remembers that the original book he read contains some information that was not in the final version. Interview with Brendan O'Brien, by Constance Backhouse and Nancy Backhouse, Toronto, 13 April 2001 (copy on file with authors). The possibility of more than one edition is also supported by several of the people we interviewed, who remember reading two distinct versions of *Where Angels Fear to Tread,* one of which was considerably less professional in binding and appearance than the 1940 publication. The 1940 printing encompassed both softcover and hardcover versions. Katharine Cipolla, parish historian at St. John's Episcopal Church, advised that one of the copies she located was numbered "#x out of 1,000," which led her to believe that one thousand copies were published. Whether this constitutes the total number published or merely the print run for the first, or second, edition, is unclear. Katharine Cipolla indicated that she had no information regarding who published the book, what the cost was, or who paid for the publication.

It appears that Mrs. Campbell distributed a copy to every family in the parish. It is unclear whether she sold or gave away the copies, but everyone Katharine Cipolla spoke with recalled that "their mother had a copy." Some of the copies found their way into the hands of lawyers and judges in Canada. D'Alton Lally McCarthy mentions in his draft autobiography that he had been "fortunate enough to get a copy of the book, which I deeply prize." One copy recently retrieved had been owned by a lawyer in British Columbia (M.W. Panet of Victoria), who had pasted two law reports (from the Ontario Weekly Notes) into the volume. Another contains the entry: "From the Library of Mr. Justice (L.McC.) Ritchie, Saint John." We have not discovered any published contemporary reviews of the book in Canada or in England. Anne Innis Dagg, *The Feminine Gaze: A Canadian Compendium of Non-Fiction Women Authors and Their Books, 1836-1945* (Waterloo: Wilfrid Laurier University Press, 2001) lists *Where Angels Fear to Tread* in her remarkable effort to compile an encyclopaedic reference to many important books that have become "edited out of the public history of our culture" (viii, 56-71). Peter Campbell Brooks, Mrs. Campbell's grandson, donated a copy to Harvard University's Widener Library. Katharine Cipolla found two copies in the Boston Atheneum and one copy in the Boston Public Library. There are copies in the Great Library of the Law Society of Upper Canada, University of Alberta and Queen's University libraries, the National Library of Canada, and the Parliamentary Library of Canada. Peter

Campbell Brooks recalls many copies of the book lying around his childhood home; apparently a number were used to prop up the couch! Interview with David Mittell and Katharine Cipolla, by Constance Backhouse, Boston, 13 August 2001 (copy on file with authors). For information on Mittell and Cipolla, see the Acknowledgments, p. xiv.

2 Birth Certificate for Elizabeth L. Bethune, Archives of Ontario, MS 929, Reel 47, vol. 17, Registration No. 041726. The birth certificate indicates that a Toronto doctor named Spragge was present at the birth. See also Mormon files on the 1881 Census of Canada: Census Place: St. Andrew's Ward, Toronto, York, Ontario, Canada; Source: FHL Film 1375883, NAC C-13247, Dist 134, SubDist G, Div 1, p. 134, Family 687. Stormont Lodge appears to have been named for the provincial electoral district formerly represented by James Bethune.

3 Toronto *Globe*, 15 August 1924. James Bethune was born in Charlottenburgh, Glengarry County, Ontario, on 7 July 1840. His paternal Scottish ancestors had first settled in Canada when his great-grandfather, Angus Bethune, came with other United Empire Loyalists to Glengarry in 1778. His grandfather, John Bethune, was chaplain to the First Battalion, Eighty-fourth Regiment of Foot. His grandmother was Veronique Bethune. James Bethune's father, also named Angus Bethune, born on 9 September 1783, was appointed the deputy sheriff of the united counties of Stormont, Dundas, and Glengarry. James's mother was Ann Mackenzie. James seems to have been the eldest of seven brothers and sisters and one half-sister. See St. Andrew's Church, Williamstown, Register of Births, Marriages and Deaths 1779-1914, Archives of Ontario, MS 107.

James Bethune studied at Queen's College in Kingston and University College in Toronto, graduating with an LL.B. in 1861. He began his articles in Cornwall with another Scottish lawyer, Jacob Ferrand Pringle, who would later become a county judge of Stormont, Dundas, and Glengarry. He concluded them with the Hon. Edward Blake in Toronto. Called to the bar of Ontario in 1862 as well as to the bar of Quebec, Bethune first practised in Cornwall, where he took an appointment in 1865 as county Crown attorney. From 1872 to 1878, he served in the provincial legislature as a Liberal for the riding of Stormont. For details of the partners who practised with Bethune in Toronto, see n. 50 below. Bethune lectured at Osgoode Hall Law School from 1864 to 1874 and served as bencher from 1875 to 1884. A Presbyterian and an elder with St. Andrew's Church, Bethune was described in his obituary as occupying "a high social position." As to Bethune's reputation, D'Alton Lally McCarthy's draft autobiography notes: "In his lifetime Mr. James Bethune was recognized as one of the ablest Lawyers at the Ontario Bar." Bethune's obituary described him as a man of "indefatigable industry," "a most formidable opponent at the bar," and a man whose "career as a lawyer has been remarkable even in this city where successful lawyers abound." James Bethune appeared regularly before the Supreme Court of Canada and, as the Toronto *Globe* noted on 15 August 1924, p. 9, was "among the first of Canadian counsel who went regularly to the sittings of the Judicial Committee of the Privy Council" in London, England, often travelling with his wife. As was the case with some of the more prominent Canadian barristers, Bethune was permitted to store his Queen's Counsel wig in a private receptacle at the Privy Council Office during his legal career. *Where Angels Fear to Tread,*

124-5. See "James Bethune, Q.C.," Toronto *Globe*, 19 December 1884, p. 6; W.J. Rattray, *The Scot in British North America* (Toronto: Maclear and Company, 1882), 757-8, 921; Law Society of Upper Canada Archives, Draft Autobiography of D'Alton Lally McCarthy, sous-fonds 1, D'Alton McCarthy sous-fonds, William G.C. Howland fonds, 994001SF1-1-4; *Toronto City Directory*, 1873, 1874, 1875, 1877, 1879, 1880; Christopher Moore, *The Law Society of Upper Canada and Ontario's Lawyers, 1797-1997* (Toronto: University of Toronto Press, 1997), 141-2, 161; Henry James Morgan, ed., *The Canadian Men and Women of the Time* (Toronto: William Briggs, 1898). For reference to James Bethune as "so well known in legal circles in Toronto for many years" see Toronto *Globe*, 15 November 1907, p. 6. His later Supreme Court cases included *Nicholls* v. *Cumming*, [1878] 1 S.C.R. 395; *Liverpool and London and Globe Insurance Co.* v. *Wyld and Darling*, [1878] 1 S.C.R. 604; *Gray* v. *Richford*, [1879] 2 S.C.R. 431; *Moore* v. *Connecticut Mutual Life Insurance Company*, [1882] 6 S.C.R. 634; and *McLaren* v. *Caldwell*, [1884] 8 S.C.R. 435. His later Privy Council cases included *Connecticut Mutual Life Insurance Company* v. *Moore*, [1881] 6 A.C. 644; 8 C.R.A.C. 391; and *Caldwell* v. *McLaren*, [1884] 9 A.C. 392; [1883-1888] 9 C.R.A.C. 73, the latter of which he had argued successfully just before his death.

4 "Lady Howland Dies after Long Illness," Toronto *Globe*, 15 August 1924, p. 9. Elizabeth Mary (Rattray) Bethune was the eldest daughter of Dr. Charles Rattray, a Cornwall physician, and Louisa Chesley Rattray. Dr. Rattray took his medical training at Edinburgh University and served as surgeon in the Royal Navy, stationed with the Atlantic Squadron. Louisa Chesley was a descendant of a prominent United Empire Loyalist family. Elizabeth Mary Rattray had five other siblings: David, Agnes, Helen, Frederick, and Robert. The Mormon files on the 1881 Census of Canada indicate Elizabeth Mary Rattray was born in 1843 but list her origin as "Spanish" in what must be a clerical error. St Andrew's Ward, Toronto, York, Ontario, FHL film 1375883, NAC C-13247, Dist 134, SubDist G DIV 1, p. 134, Family 687. Her obituary indicated she was born in 1840. It also described her as "an honorary member" of the Imperial Order Daughters of the Empire, "having taken part in the initiation of that order."

The doctor's family did not appear to have been particularly financially well off. In 1872 Dr. Rattray's estate amounted to less than $1,500, an amount that had been reduced to $1,200 by the time his wife died, one year later. Last Will and Testament of Charles Rattray, deceased 1872, Archives of Ontario, RG22, GS1, Reel 1255, no. 222; Last Will and Testament of Louisa Rattray, deceased 1873, Archives of Ontario, RG22, GS1, Reel 1255, No. 262.

5 Mrs. Campbell's parents would have both been around forty years old when she was born; in her book, Mrs. Campbell describes herself as "the child of [my mother's] old age." At her birth, there were four elder siblings: Lena, age eighteen; Cora, age sixteen; Annie, age thirteen; and Charles, age eight. Lena died at some point between the deaths of her father and her mother. Charles James Rattray Bethune, the only brother, died on 6 April 1921. Charles practised law during his short-lived career. He began as a student-at-law in 1892, working with his brother-in-law's law firm of Lindsey and Lindsey in Toronto. He was called to the bar in 1895; by 1897 he had moved to Ottawa, where he practised with Chrysler and Bethune at 46 Elgin Street. His partner, Francis Henry

Chrysler, was known to be a "confidante of Sir Wilfrid Laurier" and a "tenacious advocate." The firm had taken a new partner, Norman G. Larmonth, by 1907 and was known as Chrysler, Bethune and Larmonth. Russell M. Dick joined them when Chrysler left by 1915. The firm, now known as Bethune, Larmonth and Dick, practised at 75 Sparks Street, advertising itself in the *Canadian Law List 1918* (Toronto: Canadian Law List, 1918), xxxiii, as "Supreme Court, Parliamentary and Departmental Agents, and Agents in Practice before the Board of Railway Commissioners." Correspondence between William Drummond Hogg and Lady Howland indicates that Charles had serious alcoholism for some years before his death.

William Lyon Mackenzie King, who had studied law at the same time as Charles Bethune, and treated him as a great confidante and friend, wrote at some length in his diary about Charles's death. King notes on 6 April 1921: "When I reached the office this afternoon I rec'd word that Charlie Bethune was very ill at St. Luke's ... [I was later advised that] Charlie was dead. It appears he took an overdose of phenacatine at the Roxborough last Friday, had been found unconscious in his room by Betty Cronyn, and recovered consciousness but slightly at the hospital. He had been taking treatment at Guelph & Preston, been steady for nearly three months, got on a spree for a few days after a week in Ottawa & was gone a week later. It was his only fault, in other respects he was a splendid type of man—able, kind, affectionate & honorable. Another case of a man who should have married." For multiple references to social events, including Christmas dinners, that King attended with Charles Bethune, Charles's death, and subsequent dreams that included visions of Charles, see King, William Lyon Mackenzie, MG26, J13 diaries [Ottawa], National Archives of Canada, Manuscript Division, Prime Ministers Archives Section, 1981, 12 October 1893 (at G12), 28 November 1893 (at G30), 25 December 1893 (at G40), 8 June 1894 (at G108), 12 June 1894 (at G169), 11 and 13 January 1896 (at G337), 3 January 1901 (at G1550), 16 January 1904 (at G1821), 14 March 1915 (at G2539), 6 April 1921 (at G3486), 7 and 8 April 1921 (at G3487), 7 October 1947 (at 705). See also Privy Council Archives, "Record of Proceedings," Campbell v. Hogg, No. 56 of 1929, pp. 241-7. "Charles J. Bethune, Popular Ottawa Lawyer Is Dead," Ottawa *Citizen,* 7 April 1921, p. 2; *Where Angels Fear to Tread,* 38; *Ottawa City Directory,* 1897-8, 1898-9, 1899, 1900, 1905, 1907, 1910, 1915, 1920; Mormon files on the 1881 Census of Canada, St Andrew's Ward; William C.V. Johnson, ed., *The First Century: Essays on the History of the County of Carleton Law Association by Various Hands on the Occasion of the Association's Centenary, 1888-1988* (Ottawa: Bonanza Press, 1988), 14; Law Society of Upper Canada Archives, Past Member Record Files.

6 By the time of the legal proceeding, there were only two other surviving sisters, both described as "a generation older" than Mrs. Campbell. Cora Ann Bethune had married George Goldwin Smith Lindsey, the grandson of William Lyon Mackenzie, who was a lawyer with Lindsey, Lindsey and Evans (G.G.S. Lindsey, Lyon Lindsey, and John W. Evans). Cora Ann and George resided at 21 Rusholme Road in the 1890s, and at 145 Tyndall Avenue in Parkdale, Toronto, from about 1905 until 1928. George died on 27 May 1920. In 1928 Cora Ann moved to an apartment at 98 Charles Street East, where she remained

throughout the rest of the estate dispute. Cora Ann opposed Mrs. Campbell in the litigation, as did her sister, Annie Bethune McDougald, who was married to Alfred W. McDougald. The McDougalds resided in Montreal, initially at 210 Milton, but had moved to 64 Rosemont Avenue in Westmount by 1915. Alfred worked with the Pelican Canada and British Life Assurance Company, later going into real estate. *Campbell* v. *Hogg,* [1930] 3 D.L.R. 673 (P.C.) at 674; "Campbell-Bethune," Toronto *Star,* 14 November 1907, p. 11; *Toronto City Directory,* 1894, 1905, 1910, 1915, 1920, 1925, 1926, 1927, 1928, 1930, 1935; *Montreal City Directory,* 1907-8, 1909-10, 1914-15; "Avers Lady Howland Intended Destroy Will," Toronto *Star,* 27 June 1925, p. 3; Last Will and Testament of G.G.S. Lindsey, Archives of Ontario, RG22, MS584, Reel 332, Grant No. 40981.

7 The Privy Council indicated that James Bethune died on 18 December 1884. See *Campbell* v. *Hogg,* [1930] 3 D.L.R. 673 (P.C.) at 674, and the obituary "James Bethune Q.C.," Toronto *Globe,* 19 December 1884, p. 6.

8 The Privy Council decision noted that James Bethune's will, duly proved on 13 January 1885, bequeathed all his property, real and personal, to Elizabeth Mary Bethune, who was appointed sole executrix and guardian of the infant children. The estate was sizeable for the time. Bethune's property, exclusive of realty, amounted to $39,850, with the bulk of that sum ($30,000) secured by life insurance policies. The Last Will and Testament of James Bethune, Archives of Ontario, RG22, GS1, Reel 998, Estate Grant 55472, breaks down the personal property as follows: household goods and furniture, $4,000; book debts and promissory notes, $3,000; moneys secured by life insurance, $30,000; cash in bank, $350; library, $2,500. At James Bethune's death, William Drummond Hogg (Mrs. Bethune's brother-in-law) went to Toronto several times to help his wife's sister deal with the Surrogate Court, to obtain payment of the life insurance policy moneys, to help dispose of the testator's law library, and to negotiate the sale of Bethune's real estate. No records remain regarding the value of the real estate. Mrs. Campbell claimed that the total estate would have amounted to at least $60,000 in 1885. See *Campbell* v. *Hogg,* [1930] 3 D.L.R. 673 (P.C.) at 674-76; *Where Angels Fear to Tread,* 78.

9 Hogg agreed to manage the investment of these moneys, and did so until 1922, when a trust company was appointed in his stead. See *Campbell* v. *Hogg,* [1930] 3 D.L.R. 673 (P.C.) at 674-76; *Where Angels Fear to Tread,* 78. With widowhood, Mrs. Campbell's mother moved out of the family home to 2 Wellington Place, accompanied by her two youngest children, Elizabeth and Charles, a law student. By 1893 Mrs. Campbell's mother was renting at 32 John Street, but in 1894 she moved to 125 Bedford Road, where she lived with Elizabeth and Charles. Upon her remarriage the following year, Sir William Howland moved in to join them. *Toronto City Directory,* 1889, 1890, 1893, 1894.

10 The upper-class status of the Bethunes is indicated in part by the servants they employed. The Mormon files on the 1881 Census of Canada show that the live-in servants included a cook, a nursemaid, and two domestic servants: Elizabeth Longhouse (age thirty-one, born in Ontario, nationality German, occupation cook); Janet Reed (age twenty-one, born in Ontario, nationality Irish, occupa-

tion nurse); Fanny Cohoon (age twenty, born in Ireland, nationality Irish, occupation servant); Elizabeth Waters (age thirty-three, born in Scotland, nationality Scottish, occupation servant). On Mrs. Campbell's education see Katharine G. Cipolla, "The Privy Council's First Portia," *Eagle's Eye* (September 1992), St. John's Episcopalian Church, Jamaica Plain, p. 6. Mrs. Campbell attended the Couvent de l'Assomption in Paris. *Where Angels Fear to Tread,* 157.

11 Sir William Howland was born on 29 May 1811 in Paulings, New York, of Quaker parents Jonathan Howland and Lydia Pearce, and educated at Kinderhook Academy. He moved to Upper Canada in 1830 and, by the late 1850s, became one of its wealthiest millers and wholesale grocers. First elected to the legislature in 1857 under the auspices of George Brown's Reformers, he later served as minister of finance, receiver general, and postmaster general. The only American-born person to be designated a "father of confederation," Howland was appointed lieutenant governor on 15 July 1868, a post he held until 11 November 1873. He received a K.C.M.G. (Knight Commander of the Order of St. Michael and St. George) "in recognition of his contributions to Canadian life" in May 1879. After leaving the position of lieutenant governor, Howland served as president of the Toronto Board of Trade, the Confederation Life Assurance Company, the Anchor Marine Insurance Company, the London and Canadian Loan Agency Company, and the Ontario Bank. Howland's first marriage was in 1843 to Mary Anne Blythe, who predeceased him in 1860. In 1865 he married Susanna Julia Shrewsbury, who died in 1886. On 15 August 1895 he married Elizabeth Mary Rattray Bethune. He was a lifelong adherent of the Church of England. "Howland, Sir William Pearce," *Dictionary of Canadian Biography* (Toronto: University of Toronto Press, 1994), 13:484-7; "Sir W.P. Howland Has Passed Away," Toronto *Globe,* 2 January 1907, p. 1; "Sir Wm. Howland Has Passed Away," Toronto *World,* 2 January 1907, p. 1; "Pioneer Canadian Removed by Death," Toronto *Daily Mail and Empire,* 2 January 1907, pp. 1-2; "Sir W.P. Howland Has Passed Away," Toronto *News,* 2 January 1907, p. 7.

12 Sir William Howland lived at 215 Simcoe Street before the wedding; after it he moved into the new Lady Howland's home at 125 Bedford Road. It is difficult to date their separation with certainty, but city directories indicate that Sir William Howland moved out of 125 Bedford to 24 Isabella Street in 1904. By 1905, 125 Bedford was owned by David B. Hann. By 1906 Sir William had moved to 152 Bloor Street East. By this time, Lady Howland was no longer listed in the Toronto directory and may have moved to St. Catharines. Sir William Howland's obituary listed him as living at the home of his recently deceased brother, Peleg Howland, at 236 Bloor Street East, and attended in his final hours by his only surviving child, a daughter from Maryland, Mrs. H.K. (Florence) Merritt. On the separation, and Howland's death on 1 January 1907 at the age of ninety-six, see "Howland, Sir William Pearce," *Dictionary of Canadian Biography,* 13:484-7; *Toronto City Directory,* 1894-1907; "Sir William Howland," Toronto *Globe,* 16 August 1895, p. 8; "Sir W.P. Howland Has Passed Away," Toronto *Globe,* 2 January 1907, p. 1; "Sir Wm. Howland Has Passed Away," Toronto *World,* 2 January 1907, p. 1; "Pioneer Canadian Removed by Death," Toronto

Daily Mail and Empire, 2 January 1907, pp. 1–2; "Sir W.P. Howland Has Passed Away," Toronto *News*, 2 January 1907, p. 7. The Last Will and Testament of Sir W.P. Howland, Archives of Ontario, RG22, MS 584, Reel 1796, Estate Grant 19447, shows that Sir Howland's real and personal property, composed primarily of bank shares and real estate and valued at $24,936.28, was smaller than James Bethune's estate upon his death some thirty years earlier. The Toronto General Trusts Corporation acted as executor and trustee.

13 The Privy Council noted that the marriage to Sir William Howland "apparently did not affect in any way Lady Howland's propriety rights which remained intact." *Campbell* v. *Hogg*, [1930] 3 D.L.R. 673 (P.C.) at 674. Lady Howland had also signed a marriage settlement with Sir William Howland, which gave her a life claim to interest from the Lambton Mills property owned by Howland. The Surrogate Court file on the Last Will and Testament of Sir W.P. Howland, Archives of Ontario, RG22, MS 584, Reel 1796, Estate Grant 19447, contains documentation on the deed of settlement dated 23 December 1898, indicating that Lady Howland was paid $1,236.65 in mortgage interest between 1908 and 1910, well after her separation from Howland and his death. On the Ontario law relating to married women's property, see Constance Backhouse, "Married Women's Property in Nineteenth-Century Canada," *Law and History Review* 6, 2 (1988): 211; Lori Chambers, *Married Women and Property Law in Victorian Ontario* (Toronto: University of Toronto Press, 1997).

14 C.P. Stacey, *A Very Double Life: The Private World of Mackenzie King* (Toronto: Macmillan, 1977), 35–40. Peter Campbell Brooks, Mrs. Campbell's grandson, explained that he was told that his grandmother had "almost married" William Lyon Mackenzie King but that "the relationship went off the rails and she married Tom Campbell." Six years older than Mrs. Campbell, King was at this time something of "a ladies' man," with an active social life, fond of dancing and the company of "blushing young ladies." The women he courted were often from "families connected with the law." King became the deputy minister of labour in 1900, and would win his first seat in the House of Commons in 1908, becoming prime minister in 1921. The political Liberal connections between the Bethune family and King would have been an important bond. King also had close family connections with Mrs. Campbell: Cora Ann Lindsey's husband and King were both grandsons of William Lyon Mackenzie.

King's diary describes numerous social engagements with Charles Bethune (see note 5 above), and a dream King had of being asked to consider appointing James Bethune to the Senate. The diary also reveals a very close relationship with Cora Ann Lindsey. See King, William Lyon Mackenzie, MG26, J13, diaries [Ottawa], NAC, Manuscript Division, Prime Ministers Archives Section, 1981, 25 December 1893 (at G40), 8 June 1894 (at G108), 12 June 1894 (at G169), 14 March 1915 (at G2539), 6–8 April 1921 (at G3486–7), 26 April 1921 (at G3493), 12 February 1922 (at G3668), 18 January 1930 (at G5624), 1 August 1931 (at 617), 24 April 1944 (at 372), 24 October 1944 (at 1021), 25 August 1945 (at 819), 17 July 1948 (at 695), and 19 July 1945 (at 704). There are also references to socializing with the Hoggs (Mrs. Campbell's aunt and uncle), occasionally at their home; see 3 January 1901 (at G1550), 6 March 1926 (at G4459), 13

September 1932 (at 251). King mentions in his diary that the Hogg and Bethune families had experienced "such unpleasantness," an apparent reference to Mrs. Campbell's litigation, as well as a dream he had in which Charles Bethune and George Lindsey had appeared to him, in which George advised Cora Ann Lindsey "not to go on with a certain lawsuit." See 6 February 1927 (at G4783), 13 September 1932 (at 251), 7 October 1937 (at 705).

Prime Minister Mackenzie King would send a floral tribute to Lady Howland's funeral. Interview with Peter Campbell Brooks, by Constance Backhouse, San Francisco, 23 July 2002 (copy on file with authors); R. MacGregor Dawson, *William Lyon Mackenzie King: A Political Biography* (London: Methuen, 1958), 39-40; *Canada's Prime Ministers, 1867-1994: Biographies and Anecdotes* (Ottawa: National Archives of Canada, 1994), 20, 40.

15 We have been unable to discover how Mrs. Campbell met Thomas, although family lore has it that he proposed to her on the "end of the Heinz Pickle Pier in Philadelphia." Thomas Campbell was born on 14 October 1875 in Port Jervis, New York, to Archibald Henderson Campbell (a civil engineer who held no university degrees, born on 25 February 1832 in Toronto) and Deusa Ann Jansen (born in Mattamorres, Pennsylvania, married 1870). He graduated from Princeton University in 1899, and taught at Groton School from 1900 to 1901. He received a bachelor of divinity degree from the Episcopal Theological School, Cambridge, in 1903. He served as curate of St. Stephen's Church in Lynn, Massachusetts, from 1903 to 1904, and as associate rector of Christ Church, Cincinnati, from 1904 to 1908. The recollections of Reverend Campbell's personality and athletic prowess are from David Mittell. *The Church Militant* (May 1943): 16; "Campbell, Thomas Clyman," *Stowe's Clerical Dictionary, 1941,* 46; "Individual Record," "Family Record," and "University Record," Thomas Clyman Campbell, Princeton University Archives; correspondence between David A. Mittell and Kurt Kehl, Princeton University, 13 March 1993; correspondence between David A. Mittell and Rev. George Blackman, 12 April 1996; interview with David Mittell, by Constance Backhouse, Boston, 13 August 2001 (copy on file with authors); interview with Peter Campbell Brooks, by Constance Backhouse, San Francisco, 23 July 2002 (copy on file with authors).

16 The Toronto *Star,* 14 November 1907, p. 11, describes the Campbell-Bethune wedding in some detail. The bride's wedding gown was "of white Liberty satin, made semi-Empire, with exquisite lace trimmings and long court train. Her long tulle veil was hemmed with pearls caught with a chaplet of orange blossoms, and she carried a shower of lilies and roses. Her only ornaments were a pearl necklace and diamond and pearl pendant, the gift of the groom." The wedding party included (as bridesmaid) the bride's niece Miss Elizabeth McDougald, and (as flower girl) Miss Ethel Kirkpatrick, who was the granddaughter of Sir William and Lady Mulock. The newspaper noted that the illustrious guests—all "intimate friends and relatives"—included "the Rev. Canon and Mrs. Cody, Chief Justice and Mrs. Falconbridge, Mr. and Mrs. John L. Blaikie, Miss F. Blaikie, Mr. Justice Osler, the Chief Justice of Ontario and Lady Moss, Mr. and Mrs. F.H. Chrysler and Miss D. Chrysler, Ottawa; Mr. and Mrs. W. Drummond Hogg, Ottawa; Mr. and Mrs. A.W. McDougald, Chief Justice Sir Wm. and Lady

Mulock, Mr. and Mrs. Cawthra Mulock, Hon. Robt. Jaffray, Mr. Charles Bethune, Lindsay [sic]; Mr. and Mrs. Arthur E. Kirkpatrick, Mr. and Mrs. Wallace Jones, Mr. and Mrs. Herbert M. Mowat, Mrs. Walter Beardmore, the Premier of Ontario and Mrs. Whitney, Mr. and Mrs. Z.A. Lash, Mr. and Mrs. Miller Lash, Mr. and Mrs. Robert Cassels, the Rev. and D. Bruce Macdonald, Mrs. J.K. and Miss Helen Macdonald, Mr. and Mrs. Chas. Macdonald, Mr. Herbert H. Collier and Mrs. Camp, St. Catharines; Mrs. H. Inksater and Miss Helliwell, Mr. and Mrs. Gordon Mackenzie and Miss Mackenzie, Mr. and Mrs. C.H. Ritchie, Mr. and Mrs. J.J. Willison, Mr. Harold and Miss Ethel Baldwin, Dr. Edmund Walker and Miss Ethel Walker, Dr. J.H. and Mrs. McPherson, the Misses Wright, Miss Helen Douglas, Mr. and Mrs. Wellington Cameron and Mrs. J.Y. Cameron, Miss A. Ault, Dr. and Mrs. Percy Parker, Mr. Philip G. Kiely, Mr. and Mrs. W.R. Wadsworth, Mr. and Mrs. Vernon B. Wadsworth, Dr. and Mrs. Thistle, Mrs. Hugh Campbell, Dr. Brefney O'Reilly, Miss Gordon, Miss King, Miss Laidlaw, Mr. Walter H. Green and Miss Green, Miss E. Doroche, Napanee; Mrs. McArthur and Miss McArthur, the Misses Sinclair, Dr. L.L. and Mrs. Palmer."

Lady Howland hosted a reception at the Queen's Hotel after the ceremony, in a large room decorated with a profusion of chrysanthemums and ferns. The reception was presided over by Lady Howland, Mrs. McDougald (the bride's sister), and Mrs. W.D. Hogg (the bride's aunt). Mrs. G.G.S. Lindsey, the bride's sister, was in Atlantic City and unable to attend. The Toronto *Globe*, 15 November 1907, p. 6, notes that Charles J.B. Bethune gave away the bride, and that "after dejeuner, Mr. and Mrs. Campbell left for New York, the going-away dress being of purple chiffon velvet, purple toque, and white [fox fur] stole and muff." See also Toronto *Globe*, 14 November 1907, p. 6. St. Paul's Anglican Church was one of the most prominent in the city, described as "wealthy St. Paul's on fashionable Bloor Street below Rosedale." J.M.S. Careless, *Toronto to 1918: An Illustrated History* (Toronto: Lorimer, 1984), 166.

17 On the history of Jamaica Plain, see Anthony Mitchell Sammarco, *Images of America: Jamaica Plain* (Dover, NH: Arcadia Tempus Publishing, 1997); "Historical Jamaica Plain," travel brochure (n.p., n.d.), copy on file with authors; interview with Katharine Cipolla, by Constance Backhouse, Boston, 13 August 2001 (copy on file with authors). St. John's Episcopal parish was founded in 1841. Foundation work for the present church was begun in 1881, the cornerstone laid in 1882, and first services held in 1883. Reverend Campbell served as the second rector of St. John's Episcopal Church, from 1908 to 1943. Efforts to have him elevated to the post of Suffragan bishop in the mid-1930s failed, although Reverend Campbell received quite a few votes at the convention. Boston *Herald,* 31 August 1941, p. 4B; correspondence from Katharine Cipolla, 29 July 2002 (copy on file with authors); interview with David Mittell, by Constance Backhouse, Boston, 13 August 2001 (copy on file with authors); interview with Peter Campbell Brooks, by Constance Backhouse, San Francisco, 23 July 2002 (copy on file with authors).

18 The rectory was built as a result of a gift from the Morville family; see Katharine G. Cipolla, "The Privy Council's First Portia," *Eagle's Eye* (September 1992), St. John's Episcopalian Church, Jamaica Plain, p. 6.

19 "Individual Record," Thomas Clyman Campbell, Princeton University Archives.

20 "War Records," Thomas Clyman Campbell, Princeton University Archives.

21 For details of the children's education, see interview with David Mittell and Katharine Cipolla, by Constance Backhouse, Boston, 13 August 2001 (copy on file with authors); interview with Peter Campbell Brooks, by Constance Backhouse, San Francisco, 23 July 2002 (copy on file with authors); *The Church Militant* (May 1943): 16; *Harvard College Class of 1931, 30th Anniversary Report*; *35th Anniversary Report* (Cambridge, MA, 1956), 172; *Princeton Alumni Weekly,* 3 May 1935. On the financial help offered by Mrs. Chapin, see correspondence from Katharine Cipolla to Sydney Harris, 3 May 1992 (copy on file with authors). For information on Sydney Harris, see the Acknowledgments, p. xiv. For details of James's and Thomasine's subsequent marriages and careers, see the Epilogue.

22 Interview with Margaret Tyng Lawson, a former friend and neighbour of the Campbells, by Constance Backhouse, by telephone, Providence, Rhode Island, 14 August 2001 (copy on file with authors). Correspondence from David A. Mittell to Rev. Henry W. Sherrill, 7 April 1997 (copy on file with authors).

23 Interview with David Mittell and Katharine Cipolla, by Constance Backhouse, Boston, 13 August 2001 (copy on file with authors).

24 Interview with David Mittell and Katharine Cipolla, by Constance Backhouse, Boston, 13 August 2001 (copy on file with authors); interview with Margaret Tyng Lawson, by Constance Backhouse, by telephone, Providence, Rhode Island, 14 August 2001 (copy on file with authors). Mrs. Campbell was not listed among the members of the elite Boston women's organization, the Chilton Club, although Susan Revere Chapin was: telephone conversation with Mrs. Keenan, secretary of the Chilton Club, 3 June 2002.

25 Sir William Howland may have introduced Lady Howland to St. Catharines, for he was familiar with the international reputation that the city had acquired as a "great resort for invalids and fashionable people." He had invested in the Stephenson House, one of the elite three spas in the city, as early as the 1850s, and had once taken up residence there in 1867 to recuperate from illness. The Welland Hotel had opened with a celebrity ball in 1856, and in its early decades accommodated visitors between April and October. By the turn of the century, the Welland was open year round, and many of its visitors used the facility as a full-time residence. The hotel boasted baths where guests could obtain "treatment with the waters of the famous well." A two-storey bathhouse was erected on a wing that ran across the front of the hotel on Ontario Street, and older houses around the other wings of the hotel were torn down to provide for a bowling green. In 1910 a fifth storey was added with an open promenade and a sixty-foot solarium with skylight. The Welland also had a private hospital (the Wellandra) attached, which offered private nurses and attendants for hire. See correspondence with Arden Phair, Curator of Collections, St. Catharines Museum (copy on file with the authors); Sheila M. Wilson, ed., *Taking the Waters: A History of the Spas of St. Catharines* (St. Catharines, ON: Paul Heron, 1999), 29-31, 52-9.

26 *Campbell* v. *Hogg,* [1930] 3 D.L.R. 673 (P.C.) at 674 notes that by 1915 there were "not obscure indications" that Lady Howland's mental powers "had begun

to fail." She "ceased to attend to the accounts which hitherto she had kept methodically and regularly. No voucher from her after 1918 is forthcoming."

27 "Committee" was the legal term that referred to the status of the corporation or person appointed by the court to take control over financial or personal-care decisions. The incompetence was determined by an order of Mr. Justice William Edward Middleton of the Supreme Court of Ontario, issued pursuant to an application by Cora A. Lindsey and in the presence of Mrs. McDougald and Mrs. Campbell; as noted in *Campbell* v. *Hogg*, [1930] 3 D.L.R. 673 (P.C.) at 675. *Where Angels Fear to Tread*, 48, notes that Arthur Courtney Kingstone of Ingersoll, Kingstone, and Seymour, Barristers and Solicitors, from St. Catharines, and Mrs. Lindsey attended to the swearing of affidavits: two by physicians, one by Lady Howland's constant attendant, one by each of her daughters, and others by friends. The decision was not reported, and only partial records survive in the Privy Council Archives, "Record of Proceedings," Campbell v. Hogg, No. 56 of 1929, p. 321. Mrs. Campbell's "strenuous objection" to the Toronto General Trusts Corporation, and her preference for the appointment of another company, are noted in subsequent proceedings: *Re Howland*, [1935] O.W.N. 340 (Ontario Court of Appeal), per Riddell, J.A., at 341.

28 The date of death is listed in the Last Will and Testament of Elizabeth Mary Howland, Archives of Ontario, RG22, MS 584, Reel 43, Estate Grant 50634, No. 1784/24, 29 September 1924. Floral tributes were sent to the funeral from family members, including Mr. and Mrs. William Drummond Hogg, Mrs. W.R. Wadsworth, the Right Hon. Prime Minister William Lyon Mackenzie King, and the Toronto Women's Liberal Association. On the age at death, see *Campbell* v. *Hogg*, [1930] 3 D.L.R. 673 at 675 (P.C.). The age stipulated in the decision is several years older than that found in the Mormon files on the 1881 Census of Canada, which gives her date of birth as 1843. See Census Place: St. Andrew's Ward, Toronto, York, Ontario, Canada; Source: FHL Film 1375883, NAC C-13247, Dist 134, SubDist G, Div 1, p. 134, Family 687. For obituaries, see "Lady Howland Dies after Long Illness," Toronto *Globe*, 15 August 1924, p. 9; "Pay Last Tributes to Esteemed Woman," Toronto *Globe*, 19 August 1924, p. 9; "Lady Howland Dead at Age of 84 Years," Ottawa *Citizen*, 15 August 1924, p. 12.

29 At Lady Howland's death, the Surrogate Court records indicated that her estate totalled $17,450, broken down as follows: clothing and jewellery, $50; moneys secured by mortgage, $6,600; bank stock and other stocks, $10,800. See *Campbell* v. *Hogg*, [1930] 3 D.L.R. 673 (P.C.) at 674-6; *Where Angels Fear to Tread*, 78; Last Will and Testament of James Bethune, Archives of Ontario, RG22, GS1, Reel 998, Estate Grant 55472; Last Will and Testament of Elizabeth Mary Howland, Archives of Ontario, RG22, MS 584, Reel 43, Estate Grant 50634, No. 1784/24, 29 September 1924.

30 Arthur Slaght was the son of Florence Louise Wilson Slaght and Thomas Rowell Slaght, a Norfolk Crown attorney. Slaght was educated at Simcoe public high schools, articled with Charles J. Holman, K.C., and was called to the bar in 1898. He practised with a series of Toronto law firms until 1906, when he left for the mining country of Cobalt and set up law practice with his brother, Leroy, in Haileybury, for ten years. The field was lucrative, as the new mineral discoveries of northern Ontario and the emerging market for hydroelectricity com-

manded expanding legal services. Slaght returned to Toronto in 1916 and took up practice with James Cowan and R. Irvin Ferguson. At the time of the case, he was practising with the firm of Slaght and Cowan on the fourteenth floor of the Royal Bank Building at 6 King Street East in Toronto. Famous for his merciless cross-examinations, Slaght spellbound all who observed him—witnesses, jurors, opposing counsel, court officials, and reporters alike. He was described as "eloquent, incisive, witty and brilliantly manipulative." D'Alton Lally McCarthy would characterize him as "clever and vigorous" and "one of our outstanding pleaders." The press boasted that the flamboyant barrister had successfully defended nineteen murder trials in a row. A key organizer behind Premier Hepburn's election campaign, Slaght was described as "the brilliant courtroom lawyer whose eloquence had often swayed jurors, judges, and even hardened crown prosecutors, who played to the jurors of the province. Night after night that summer, sweat glistening on his forehead, hands punctuating every point, Slaght roused his audience to cheers, boos and foot-stamping ... [Mitch and Arthur] walked out of countless halls to standing ovations and into the night to unwind with congenial companions and a bottle of Dewars." See "Slaght, Arthur Graeme K.C.," in *Prominent Men of Canada, 1931-32*, ed. Ross Hamilton (Montreal: National Publishing, 1932), 291-2; "Slaght, Arthur Graeme," in *The Canadian Who's Who, 1961-63* (Toronto: University of Toronto Press, 1985), 1029; Slaght, Arthur Graeme, *The Canadian Who's Who, 1936-37* (Toronto: University of Toronto Press, 1985), 1000; Law Society of Upper Canada Archives, Past Member Record Files; Obituaries—St. Thomas *Times-Journal*, 24 January 1964; Kirkland Lake *Northern Daily News*, 24 January 1964; Toronto *Globe and Mail*, 24 January 1964; Law Society of Upper Canada Archives, Draft Autobiography of D'Alton Lally McCarthy, sous-fonds 1, D'Alton McCarthy sous-fonds, William G.C. Howland fonds, 99400ISF1-1-4; John T. Saywell, *"Just Call Me Mitch": The Life of Mitchell F. Hepburn* (Toronto: University of Toronto Press, 1991), 107, 119, 128, 139, 184.

31 McCarthy was born on 5 December 1870, and educated at Trinity College School in Port Hope, and at Marchiston Castle School in Edinburgh. He received a B.A. at the University of Trinity College in Toronto, 1892, and was called to the bar three years later. The other partners in the McCarthy and McCarthy law firm were H.A. Harrison, W.J. Beattie, William Ralph West, and S.A. Hayden. In 1929 Lally McCarthy left the firm, in part because he was not interested in the solicitors' corporate practice that was becoming the firm's main specialty; he practised as a solo litigation barrister thereafter. "Gregarious, civilized, never at a loss, he knew all the courtrooms of the province, and he sailed regularly on the Atlantic liners to plead Privy Council cases in London" (correspondence from Christopher Moore, 4 and 15 July 2002, copy on file with authors). A young lawyer who admired him once commented: "He liked his women and his liquor and society and he liked his law, maybe I have given that in the wrong order. He had a flair for appearance." McCarthy played polo until he was age seventy, and rode to hounds until he retired at age seventy-five. He died on 3 September 1963. For further biographical details, see the Epilogue. Law Society of Upper Canada Archives, Past Member Record Files; "D'Alton L. McCarthy Lawyer Half Century," Toronto *Star*, 7 September 1963; Moore, *Law*

Society of Upper Canada, 174, 223-6; Henry Morgan, *The Canadian Men and Women of the Time,* 2nd ed. (Toronto: William Briggs, 1912), 749.

32 Hogg's parents were David Hogg, who had settled in Perth in 1835, and Isabella Inglis. "Of Scottish descent," he was educated at the Perth High School, admitted as a student-at-law in 1869, and won several scholarships while at Osgoode Hall Law School. After his call, he began practice with John Bain, K.C., of Toronto, but was soon lured to Ottawa to become partner to Daniel O'Connor, K.C., who was "the Chief Legal Agent for the Dominion Government." There, he conducted much of the litigation work of the government until the retirement of the Tupper Administration. Law Society of Upper Canada Archives, Past Member Record Files; Morgan, *Canadian Men and Women* (1898), 471.

33 On the history of the St. Andrew's Society, see John Thorburn, *Sketch of the First Half Century of the St. Andrew's Society of Ottawa, 1846-1897* (Ottawa: Haldane, 1898).

34 For details of the will, see Book One n. 5. In 1884 Hogg resided at 261 Somerset Street West in Ottawa, but moved by 1897 to 221 Somerset West. The Mormon files on the 1881 Census of Canada show Agnes to be twenty-seven years old, and their son Frederick, two. Wellington Ward, Ottawa, Carleton, Ontario, FHL Film 1375865, NAC C-13229, Dist 105, SubDist A, Div. 2, p. 165, Family 782. There was also a second son, William Chesley Hogg, who moved to Edmonton after reaching adulthood. Law Society of Upper Canada Archives, Past Member Record Files; *Ottawa Directory,* 1884, 1889-90, 1894-5, 1896-7, 1897-8, 1898-9, 1899, 1900, 1905, 1907, 1910, 1920, 1927, 1928, 1929, 1930; "Striking Tribute by Bench and Bar to W.D. Hogg, K.C.," Ottawa *Citizen,* 5 January 1940, p. 2. On the close relationship between the Hogg and Bethune families, see *Where Angels Fear to Tread,* 68, and the press coverage of Mrs. Campbell's wedding, Toronto *Globe,* 15 November 1907, p. 6. The transcript of the Surrogate Court proceeding in January 1927, found in the Privy Council Archives, "Record of Proceedings," Campbell v. Hogg, No. 56 of 1929, p. 156, notes that the two families had "very intimate relations, constant visiting back and forth," that Lady Howland stayed at the Hoggs for several months after James Bethune's death, and that Charles lived with the Hoggs for almost the full year in 1885.

35 The source of the federal government contract work was O'Connor and Hogg's Conservative Party connections; both were active in the Ottawa Conservative Association. From 1878 to 1896, while the Conservatives were in power, Hogg was engaged "almost continuously in Counsel work for the Crown in the Exchequer and Supreme Courts of Canada," according to the remarks recorded at the Law Society Convocation of 21 March 1940 upon Hogg's death. Frederick A. Magee joined the firm in 1897, and after the death of O'Connor, the firm was known as Hogg and Magee. Magee was later appointed the local master of the Supreme Court at Ottawa, and, in 1907, the firm was redrawn as Hogg and Hogg, when William Hogg's son Frederick Drummond Hogg joined him. From 1911 to 1934, the firm operated from 48 Sparks Street, and developed a solid reputation among the other members of the Ottawa bar. Frederick Hogg, called to the bar in 1904, was appointed K.C. in 1928 and served as the president of the Carleton Law Association. *Ottawa Directory,* 1884, 1889-90, 1894-5, 1896-7, 1897-8, 1898-9, 1899, 1900, 1905, 1907, 1910, 1920, 1927, 1928, 1929, 1930,

1935; Law Society of Upper Canada Past Member Record Files; interview with E. Peter Newcombe, by Constance Backhouse, Ottawa, 13 August 2002 (copy on file with authors). The *Canadian Law List 1924* (Toronto: Canadian Law List, 1924), xlii, includes an advertising card for Hogg and Hogg that states: "Solicitors for La Banque Nationale, The British American Bank Note Co., The Home Building and Savings Association, The North American Life Assurance Co. &c."

36 In 1895 William Drummond Hogg had been elected president of the Carleton County Law Association. One year later, he was first elected bencher. While a bencher, Hogg served on the following committees: Reporting Committee 1896-1908; Discipline Committee 1896-1911, 1917-21; Library Committee 1899-1900; Finance Committee 1916-24; County Libraries Committee 1917-26; Journals and Printing Committee 1924-6. Law Society of Upper Canada Archives, Past Member Record Files.

37 On Hogg's age, see *Campbell v. Hogg,* [1930] 3 D.L.R. 673 at 675 (P.C.). The "prominent" comment was from William Renwick Riddell of the Ontario Court of Appeal. See *Re Howland,* [1935] O.W.N. 340 at 341. Johnson, *The First Century,* 15, lists Hogg among the leading early Ottawa solicitors, and remarks on "his distinctive white beard."

38 Trust companies first appeared in India, when the East India Company established various agency houses to transact business as trustees. The 1870s witnessed their initial establishment in the United States. J.W. Langmuir, the inspector of prisons and public charities for Ontario, was the founder of the Toronto General Trusts Corporation (TGTC). The charter of incorporation authorized the TGTC to serve as trustee, executor, administrator, agent, and receiver for managing and winding up estates, and investing money. It also managed safety deposit boxes. It advertised itself as "a well organized company possessing ample capital and the necessary equipment, including a staff of trained officials, for carrying on its operations systematically and economically, on strict business principles." Offices were established in Toronto, Montreal, Ottawa, Windsor, Winnipeg, Regina, Saskatoon, Calgary, and Vancouver. On the life and legacy of Reuben Wells Leonard, whose trust bestowed scholarships solely available to white Protestants of British nationality or parentage, see Bruce Ziff, *Unforeseen Legacies: Reuben Wells Leonard and the Leonard Foundation Trust* (Toronto: University of Toronto Press, 2000). See also *The Toronto General Trusts Company* (Toronto: n.p., 1892); John Cowan, "Canada's Oldest Trust Company," *The Canadian Magazine,* October 1922.

39 See Moore, *Law Society of Upper Canada,* 199.

40 Advertisement for TGTC in John Cowan, *Surrogate Court Rules of Ontario,* 8th ed. (Toronto: Ontario Publishing Co., 1942). Other page-length advertisements appeared in various city directories across the country.

41 "Chiselling Trust Co.," Toronto *Hush* 7, 41 (13 October 1934), 7 also notes: "No potential client of the Toronto General Trusts Corporation can expect any better treatment from this corporation than has been given to Mrs Campbell. The earnest advice of 'Hush' is to keep their affairs out of the hands of ... the Toronto General Trusts Corporation" (copy on file with authors).

42 Two of Sir William's sons served as mayor of Toronto. The eldest, William Holmes Howland, served from 1886 to 1888 but retired from office in part

because his father, who was "old and ailing, needed his help with his business." He predeceased his father in 1893. Oliver O. Howland, who served a two-year term as mayor, also predeceased his father in 1905. Desmond Morton, *Mayor Howland: The Citizen's Candidate* (Toronto: Hakkert, 1973), 15, 85, 107. For references on the history of Toronto, see generally Careless, *Toronto to 1918*; William Kilbourn, *Toronto Remembered: A Celebration of the City* (Toronto: Stoddart, 1984); Frederick Armstrong, *A City in the Making: Progress, People and Perils in Victorian Toronto* (Toronto: Dundurn, 1988); George P. de T. Glazebrook, *The Story of Toronto* (Toronto: University of Toronto Press, 1971); Victor Russell, ed., *Forging a Consensus: Historical Essays on Toronto* (Toronto: University of Toronto Press, 1984).

43 Glazebrook, *Story of Toronto*, 161.

44 For some discussion of the social lives of Toronto's elite, including references to dinner parties and balls hosted by "wealthy business families such as ... the Howlands," see Peter Oliver, *The Conventional Man: The Diaries of Ontario Chief Justice Robert A. Harrison, 1856-1878* (Toronto: University of Toronto Press, 2003), 52.

45 See generally Catherine L. Cleverdon, *The Woman Suffrage Movement in Canada* (Toronto: University of Toronto Press, 1950); Alison Prentice et al., *Canadian Women: A History* (Toronto: Harcourt Brace Jovanovich, 1988); Careless, *Toronto to 1918*.

46 Edgar McInnis, *Canada: A Political and Social History* (Toronto: Holt, Rinehart and Winston, 1982), 481-3, 510, 518, 520; Careless, *Toronto to 1918*; Glazebrook, *Story of Toronto*, 205-7.

47 Moore, *Law Society of Upper Canada*, 185, 187, 196, 200. Moore notes that half of new Ontario lawyers in the 1920s held a university degree, when higher education was available to only 3 percent of Canadian youth. The expansionist decade of the 1920s broke through the stagnation of lawyer numbers that had reigned since the turn of the nineteenth century, spawning an increase by about a third between 1921 and 1931, but witnessing little change in social caste.

48 Ibid., 106, 203, 232.

49 Elections for benchers began in Ontario in 1871, after the legislature passed a statute terminating the life appointments of the existing benchers and empowering all members of the bar to elect thirty benchers-at-large to five-year terms. Bencher elections were based largely on name recognition, and convocation tended to be dominated by elite lawyers who were older, wealthier, and more urban than the lawyers they governed, as well as more likely to come from large firms. Incumbents tended to win re-election. In 1912 the number of benchers was enlarged when long-term incumbents were permitted to become life benchers. They did not lose voting rights, but they were no longer counted among the thirty elected benchers. It was not until 1970 that life appointments for long service became non-voting positions. Ibid., 71-2, 75, 132, 138-9, 203, 210. See also John George Lambton Durham, *Lord Durham's Report,* ed. Gerald M. Craig (Toronto: McClelland and Stewart, 1963).

50 Bethune's principal, the Hon. Edward Blake, was a pillar of the Liberal party and a renowned barrister, often referred to as "the greatest lawyer in Canada." By the 1870s, Bethune practised in Toronto in partnership as Blake, Kerr and Bethune, a

law firm that later became the prestigious Blake, Kerr, Lash, and Cassels. James Bethune left the firm in 1873 to practise as Bethune and Hoyles. By the mid-1870s, that firm had merged into a new partnership as Bethune, Osler and Moss, in which James Bethune became the "chief partner" of a firm that included a roster of illustrious lawyers: Featherston Osler, Charles Moss, William Glenholme Falconbridge, Newman W. Hoyles, J.H. Thom, Walter Barwick, Sir Allen Bristol Aylesworth, and William J. Franks. The firm underwent name and personnel changes, as many of its senior members were elevated to the bench. By 1880 it was known as Bethune, Moss, Falconbridge, and Hoyles. Morgan, *Canadian Men and Women* (1898), 37, 319, 482, 530, 788, and (1912), 47, 384, 533, 609, 875.

WHERE ANGELS FEAR TO TREAD

PROLOGUE

1 The date was 1 May 1930. The London *Daily Herald,* 1 May 1930, p. 3, describes the weather as "fair generally, and warm locally, light variable wind." The reference in the book title is to a quotation of English poet Alexander Pope (1688-1744). The full quotation is: "For fools rush in where angels fear to tread." It appeared first in *The Poetical Works of Thomas Gray and an Essay on Criticism, The Rape of the Lock, and An Essay on Man* (1711). See Charles Dudley Warner, ed., *Biographical Dictionary and Synopsis of Books Ancient and Modern* (Akron, OH: Werner, 1965), 436; *The Concise Oxford Dictionary of Quotations,* 2nd ed. (Toronto: Oxford University Press, 1981), 184-5.

2 Mrs. Campbell's argument before the Privy Council began on 3 February 1930, continued on 4 and 5 February, and then adjourned until 13 and 14 February, when she made her final arguments.

3 We have searched the following newspapers: Toronto *Globe, Daily Mail and Empire, Evening Telegram, Star;* Ottawa *Citizen*; Montreal *Gazette*; Halifax *Chronicle*; Winnipeg *Free Press*; London *Times, Daily Herald*. We have been unable to find references with these specific titles, but found many similarly titled: "Woman Makes History: Portia Wins Appeal to Privy Council," London *Daily Herald,* 2 May 1930, p. 4; "Privy Council Allows Woman Her Own Appeal," Toronto *Star,* 1 May 1930, p. 2; "Canada's Portia Is Child of Man Who Never Knew When He Was Beaten," Toronto *Evening Telegram,* 3 May 1930, p. 3; "Toronto Woman First before Privy Council: Canadian-Born Portia Makes Legal History in Appeal to Peers," Toronto *Daily Star,* 28 January 1930, p. 1; "Canadian Portia Is Calm in Plea to Privy Council," Toronto *Star,* 3 February 1930, p. 19; "Canadian Portia Is Complimented by Privy Council," Toronto *Star,* 20 February 1930, p. 1.

4 After the unprecedented stresses of the First World War and its frightful military casualties, London celebrated the declaration of peace by according honour to those who had given their lives. The Cenotaph was designed by Sir Edwin Lutyens and erected in 1920 at the bottom of Whitehall to the memory of the dead in the armed forces. It consists of a thirty-three-foot-tall pylon with sculptured wreaths of green South African stone and the inscription, "The Glorious

Dead." Harold P. Clunn, *The Face of London* (London: Spring, 1962), 237; James
L. Howgego, *London in the 20s and 30s from Old Photographs* (London: Batsford,
1978), 2, photo 119.

5 The three Law Lords of the Judicial Committee of the Privy Council who sat
on the case were Lord Blanesburgh, Lord Tomlin, and Lord Russell of Killowen.
The eight Law Lords of the Judicial Committee of the Privy Council were Lord
Dunedin, Lord Blanesburgh, Lord Darling, Lord Atkin, Lord Tomlin, Lord
Thankerton, Lord Russell of Killowen, and Lord Macmillan.

6 This was Eugene Lafleur, K.C., LL.D., who was described as "the leader of the
Canadian Bar.""The Late Mr. E. Lafleur, K.C.," London *Times*, 2 May 1930, p. 5.

7 William Norman Tilley, K.C., described Lafleur as "a great advocate" and "a
man of great culture and refinement.""The Late Mr. E. Lafleur, K.C.," London
Times, 2 May 1930, p. 5. Tilley sat through Mrs. Campbell's entire argument
before the Privy Council, and later was the source of much of the information
the Ontario legal community received about the proceeding in England; see
Law Society of Upper Canada Archives, Draft Autobiography of D'Alton Lally
McCarthy, sous-fonds 1, D'Alton McCarthy sous-fonds, William G.C. Howland
fonds, 994001SF1-1-4. For further reference to Tilley's law firm's involvement in
Mrs. Campbell's case, see Book One, nn. 17 and 18.

8 Reasons for judgment in *Campbell* v. *Hogg et al.* were published as [1930] 3
D.L.R. 673 (P.C.).

BOOK ONE: THE LOST WILL

1 For biographical details of James Bethune, see the Introduction. Old
Government House was located at King and Simcoe Streets on the site of the
former Elmsley House. Construction was completed in 1870, and Lieutenant
Governor Howland was the first resident. In 1910 the property was sold to the
Canadian Pacific Railway, and the site was cleared in 1912. It is now occupied
by office buildings, a housing complex, and Roy Thomson Hall. See R.H.
Hubbard, *Ample Mansions: The Viceregal Residences of the Canadian Provinces*
(Ottawa: University of Ottawa Press, 1989), 114-16, 122. Construction of the
new Government House, on the Rosedale Ravine at Chorley Park, took place
from 1912 to 1915, at a cost of two and a half million dollars. It was closed in
1937, and the building was later leased as a military hospital, a training base for
reserve army units, a mounted police headquarters, and a haven for Hungarian
refugees. It was demolished in 1961, and the property became a public park. See
ibid., 123-8.

2 Sir William Howland's portrait, a commissioned work by George Theodore
Berthon (1806-92), oil on canvas, 109.2 x 81.3 cm, hangs in the Lieutenant
Governor's Suite in the Ontario Legislature, Queen's Park, along with portraits
of other former lieutenant governors. A second portrait, by Andrew Dickson
Patterson (1854-1930), oil on canvas, 124.5 x 87.6 cm, is housed in the art storage
area. Correspondence from Gillian Reddyhoff, curator, Archives of Ontario, 30
July 2002 (copy on file with authors).

3 For biographical references to Elizabeth Mary Rattray Bethune, later Lady
Howland, see the Introduction.

4 The order of Mr. Justice William Edward Middleton of the Supreme Court of Ontario appointing the Toronto General Trusts Corporation committee of Lady Howland's estate was signed 6 October 1922. The only surviving records are found in the Privy Council Archives, "Record of Proceedings," Campbell v. Hogg, No. 56 of 1929, p. 321. After his elevation to the Ontario Court of Appeal, Judge Middleton would sit on further legal proceedings regarding Lady Howland's estate in 1929. Lady Howland died on 14 August 1924. This is the date mentioned in the Surrogate Court records, Archives of Ontario, RG22, MS 584, Reel 43, Estate Grant 50634, No. 1784/24, 29 September 1924. The date mentioned in the Privy Council decision, 4 August 1924, appears to be a misprint; *Campbell* v. *Hogg,* [1930] 3 D.L.R. 673 at 679. For details about the sisters, their husbands, and their places of residence, see Introduction n. 6.

5 The document, dated 29 June 1915, which was later filed in the Surrogate Court of the County of York, reads:

THIS IS THE LAST WILL AND TESTAMENT of me LADY ELIZABETH MARY HOWLAND of the City of Toronto in the County of York, Widow of the late Sir William Pierce [sic] Howland K.C.M.G. deceased.

I GIVE AND BEQUEATH to my son Charles James Rattray Bethune the sum of One thousand dollars, one plain solitaire diamond ring, one old fashioned ring which belonged to his grand-father Doctor Rattray, one library writing table and bookcase (mahogany).

I GIVE AND BEQUEATH to my daughter Cora Ann Lindsey the sum of Two thousand dollars, my onyx locket set with pearls, my blue and gold enamelled locket containing painted portrait of her father and sister Lena.

I GIVE AND BEQUEATH to my daughter Annie McDougald, the sum of Two thousand dollars, one diamond and ruby ring (twin setting), one gold bracelet, gold thimble, one large antique brass lamp, one gold brooch set with cairngorm, lace scarf.

I GIVE AND BEQUEATH to my sister Agnes Louisa Hogg of the City of Ottawa the sum of One thousand dollars, my gold and onyx chain, one of my water-colour paintings by myself (Beggar Girls) and an old bed-room chair.

I GIVE AND BEQUEATH to my brother-in-law W.D. Hogg, K.C. of the City of Ottawa the sum of One thousand dollars, and my best thanks and love for all the kindnesses and assistance he has given me for many years.

I GIVE AND BEQUEATH to my daughter Elizabeth Louisa Bethune Campbell my diamond and ruby ring (two rubies), my long gold watch chain, mourning brooch containing Grand-mother's hair, sapphire and diamond brooch, point lace cape and flounce, mahogany card table, Bulique china, table ornament.

I GIVE AND BEQUEATH all other my remaining furniture, ornaments, jewellry [sic], clothing, household goods, pictures, china, books to my children to be divided between them as they may agree.

I GIVE, DEVISE AND BEQUEATH all other my real and personal estate not hereinbefore disposed of and of whatever nature and kind and wheresoever situate to my Executors and Trustees hereinafter named IN TRUST to sell and dispose of the same and invest the proceeds or if invested to keep the same invested with full power to vary the investments and to call in moneys invested and re-invest the same as they in their discretion may deem prudent, and to pay the income arising therefrom to my daughter Elizabeth Louisa Bethune Campbell, wife of Thomas C. Campbell, half-yearly until she attain [sic] the age of thirty-eight years, and then to pay her the whole of the residue of my estate.

I DESIRE my body to be place [sic] in St. James' Cemetery, Toronto, beside my husband James Bethune, and I request my Executors and my said daughter Elizabeth Louisa Campbell to keep the plot in the Cemetery in good order in memory of her father and mother.

I HEREBY REVOKE all former wills heretofore at any time made by me and I HEREBY APPOINT the Toronto General Trusts Corporation to be the Executors and Trustees of this my Will.

IN WITNESS whereof I have hereunto set my hand this twenty-ninth day of June, 1915.

[Archives of Ontario, RG22, MS 584, Reel 43, Estate Grant 50634, No. 1784/24, 29 September 1924.]

6 The law firm that had drawn the will for Lady Howland was Ingersoll, Kingstone, and Seymour of St. Catharines, Ontario. The leading counsel would probably have been J. Hamilton Ingersoll, who was called to the bar in 1882, and practised in St. Catharines until his death in 1933. Law Society of Upper Canada Archives, Past Member Record Files.

7 Mrs. Campbell was married to Rev. Thomas Clyman Campbell, rector of St. John's Episcopal Church in Jamaica Plain, Massachusetts. The rectory, built down the street from the church, was located at 24 Alveston Street. For information about Mrs. Campbell's two children, see the Introduction.

8 The summer home was in Chester, Nova Scotia. Interview with Peter Campbell Brooks, by Constance Backhouse, San Francisco, 23 July 2002 (copy on file with authors).

9 Archibald D. Langmuir was the general manager of the Toronto General Trusts Corporation, a position he took over from founder J.W. Langmuir in 1914. Some years earlier, he had acted as executor for Sir William Howland's estate. See John Cowan, "Canada's Oldest Trust Company," *The Canadian Magazine,* October 1922, as reprinted by the Toronto General Trusts Corporation, 3. William G. Watson was the assistant general manager of the Toronto General Trusts Corporation, a position he had held since 1914. Hector M. Forbes was

the estates manager of the Toronto General Trusts Corporation. For information on the management of the corporation, see entry in the *Toronto City Directory* (1924), 789, 1427, 1469.

10 This would have been Cora Ann Lindsey's residence, at 145 Tyndall Avenue.

11 Arthur Courtney Kingstone was born on 24 October 1874 in Toronto. His parents were Frederick William Kingstone and Henrietta Georgina Grassett. He was educated at Upper Canada College and Ridley College, and obtained a B.A. at the University of Toronto in 1896. He articled with Jones, Du Vernet in Toronto and was called to the bar in 1899. He would serve as a bencher of the Law Society of Upper Canada from 1921 to 1932, when he was appointed to the Supreme Court of Ontario. His wife, Marion Parmenter, came from the Parmenter legal family. (Reginald Holland Parmenter, Q.C., Marion's brother, was a partner with the Tilley, Johnston, Thomson and Parmenter Toronto law firm.) Kingstone would die of a heart attack on 5 January 1938, while on a holiday in Vancouver. Law Society of Upper Canada Archives, Past Member Record Files.

12 Some time around 1914, Lady Howland retired to St. Catharines, Ontario, where she made her home in the Welland Hotel. For more details, see the Introduction.

13 Although Mrs. Campbell does not give the date, it must have been shortly after Lady Howland's death on 14 August 1924.

14 For information on J. Hamilton Ingersoll, see n. 6 above.

15 For information on Mrs. Campbell's brother, Charles James Rattray Bethune, see the Introduction.

16 There was no one of the appropriate age named Cummings during this period in the Law Society of Upper Canada Archives, Past Member Record Files. It is possible that Mr. Cummings was temporarily sojourning in Canada and was not formally registered with the Ontario legal profession.

17 William Norman Tilley was born on 11 March 1868 at Tyrone, in Durham County, Ontario. His parents were William Edward Tilley, a school inspector, and Selina Ann Vanstone. Norman Tilley taught school for several years in the 1880s and, according to lawyers' lore, when he left for Osgoode Hall, the school trustees of rural Cainsville advised him that "if ever there was a person we thought was ill-conceived to be a lawyer, it would be you." Rumour goes that Tilley "kept the letter all his life." He articled with Allan Aylesworth, a former partner of James Bethune, and obtained the gold medal at Osgoode Hall Law School. He was called to the bar in 1894, and practised with Tilley, Johnston, Thomson and Parmenter (partnered by Strachan Johnston, K.C., Reginald Holland Parmenter, K.C., Arthur J. Thomson, and W.S. Morlock). The firm had been located in the Toronto General Trusts Building at 85 Bay Street in 1918, and would move with the Trust Company by 1924 to 255 Bay Street. Tilley obtained a K.C. in 1915 and served as bencher from 1916 to 1930. He would be elected treasurer of the Law Society of Upper Canada from 1930 to 1935. He acted as director of the Canadian Pacific Railway, Bank of Montreal, Canadian Life Assurance Co., and Royal Trust before his death in 1942. Chief Justice Sir William Mulock once described him as one of Canada's "most brilliant lawyers," and he was widely reputed to be "the dominant Canadian litigator of his time."

See Christopher Moore, *The Law Society of Upper Canada and Ontario's Lawyers, 1797–1997* (Toronto: University of Toronto Press, 1997), 156–7, 204; Law Society of Upper Canada Archives, Past Member Record Files; *Canadian Law List 1918* (Toronto: Canadian Law List, 1918); *Toronto City Directory, 1924*.

18 John Strachan Johnston, K.C., was a partner in the Tilley, Johnston, Thomson and Parmenter law firm. By 1930 it would be located at 8 King Street West, and would add the following to its roster: S.E. Wedd, B.V. McCrimmon, C.F.H. Carson, J.G. Middleton, E.P. Tilley, and J.S.D. Tory. Johnston received a B.A. from the University of Toronto in 1889 and an LL.B. in 1890. He was admitted as a student-at-law in 1889 and called to the bar in 1892. He resided at 1 Dale Avenue, Toronto. He would die 14 September 1941. Law Society of Upper Canada Archives, Past Member Record Files; *Toronto City Directory, 1924*; *The Canadian Who's Who, 1936-37* (Toronto: Times Publishing, 1937), 565.

19 For an example of such a case, see *Howith* v. *McFarlane* (1924), 56 O.L.R. 375 (C.A.), which admitted a lost will to probate based on the testimony of the plaintiff who had drawn it, was present at its execution, and was named the executor. The plaintiff testified that the lost will had been executed in accordance with the legislation, and proved the contents by the production of his memorandum of instructions and a carbon copy of the will. R.E. Kingsford, *The Law Relating to Wills: Adapted to the Provinces of the Dominion of Canada*, 6th ed. (Toronto: Carswell, 1913), notes on p. 84, "where a will has been lost or destroyed ... the contents of the will may be proved by secondary evidence: such as a draft or copy." Kingsford cites *Johnson* v. *Lyford* (1868), L.R. 1 P. and D. 546, to illustrate that written statements made by the testator, along with actions in relation to the statement, were admissible as the contents of the will.

20 Reginald Holland Parmenter was admitted as a student-at-law in 1899 and called to the bar in 1902. He practised in Toronto with the Tilley, Johnston, Thomson and Parmenter law firm. He died on 22 July 1939.

21 Thomasine would have been attending Miss Souther's Dancing School in Jamaica Plain, at which Miss Marguerite Souther dispensed lessons in etiquette, decorum, and ballroom dancing to the elite girls from Jamaica Plain and the freshmen boys from Harvard University. See interview with Katharine Cipolla, by Constance Backhouse, Boston, 14 August 2001 (copy on file with authors).

22 For details of Slaght's background and career, see the Introduction and Book Two n. 32.

23 The trial took six days in June and July 1925, before Mr. Justice Hugh Thomas Kelly of the Supreme Court of Ontario, and the decision came out 20 October 1925. Judge Kelly was born in Adjala Township, Simcoe County, on 1 March 1858, the son of Irish Roman Catholic immigrant farmers John and Annie McLaughlin Kelly. He was educated at St. Michael's College in Toronto and Toronto University, called to the bar in 1886, and carried on practice with Foy and Kelly in Toronto. He also served as president of the York County Law Association and the Toronto Bar Association. He would die 7 December 1945. See Henry J. Morgan, ed., *Canadian Men and Women of the Time* (Toronto: William Briggs, 1912), 603; *The Canadian Who's Who, 1938-39* (Toronto: University of Toronto Press, 1985), 365; Law Society of Upper Canada Archives, Past Member Record Files.

24 William Ridout Wadsworth appeared for Cora Lindsey. William James Elliott, K.C., represented Annie McDougald. Ewart Victor McKague appeared for the Toronto General Trusts Corporation. "Osgoode Hall News," Toronto *Globe,* 20 October 1925, p. 7.

25 Kingstone was appointed to the Supreme Court of Ontario, High Court of Justice, in 1932.

26 For biographical details on William Drummond Hogg, see the Introduction.

27 This appears to be a misprint. James Bethune died in Toronto on 18 December 1884. His will was probated in 1885.

28 The only surviving information on this judgment, in the absence of archival court records, comes from the press coverage. The Toronto *Evening Telegram,* 20 October 1925, p. 15, in an article titled "Lady Howland Revoked Will: Action Fails," reported that Judge Kelly found that the will was actually made, but revoked while Lady Howland was still mentally competent:

> His Lordship says ... there was no question that a will was prepared and executed in 1915 and if revocation was not established there would be no question as to its contents, a copy of the will having been produced. The onus was upon the defendants to show that revocation was effected during a period of mental competency. There were two features to be considered: whether the will itself was in the possession of the testatrix, and secondly, if so, whether she was at any time after it came into her possession mentally unfit to revoke the will, and if so, was revocation effected during a lucid interval.
>
> His Lordship refers to the court declaration vesting Lady Howland's affairs in a committee, but he points out that that declaration was of incapability to manage her own affairs. He questions whether that order would have been made on "mental incapacity" ... As to the destruction of the will, his Lordship says that, while it cannot be determined, he believes it a fair and reasonable presumption that the will was destroyed with the intention of revoking it within a short time after it was brought to her from the solicitor's office and while Lady Howland had mental capacity to effect revocation.

The coverage in the Toronto *Globe,* 20 October 1925, p. 7, "Osgoode Hall News" column was shorter, and somewhat more confusing:

> Action to establish a will of Lady Howland bearing date June 29, 1915, for the appointment of the said Trust Corp. as executor and for the revocation of the letters of administration.
>
> Judgment: The will sought to be established is not produced, and has not been discovered since the death of Lady Howland. On Oct. 6, 1922, an order was made by a court declaring Lady Howland, on account of her age and mental and physical infirmity, incapable of managing her own affairs, and that she should be placed in the custody of a guardian as to her person, etc. My opinion is that the facts of this case do not rebut the presumption of revocation. While the actual date cannot be determined, I

believe it is a fair and reasonable presumption that the will was destroyed with the intention of revoking it within a short time after it was brought to her from her solicitor's office and while she had mental capacity to effect a revocation. Action dismissed with costs. Fifteen day's stay.

The decision was rendered within the framework of the common law, which provided that when a will was not found at the death of the testator, a presumption arose that the will had been destroyed for the purpose of revoking it. The presumption could be rebutted with evidence about the actions or statements of the testator before death. See *Sudgen* v. *Lord St. Leonards,* [1875-76] 1 P.D. 154 (C.A.) at 217; *Lefebvre* v. *Major,* [1930] S.C.R. 252; *Re Perry,* [1925] 1 D.L.R. 930 (Ont. C.A.); *In Re Sykes, Drake* v. *Sykes* (1907), 23 Times L.R. 747. Kingsford, *Law Relating to Wills,* 83, notes that it was "difficult to lay down any general rule as to the nature of evidence which is required to rebut the presumption of destruction ... Where the will makes a careful and detailed disposition of the testator's property, and nothing happens to make it probable that he wishes to revoke it, the presumption raised by the disappearance of the will may be rebutted by slight evidence, especially if it is shewn that access to the box, or other place of deposit where the will was kept, could be obtained by persons whose interest it is to defeat the will." Where the testator had become mentally incompetent, the rebuttable presumption no longer applied. Instead, the burden of proof shifted to those who claimed that the will had been set aside, to prove that the testator was of sound mind at the time of revocation. See *Sprigge* v. *Sprigge* (1868), L.R. 1 P. and D. 608; Kingsford, *Law Relating to Wills,* 84.

29 There are no surviving court records for the Ontario Court of Appeal prior to 1941; conversation with Paul McIlroy, legal records archivist, Archives of Ontario, 11 July 2002. Counsel appeared as follows: W.J. Elliott, K.C., for Annie McDougald; E.V. McKague for the trust company; W.R. Wadsworth for Cora Ann Lindsey. Argument appears to have been heard 20 April 1926. The judges who heard the case were Chief Justice Sir William Mulock, Mr. Justice Frank Egerton Hodgins, Mr. Justice James Magee, Mr. Justice William Nassau Ferguson, and Mr. Justice Robert Cooper Smith. All appear to have had significant linkages either to the Bethune/Howland/Campbell families or to William Hogg. Mulock was a close family friend and had attended Mrs. Campbell's wedding. Hodgins's legal practice would have overlapped with Hogg's, since he acted as the legal agent for the Dominion government in Toronto, and Hodgins's term as bencher from 1910 to 1912 also overlapped with Hogg's. Magee would speak "charmingly" to Mrs. Campbell of her father and mother, both of whom he had known. Ferguson had articled with Mulock and served alongside Hogg after he was elected bencher in 1916. Smith would have been familiar with the Bethune family, as he had served as the M.P. for the federal riding of Stormont from 1908 to 1911. Law Society of Upper Canada Archives, Past Member Record Files; *Where Angels Fear to Tread,* 95; "Campbell v. Lindsey," Toronto *Globe,* 20 April 1926, p. 5.

30 According to the press coverage, Slaght argued that the mere fact that a will could not be found was not proof that it had been revoked. He also brought out in evidence that no one had ever made a "very thorough search" for the will.

Slaght contended that the revocation of a will was as serious a matter as the execution of such a document and required as definitive proof. He argued that there was no proof that an envelope containing a will, sent to the Welland Hotel from the Ingersoll, Kingstone firm, had ever reached Lady Howland. Even if it had, he claimed, her health had failed progressively, and she had been in no condition to revoke a will. "The onus of proof of testamentary capacity lay with his opponents," he concluded. "Campbell v. Lindsey," Toronto *Globe*, 20 April 1926, p. 5; "Daughter Brings Appeal in Howland Will Case," Toronto *Star*, 20 April 1926, p. 3.

31 The architectural plan from the 1910-12 addition to Osgoode Hall by provincial government architect Francis Riley Heakes shows a "Consultation Room" adjacent to the Court of Appeal. The courtroom still exists (Courtroom 1) and is used for appeals. Correspondence from Elise Brunet, archivist, Law Society of Upper Canada, 30 July 2002 (copy on file with authors).

32 The Lunacy Act, R.S.O. 1914, c.68. Section 37(1) set the act in motion provided that an individual could be "proved to the satisfaction of the Court, that he is, through mental infirmity, arising from disease, age, or other cause, or by reason of habitual drunkenness or the use of drugs, incapable of managing his affairs." Under s.6, the application could be made by the attorney general of Ontario, by any one or more of the next of kin, by a wife or husband, a creditor, or any other person. Under s.7, the evidence had to establish the mental infirmity "beyond reasonable doubt." Section 11 provided that where a committee of the estate was appointed:

(a) The committee shall, within six months after being appointed, file in the office of the master to whom the matter is referred, or of such officer as may be appointed for that purpose, a true inventory of the whole real and personal estate of the [incompetent], stating the income and profits thereof, and setting forth the debts, credits, and effects of the [incompetent], so far as the same have come to the knowledge of the committee;

(b) If any property belonging to the estate is discovered after the filing of an inventory the committee shall file a true account of the same, from time to time, as it is discovered.

The trust company wrote on 10 October 1922 to Hogg, asking him to supply to the corporation a detailed list of Lady Howland's investment, and to advise whether the mortgage papers and other documents were in his hands. By letter dated 19 October 1922, Hogg's law firm replied: "We beg to hand you ... the several mortgages which have been in our possession as set out in the statement enclosed, amounting in all to $8,200." *Campbell* v. *Hogg*, [1930] 3 D.L.R. 673 (P.C.) at 678.

33 The election for benchers, in which all practising members of the bar voted for thirty lawyers (not fifty, as Mrs. Campbell states) to govern the legal profession, took place in April 1926. The results placed Slaght thirty-eighth, with 747 votes. Eight of the benchers who received more votes than Slaght were named life benchers because of the number of times they had been elected: Willoughby

Staples Brewster, K.C., John Cowan, K.C., Frederick Weir Harcourt, K.C., Isidore Frederick Hellmuth, K.C., William Field Kerr, K.C., Thomas Herbert Lennox, K.C., Wallace Nesbitt, K.C., and Newton Wesley Rowell, K.C. This meant that the roster of benchers in 1926 included Slaght, as the last elected member. See Law Society of Upper Canada Archives, Minutes of Convocation, vol. 17, 29 April 1926.

James Cowan had been born in Scotland, and received an LL.B. from the University of Edinburgh. His father, J.E. Cowan, became a bank manager in Toronto. James immigrated to Canada in 1911, and practised law in Saskatchewan from 1911 to 1919, when he began articling in Ontario. He was called to the Ontario bar in 1922, and practised with Slaght and Cowan in Toronto. He would be appointed a Toronto police magistrate by Mitchell Hepburn's provincial Liberal government in 1936, but ultimately forced to resign by the same government in 1938. The press coverage of the resignation did not disclose the details: "Beyond the statement that the request for Magistrate Cowan's resignation was an immediate and direct outcome of [Ontario Attorney General] Conant's unheralded inspection of city police courts, no official explanation is forthcoming at Queen's Park of the attorney-general's action. It is understood that the attorney-general's decision was approved by the Ontario government at a cabinet session late yesterday afternoon." Cowan died in Toronto on 23 June 1953. Toronto *Star,* 11 May 1939; Law Society of Upper Canada Archives, Past Member Record Files.

BOOK TWO: THE PLUNDERED ESTATE

1 Initially in 1884, Lady Howland had inherited all of James Bethune's estate, which was composed of $39,850 in personalty and an unknown sum in realty, totalling a possible $60,000. For more details, see the Introduction. On 19 October 1922, Hogg's law firm advised the trust company that the investments he was managing included "several mortgages" amounting in all to $8,200," which he handed over to the company. *Campbell* v. *Hogg,* [1930] 3 D.L.R. 673 (P.C.) at 678.

2 Newton Wesley Rowell was born on 1 November 1867 in the township of London, Middlesex County, Ontario. His British parents were Joseph Rowell, a minister, and Nancy Green. He was called to the bar in 1891, and practised in Toronto with Rowell, Reid, Wilkie and Wood. He received his K.C. in 1902 and was elected a bencher in 1911. He would serve as bencher continuously until 1935, when he became treasurer of the Law Society, a position he held until 1936. Rowell would also serve as president of the Canadian Bar Association from 1932 to 1934. The Toronto *Mail and Empire* described him as "one of the outstanding legal and constitutional authorities of the day."

Rowell was also an active politician. He was elected as a Liberal M.L.A. for North Oxford and served as leader of the Opposition from 1911 to 1917, and then as M.P. for Durham from 1917 to 1921. He served as minister of health, secretary of state and external affairs, helped to form the Union government, and was appointed vice-chairman of Prime Minister Robert Borden's war cabinet. In politics, he was an advocate of temperance, political rights for women, improved factory and worker's compensation laws, better housing, unemployment and health insurance, mother's allowances, prohibition of child labour, and reduced hours for women and youths. During the First World War, Rowell ran most of the operations of the federal government and was known as one of the "chief architects of Canada's war effort." In 1937 he was appointed co-chair of the Rowell-Sirois Commission, which produced an influential and wide-ranging report on the financial aspects of Canadian federalism. In his later years, Rowell represented Canada at the League of Nations and achieved a reputation as an international statesman.

In addition to the presidency of the Toronto General Trusts Corporation, Rowell served as director of the Globe Printing Co. and the Lake Superior Corporation. He resigned as president of the Toronto General Trusts Corporation in 1934. Rowell's firm, undermined in part by Rowell's habit of working in isolation from the other partners, fell apart after he became a judge in 1936, although junior partners eventually rebuilt it as McMillan, Binch. Rowell died on 22 November 1941. Margaret Prang, *N.W. Rowell: Ontario Nationalist* (Toronto: University of Toronto Press, 1975); "Rowell, Hon. Newton Wesley, P.C.," *Who's Who in Canada, 1936-37* (Toronto: Times Publishing, 1937), 949; "Rowell, Hon. Newton Wesley, P.C.," *The Canadian Who's Who, 1938-39* (Toronto: University of Toronto Press, 1985), 589-90; Toronto *Star,* 3 September 1983, p. H6; Christopher Moore, *The Law Society of Upper Canada and Ontario's Lawyers, 1797-1997* (Toronto: University of Toronto Press, 1997), 198; Law Society of Upper Canada Archives, Past Member Record Files.

3 Mrs. Campbell does not provide the year, but based on correspondence in the Privy Council Archives, it appears that some of Hogg's written replies to the queries of the trust company came on 6 May 1926, 14 June 1926, 26 October 1926, 9 November 1926, and 16 November 1926. The references to May, when Mrs. Campbell realized that Hogg's replies were inaccurate, and October, when she went to Ottawa, are probably to 1926. It is unlikely that they are to 1927, since the next Surrogate Court hearing into the matter, which reviewed this correspondence, concluded 14 April 1927. Privy Council Archives, "Record of Proceedings," Campbell v. Hogg, No. 56 of 1929, pp. 250-8; *Campbell* v. *Hogg,* [1930] 3 D.L.R. 673 (P.C.) at 679-81, 685.

4 The Privy Council would later confirm this, noting that Charles, who died on 6 April 1921, was deceased before Hogg's ledgers indicated that the mortgage money had been received:

> Now each of these statements [by Hogg] was unfortunately entirely incorrect. Charles Bethune was dead before the Vaillancourt moneys were received; the note in Mr Hogg's ledger was that the balance of the Dumas mortgage was "paid to Lady Howland by Charles," an impossibility, as the moneys were only received in July, 1921, three months after Charles's death: and no part of the $800 from the Campbell mortgage was ever paid to Lady Howland by cheque or otherwise. The facts were that all these three sums remained in Mr Hogg's hands uninvested, and in cross-examination in these proceedings he found himself unable to explain how he came to make the statements just set forth. Their

Lordships regret having to emphasize this slip, but Mr Hogg's carelessness of assertion, of which this is a typical example, constitutes one of the great difficulties in the case.

Campbell v. *Hogg*, [1930] 3 D.L.R. 673 (P.C.) at 680.

5 James Davey was the manager of the Ottawa branch of Toronto General Trusts Corporation. The branch was established in 1903, after the Toronto General Trusts Corporation acquired the assets of the Ottawa Trust and Deposit Company. See John Cowan, "Canada's Oldest Trust Company," *The Canadian Magazine*, October 1922, as reprinted by the Toronto General Trusts Corporation, 5.

6 William Drummond Hogg and his son, Frederick Hogg, practised from the Trusts Building at 48 Sparks Street, Ottawa.

7 Rowell was elected a bencher in 1911 and served continuously until he became treasurer in 1935. He would also be sitting as chair of the discipline committee in 1931 when Mrs. Campbell laid a disciplinary complaint against Hogg. Rowell and Hogg's terms as benchers overlapped for many years. Hogg failed to secure re-election as bencher in 1911, but upon re-election in 1916 began to serve as a life bencher until 1940. Hogg had himself sat on the discipline committee from 1896 to 1911, and 1917 to 1921. In 1926 Hogg was only sitting on the county libraries committee and the journals and printing committee. Rowell's elevation to chief justice occurred in 1936, despite his lack of previous judicial experience.

8 The overt racism in this statement was widely shared by white Canadians in the late nineteenth and early to mid-twentieth centuries. References to Chinese-Canadians as "Chinks" and promotion of stereotypes about connections with illegal drugs appeared regularly in the press and in statements made by leading figures from the legal, political, and social reform communities. See Constance Backhouse, *Colour-Coded: A Legal History of Racism in Canada, 1900-1950* (Toronto: University of Toronto Press, 1999), chs. 1 and 5; and Constance Backhouse, *Petticoats & Prejudice: Women and Law in Nineteenth-Century Canada* (Toronto: Osgoode Society and Women's Press, 1991), ch. 7.

9 There were, of course, no photocopying or duplicating machines available in 1926, so copying had to be done by hand, or by typists who recreated a document, based on the original.

10 The Privy Council would later confirm the multiplicity of contradictory letters in its decision. *Campbell* v. *Hogg*, [1930] 3 D.L.R. 673 (P.C.) at 679-82.

11 The reference to Rowell as the "Christian man" may have arisen, in part, from his electoral campaigns advocating the prohibition of alcohol. In a provincial election campaign in 1911, Rowell's platform to "abolish-the-bar" was spread through speeches in which Rowell told crowds across the province that they "could vote for organized Christianity or they could vote for the organized liquor industry." In 1916, when he travelled to France on a governmental visit to the troops, he surprised the group who met him late at night at the airport in Paris with his first question: "Is there a Methodist chapel in Paris?" A prominent Methodist, Rowell promoted the Laymen's Missionary Movement for the "evangelization of the world in this generation" and was the most influential layman to support the formation of the United Church of Canada in 1925. Rowell was

reputed to be "a mild-mannered, soft-spoken gentleman, unfailingly courteous, with a deep understanding and an awesome grasp of law, finance and international diplomacy." Donald Jones, "Incorruptible Party Leader Redeemed Ontario Liberals," Toronto *Star,* 3 September 1983, p. H6; Prang, *N.W. Rowell.*

12 The Privy Council decision confirmed this amount sent from Hogg to wrap up the estate. *Campbell* v. *Hogg,* [1930] 3 D.L.R. 673 (P.C.) at 681.

13 The right to pass accounts was statutory: Trustee Act, R.S.O. 1927, c.150, s.23. On 7 January 1927, Hogg presented his account to the Surrogate Court to be examined, audited, and passed. The style of cause was originally titled "In the matter of the agency of W.D. Hogg, K.C., and in the estate of Lady Howland," but it was amended by consent to "In the matter of the Trustee Act." The proceeding, which ultimately consumed six days, was unwieldy and complex. In the first presentment, Hogg put forward an account, commencing in June 1886, which showed total receipts of $39,972.86 and a total discharge of $39,486.86, leaving $486 due from him. The surviving records are located in the Privy Council Archives, "Record of Proceedings," Campbell v. Hogg, No. 56 of 1929. Details have also been drawn from *Campbell* v. *Hogg,* [1930] 3 D.L.R. 673 (P.C.) at 682, 685.

14 The Privy Council noted that the fee Hogg proposed to charge for his work on the estate was $1,155, calculated as $30 a year for thirty-eight and a half years. The Law Lords did not criticize the amount of the bill, but they noted that Hogg had "never before hinted at any such claim," and added that it could "hardly be doubted that the chief merit of this particular assessment of it was that it balanced the account to within a margin of $6.41 and thus relieved him of the imputation that a large sum had for years remained undisclosed in his hands." Even here, Hogg failed in accuracy, since as the Privy Council would later note, the trust had lasted only thirty-five years. *Campbell* v. *Hogg,* [1930] 3 D.L.R. 673 (P.C.) at 681.

15 On 17 January 1927, Hogg produced a second set of accounts, with approximately eighteen changes. This showed total receipts of $46,567.61 and a total discharge of $45,994.64, leaving almost $573 due from him. Judgment was reserved, and delivered on 21 October 1927. *Campbell* v. *Hogg,* [1930] 3 D.L.R. 673 (P.C.) at 682, 685.

16 This most probably refers to Susan Revere Chapin, one of the wealthiest parishioners in Reverend Campbell's congregation. She was the widow of Henry Bainbridge Chapin, one of the wardens of St. John's Episcopal Church who selected and called the Campbells. Parish records indicate that Mrs. Chapin's son was baptized in 1891, when the family lived on Centre Street. Her son died in an accident in 1908 at age sixteen. Her husband died in 1910. By 1917 Mrs. Chapin was living on Louders Lane. A great-granddaughter of Paul Revere, Chapin had family in England (her sister was the wife of Sir William Osler in Oxford) and had spent considerable time there during the First World War. Both her class and her English connections would have endeared her to Mrs. Campbell. She would have been in her early sixties when she provided so much support and financial assistance to Mrs. Campbell. She died in 1961. See William Lawrence, "Susan Revere Chapin," *The Church Militant* (November 1940), n.p. (copy on file with authors); Katharine G. Cipolla, "The Privy

Council's First Portia," *Eagle's Eye* (September 1992), St. John's Episcopalian Church, Jamaica Plain, p. 6. On the social connections between the two women and the financial help offered by Mrs. Chapin, see correspondence from Katharine Cipolla to Sydney Harris, 3 May 1992 (copy on file with authors); interview with David Mittell and Katharine Cipolla, by Constance Backhouse, Boston, 13 August 2001 (copy on file with authors).

17 James Lang, formerly the assistant secretary at Toronto General Trusts Corporation, was the estates manager in Toronto during the litigation. *Toronto City Directory,* 1927, 1932, 1937. Ewart Victor McKague was a thirty-four-year-old lawyer and not completely inexperienced. Presumably Mrs. Campbell, who was used to dealing with Tilley, Rowell, and other lawyers at the peak of their careers, had very high standards for counsel. McKague had been called to the bar seven years earlier, on 20 May 1920, and practised in Toronto with William James Elliott. McKague's father was H.H. McKague, a sales manager. He had received a B.A. from the University of Toronto in 1915 and began his articles with Elliott in 1915, at the age of twenty-two. He served in the First World War, and received a K.C. in 1945, at the close of the Second World War, in which he also served. Law Society of Upper Canada Archives, Past Member Record Files.

18 The date would have been 7 January 1927, the commencement of the Surrogate Court hearing.

19 The explicit reference to Semitic features suggests that Mrs. Campbell shared the discriminatory anti-Semitic attitudes prevalent in Canadian legal circles and the wider society. See Irving Abella and Harold Troper, *None Is Too Many* (Toronto: Lester, 1983); Alan Davies, ed., *Antisemitism in Canada: History and Interpretation* (Waterloo, ON: Wilfrid Laurier University Press, 1992); Lita-Rose Betcherman, *The Swastika and the Maple Leaf* (Toronto: Fitzhenry and Whiteside, 1975); David Rome, *Clouds in the Thirties: On Anti-Semitism in Canada 1929-1939* (Montreal: Canadian Jewish Congress, 1977); Constance Backhouse et al., "Clara Brett Martin: Canadian Heroine or Not?" *Canadian Journal of Women and the Law* 5, 2 (1992): 263-356; James W. St. G. Walker, *"Race," Rights and the Law in the Supreme Court of Canada* (Osgoode Society and Wilfrid Laurier University Press, 1997).

20 Robert Irvin Ferguson was born on 17 December 1895 in Morris Township, Ontario. He attended Wingham High School and Stratford Normal School, taught school briefly, and then served as a lieutenant with the 161 Huron Infantry in the First World War. Upon his return, he worked in a steel plant in 1919, and then obtained his B.A. from the University of Toronto in 1922. That year he began articling with Dudley Holmes in Goderich, and was called to the bar in 1925, when he began practice with Slaght. Ferguson received a K.C. in 1936 and became a judge of the Supreme Court of Ontario in 1950. He remained on the bench until his death 28 November 1969. His most notorious case was the Steven Truscott murder trial of 1959. Judge Ferguson sentenced fourteen-year-old Truscott to death for the rape and murder of twelve-year-old Lynne Harper, but the sentence was commuted to life imprisonment, and Truscott was paroled in 1969 after serving ten years. Judge Ferguson also presided over another well-known case in 1958, in which he quashed orders deporting an elderly Israeli couple and an Italian, and criticized immigration

legislation that disentitled immigrants from the protection of Canadian law. Law Society of Upper Canada Archives, Past Member Record Files; "High Court Judge R.I. Ferguson Dies," Toronto *Daily Star,* 28 November 1969; "Conducted 1959 Trial of Steven Truscott," *Globe and Mail,* 29 November 1969.

Childs was located at 279-83 Yonge Street, across the street from the Royal Bank Building, which was on the northeast corner of King Street and Yonge, Toronto. *Toronto City Directory,* 1927.

21 The Law Society records spell the barrister's name as George Frederick Macdonnell. He was admitted as a student-at-law in 1894 and called to the bar in 1898. In 1927 he was in solo practice in the Fraser Building at 53 Queen Street, Ottawa. He died in July 1939. *Canadian Law List 1927* (Toronto: Canadian Law List, 1927); *Ottawa City Directory,* 1927.

22 Built in 1912, at a cost of $2 million the Château Laurier had at that time 350 rooms, 155 with private bathrooms. Its original room rates ranged from $2 upwards. According to Joan E. Rankin, *Meet Me at the Chateau: A Legacy of Memory* (Toronto: Natural Heritage Books, 1990), 19, the hotel "typified the grandeur of the old chateau seen in the Loire Valley in France. It was built of smooth granite blocks and lightbuff Indiana limestone. Its crown, erupting with turrets, dormers and gables, was sheathed in copper which the elements would slowly oxidize to a soft shade of green to match the roofs of the Parliament Buildings next door."

23 James Arthur Mulligan, born on 24 July 1861, began his legal career as a student-at-law in 1878, and was called to the bar in 1883. The 1881 Census indicates that he was Irish Catholic; see Mormon files on the 1881 Census of Canada: Census Place: Pembroke, Renfrew North, Ontario, Canada; Source: FHL Film 1375870, NAC C-13234, Dist 114; SubDist E, p. 76, Family 309. Mulligan practised in Toronto for some years and then moved to Sudbury, where he practised alone in 1902, with A.D. Meldrum as Mulligan and Meldrum by 1904, and with T.M. Mulligan as Mulligan and Mulligan in 1915. He was appointed to the Carleton County Court in 1922 and sat on the bench until 1928. Law Society of Upper Canada Archives, Past Member Record Files; *Canadian Law List 1902, 1904, 1915.*

24 The Ottawa lawyer representing Cora Ann Lindsey was Robert Victor Sinclair, K.C. He became a student-at-law in 1880, was called to the bar in 1885, and practised with Joseph J. Gormully until 1891. He had a solo practice at 74 Sparks Street from 1891 until 1902, at which time he joined forces with Sir A.P. Caron. They continued to practise together until 1907. Between 1907 and 1913, still at 74 Sparks, Sinclair was again in solo practice. In 1914 he moved on his own to the Booth Building, 165 Sparks, and stayed there until 1939. He died on 16 February 1943. *Ottawa City Directory,* 1885-6, 1889-90, 1891-2, 1895-6, 1902, 1907, 1914, 1940; Law Society of Upper Canada Archives, Past Member Record Files; *Canadian Law List 1920,* 161; *Canadian Law List 1928,* 164; *Canadian Law List 1929,* 164.

25 Hogg practised at 832 Sparks Street until 1911, when he moved to 48 Sparks Street. *Ottawa City Directory,* 1896-7, 1900, 1907, 1910-15.

26 For details of James Bethune's will, see the Introduction.

27 The Privy Council confirmed Mrs. Campbell's account of some of this

information. It noted that, in 1905, Hogg received $2,000 on the sale of some coal stock belonging to Lady Howland. He paid $200 to her, retaining $1,800 for investment. He advised Lady Howland by letters dated 3 November 1905 and 16 January 1906 that he had taken an $1,800 mortgage with the Capital Real Estate Co., and paid Lady Howland interest half-yearly on this mortgage until 1918. In fact, Hogg was the president of Capital Real Estate Company Limited. The Law Lords concluded that Hogg had taken out a mortgage worth only $800 but paid Lady Howland interest as if it were a $1,800 mortgage, as Mrs. Campbell indicated. Hogg's testimony was to the effect that this was "all a mistake," and that when he realized it in March 1917, he met with Lady Howland to inform her. The Law Lords described Hogg's testimony as "strange." They also doubted Hogg's memory about the meeting with Lady Howland, noting that full interest was paid on 9 July 1917, and that it was not until 4 February 1918 that the reduction of interest was first made. Furthermore, they noted that if the conversation had taken place as Hogg thought he recollected, it would seem "obvious that he must then have done one of two things; he must either at once have invested the $1,000 or returned it forthwith to Lady Howland. But he did neither." Ultimately, they held Hogg not liable for any further interest, because "interest on uninvested balances [was] not chargeable in these proceedings," but held him fully "accountable for the net amount of the principal." *Campbell v. Hogg,* [1930] 3 D.L.R. 673 (P.C.) at 690-2; Privy Council Archives, "Record of Proceedings," Campbell v. Hogg, No. 56 of 1929, p. 71.

28 See Trustee Act, R.S.O. 1927, c.150, s.23. Mrs. Campbell was wrong about the statute she cites. The Privy Council decision did not comment on any statutory breach of the Trustee Act, although it did note: "It is, of course, an elementary proposition that a trustee must keep an accurate account of the trust property, and must always be ready to render it when required. This history, apart altogether from any question as to the completeness or correctness of the final account, is a striking commentary on Mr Hogg's neglect of this elementary duty. He has surely only himself to thank if a final account preceded by such a record is critically dealt with by any Court." In fact, the statutory breach seems to have been of the Surrogate Courts Act, R.S.O. 1927, c.94. Section 38 of the Surrogate Court Rules set forth stringent regulations as to the requisite contents of accounts presented to the court for passing. They were to contain "a true and perfect inventory of the whole property in question" and to include: "(1) An account showing of what the original estate consisted; (2) An account of all moneys received; (3) An account of all moneys disbursed; (4) An account of all property remaining on hand." See John Cowan, *Surrogate Court Rules of Ontario,* 3rd ed. (Toronto: Dudgeon and Thornton, 1922), 34. The Privy Council decision concluded, in *obiter,* that Hogg's accounts did not comply with this: "How easy it should have been for [Hogg] to comply with all these requirements if he had kept, even in the simplest form, a complete and separate record of his transactions on her account. Unfortunately, professional man though he was he did not do so, and the account filed having been prepared, as was contended, without reference to or attempt to comply with R. 38, it was objected by the appellant that it should not be accepted at all." Noting that the Surrogate Court had

been "indulgent" in accepting the records, the lordships added, "To their Lordships it would not have been surprising had he, however reluctantly, felt compelled to reject it altogether." The issue was no longer a live one at the Privy Council, as the parties had agreed to accept the account and confined the appeal to a discussion of the objections to particular items and omissions. *Campbell* v. *Hogg,* [1930] 3 D.L.R. 673 (P.C.) at 682-5.

29 For biographical details, see n. 24 above, Mrs. Campbell's reference to the "tie that binds these two men" is difficult to document. Both were Ottawa lawyers, but we have discovered no other connections.

30 The Privy Council confirmed some of Mrs. Campbell's suspicions in its final decision. It noted that Lady Howland's ledger book listed one loan of $1,100 made in 1885 to McAmmond at 6 percent interest, and one of $500, made in 1885 to Martin at 8 percent interest. The Law Lords indicated that it was "very extraordinary" that Hogg had held the bonds without knowing the address of either. However, they declined to find that the loans never existed, noting that this was not the question the board was called upon to answer. Dealing exclusively with the issue of whether Hogg had discharged himself of the sum of $1,600 by paying it back to Lady Howland, the Privy Council determined that there was no voucher indicating the receipt, and no trace of any payment into her bank account, and so concluded that Hogg had not discharged himself of the sum. *Campbell* v. *Hogg,* [1930] 3 D.L.R. 673 (P.C.) at 697-701.

31 The Privy Council confirmed this, noting: "It must now be taken to be admitted that the entries now appearing in his firm's ledger were interpolated by himself after the question of payment was in 1926 raised at the appellant's instance. Again, the sum said to have been received and paid over was not the proper sum." *Campbell* v. *Hogg,* [1930] 3 D.L.R. 673 (P.C.) at 700.

32 Arthur Slaght had a reputation as a man about town, a drinker, a hedonist, and a charming lady's man. Separated from his wife, Evelyn Lukes, after only a few years of marriage, he maintained a grand home in Toronto at 51 Russell Hill, in which he, apart from a chauffeur, housekeeper, and maid, was the sole resident. He would take time off in the winter to spend several months at the Breakers resort in Florida. He travelled by cruise ship with groups of his friends to Havana. In one famous trip to Bermuda with Mitchell Hepburn in 1934, Slaght docked the SS *Monarch of Bermuda* at Nassau, and the two missed their lunch with the governor of Nassau because they were ensconced in a brothel. Slaght maintained a palatial summer home in Parry Sound, on Georgian Bay. Known as the "Beau Brummel of the Commons," Slaght's "passion for fine clothes was more than matched by his enthusiasm for a good time." Lawyers who knew him recall his penchant for introducing the "charming-looking ladies" who would be with him in New York City or elsewhere as his "niece." Despite having come from modest circumstances, Slaght "was a patrician who affected elegance." The bulk of Slaght's money came from mining stock he obtained through clients from northern Ontario, particularly stock for the Macassa mines and through connections with mining financier Harry Oakes. He earned a lot through his law practice, and he apparently spent almost every penny he made.

Mitchell Hepburn and Arthur Slaght, who frequently caucused with political cronies at the King Edward Hotel, were often depicted as living "on the edge of scandal." The rumour was that Slaght had been denied the cabinet post of justice by Mackenzie King, despite his "exceptional ability," because of "having habits that might get him and others in serious trouble." Other rumours characterized Slaght as the one who rejected the cabinet, noting that he had "turned down King's invitation to join the cabinet because even at sixty-one he was unwilling to give up his 'Bohemian life.'" One Tory complained rather querulously that Slaght was "a social and moral leper of the lowest order ... such a low degenerate that his wife and family had to break up their home and leave him, on account of his immorality and drunken blackguardism." Others reported that he began a long and loving, if not always faithful, relationship with a woman less than half his age, when he turned fifty-eight. His mistress had left a bank to join the civil service at Queen's Park in 1935, and was a close friend of Mitch Hepburn's companion. Some of the more proper secretaries at Whitney Block apparently referred to the two women as "the stable." John T. Saywell, *"Just Call Me Mitch": The Life of Mitchell F. Hepburn* (Toronto: University of Toronto Press, 1991), 127-8, 192-3, 237-8, 409, 423-4; interview with Ronald Graeme Slaght, by Constance Backhouse, Nancy Backhouse, Rachel Chisholm, Toronto, 20 June 2002 (copy on file with authors); interview with Brendan O'Brien, by Constance Backhouse and Nancy Backhouse, Toronto, 13 April 2001 (copy on file with authors).

   Arthur Slaght was a serious hockey fan. He would subsequently act against Connie Smythe over the building of Maple Leaf Gardens in 1931, and to spite his opponent, purchased the best seats behind the Toronto Maple Leaf bench. Interview with Ronald Graeme Slaght by Constance Backhouse, Toronto, 20 June 2002 (copy on file with authors).

33 Norman L. Martin was a chartered accountant and authorized trustee in bankruptcy whose office was at 73 King Street West, Toronto. *Toronto City Directory,* 1927. Martin had no partners in his firm, although he had a staff of about thirty, twelve of whom were accountants. At this point, he had been in practice for twenty-five years. Privy Council Archives, "Record of Proceedings," Campbell v. Hogg, No. 56 of 1929, pp. 171, 182.

34 The Hon. William Nassau Ferguson had been appointed to the Ontario Court of Appeal in 1916. He was born on 31 December 1869 in Cookstown, Ontario, to Isaac Ferguson and Emily J. Gowan. Ferguson was educated at Upper Canada College, and articled with William Mulock (later chief justice of Ontario) in 1889. He was called to the bar in 1894 and practised in Toronto with Millar and Hunter, a firm that later became Miller, Ferguson, Hunter. He served as a bencher for eight months in 1916, until his elevation to the bench. He died on 9 November 1928.

35 This became Exhibit 44-A, "Record of Mrs. E.M. Bethune's Mortgages, March, 1890," filed on 23 May 1927, despite the conclusion of the hearing on 14 April 1927. The document contained the headings and particulars of securities from 1885 to March 1890, twenty in all, in Hogg's handwriting, and purported to be a record of early investments of Lady Howland's money. The Privy Council would later note that, "its admission without qualification or explanation from Mr. Hogg as to the extent of his responsibility for the transactions entered there-

in by him has remained something of an embarrassment." *Campbell* v. *Hogg,* [1930] 3 D.L.R. 673 (P.C.) at 685-6.

36 Judgment was delivered on 21 October 1927. It was rendered "just a few weeks prior to his death." Although the decision was unreported, it is contained in the Privy Council Archives, "Record of Proceedings," Campbell v. Hogg, No. 56 of 1929, p. 195. Mulligan largely accepted Hogg's account of 17 January 1927, finding that only $201.61 remained outstanding, an amount that had been admitted by Hogg's counsel. Mulligan rejected Mrs. Campbell's other objections, noting:

> The Trustee has reached an age approximating eighty years, and his memory, endeavouring to recall acts extending over forty years, is more dangerous than he suspected, but I have confidence in his disposition to be just. I credit the loss of his books as hampering a full accounting, and bearing this in mind, am disposed to be indulgent in enabling him to clear the account. Under the circumstances I accept the amount as filed, although not complying with the form required in the Surrogate Court, under Rule 38 ... On the question of the necessity of corroboration of the statement of the Trustee ... I hold that there has been an underlying connection between several disputed items sworn to by the Trustee, and his evidence is corroborated with respect to some of these, so as to satisfy me as to the accuracy of his testimony and his general credibility, thus satisfying the Statute as to the rest of the items.

The only point that Mulligan found in Mrs. Campbell's favour was a denial of Hogg's claim to compensation for his work on behalf of the estate. Mulligan held that "it was not the intention of either party that he should receive compensation for his services." *Campbell* v. *Hogg,* [1930] 3 D.L.R. 673 (P.C.) at 686.

Book Three: Counsel Lay Down Their Brief

1 John Galsworthy (1867-1933) wrote the play *Loyalties,* which was first presented in 1922. See John Galsworthy, *Loyalties: A Drama in Three Acts* (New York: Charles Scribner, 1924). It is set in the "rarefied atmosphere of cultivated upper-class British society in the 1920s," and the plot explores an incident of theft perpetrated by a well-liked and accepted member of the set. When accusations are made against the thief, most of his circle rally to his defence instinctively, out of loyalty to his class and professional status. See Frank N. Magill, ed., *Masterplots* (Englewood Cliffs, NJ: Salem Press, 1976), 6:3, 544-6.

2 The first lawyer Slaght recommended was William Norman Tilley, K.C. (whose biographical details are described in Book One n. 17). Since Tilley was a law partner of Strachan Johnston, who had provided such recalcitrant and unsatisfactory representation for Mrs. Campbell on the will dispute, it seems very odd that Slaght should have suggested him. Slaght took the file from Johnston, so he must certainly have known the dubious quality of the firm's services on behalf of Mrs. Campbell.

The second lawyer was Isidore Frederick Hellmuth, K.C. Hellmuth had been elected a bencher in 1916, the same year Tilley was first elected, and was re-elected continuously until 1926, when he became a life bencher, like Hogg. Hellmuth was born on 21 February 1854 in Sherbrooke, Quebec, the son of Right Rev. Isaac Hellmuth, Anglican bishop of Huron, and Catherine Evans. His father, Isaac, had converted from the Jewish faith. Hellmuth was educated at Hellmuth College in London, Ontario, received an LL.B. at Trinity College, Cambridge, in 1877, and became a member of the Inner Temple in England. He was called to the Ontario bar in 1877 and began practice with the firm of Hellmuth, Cattenach, Meredith in Toronto the same year. The firm eventually changed its name to Hellmuth, Cattenach, Ramsay. Hellmuth left Toronto to practise in London from 1892 to 1900. He returned to Toronto in 1900, where he would practise until 1936. Hellmuth's practice included frequent appellate work at the Privy Council. He died on 17 February 1944. Law Society of Upper Canada Archives, Past Member Record Files; Christopher Moore, *The Law Society of Upper Canada and Ontario's Lawyers, 1797-1997* (Toronto: University of Toronto Press, 1997), 179.

The third was D'Alton Lally McCarthy. For details on McCarthy, see the Introduction.

3 The appeal from the Surrogate Court lay to a single judge at Osgoode Hall, sitting ad hoc as a judge of the High Court; see William J. Anderson, "Where Angels Fear to Tread," *Law Society of Upper Canada Gazette* 29, 1 (1995): 18. Cornelius Arthur Masten, the Court of Appeal judge appointed to hear the appeal, had been born on 16 December 1857 in St. John's, Quebec. His parents were James and Jane Masten. Masten graduated from Victoria University in 1879 and taught as a math master at Orillia High School from 1879 to 1880, when he became a student-at-law, articling with John Bain and George F. Shepley. He was called to the bar in 1883 and practised in Ontario from 1884 to 1915. In 1915 he was appointed to the Supreme Court of Ontario; in 1923, he was elevated to the Court of Appeal. Seventy years old at the time of this hearing, Masten's "distinguishing" features were his "black spats" and his deafness, the latter often interfering with his ability to hear the argument in court. He died on 31 August 1942. Law Society of Upper Canada Archives, Past Member Record Files; A.B. McKillop, *The Spinster and the Prophet: Florence Deeks, H.G. Wells and the Mystery of the Purloined Past* (Toronto: Macfarlane Walter and Ross, 2000), 350-3.

4 William Ralph West, whose father was E.C. West, a farmer, was born in 1896. He received his B.A. from the University of Toronto in 1915, began to article in 1919, and was called to the bar in 1924, where he practised with the McCarthy law firm. He would receive a K.C. in 1946, and die 6 November 1975. Law Society of Upper Canada Archives, Past Member Record Files.

5 The case was argued on 14 and 15 December 1927. Mr. Justice Masten's Bench Books, 1927, 25-46.

6 The Toronto *Evening Telegram,* 15 December 1927, p. 27, reported in an article titled "Trustee Got $19,000; Left About $8,415" that "at the outset, Justice Masten said he had had personal relations with Mr. Hogg and had acted for him in a good many things." Masten had "been a student in Mr. Hogg's office," according to Law Society of Upper Canada Archives, Draft Autobiography of

D'Alton Lally McCarthy, sous-fonds 1, D'Alton McCarthy sous-fonds, William G.C. Howland fonds, 994001SF1-1-4. Another connection would have been Masten's and Hogg's terms as benchers of the Law Society of Upper Canada. Masten had been elected a bencher in 1908 and served for at least three years of overlap with Hogg until 1915.

7 Mephistopheles, a character in Johann Wolfgang von Goethe's *Faust,* is described as a "subordinate devil, one of many, in Lucifer's dominion," the "sum-total of all non-doing: laziness, procrastination, indifference, self-indulgence, cynicism, idle mockery, frivolity, doubt, self-doubt, disinterest, purposeless activity, wanton destructiveness of nature and beast and man." As complex as he is evil, Mephistopheles is also "a polished courtier, a salon gallant and a backstairs gallant, immensely intelligent, witty." Mount Brocken, in the Harz Mountains in Germany, is the location to which Mephistopheles brings Faust to witness the celebration and revelry of witches. See Charles E. Passage, ed., *Johann Wolfgang von Goethe's Faust, Part One and Part Two* (New York: Bobbs Merrill, 1965), xli-xlii; Richard K. Cross, "Climbing the Brocken," *Modern Age* 36, 4 (1994): 308.

8 The only surviving records for Masten's judgment are found in the Privy Council Archives, "Record of Proceedings," Campbell v. Hogg, No. 56 of 1929, p. 203. Press coverage of the decision is contained in "Masten Gives Reasons in Dismissing Appeal," Toronto *Star,* 23 December 1927, p. 27; "Trustee Got $19,000; Left about $8,415," Toronto *Evening Telegram,* 15 December 1927, p. 27; "Judgments in Probe of Trusteeship," Toronto *Evening Telegram,* 23 December 1927, p. 21. In his order dated 19 December 1927, Masten, J.A., dismissed all of Mrs. Campbell's claims, making factual findings that the Privy Council subsequently ruled were "wrong." Mrs. Campbell states that Judge Masten "found that Mr. Hogg had been guilty of retaining trust funds," even though the gain was "scarcely over eleven hundred dollars." The relevant portion of the judgment held that Hogg had retained "out of the capital in his hand the sum of $1155.00, which he considered ought properly to be retained as a very modest compensation for his services during the forty years that he acted as trustee." Masten noted that Hogg's claim to this compensation had been disallowed by Judge Mulligan, and added that, "upon the best consideration I was able to give it, I found myself unable to allow the cross-appeal [on this issue]." Judge Masten then made an error by amending the order of Surrogate Court Judge Mulligan to add the sum of $1,155 to the balance found in favour of the estate. The Privy Council would later decide that Masten's amendment was "due to a misapprehension on the part of the Judge," who "mistakenly supposed that Mr. Hogg had entered in his account of January 17, 1927, $1,155 for his compensation and his order was intended to make his disallowance of any sum for compensation effective." *Campbell v. Hogg,* [1930] 3 D.L.R. 673 (P.C.) at 688.

One of the most interesting paragraphs of the judgment is the positive assessment of Hogg: "I have no doubt regarding the substantial services rendered by Mr. Hogg nor regarding the complete honesty of all his actions. The questions before the Court have arisen, in my opinion, from intimate family relations which existed and which naturally, perhaps, induced a certain looseness in recording the transactions. No claim was ever suggested by Lady Howland during her lifetime, and I have no doubt if she were alive, no such claim would now be put forward."

9 Lally McCarthy's draft autobiography confirms that Judge Masten had contacted McCarthy about scheduling a "re-hearing before him in regard to one point which apparently worried him." It is possible that his error in adding $1,155 to the balance of the estate inspired his wish to speak with counsel and parties, and to revise the original decision. Law Society of Upper Canada Archives, Draft Autobiography of D'Alton Lally McCarthy, sous-fonds 1, D'Alton McCarthy sous-fonds, William G.C. Howland fonds, 994001SF1-1-4.

10 James McGregor Young had been born in Hillier, Prince Edward County, on 6 June 1864. His father was John Young, and his mother, Letitia Jane Whitten. He was educated at Picton High School and the University of Toronto. In 1884 he began articling with the Toronto firm of Blake, Lash and Cassels, a reconfiguration of James Bethune's old firm. He was called to the bar in 1887 and practised with the Blake firm until 1895. At that point he became a full-time lecturer in law for many years, first at the Law Society of Upper Canada, and subsequently at the University of Toronto. He received a K.C. in 1908 and was elected a bencher in 1926. Eventually Young returned to law practice in Toronto for several years with Young and McEvoy but was then appointed official guardian in 1928. He died on 1 April 1942. Law Society of Upper Canada Archives, Past Member Record Files.

11 Edmund Harley was the senior registrar for the Supreme Court of Ontario at the time. *Canadian Law List 1927* (Toronto: Canadian Law List, 1927).

12 John Joseph Daley, the chief librarian of the Great Library at Osgoode Hall, had worked with the library since 1882. Daley would have had little first-hand knowledge of Mrs. Campbell's father, since he worked only temporarily with the library until 1884. The year that James Bethune died, Daley was promoted to the position of assistant librarian. In 1895 he was elevated to the post of chief librarian, a position he held until retirement in 1939. Leonard Wrinch, the assistant librarian, would never have known Bethune. He began work at the Great Library in 1916, was appointed assistant librarian in 1923, and died in 1956.

13 Leonard D'Arcy Hinds was born in Barrie in 1868, to Bernard Hinds and Anna Leonard. He studied at the separate school and Barrie Collegiate, and graduated from St. Michael's College. He was one of the founders of the 208th Irish Regiment, and retired with the rank of major. In 1905 he became judgment clerk at Osgoode Hall, but it was not until the age of fifty that he completed studies at Osgoode Hall. He was called to the bar in 1920. Hinds, famous for his colourful personality, became known as "Toronto's most famous Irishman." He was a writer of Irish songs and poetry, and served as secretary of the United Irish League and president of the Gaelic League. He served as assistant registrar and registrar of the Supreme Court of Ontario for forty years, retiring in 1938. Law Society of Upper Canada Archives, Past Member Record Files; "Noted Court Registrar D'Arcy Hinds Is Dead," and "A Charming Fighter," Toronto *Globe,* 26 and 29 March 1948.

14 The First Divisional Court of the Appellate Division was composed of Chief Justice Rt. Hon. Sir William Mulock, Hon. James Magee, Hon. Frank Egerton

Hodgins, Hon. William Nassau Ferguson, and Hon. David Inglis Grant. Chief Justice Mulock and Judges Magee and Hodgins had sat on the earlier will dispute, in which the infamous settlement was negotiated. Chief Justice Mulock was a close family friend.

Sir William Mulock was born on 19 January 1844 at Bond Head, Ontario, of Dr. Thomas Holman Mulock and Mary Cawthra. He obtained a B.A. from the University of Toronto in 1863, and was called to the bar in 1868. He practised with the firm of Mulock, Tilt, Miller and Crowther in Toronto, and had the distinction of taking as an articling student Clara Brett Martin, Canada's first female lawyer. Mulock was elected a Liberal M.P. for North York from 1882 to 1905, and served as postmaster general and minister of labour. He was appointed chief justice of the Supreme Court of Ontario High Court (Exchequer) in 1905, and chief justice of the Supreme Court of Ontario High Court of Justice in 1923. He died on 1 October 1944. On the linkages with the Bethune/Howland/ Campbell families, see Book One n. 29.

Judge Magee was born in 1846 in Liverpool, the son of Richard Magee. He emigrated to Canada in 1855 and was educated at the London, Ontario, Grammar School. He was called to the bar in 1867 and practised in London. In 1893 he was appointed Middlesex County Crown Attorney. He was elected bencher from 1891 to 1896, missing Hogg's election by just one term. Judge Magee was appointed to the Supreme Court of Ontario in 1904, and elevated to the Court of Appeal in 1919, where he sat until 1933. On the linkages with the Bethune/Howland/Campbell families, see Book One n. 29.

Judge Hodgins was born on 27 March 1854. Educated at Toronto's University of Trinity College, he was called to the bar in 1878 and practised in Toronto. He served as president of the Ontario Bar Association and was elected bencher in 1910. Judge Hodgins was appointed to the Ontario Court of Appeal in 1912, where he sat until 1932. On the linkages with Hogg, see Book One n. 29.

Judge Ferguson was born on 31 December 1869 in Cookstown, Ontario, of Isaac Ferguson and Emily J. Gowan. Educated at Upper Canada College, he articled with William Mulock. He was called to the bar in 1894 and practised in Toronto with Millar and Hunter, a firm that later became Millar, Ferguson, Hunter. He died on 9 November 1928. On the linkages with Hogg, see Book One n. 29.

Judge Grant was born on 22 August 1872. He was called to the bar in 1895 and practised in Orillia and, later, Toronto. He was appointed to the Supreme Court of Ontario in 1925 and elevated to the Court of Appeal in 1927. He died on 1 January 1933.

Law Society of Upper Canada Archives; Henry Morgan ed., *Canadian Men and Women of the Times* (Toronto: William Briggs, 1898), 599, 665-6; 2nd ed. (1912), 391, 538, 723-4, 833-4; *The Canadian Who's Who, 1936-37* (Toronto: Times Publishing, 1937), 700, 811-12.

15 Barristers who had received the distinction of being appointed King's Counsel were allowed to wear silk gowns and to sit at a table closer to the bench in the court.

16 "Lady Howland Case Decision Is Appealed," Toronto *Star*, 13 February 1928, p. 3, notes that Mrs. Campbell argued that N.L. Martin, her accountant, had found "on Hogg's own admissions that he owed more than $27,000 to Lady Howland's estate, capital and interest." Chief Justice Mulock then requested the matter be simplified by asking an accountant to "find how matters stand," and Mrs. Campbell replied she had "spent all her money" and could not "have anything else looked into." The court then permitted Mrs. Campbell to "go over the matter item by item."

17 Judge Ferguson died on 9 November 1928. For details of the judgment, see n. 22 below.

18 The Flying Scotsman was built by the London and North Eastern Railway in 1923. It was chosen by that railway to represent the latest in steam locomotive design at the British Empire Exhibitions in Wembley in 1924 and again in 1925. In 1928 it began a non-stop run from London to Edinburgh, the longest non-stop train trip in the world at the time. By 1934 it was the first train to be able to travel 100 mph. C. Hamilton Ellis, *The Flying Scotsman, 1862-1962* (London: George Allen and Unwin, 1962).

19 Eighty-four-year-old Sir William Mulock's long tenure as chief justice had earned the six-foot-tall, venerable jurist this nickname, and he was described by lawyers as "a God-like figure with his flowing beard and high-domed forehead." Lita-Rose Betcherman, *The Little Band: The Clashes between the Communists and the Canadian Establishment, 1928-1932* (Ottawa: Deneau, 1983), 207-8.

20 This is a reference to the tangled quagmire of a seemingly endless lawsuit over an estate that formed the centrepiece of Charles Dickens's *Bleak House* (London: Bradbury, 1853).

21 The 29 November 1928 judgment was reported in summary fashion as *Re Howland* (1928), 35 O.W.N. 175 (C.A.). Counsel for Hogg and Mrs. Lindsey was Robert Victor Sinclair, K.C. Ewart Victor McKague was counsel for the Toronto General Trusts Corporation. The majority decision, written by Judge Hodgins, dismissed Mrs. Campbell's claim primarily because Hogg had never taken the position of trustee. Although Hogg had voluntarily assumed the position of trustee when he attempted to pass his accounts before the Surrogate Court, Judge Hodgins found that an individual could not "constitute himself a trustee," by "mere ipse dixit." The court characterized the relationship between Lady Howland and Hogg as "that of principal and agent." Relying substantially on Mrs. Lindsey's memorandum that Hogg had never acted as trustee, the majority judgment stated: "She says that after the death of her father, the late James Bethune, Lady Howland's first husband, Mrs. Bethune naturally turned to her brother-in-law for assistance in procuring investments for a portion of the moneys realised from the estate of Mr. Bethune." In conclusion, Judge Hodgins noted: "No one can make substantive law for himself; and unless the circumstances in which he stands warrant the conclusion which he desires, he has no right to invest himself with it." Like the dissenting decision, the majority conceded that Hogg's accounts were incomplete, with records extending from 1886 to 1926 lost, one of the parties dead, and the other seriously handicapped by the loss of his books, vouchers, and papers. Instead of criticizing Hogg for the

incomplete records, the majority decided it would be "useless to attempt to arrive at an accurate result based on figures admittedly incomplete," and that it was better to let the Surrogate Court decision, affirmed by Judge Masten, stand. However, Judge Hodgins noted that Judge Masten's decision to increase the amount of the estate by $1,155 to disallow Hogg's costs had been erroneous, because the Surrogate Court had never allowed compensation in the first place.

The last portion of the majority judgment held that an amount of $1,000 was to be added to the estate. The justification for this seems quite peculiar in retrospect:

> It may be that the costs and expense of taking the accounts in the way adopted by Mr. Hogg has materially increased the burden on the appellant; and it may also be a more satisfactory ending to the case if some amount, in addition to that found by the Surrogate Court Judge, is allowed to Mrs. Campbell as compensation for the expenses which these proceedings have entailed. The amount allowed by the Surrogate Court Judge should be increased by $1,000 if Mrs. Campbell is willing to accept the total sum in full of her claim against Mr. Hogg and as a settlement of the matter.

Re Howland (1929), 35 O.W.N. 175 (C.A.) at 175-7. The $1,000, which Mrs. Campbell says seemed to her "to savor of a bribe," was considered "an extraordinary provision" by subsequent judicial observers; see Anderson, "Where Angels Fear to Tread," 19. Even the Privy Council was prepared to intimate that it was problematic: "The refusal by the appellant of the additional sum mentioned makes it unnecessary for their Lordships to consider whether the Appellate Division had in that matter jurisdiction to act as it proposed to do." *Campbell* v. *Hogg,* [1930] 3 D.L.R. 673 at 689.

Judge Magee's dissenting judgment assumed Hogg had been acting as trustee, since he had come to court under the Trustee Act to pass his accounts. Judge Magee was very critical of the decisions of the Judges Mulligan and Masten, which had made findings "contrary to the evidence." The judges had failed to consider that Mr. Hogg himself had testified that "large sums had come into his hands and that investments had been made both before and after the commencement of the account," and that "no means" was afforded to the court "to ascertain how much capital Mr. Hogg had received." Judge Magee would have allowed the appeal, and sent the matter back to the Surrogate Court to reconsider, based on any further evidence either side might care to adduce. He was careful to add that he wished at this point to decide "nothing beyond the fact that there are unexplained or partly explained matters which require to be straightened out," and that he recognized that Hogg was "under the serious disadvantage of the lapse of many years and the loss of books and papers, and it would be unjust to him that without further inquiry the questions should be determined upon the evidence as it stands, shewing considerable sums received by him outside of his account and also considerable sums invested by him." Lastly, Judge Magee joined his colleagues in the peculiar suggestion that Mrs.

Campbell consider taking the $1,000 in settlement. While characterizing it as "only a tentative suggestion," Judge Magee ventured that it "might be accepted as a family settlement of a troublesome difficulty." *Re Howland* (1929), 35 O.W.N. 175 (C.A.) at 178-9.

22 The Ontario Court of Appeal records no longer survive, but the National Archives of Canada, Blake and Redden fonds, R3485-0-9-E, vol. 62, file 6, indicate that there were three appeal decisions: 19 November 1928, 29 November 1928, and 18 March 1929. The Privy Council Archives, "Record of Proceedings," Campbell v. Hogg, No. 56 of 1929, containing the 29 November 1928 judgment, notes at p. 219: "This judgment supersedes the judgment announced on the 19th of November, 1928, the form of which was due to a misunderstanding." Since the 19 November 1928 version no longer survives, it is difficult to know how the first and second judgments differed from each other. The 18 March 1929 judgment was an order instructing that a memorandum be attached to the reasons for judgment. The memorandum stated: "The memorandum filed on behalf of Mrs. Cora Ann Lindsay [sic] was withdrawn on the 18th of February 1928, before the argument was proceeded with." No records of the memorandum survive. A summary of the 29 November decision was reported as *Re Howland* (1928), 35 O.W.N. 175 (C.A.). Counsel for Hogg and Mrs. Lindsey was Robert Victor Sinclair, K.C.; counsel for the Toronto General Trusts Corporation was Ewart Victor McKague. Judge Hodgins wrote the majority judgment, with Judge Magee dissenting.

23 One account of the letter was printed in "Refuses Court Offer of $1,000," Toronto *Evening Telegram,* 30 November 1928, p. 1. The letter survives in full in the Privy Council Archives, "Record of Proceedings," Campbell v. Hogg, No. 56 of 1929, pp. 226-7.

BOOK FOUR: MY STRUGGLE FOR ENGLAND

1 Norman Bentwich, *The Practice of the Privy Council in Judicial Matters,* 2nd ed. (Toronto: Carswell, 1926). The book outlines the civil procedure or "Rules of the Judicial Committee" to appeal a case to the Privy Council. Part I outlines jurisdictional matters, including brief histories of the British colonies of Canada, India, Australia, and South Africa, as well as their distinct legal systems and procedural requirements. Part II details the conditions and rules of appeal. Part III examines the practice in appeals in admiralty, prize court, and ecclesiastical matters.

2 We have been unable to locate a newspaper report with this headline, but "Canada's Portia Is Child of Man Who Never Knew When He Was Beaten," Toronto *Evening Telegram,* 3 May 1930, p. 3, contains several paragraphs of humorous anecdote about the $11.75 law book.

3 Bentwich, *Practice of the Privy Council,* 37, quoting *Prince v. Gagnon,* [1882-83] 8 A.C. 103 (P.C.) at 105.

4 Bentwich, *Practice of the Privy Council,* 38, quoting *Clergue v. Murray,* [1903] A.C. 521 at 522-3. The wider access for appeals from provincial courts was reflected in the number of cases that were appealed. Over the seventy-five years between

Confederation and the patriation of judicial authority, the Judicial Committee would hear a total of 667 Canadian appeals, 253 from the Supreme Court itself and 414 that bypassed the Supreme Court and came directly from the provincial courts of appeal. Peter McCormick, *Supreme at Last: The Evolution of the Supreme Court of Canada* (Toronto: Lorimer, 2000), 9.

5 The Privy Council Appeals Act, R.S.O. 1927, c.86, s.1, provided: "Where the matter in controversy in any case exceeds the sum or value of $4,000, as well as in any case where the matter in question relates to the taking of any annual or other rent, customary or other duty, or fee, or any like demand of a general and public nature affecting future rights, of what value or amount soever the same may be, an appeal shall lie to His Majesty in His Privy Council; and except as aforesaid, no appeal shall lie to His Majesty in His Privy Council." Section 2 provided: "No such appeal shall be allowed until the appellant has given security in $2,000, to the satisfaction of the court appealed from, that he will effectually prosecute the appeal, and pay such costs and damages as may be awarded in case the judgment appealed from is confirmed." Section 4 provided: "Subject to the provisions of The Guarantee Companies Securities Act, the security shall be by bond of two sufficient sureties, each of whom shall make affidavits of justification." Section 5 provided: "Where security is to be given for payment of money, directed by the judgment or order appealed from to be paid, either as a debt or for damages or costs, the bond shall be in double the amount by the judgment or order directed to be paid."

6 Bentwich, *Practice of the Privy Council,* 45, notes: "It will be observed that no leave has to be asked or obtained on appeal from Ontario. The provision is that 'an appeal shall lie.'" The provision quoted is s.1 of the Privy Council Appeals Act, R.S.O. 1914, c.54, an exact precursor to the R.S.O. 1927, c.86, s.1.

7 Bentwich, *Practice of the Privy Council,* 201, quotes Rule 13 of the Rules of the Judicial Committee issued in 1925, that where the record was printed abroad, forty copies were required to be transmitted to the Registrar of the Privy Council. Mrs. Campbell appears to have forgotten that only forty copies were required, not sixty. Bentwich, *Practice of the Privy Council,* 368, notes the list of "Council Office Fees." For example, entering appearance, £1; lodging petition of appeal, £3; and setting down appeal (chargeable to Appellant only), £5.

8 Bentwich notes on pp. 169-70 that Rule 8 provided: "Rules 3 to 7 (both inclusive) shall apply *mutatis mutandis* to petitions for leave to appeal *in forma pauperis,* but in addition to the affidavit referred to in Rule 4 every such petition shall be accompanied by an affidavit from the petitioner stating that he is not worth 25l. in the world excepting his wearing apparel and his interest in the subject-matter of the intended appeal, and that he is unable to provide sureties, and also by a certificate of counsel that the petitioner has reasonable ground of appeal."

9 The objection to allowing Mrs. Campbell to have her motion made before a single judge, Judge Magee, was offered by Robert Victor Sinclair, counsel for Hogg. *Re Howland* (1929), 35 O.W.N. 319 (C.A.) notes at 329 that "objection however being taken by the respondent to the matter being dealt with by a single judge, as provided by the statute, the motion was enlarged before the full Court." The Privy Council Appeals Act, R.S.O. 1927, c.86, s.10, provided: "A

judge of the Supreme Court shall have authority to approve of and allow the
security to be given by a party who intends to appeal to His Majesty in His
Privy Council." The case was heard by Chief Justice Mulock and Judges Magee,
Hodgins, and Middleton.

10 William Edward Middleton had been born in Toronto on 2 March 1860. His
parents were William Middleton, a bookkeeper, and Mary Noverre. Middleton
studied at Toronto Grammar School, and apprenticed as student-at-law with the
Toronto firm of Macdonald, Merritt, Shepley and Geddes. He was called to the
bar in 1884, and made K.C. in 1908. In 1910 he was appointed to the Supreme
Court of Ontario, and it was in that capacity that he had presided over the 1922
hearing into the mental competence of Lady Howland, ultimately ruling her
incompetent, and transferring her assets to the Toronto General Trusts
Corporation. In 1923 he was elevated to the Court of Appeal. Judge
Middleton's wife, Isobel Brown, had been diagnosed with cancer early in 1929,
just as Mrs. Campbell's case came before the court; she died on 20 May 1929.
Middleton's politeness toward fellow judges, counsel, and litigants was legendary.
He has also been described as "short, about five foot five, and chubby, clean
shaven, and almost cherubic in appearance," with "puckish wit, and in the priva-
cy of his chambers, an infectious chuckle." He died on 17 February 1948. *The
Canadian Who's Who, 1936-37* (Toronto: Times Publishing, 1937), 781-2; John D.
Arnup, *Middleton: The Beloved Judge* (Toronto: McClelland and Stewart, 1988), 7,
57, 157.

11 There are no surviving archival court records, but a summary of the decision,
dated 1 February 1929, was reported as *Re Howland* (1929), 35 O.W.N. 319
(C.A.). The motion by Mrs. Campbell was "for the allowance of security upon
the proposed appeal, and for an order admitting the appeal." No question had
been raised as to the adequacy of the security, since the money had been
deposited in court. Sinclair had opposed the right of appeal for two reasons.
First, he argued that the matter in controversy did not exceed the sum of $4,000.
Middleton dismissed this argument: "It is true that no specific amount has yet
been determined which would flow from the success of the appellant, but there
is no room for doubt that, if the appellant is right in her contentions, the amount
involved far exceeds the named sum." Sinclair's second objection was that a controversy arising from the passing of accounts in the Surrogate Court was not a
"case" within the meaning of the statute. Middleton also dismissed this claim:
"In the view of this Court, the word is used in the widest possible sense, and an
appeal is always competent where the decision is that of the Court or a judicial
officer acting in a judicial capacity. The appeal to this Court was heard by the
Court in the ordinary course of its judicial duty." Accordingly, Middleton admitted the appeal (at 319-20). There were no dissenting opinions.

The censure of Mr. Hogg appeared in Middleton's order as to costs (at 320):
"The respondent being solely responsible for the expense occasioned by the
hearing of the appeal in the full Court, he should not be allowed any costs of
that argument." In the absence of surviving archival records, it is not possible to
verify whether a memorandum was appended to Middleton's judgment "to the
effect that certain evidence used therein had been withdrawn before the argument of the case." The reported decision contains no reference to this.

The Latin *functus officio* means "having performed his or her office (of an officer or official body) without further authority or legal competence because the duties and functions of the original commission have been fully accomplished." B.A. Barner, ed., *Black's Law Dictionary,* 7th ed. (St. Paul, MN: West Group, 1999), 682.

12 Bentwich, *Practice of the Privy Council,* 200-2, sets forth Rules 12-14 of the Rules of the Judicial Committee regarding the printing of the record.

13 The removal of the transcript and its closure to the public was confirmed by *Re Howland* (1929), 36 O.W.N. 53 (C.A.).

14 William Herbert Price, who was born in Owen Sound, began his legal career as an articling student in 1899. He was called to the bar in 1904 and practised in Sarnia. He served in the First World War, and received a K.C. in 1921. He was elected to the provincial legislature in 1923 and served as both provincial treasurer and attorney general. He died on 21 December 1963. Law Society of Upper Canada Archives, Past Member Record Files.

15 A summary of the decision by Judge Hodgins, dated 18 March 1929, was reported as *Re Howland* (1929), 36 O.W.N. 53 (C.A.). The motions were heard by Chief Justice Mulock and Judges Magee, Hodgins, and Fisher. W.R. Wadsworth represented Hogg; E.V. McKague appeared for the Toronto General Trusts Corporation. Judge Hodgins described the transcript (at 53) as "stenographic notes taken by one of the Judges' secretaries or stenographers for private use and convenience of the Judges should they need anything beyond their personal notes of the argument." He asserted (at 53) that the transcript had "by inadvertence, found its way into the files in the Registrar's office containing the papers on the appeal." He refused Mrs. Campbell's motion for delivery of the transcript, "with costs payable by her to the respondent in any event of the appeal to the Privy Council" (at 54). See also "Transcript Refused," Toronto *Star,* 19 March 1929, p. 28; "At Osgoode Hall," Toronto *Globe,* 20 March 1929, p. 29.

16 The motion Mrs. Campbell put before the Court of Appeal was "for an order declaring that Cora A. Lindsey was and still is a party to the applicant's appeal to the Privy Council." The argument was heard by Chief Justice Mulock and Judges Fisher, Hodgins, and Magee. The decision, dated 18 March 1929, was reported in *Re Howland* (1929), 36 O.W.N. 53 (C.A.). Judge Hodgins (Chief Justice Mulock and Judge Fisher concurring) refused the motion, noting at 54: "As to the motion in regard to Mrs Lindsey, it appears that she was not made a party to the appeal to this Court by the applicant or by the respondent's cross-appeal, and she took no part in the appeal or cross-appeal. This motion is ... refused." The report notes that Judge Magee had agreed in the result for reasons briefly stated in writing; these were not included in the report. See also "At Osgoode Hall," Toronto *Globe,* 20 March 1929, p. 29.

17 The entire record had to be reproduced through typescript, including the transcript of evidence, and exhibits such as cheques, vouchers, and books of accounts. Once typed, the appeal record was then sent for printing.

18 This is still 1929.

19 Bentwich, *Practice of the Privy Council,* 202, quoting Rule 17 of the Rules of the Judicial Committee.

BOOK FIVE: DOWNING STREET, THE PRIVY COUNCIL

1 For Susan Chapin, see Book Two n. 16.
2 "Canada's Portia Is Child of Man Who Never Knew When He Was Beaten," Toronto *Evening Telegram*, 3 May 1930, p. 3, reports: "Mrs. Campbell was very indignant when the rumor was mentioned that a wealthy American had financed her appeal. 'It is idle and idiotic,' she said. 'I have received no outside help whatsoever, but a few personal friends, keen to see justice done in a woman's single-handed fight, have been generous.'"
3 Lawrence was the Massachusetts Episcopalian bishop. He resided in Brookline, and came from the family for whom the town of Lawrence, Massachusetts, was named. As to Bishop Lawrence's affinity for Britain, the Episcopalian church in Boston was described as "almost a British church ... the closest thing to Anglican, although that was a term that would not have been used in Jamaica Plain." Interview with Katharine Cipolla, 14 August 2001, Boston (copy on file with authors).
4 The *Canadian Law List 1920* lists Blake and Redden as Privy Council agents, with two counsel: S.V. Blake (barrister and solicitor of Ontario) and Frederick Adam Corrie Redden (solicitor of Ontario and England), practising from 17 Victoria Street S.W. 1. See also *The Law List, 1929* (London: Stevens and Sons, 1929).
5 The case referred to may be *Caldwell* v. *McLaren,* [1884] 9 A.C. 392; [1883-1888] 9 C.R.A.C. 73, an appeal from the Supreme Court of Canada, which James Bethune had argued successfully just before his death. Opposing counsel were Solicitor General Sir F. Herschell and D'Alton McCarthy senior. The case involved the complaint of a property owner who sought to enjoin Bethune's client from floating timber and logs downstream. The Privy Council held that the right of Bethune's client, the lumberer, to free passage of his logs, extended to streams in their natural state as well as streams that had been "improved" by adjacent property owners. The litigants were equally prominent stakeholders. Caldwell (the lumberer) had a nephew who was the Liberal member for Lanark in the provincial legislature over which Oliver Mowat presided. McLaren, the riparian stream improver, was a long-time friend and supporter of Canada's prime minister, John A. Macdonald. Mowat had promoted economic development over the interests of private property owners for years; Macdonald had long objected to undue interference with private rights. See Jamie Benidickson, "The Culture of Flushing," draft manuscript, June 2002. Bethune argued the case on 4-6 March 1884, the decision was rendered on 7 April 1884, and Bethune died on 18 December 1884. Although this does not appear to have been an "international law" case, it was mentioned in his obituary as the "famous 'streams case,'" the case by which Bethune "won the greatest fame, and that by which he will always be remembered." "James Bethune Q.C.," Toronto *Globe,* 19 December 1884. There were no other Privy Council cases published in the law reports in which Bethune appeared as counsel after this one.

In his draft autobiography, D'Alton Lally McCarthy provides some sense of the social circumstance that surrounded the appearance of Canadian counsel before the Privy Council, which may help explain the familiarity of British lawyers, judges, and clerks with Mrs. Campbell's father:

> In the old days July was a great meeting time for Counsel from all over Canada, who usually arranged to have their appeals set down for the July sittings of the Privy Council, so that they could combine business with pleasure. This really worked out remarkably well, because our High Commissioner was always able to arrange for us to get into the Royal Enclosure at Ascot and also secured us invitations to the Garden Party at Buckingham Palace, and one of the Inns of Court always gave a banquet for Canadian Counsel. In addition to this Sir Charles Russell [the eldest son of Lord Russell of Killowen], whose firm of Solicitors were, and still are, the agents for the Justice Department at Ottawa, always gave a private dinner at Claridges. In the early years he used to ask the wives of Counsel to dinner also, and I can well remember these delightful entertainments and the amusement we got afterwards by the introduction of Houdini, the magician, who always entertained us.

Law Society of Upper Canada Archives, Draft Autobiography of D'Alton Lally McCarthy, sous-fonds 1, D'Alton McCarthy sous-fonds, William G.C. Howland fonds, 994001SF1-1-4.

6 For some references, see "Transcript Refused," Toronto *Star,* 19 March 1929, p. 28; "At Osgoode Hall," Toronto *Globe,* 20 March 1929, p. 29. Further descriptions of the relations between Mrs. Campbell and Osgoode Hall officials appear in "Canada's Portia Is Child of Man Who Never Knew When He Was Beaten," Toronto *Evening Telegram,* 3 May 1930, p. 3.

7 The *Canadian Law List 1929* lists this firm under "Foreign Counsel," practising from 4 Great Winchester St., and including P.H. Coxe, C.E. Bischoff, J.A.P.P. Thompson.

8 This was L.W.S. Upton.

9 Mrs. Campbell sailed in May 1929, so this would have been June of 1929.

10 Russell Square contained shops and many hotels, some large and imposing, as well as numerous smaller ones. Bloomsbury was famous as a centre for large temperance hotels and boarding houses, some of them containing upwards of two hundred rooms. Several fine blocks of flats were arrayed along Great Russell Street and Bedford Avenue. Harold P. Clunn, *The Face of London* (London: Spring, 1962), 144, 149.

11 In Greek mythology, Cerberus is the three-headed watchdog that guards the entrance to Hades, preventing the departure or entry of unauthorized souls. It was fabled that the ferocity of Cerberus could be appeased by throwing him a special honey-cake, the "sop to Cerberus." The Greeks and Romans developed a tradition of putting a cake in the hands of the dead, to allow them to pass without molestation. Meyer Reinhold, *Past and Present: The Continuity of Classical Myths* (Toronto: Hakkert, 1972), 147; E.C. Brewer, ed., *Brewer's Dictionary of Phrase and Fable* (London: Cassell, 1959), 844.

12 Jerome Klapka Jerome wrote this short story in 1900 and later turned it into a stage play. It premiered at the St. James's Theatre in London on 1 September 1908. The story takes place in a disreputable boarding house in Bloomsbury,

where the lead character, a Christ-like figure, transforms the lives of his fellow occupants by forcing them to see their true selves and change their ways. The eminent Shakespearean actor Sir Johnston Forbes-Robertson, known as one of the best Hamlets of the day, was the first to star in the leading role. See Jerome K. Jerome, *The Passing of the Third Floor Back: and Other Stories* (London: Hurst and Blackett, 1900); Donald Brook, *A Pageant of English Actors* (Freeport, NY: Books for Libraries Press, 1972), 234, 240-1.

13 Sir Charles H.L. Neish, K.B.E., C.B., was the registrar of the Privy Council and the registrar of Ecclesiastical Causes.

14 Hogg's counsel, Ronald Smith, practised with Bischoff, Coxe, Bischoff, and Thompson, at 4 Great Winchester Street. See National Archives of Canada, Blake and Redden fonds, R3485-0-9-E, vol. 62, file 6.

15 The British Museum, on Great Russell Street, to the north of Bloomsbury Way, originated in 1753 when a public lottery raised sufficient funds to purchase the library of Sir Hans Sloane. The building was erected on the site of Montague House between 1823 and 1847 at a cost of one million pounds. The opening ceremony was performed by King George V in 1914. Clunn, *Face of London*, 148. The reading room became the centre of London's intellectual life in the late nineteenth and early twentieth centuries. Virginia Woolf describes herself entering the room in her 1929 *A Room of One's Own* (New York: Harcourt, Brace, 1929), 44: "The swing-doors swung open; and there one stood under the vast dome, as if one were a thought in the huge bald forehead which is so splendidly encircled by a band of famous names." Famous male readers included Thomas Hardy, Arnold Bennett, Samuel Butler, W.E. Gladstone, Leslie Stephen, A.C. Swinburne, George Bernard Shaw, W.B. Yeats, and Bram Stoker. Famous female patrons included Eleanor Marx, Clementina Black, Annie Besant, E. Nesbit, Olive Schreiner, Charlotte Wilson, Beatrice Potter, Alice Zimmern, Emma Brooke, Beatrice Harraden, Charlotte Despard, and Dorothy Richardson. See Ruth Hoberman, "Women in the British Museum Reading Room during the Late-Nineteenth and Early-Twentieth Centuries: From Quasi- to Counter-public," *Feminist Studies* 28, 3 (2002): 489.

The books Mrs. Campbell refers to were probably Walter Banks, ed., *Lewin's Practical Treatise on the Law of Trusts*, 13th ed. (London: Sweet and Maxwell, 1928); Sir Arthur Underhill, *The Law Relating to Private Trusts and Trustees*, 8th ed. (London: Butterworth, 1926); Norman Bentwich, *The Practice of the Privy Council in Judicial Matters*, 2nd ed. (Toronto: Carswell, 1926); William Bowstead, *A Digest of the Law of Agency*, 6th ed. (London: Sweet and Maxwell, 1919).

16 It is possible that Mrs. Campbell is referring to Great Britain, *The Complete Statutes of England: Classified and Annotated, in Continuation of Halsbury's Laws of England; and for Ready Reference Entitled: Halsbury's Statutes of England* (London: Butterworths, 1929-31) or Earl of Halsbury, *The Laws of England* v. 28 (London: Butterworths, 1914).

17 See Herbert Bentwich, "The Judicial Link of Empire," *The English Review* 43 (July-December 1926), 393.

18 Albert Venn Dicey, *The Privy Council* (London: Macmillan, 1887; reprint, Westport, CT: Hyperion Press, 1979), 5-6, 12-13, 146 (page citations are to the original edition).

19 The *Canadian Law List 1929* mentions ten "judges from the Dominions beyond the Seas" who were members: Rt. Hon. Sir Charles Fitzpatrick, G.C.M.G. (Canada); Rt. Hon. Sir James Rose Innes, K.C.M.G. (South Africa); Rt. Hon. Mr. Justice Lyman Poore Duff (Canada, Supreme Court); Rt. Hon. Chief Justice Sir Adrian Knox, K.C.M.G. (Australia, High Court); Rt. Hon. Sir Robert Stout, K.C.M.G. (New Zealand); Rt. Hon. Mr. Justice Isaac Alfred Isaacs, K.C.M.G. (Australia, High Court); Rt. Hon. Chief Justice Francis Alexander Anglin (Canada, Supreme Court); Rt. Hon. Chief Justice Sir William Mulock, K.C.M.G. (Ontario); Rt. Hon. Sir Lancelot Sanderson (Bengal); Rt. Hon. Chief Justice Sir William Henry Solomon, K.C.S.T., K.C.M.G. (South Africa).

20 This was reported as *Reverend John Wakeford* v. *The Bishop of Lincoln,* [1921] 1 A.C. 813 (P.C.).

21 This was the famous "Persons Case," in which the Privy Council overturned the Supreme Court of Canada decision that had held that women were not qualified to sit in the Senate. *Henrietta Muir Edwards et al.* v. *Attorney-General for Canada,* [1930] A.C. 124 (P.C.). Newton Wesley Rowell, K.C., was counsel for the women, as well as for the government of Alberta, which supported the women's claim. The women chose him specifically because they wanted "the best legal representation they could secure," and because they knew Rowell was personally committed to their cause. Rowell was opposed by W.N. Tilley. Lord Sankey, who set down Mrs. Campbell's case for an early hearing in the Privy Council, was the judge who rendered the "Persons Case" decision. Margaret Prang, *N.W. Rowell: Ontario Nationalist* (Toronto: University of Toronto Press, 1975), 444, 452-8.

22 The Privy Council overruled the Quebec Court of King's Bench and held that a marriage between persons domiciled in Quebec, solemnized in France according to the rites of the Roman Catholic Church, but without a civil ceremony, was a nullity in France, and would therefore also be a nullity in Quebec. *Eugene Berthiaume* v. *Dame Dastous,* [1930] A.C. 79 (P.C.). Blake and Redden acted as solicitors for the appellant.

23 The decision was reported as *Benjamin Knowles* v. *The King,* [1930] A.C. 366 (P.C.).

24 The decision was reported as *In re Southern Rhodesia,* [1919] A.C. 211 (P.C.).

25 The case was reported as *Labrador Boundary Case* (1927), 43 Times Law Reports 289.

26 This is still 1929.

27 The theory Mrs. Campbell refers to was that the holiday developed because servants were required to work on Christmas Day, taking the following day off. As they prepared to leave to visit their families, their employers would present them with gift boxes. Jack Dempsey and Gene Tunney were professional boxers. See Bob Burrill, *Who's Who in Boxing* (New Rochelle, NY: Arlington House, 1974), 55, 188; see generally Mel Heimer, *The Long Count* (New York: Atheneum, 1969).

28 See, for example, "Canadian Portia Is Calm in Plea to Privy Council," Toronto *Star,* 3 February 1930, p. 19, and "No Legal Training," Yorkshire *Evening News,* 3 February 1930, the details of which are discussed in the Epilogue.

29 Mrs. Campbell's legal argument before the Privy Council began 3 February 1930.

30 See, for example, "Canadian Portia Is Calm in Plea to Privy Council," Toronto
   Star, 3 February 1930, p. 19, which quotes Mrs. Campbell as follows: "'I am
   thrilled to be here after all this time,' Mrs. Campbell told *The Star*, as she waited
   in an ante-room before the opening of the appeal." See also "Toronto Woman
   First before Privy Council," Toronto *Daily Star*, 28 January 1930, p. 1, in which
   Mrs. Campbell is quoted as saying: "I feel very great confidence and believe that
   when one has to do something, one receives the strength to do it." Similarly, "No
   Legal Training," Yorkshire *Evening News*, 3 February 1930: "'This is a thrilling
   experience for me,' she said to one of the officials as she waited in the ante-room
   for the case to be called. 'Your Judicial Committee is the highest tribunal in the
   Empire, is it not?'"

31 The only physician in Mrs. Campbell's family history was Dr. Charles Rattray,
   Lady Howland's father. As he was Scottish, he was probably the graduate. Her
   son, James Bethune Campbell, would indeed become a physician, but would
   obtain his degree from Harvard. For details of James Bethune Campbell's medical education and career, see the Epilogue.

32 Legal impediments prevented many women from practising law in England
   prior to the enactment of the Sex Disqualification Removal Act, 1919 (U.K.), 9
   and 10 Geo. V, c.71. Elizabeth Orme appears to have been the first to seek legal
   qualification, in the early 1870s. She attended lectures on law at University
   College, London, and apprenticed in the chambers of a barrister at Lincoln's Inn.
   Orme won a first prize in Roman law and the Hume Scholarship at University
   College in 1876, although her LL.B. was not bestowed until 1888. During the
   1870s until after the turn of the century, Orme practised with a series of female
   partners, doing commissioned work for male solicitors, although she never formally applied for admission to the bar.
       Cornelia Sorabji from India studied at Oxford from 1888 to 1892, passing the
   bachelor of Civil Laws (B.C.L.) examination but failing to receive the degree, as
   was the case with all Oxbridge women at the time. She returned from India to
   collect the degree and gain admission to the British bar many years later.
   Lincoln's Inn rejected the application of Miss Day in 1891. The courts decided
   that Margaret Hall was not a "person" for the purposes of the Solicitors' Act in
   Scotland in 1900. Gray's Inn was prepared to admit Bertha Cave in 1902, until
   they determined that they could not do so without the permission of the judges.
   An appeal tribunal chaired by the Lord Chancellor refused the admission, forging a precedent that would impede the admission of Cristabel Pankhurst (who
   completed her LL.B. at Victoria in 1904) and Ivy Williams (who passed the
   B.C.L. examination in Oxford in 1902 and earned an LL.D. from the University
   of London in 1903). Gwyneth Bebb appealed her rejection from the Law
   Society to the courts, and lost when the judges cited Sir Edward Coke on the
   unfitness of women to be lawyers and ruled that they were not "persons."
       After the passage of the 1919 admission statute, the first two women in the
   United Kingdom to qualify as barristers did so in Dublin. Ivy Williams became
   the first woman to be called to the English bar, by the Inner Temple in May
   1922. Helena Normanton, who was actually the first female bar student (29
   December 1919 at the Middle Temple) was called in November 1922; she was
   also the first woman to practise as a barrister. Throughout these years, the Law

Society lobbied vigorously against the admission of women, male law students exhibited hostility toward female students, and many commentators expressed misogynistic rhetoric over the prospect of women in law. See Helena Kennedy, *Eve Was Framed: Women and British Justice* (London: Chatto and Windus, 1992), 57; Inner Temple Library Records; James C. Albisetti, "Portia Ante Portas: Women and the Legal Profession in Europe, c. 1870-1925," *Journal of Social History* 33, 4 (2000): 825; Rose Pearson and Albie Sachs, "Barristers and Gentlemen: A Critical Look at Sexism in the Legal Profession," *Modern Law Review* 43 (1980): 400; Albie Sachs and Joan Hoff Wilson, *Sexism and the Law* (New York: Free Press, 1978). Richard L. Abel, *The Legal Profession in England and Wales* (Oxford: Basil Blackwell, 1988), 329-30, compiled tables showing 10 women called in 1922, 10 in 1923, 18 in 1924, 9 in 1925, 10 in 1926, 15 in 1927, 16 in 1928, and 13 in 1929, for a total of 101 at the time Mrs. Campbell's Privy Council case was heard. Abel also notes (pp. 79-80) that the number of women lawyers fluctuated between 2 and 6 percent of calls during the 1920s and 1930s.

33 See, for example, "Toronto Woman First before Privy Council: Canadian-Born Portia Makes Legal History in Appeal to Peers," Toronto *Daily Star,* 28 January 1930, p. 1; "Canadian Portia Is Calm in Plea to Privy Council," Toronto *Star,* 3 February 1930, p. 19; "No Legal Training," Yorkshire *Evening News,* 3 February 1930; "Mrs. Campbell Talks Five Hours to Peers," Toronto *Star,* 4 February 1930, p. 1; "First of Her Sex to Plead in Suit," Ottawa *Evening Citizen,* 4 February 1930, p. 1; "Canadian Portia Is Still Arguing Estate Case before Privy Council," Toronto *Star,* 13 February 1930, p. 23; "Canadian Portia Is Complimented by Privy Council," Toronto *Star,* 20 February 1930, p. 1.

34 Mrs. Campbell had argued on 3 and 4 February, adjourning on 5 February, and continuing the adjournment due to Lord Blanesburgh's cold until 13 and 14 February, when she returned and finished her argument.

35 Frank Gahan was counsel, although the reported case indicated in error that it was Mr. Frank Graham. See National Archives of Canada, Blake and Redden fonds, R3485-0-9-E, vol. 62, file 6; *Campbell* v. *Hogg* (1930), 39 O.W.N. 85 (P.C.).

36 The passage missing between the two quotations in Mrs. Campbell's book, found at 690 of *Campbell* v. *Hogg,* [1930] 3 D.L.R. 673, reads:

> The appellant's case with reference to these mortgages is put thus. In the book in question there are entered by Mr Hogg six Ottawa mortgages and two mortgages (McAmmand [sic] and Martin) not charged on real estate, for all of which he accepts full responsibility. There is in the form of entry no difference in the book between what may be called the Toronto mortgages and these others. The first mortgage entered is a Toronto mortgage. Mr Hogg stated in evidence that he did not know what Lady Howland did with her money which she did not entrust to him. Clearly, he was not ignorant of these Toronto mortgages. Again the book 44A is to avail as evidence on behalf of all parties interested: he must therefore be charged with the same responsibility in regard to the moneys secured by these Toronto mortgages that he has accepted with regard to the others. The general answer made on behalf of Mr Hogg to all this — there may be further answers in respect of individual securities — is that

he had no concern in or responsibility for any Toronto mortgages of Lady Howland. Other advisers acted for her in Toronto. He did not. These mortgages were no concern of his. Now, as an answer, this does not strike their Lordships as completely satisfactory. It is not Mr Hogg's personal response, and it is unfortunate that he did not himself make it either by a reservation to that effect when tendering 44A in evidence or on affidavit.

37 George du Maurier was a famous *Punch* artist. He wrote his first novel, *Peter Ibbetson,* in 1891, at the age of fifty-five. Like the author, the main character spends his childhood in the Paris suburb of Passy; when his parents both die within a week of one another, he moves to London with his uncle. As an adult he returns to Paris but finds his neighbourhood no longer the same. At the end of the novel, the main character murders his uncle and goes to jail, where he dies in his cell. See George du Maurier, *Peter Ibbetson* (London: Osgood McIlvaine, 1891); Frank N. Magill and Dayton Kohler, eds., *Masterplots: English Fiction Series* (New York: Salem Press, 1964), 57-62; Richard Kelly, *George du Maurier* (Boston: Twayne Publishers, 1983), 655-7.

38 The Canadian courts had found Hogg's assertions and his testimony credible, despite the high onus of proof demanded by statute. The Evidence Act, R.S.O. 1927, c.107, s.11, provided that "in an action by or against the heirs ... of a deceased person an opposite or interested party shall not obtain a judgment or decision on his own evidence in respect of any matter occurring before the death of the deceased person unless such evidence is corroborated by some other material evidence." The Surrogate Court had specifically found corroboration with respect to four mortgages (a finding that would be reversed in the Privy Council), and then made a general assessment regarding the rest of the accounts. The Law Lords objected to the Surrogate Court's assessment that a general finding of credibility could apply to the estate as a whole, declaring that they were not prepared "to subscribe to the doctrine that each of the substantive items in Mr. Hogg's account is not an independent transaction standing upon its own merits." Furthermore, they also dismissed the Surrogate Court's finding of credibility as such. "The connected items in this case, if any such there be, have not been proved by the evidence of Mr. Hogg, corroborated by Lady Howland's vouchers. They have been established on Lady Howland's vouchers alone without any supportive evidence to speak of from Mr. Hogg. Lastly, their Lordships feel bound to add, although they greatly regret having to do so, that Mr. Hogg's evidence, even as described by the Judge, did not reach the class of testimony which is required for the rule to apply." Consequently, the Privy Council decided that the concurrent findings of the courts below "were based on an erroneous proposition of law to such an extent that with that proposition corrected they disappear. Within the Board's rule there has been no finding at all. The complaints made by the appellant must therefore be investigated by their Lordships afresh." *Campbell* v. *Hogg,* [1930] 3 D.L.R. 673 at 686-9. For further discussion of the findings, see the Epilogue.

39 The passages of the judgment dealing with the facts and analysis supporting the finding of trusteeship read:

No capital account is available, showing either how much was received from or was returned to Lady Howland and the absence of such an account has occasioned in these proceedings difficulties of its own to which their Lordships must again recur. Mr. Hogg, however, it should at once be stated, disclaims sole responsibility for these difficulties. He explains that it was as a friend that Lady Howland sought his assistance. Transactions on her account and payments made to her were accordingly less formal than in the case of an ordinary client. In many instances the only existing record of payments made is to be found in the receipts which she insisted upon giving and which fortunately have been preserved. No question with reference to accounts ever arose, he says, between Lady Howland and himself during her life, and he feels it to be a hardship that he should have to deal particularly with these matters so long since the event, after the loss or destruction in 1911 of so many of his books and papers, and after the death of Lady Howland herself. Their Lordships will not fail throughout their consideration of the case to bear these matters in mind and attach to them such weight and effect as in the circumstances they deserve. Their Lordships deem it sufficient for the moment to observe that while a trustee may if he chooses renounce any of his privileges as such, a *cestui que trust* like Lady Howland is not without her own consent to be deprived of any protection to which the law entitles her and it does not lie in the mouth of a trustee to suggest that she should be ...

[Hogg] retained no remuneration for his services during his association with Lady Howland ... The selection of the securities and their management remained exclusively in Mr. Hogg's care. He collected the principal and interest ... All payments were made to Mr. Hogg; everything passed through his hands ...

And, in these proceedings at all events, initiated as they were by Mr. Hogg himself, and with ample warrant from the facts and course of business disclosed, it is as a trustee of the funds entrusted to him that he seeks to have taken the accounts of his receipts and payments rendered to the Court. And their Lordships have been unable to find any reason why in this respect Mr. Hogg should not be taken at his word, although they are fully conscious that not a few of his difficulties in the case flow from a certain inconsistency in the attitude at different times taken up by him in this regard ...

It is, of course, an elementary proposition that a trustee must keep an accurate account of the trust property, and must always be ready to render it when required. This history, apart altogether from any question as to the completeness or correctness of the final account, is a striking commentary on Mr. Hogg's neglect of his elementary duty ...

The application by Mr. Hogg to have his account taken invoked a jurisdiction which is somewhat special ... The jurisdiction is conferred by the Trustee Act, R.S.O. 1927, c.150, s.23 ... The proceedings ... were at the hearing in the Surrogate Court, by consent amended by being intituled "In the matter of the Trustee Act." "It is a matter of trusteeship," Mr.

Hogg said, "the money came into my hands and was invested." And at a later stage in answer to a suggestion by Mrs. Campbell's counsel ... he added, and as their Lordships think, he rightly added, "Certainly there is no doubt about that" ...

Their Lordships cannot doubt that the Judges in the Appellate Division would have been vigilant to animadvert upon these irregularities on the part of a trustee had it not been for the view taken by them—a mistaken view as their Lordships think—that Mr. Hogg's relation to Lady Howland was one of agency without fiduciary responsibility.

Campbell v. *Hogg,* [1930] 3 D.L.R. 673 at 676-8, 682-3, 701.
The Privy Council reversed a number of the Surrogate Court findings of fact, and found $7,027.34 owing on a series of loans and mortgages; for details see the Epilogue. *Campbell* v. *Hogg,* [1930] 3 D.L.R. 673 at 694-703.

40 The judgment noted: "The question whether the balance of the appellant's costs, in whole or in part should, before division, be paid out of the fund recovered as the result of these proceedings, is one beyond the jurisdiction of their Lordships. Its solution must and can only be a matter of agreement between the appellant and her sisters." *Campbell* v. *Hogg,* [1930] 3 D.L.R. 673 at 703.

41 The Privy Council noted that Mr. Hogg had never hinted at any claim for remuneration prior to having to pass his accounts before the Surrogate Court: "It was rejected in the Canadian Courts, and was not revived before the Board." *Campbell* v. *Hogg,* [1930] 3 D.L.R. 673 at 681.

42 The Privy Council decision made reference, at one point, to Hogg's letter of 19 October 1922, reporting the status of Lady Howland's estate to the trust company:

Mr. Hogg, their Lordships feel, must now regret the form of that letter. It is not too much to say that it left him with regard to the whole matter in a thoroughly false position, not improved by his attempt, in the early part of his evidence in these proceedings, to explain it away. The letter ignores altogether his own personal responsibility undertaken towards Lady Howland over a long term of years: it has no regard to the existence of unsettled accounts of his in that character upon which must now be taken to be admitted a very substantial further balance was then owing to her estate. The letter, indeed, purports to treat Lady Howland as having been a mere client of Mr. Hogg's firm, who, in response to the request of her legally constituted representative are handing over her securities and money left in their custody as her solicitors. And that mistaken attitude was the more unfortunate for the reason that almost any statement of Mr Hogg's who was a local director of the corporation would unreservedly be accepted by its manager. It behoved him therefore to be specially careful to see that his answer was both accurate and complete. As was only to be expected the letter was accepted without observations and for four years no further information was either asked from or volunteered by Mr. Hogg. Their Lordships find it difficult to justify Mr. Hogg's silence during this long period. Consistently with his *bona fides,* which their

Lordships would be slow to impugn, it presents one of many indications of a failure on his part to treat seriously his undoubted responsibilities in this matter.

Campbell v. *Hogg,* [1930] 3 D.L.R. 673 at 679.

43 The Privy Council decision stated:

> The Surrogate Court Judge, however, crediting the loss of Mr. Hogg's books as hampering a full accounting was, as he said, disposed to be indulgent in enabling him to clear the account. Accordingly he accepted it. To their Lordships it would not have been surprising had he, however reluctantly, felt compelled to reject it altogether, as indeed Magee J.A., later on in effect did. But their Lordships need not pursue this matter further, because the appellant before the Board no longer asked that the account should be thrown out. She was content to accept the position to which in the Canadian Courts she had been relegated and she confined her appeal to the discussion of detailed objections to particular items therein or omissions therefrom. And their Lordships have acquiesced in that course being taken before them. But their acquiescence must not be supposed to indicate any sympathy on their part with the view, if such a view be anywhere entertained, that the rule of the Surrogate Court on this matter is one that need only be lightly observed. On the contrary their conviction is that the strict enforcement of the rule [that the accounts presented were to contain a true and perfect inventory of the whole property in question] is essential for the protection of trust property throughout Ontario.

Campbell v. *Hogg,* [1930] 3 D.L.R. 673 at 684-5, 689.

44 In Greek mythology, Scylla is a sea monster who lives underneath a dangerous rock at one side of the Strait of Messia, opposite the dangerous whirlpool Charybdis. Both threaten passing ships; the expression one's "Scylla and Charybdis" denotes opposite dangers that beset one's course. See Thomas Bulfinch, *Bulfinch's Mythology* (New York: Thomas Y. Crowell, 1970), 243-5.

45 The Privy Council noted that the "refusal by the appellant of the additional sum mentioned makes it unnecessary for their Lordships to consider whether the Appellate Division had in that matter jurisdiction to act as it proposed to do." *Campbell* v. *Hogg,* [1930] 3 D.L.R. 673 at 689.

46 See Book Two n. 27.

47 This was almost a direct quotation from the decision, at 702, where the Law Lords were critical of Hogg's "practice, increasing in the later years, of leaving her balances in his own hands or in those of his firm uninvested and carrying no interest for periods of indefinite duration." The Privy Council noted that even Hogg had admitted that "there were moneys of Lady Howland's in his hands uninvested." Itemizing a mortgage by Phillip Vaillancourt for $450, a mortgage by Charles Dumas for $1,200, and a mortgage by Donald Campbell for $800, it concluded that "all these three sums remained in Mr. Hogg's hands uninvested, and in cross-examination in these proceedings he found himself unable to

explain how he came to make the statements [that the balance had been paid out]. Their Lordships regret having to emphasize this slip, but Mr. Hogg's carelessness of assertion, of which this is a typical example, constitutes one of the great difficulties in the case." As for the Capital Real Estate transactions, the Privy Council found a sum of $1,000 "as an uninvested balance carrying no interest since July, 1917." *Campbell* v. *Hogg*, [1930] 3 D.L.R. 673 at 680, 692.

The partnership of Hogg and Hogg dissolved when Frederick Drummond Hogg was appointed to the bench; for details see the Epilogue. *The Canadian Who's Who, 1936-37* (Toronto: Times Publishing, 1937), 516, notes that William Drummond Hogg retired in 1934.

48 The Privy Council did not explain why it found that the legislation did not countenance the award of interest. Section 65(3) of the Surrogate Courts Act, R.S.O. 1927, c.94, which appears to have been the relevant section, provided: "The judge, on passing the accounts of an executor, administrator or such a trustee, shall have jurisdiction to enter into and make full enquiry and accounting of and concerning the whole property which the deceased was possessed of or entitled to, and the administration and disbursement thereof in as full and ample a manner as may be done in the Master's office under an administration order, and, for such purpose, may take evidence and decide all disputed matters arising in such accounting subject to appeal." *Campbell* v. *Hogg*, [1930] 3 D.L.R. 673 at 683, 701. When Mrs. Campbell returned to Ontario and attempted to enforce her judgment, the issue of jurisdiction to award interest sparked differing judicial opinions and legislative attention. For further details, see the Epilogue.

49 See An Act to Amend the Surrogate Courts Act, S.O. 1933, c.63, s.3.

50 On the litigation surrounding the entitlement to interest, see the detailed discussion in the Epilogue.

51 On the litigation surrounding the enforcement of the judgment, and the battle over Mrs. Campbell's costs, see the detailed discussion in the Epilogue.

52 Johnson was a London aviator who became the first woman to fly alone from London to Australia, in 1930. She would set additional records with flights to India, Japan, South Africa, and America in the early 1930s. She received the president's gold medal from the Society of Engineers, the Egyptian gold medal for valour, the International League of Aviators' women's trophy, and the Royal Aero Club's gold medal. She would soon become the president of the Women's Engineering Society. See Charles Dixon, *Amy Johnson—Lone Girl Flyer* (London: Sampson Low, Marston, 1930); "Johnson, Amy," *Who's Who, 1940* (Toronto: Macmillan, 1940), 1678.

53 See the *Law Journal* (London), 10 May 1930.

54 The Privy Council eventually awarded Mrs. Campbell £463 19s. 6d. as "three-fourths of her costs thereof incurred in England." The decision also stated that Hogg should pay her "three-fourths of her costs incurred in all the Courts of Ontario, [and] three-fourths of her costs in this Appeal incurred in the Appellate Division of the [Ontario] Supreme Court." The Toronto General Trusts Corporation was to recover from Hogg "their costs incurred in all the Courts of Ontario, their costs of this Appeal incurred in the Appellate Division of the [Ontario] Supreme Court, and the sum of L428 11s. 2d. their costs thereof incurred in England." Privy Council Board Judgment, At the Court at

Buckingham Palace, 15 May 1930. For further discussion about the protracted litigation that subsequently ensued in Canada over the Ontario portion of these costs, see the Epilogue.

55 Mrs. Campbell's son, James Bethune Campbell, was studying for his B.A. at Harvard University while she argued her case. For further details of James's education and career, see the Epilogue.

56 The right to appeal provincial superior court decisions as well as Supreme Court of Canada decisions had posed concerns for Canadian politicians as early as 1875, when Hamilton M.P. Aemilius Irving first proposed to prohibit such appeals. In 1895 the British government agreed to begin appointing senior justices from Canada to the Judicial Committee, although their participation was limited. The Privy Council jurisdiction raised considerable controversy after the turn of the nineteenth century. Supporters of the Judicial Committee pointed to the "high calibre of its personnel and to its neutrality on emotive Canadian issues." Opponents objected to the colonial symbolism of not having a court of last resort on Canadian soil, the Privy Council's lack of knowledge of Canadian conditions, the cost, and the delay. Recent academic review of the role of the Privy Council in shaping Canadian jurisprudence suggests that the Judicial Committee "virtually eliminated some of the critical legislative powers of the federal government and destroyed its capacity to act on the economic and social problems of the twentieth century." See John T. Saywell, *The Lawmakers: Judicial Power and the Shaping of Canadian Federalism* (Toronto: University of Toronto Press, 2002). A bill to abolish appeals to London was presented to the Supreme Court of Canada by way of referendum in 1939. It was upheld as constitutional in [1940] S.C.R. 76, a decision affirmed by the Judicial Committee in 1946 in [1947] A.C. 127. Legislation eliminating appeals was passed in 1949; An Act to Amend the Supreme Court Act, S.C. 1949 (2nd Sess.), c.37, s.3. The statute was not retroactive, and it took some years for the last cases to work their way through the system. The last Canadian appeal was decided in 1959. James G. Snell and Frederick Vaughan, *The Supreme Court of Canada: History of the Institution* (Toronto: University of Toronto Press, 1985), 178-95; Peter McCormick, *Supreme at Last: The Evolution of the Supreme Court of Canada* (Toronto: Lorimer, 2000), 6-11.

EPILOGUE

1 Mrs. Campbell submitted a bill of costs for $2,000 before Taxing Officer A.J. McGillivray. He slashed this to $800, and this was then reduced to $600 because Mrs. Campbell had been allowed only three-quarters of her costs. "Won Case at Privy Council, Costs Are Taxed in Toronto," Toronto *Evening Telegram,* 10 October 1930, p. 3. Mrs. Campbell appealed against the disallowance of the accountant's fees, and Hogg cross-appealed against the allowance of Slaght's fees. The appeal was heard first by Carleton County Court judge Edward J. Daly. Judge Daly refused to allow the accountant's fees and reversed the previous decision to allow Arthur Slaght's legal fees, allowing only $100 for the passing of accounts. Mrs. Campbell appealed again to the High Court, and Chief Justice Hugh Edward Rose upheld the denial of accountant's fees, noting that there was

"nothing in the tariff to authorize any such item." However, Chief Justice Rose restored the counsel fees, granting $500 for Slaght's efforts before the Surrogate Court. He noted that the estate was "to benefit very largely" through Mrs. Campbell's efforts and the services of her counsel. It was clear that the reversal was in response to the Privy Council comment that Mrs. Campbell "should as nearly as it is practicable be reimbursed to the extent of three-quarters" of her costs. "The Court would not be proceeding in accordance with the evident intention of their Lordships of the Privy Council if unnecessarily Mrs. Campbell was left to bear any very great portion of the costs properly incurred by her in retaining counsel and solicitors," concluded Chief Justice Rose. "Even so," he added, "Mrs. Campbell's fee will fall short of covering her expenses ... for she will not be receiving anything in respect of the services of the accountant whom she has had to pay, or in respect of her own travelling expenses and expenses of living in Ottawa, or in respect of sums paid to Mr. Slaght in respect of consultations." The amount Chief Justice Rose awarded was $501.95. W.J. Elliott, K.C., acted for Toronto General Trusts Corporation, and W.R. Wadsworth, K.C., for Hogg. See *Re Howland; Re Campbell and Hogg* (1930), 39 O.W.N. 292 (Ontario High Court) at 292-5. Hogg then appealed to the Ontario Court of Appeal. Elliott continued to act for the trust company, and Wadsworth, for Hogg. The decision of Judge William Renwick Riddell, delivered on 6 March 1931, was that the Ontario Supreme Court had no jurisdiction to overrule a Surrogate Court taxation of costs. He set aside Chief Justice Rose's order, thus reinstating Judge Daly's decision. The final costs recoverable would have been approximately $200, after the amount was adjusted by the reduced counsel fee. See *Re Howland, Re Campbell & Hogg,* [1932] 3 D.L.R. 623 (Ontario Court of Appeal).

2　The activity may have been prompted in part by a motion that Mrs. Campbell filed for removal of the Toronto General Trusts Corporation as executor of Lady Howland's estate; "Move for Removal," Toronto *Star,* 14 October 1930, p. 26. The Toronto *Star,* 24 October 1930, p. 9, reports that the motion was adjourned because Mrs. Campbell had failed to serve her sisters. "Howland Estate Case Motion Is Dismissed," Toronto *Evening Telegram,* 14 November 1930, p. 3, notes that Mrs. Campbell advised the court that she wished her motion to be adjourned indefinitely, because she now believed that the "trust company was endeavoring to recover monies owing to her mother's estate." Chief Justice Rose dismissed, rather than adjourned, the motion.

3　These statements, set forth in the statement of claim issued by the trust company, were quoted in a decision arising from subsequent litigation: *Toronto General Trusts Co.* v. *Hogg,* [1932] 4 D.L.R. 465 (Ontario Court of Appeal), per Magee, J.A., at 468.

4　*Re Howland* (1930), 33 O.W.N. 78. W.J. Elliott, K.C., appeared for the trust company, and R.V. Sinclair, K.C., for Hogg. Judge Garrow noted at 78-9, in a decision delivered on 17 September 1930, that there was in the judgment of the Privy Council "no adjudication directing payment, but merely a finding or a declaration that there is so much money in the hands of the trustee ... Undoubtedly the applicant is entitled to carry the judgment into operation so far as it goes, but, as is pointed out, it does not direct payment, and if the learned

Judge is, in effect, asked to do now what neither the Privy Council nor the Appellate Division has done and direct payment of the amount found due in order that execution may issue, he holds that I have no power to do so." He subsequently dismissed the application with no order as to costs. The Toronto *Star* noted in "Reaps No Award From Her Victory at Privy Council," 17 September 1930, p. 2, that upon receipt of the judgment, Mrs. Campbell "wired the authorities in London, England," and appealed for assistance to Attorney General Price.

Clarence Garrow was born on 12 June 1875, to James Thompson Garrow, a judge, and M.B. Fletcher. He was admitted as a student-at-law in 1896 and called to the bar in 1899. He practised in Goderich until made a master of the Supreme Court of Ontario in 1923. In 1929 he was elevated to the Ontario High Court of Justice. He died on 25 May 1934. Law Society of Upper Canada Archives, Past Member Record Files.

5 Hogg and his counsel would subsequently argue against the award of interest. But even they would concede that it was potentially available. In the subsequent Supreme Court of Canada appeal on the issue of interest (see further discussion below), Hogg's counsel stated that he was not suggesting that the Privy Council had held that there was no jurisdiction but that, "in view of all the circumstances disclosed by the evidence … this is not a case in which the appellant *should* be charged with interest." See Toronto General Trust Co. v. Hogg, "Appellant's Factum" in the Record, held in the Supreme Court of Canada Archives. For an example of judicial surprise, see, for example, *Re Johnson,* [1932] O.R. 385 (Ontario Court of Appeal), per Riddell, J.A., at 388-9, and further discussion below.

6 Hugh Edward Rose was born on 16 September 1869 in Toronto, to John Edward Rose, a judge of the Supreme Court of Ontario, and Kate Macdonald. He obtained a B.A. from the University of Toronto in 1891 and was admitted as a student-at-law the same year. He was called to the bar in 1894 and practised in Toronto. He obtained a K.C. in 1908 and was appointed to the Supreme Court of Ontario, High Court of Justice, in 1916. He served as chief justice from 1930 to 1945. He died on 13 October 1945. Law Society of Upper Canada Archives, Past Member Record Files.

7 *Toronto General Trusts Corporation* v. *Hogg* (1930), 39 O.W.N. 296 (High Court) at 296-8. W.J. Elliott, K.C., continued to act for the trust company, but R.V. Sinclair, K.C., was back to represent Hogg. The decision was issued on 13 November 1930. After the ruling, Hogg launched an appeal, claiming that Chief Justice Rose had "erred in holding that the Privy Council had found Mr. Hogg a trustee for Lady Howland, and in holding that the defendant was not entitled to adduce new evidence in the Ontario courts." There was no reported decision of the result on this appeal, but given that the main action continued, it must have been dismissed. See "Sum Awarded Howland Estate," Toronto *Evening Telegram,* 14 November 1930, p. 3; "Litigation Resumes with Hogg's Appeal," Toronto *Star,* 22 November 1930, p. 1.

8 Christopher Moore has noted that although barristers had been disbarred for "ungentlemanly behaviour as early as 1820, in 1876 explicit disciplinary powers were spelled out legislatively." An Act to Amend the Laws Respecting the Law

Society, S.O. 1876, c.31, ss.1 and 2 provided that the benchers could "make all necessary rules, regulations and by-laws and dispense therewith" regarding "matters relating to the interior discipline and honour of the members of the Bar" and "discipline and practice of such attorneys, solicitors and articled clerks." This was clarified in An Act to Extend the Powers of the Law Society of Upper Canada, S.O. 1881, c.17, s.1:

> Whenever any person, being a barrister or attorney-at-law, or a solicitor of the Court of Chancery, or a student-at-law, or attorney's clerk serving under articles, has been or may hereafter be found by the Benchers of the Law Society, after due inquiry by a committee of their number or otherwise, guilty of professional misconduct, or of conduct unbecoming a barrister, attorney, solicitor, student-at-law, or articled clerk, it shall be lawful for the said Benchers in Convocation to disbar any such barrister, and to resolve that any such attorney or solicitor is unworthy to practise as such attorney or solicitor; to expel from the society, and the membership thereof, any such student or articled clerk, and to strike his name from the books of the society.

The power to suspend barristers from practice for a set period was added in An Act to Amend Various Statutes in View of the Statute Revision, S.O. 1897, c.15, Schedule A (29, 31). For the first few decades, it was the general practice of the Law Society to advise those who made complaints that their remedy "lay with the courts." But by the turn of the nineteenth century, the disciplinary committee had become a forum in which practitioners worked out ethical norms for the changing conditions of legal practice. Christopher Moore, *The Law Society of Upper Canada and Ontario's Lawyers, 1797-1997* (Toronto: University of Toronto Press, 1997), 149-51.

9 The notice of motion of Mrs. Campbell "In the Supreme Court of Ontario, in the Matter of an application by Elizabeth Bethune Campbell to the Court, for the removal of W.D. Hogg, K.C., from the Rolls of the Law Society of Upper Canada," 9 June 1931, and the affidavit by Hogg, "In the Supreme Court of Ontario, in the Matter of an application by Elizabeth Bethune Campbell, to the Court, for the removal of W.D. Hogg, K.C., from the Rolls of the Law Society of Upper Canada," 15 June 1931, were found in the Archives of Ontario, RG22-5800, No. 2612/30, as part of the Supreme Court of Ontario file on *Toronto General Trusts Corporation* v. *William D. Hogg*. The documents were also quoted in the copy of the motion and portion of the transcript of the hearing located in the Law Society of Upper Canada Archives, Disciplinary Files, W.D. Hogg, 15 October 1931 to 18 October 1934. (We are indebted to Brendan O'Brien for providing a copy of these latter records to us.)

10 Law Society of Upper Canada Archives, Disciplinary Files, W.D. Hogg, 15 October 1931 to 18 October 1934. (We are indebted to Brendan O'Brien for providing a copy of these records to us.)

11 There are no surviving legal records as to the judicial response to the motion.

12 In support of her complaint, Mrs. Campbell filed a copy of the notes she had used in the application she had made before Chief Justice Rose in 1930, as well

as a copy of the notice of motion she had filed the previous June in the Ontario Supreme Court. Hogg sat as a member of the discipline committee from 1896 to 1911 and from 1917 to 1921. Law Society of Upper Canada Archives, Past Member Record Files; Disciplinary Files, W.D. Hogg, 15 October 1931 to 18 October 1934; Discipline Committee Minutes, 18 March 1915 to 12 November 1936, dated 15 October 1931, p. 391. (We are indebted to Brendan O'Brien for providing a copy of these records to us.)

13 The decision was reported as *Toronto General Trusts* v. *Hogg* (1932), 41 O.W.N. 102 (Ontario High Court), but the summary account was somewhat misleading in comparison with the full decision; see "Case on Appeal," *William D. Hogg* v. *Toronto General Trusts Corporation,* located in "The Record" of the Supreme Court of Canada Archives for the subsequent Supreme Court appeal. W.J. Elliott, K.C., acted for the trust company, and R.V. Sinclair, K.C., for Hogg. Hogg had argued that he owed no interest until the date of the Privy Council judgment, and that even that should be calculated as simple interest. The decision, issued on 26 March 1932, stated that the judgment of the Privy Council

> has not the effect of overruling the Judgments of our Courts in Re McIntyre, so long followed in practice, but simply restricts the jurisdiction of the Surrogate Court Judge when Accounts are brought before him in proceedings initiated under Section 23 of the Trustee Act. The distinction, I think, is drawn between a Trustee, such as the Defendant Hogg was, and a Trustee appointed by Will. Thus, construing the Judgment of the Privy Council, I am of opinion the Plaintiffs are not concluded from obtaining interest if, in the circumstances, they are entitled to charge the same on uninvested balances in the hands of the Trustee. The defence of Res Judicata fails.

Judge Jeffrey noted that it was incontestable that Hogg had served as a trustee, and that he had committed "breaches of trust." Interest was awarded at the statutory rate of 5 percent. Judge Jeffrey's explanation for awarding interest compounded half-yearly related to the gravity of Hogg's misdoing:

> Then, what reason is there for depriving the Plaintiff of interest? ... Their Lordships took into consideration the age of the Defendant, the fact that the accounting was asked for after the lapse of many years, and the further fact that it was alleged by him that vouchers, receipts and books of account had been destroyed. Yet, notwithstanding that, they came to the conclusion that the Defendant had been guilty of breaches of trust ... I have given this aspect of the case very grave consideration and I cannot see my way clear to relieve the Defendant by simply awarding interest at the usual Statutory rate without rests. There can, as I stated before, be no doubt that the breaches of trust were grave. Large sums of money remained in the Defendant's hands uninvested, and when inquiry was made of him he failed to disclose this fact ... No good purpose would be served by dealing further with these breaches of trust, save to say, as I have

set out, that they were of a grave nature, and of such gravity as to dis-entitle the Defendant to escape interest with rests.

Nicol Jeffrey was born on 21 October 1867, and admitted as a student-at-law in 1887. He was called to the bar in 1894 and practised in Fergus and Guelph. He was appointed to the Supreme Court of Ontario High Court of Justice in 1928, and served in that position until his death on 20 July 1940. Law Society of Upper Canada, Past Member Record Files.

14 In *Toronto General Trusts Co.* v. *Hogg,* [1932] 4 D.L.R. 465 (Ontario Court of Appeal), two of the appellate judges spoke to the issue. Judge Riddell noted at 473 that the Judicial Committee appeared to have decided that interest could not be awarded in such proceedings, but mused: "Whether this adjudication is in accordance with what was considered by our Courts as the law in this Province, I do not consider." Judge Masten noted at 476-9:

> I agree with the opinion expressed by my brother Riddell that an infer-ence may be drawn from some of the expressions used in the reasons for judgment of the Judicial Committee, that the Committee thought that the Surrogate Court was without jurisdiction to award damages by way of interest against Hogg on the taking of accounts in the Surrogate Court. Such an opinion is not categorically stated in the reasons, nor does it appear in the formal order of the Privy Council, but the inference as to the view entered by the Committee seems reasonably plain ... In my opinion, however, the observations in the reasons of judgment of the Judicial Committee are *obiter,* because no claim to interest was ever raised in those proceedings unless it was by way of some general suggestion, which appears to have been put forward for the first time in the argument before their Lordships ... The settled practice of the Surrogate Courts of Ontario of permitting surcharge and falsification of accounts and of awarding interest against defaulting trustees or executors is well founded in the provisions of the Surrogate Court Act and the Rules of Court applicable thereto; also that on the ground that the observations of their Lordships were made in respect of a question not properly argued before them, and on which no opportunity of adequate argument had been afforded to the present appellant, I would decline to consider the infer-ence from the observations in their reasons as binding on this Court in the present proceeding.

Shortly thereafter, on 4 May 1932, a differently constituted Court of Appeal bench considered the issue in *Re Johnson,* [1932] 3 D.L.R. 164. Judges Magee, Riddell, and Hodgins expressed the view that due to the judgment of the Judicial Committee, the Surrogate Court had no jurisdiction to entertain a claim for interest in taking such an account. Judge Riddell added at 166-7 that the Privy Council ruling was "contrary to our settled practice for many years," and that legislation was "loudly called for to correct what I conceive to be a reversal, a revolutionary change, in our settled practice." This prompted Judge Masten to add a postscript to his original *Hogg* decision at 483, noting that he was "unable to agree with that view." It also prompted a subsequent legislative amendment to clarify that the Surrogate Court did have jurisdiction to award interest. See An Act to Amend the Surrogate Courts Act, S.O. 1933, c.63, s.3.

15 *Toronto General Trusts Co.* v. *Hogg,* [1932] 4 D.L.R. 465 (Ontario Court of Appeal), per Magee, J.A., at 469.

16 See, for example, William J. Anderson, "Where Angels Fear to Tread," *Law Society of Upper Canada Gazette* 29, 1 (1995): 24. W.J. Elliott, K.C., and E.V. McKague represented the trust company. R.V. Sinclair, K.C., represented Hogg. The decision was delivered on 7 April 1932.

17 *Toronto General Trusts Co.* v. *Hogg,* [1932] 4 D.L.R. 465 (Ontario Court of Appeal) at 474-83. Judge John Fosberry Orde concurred in Judge Masten's dissenting opinion. In a decision that has been characterized by Anderson, "Where Angels Fear to Tread," 25, as, "to put it mildly, remarkable," making it "hard to avoid the conclusion that he was carrying forward the bias he had earlier displayed in favour of his friend of forty years," Judge Masten wrote at 478, 482-3:

> I can say from personal recollection of the argument of the case when it came before me on appeal from the Surrogate Judge, that no suggestion of a claim to interest was put forward on behalf of Mrs. Campbell or on behalf of the Trust Corporation, and I am informed by the members of the Court of Appeal, who heard the subsequent appeal, that no such claim was put forward before them ... The Surrogate Court had and has jurisdiction to entertain a claim for interest against an accounting trustee and any different view suggested in the reasons of the Judicial Committee was *obiter* and is not binding on this Court ... The present respondent was bound to put forward in the Surrogate Court its claim to interest, and, having failed to do so, is estopped from asserting in this action any claim beyond the capital sum of $7,027.34 ... The appeal should be allowed, the claim of interest disallowed ... [and] the appellant should be entitled to his costs.

18 *Toronto General Trusts Co.* v. *Hogg,* [1932] 4 D.L.R. 465 (Ontario Court of Appeal) at 466-7. Chief Justice Mulock explained his ruling at 467:

> There is no fixed rate of interest chargeable under all circumstances against a trustee in respect of trust funds in his hands and not properly employed ... In Ontario, the rate paid on such deposits is, generally, less than the legal rate or that procurable on permanent investments. If the circumstances warrant the trust funds being so temporarily deposited, the trustee would not be chargeable with a higher rate. If the trustee negligently fails to more profitably invest the trust funds, then he will be chargeable with interest at a higher rate. If he uses them in his own business, then, at the option of the *cestui que trust* he will be chargeable with whatever profits they earned. Thus, under varying circumstances, he is chargeable with varying rates of interest and with or without annual or semi-annual rests, not by way of punishment to the trustee, but in order to compensate the *cestui que trust* to the extent of the estimated earnings

of the fund if properly invested. I make these observations by way of showing that the Court, in determining what interest is chargeable against a trustee who fails in his duty to properly invest trust funds, must know the nature of such breach of trust. There is no such evidence before the trial Judge in this case, and I therefore think that the judgment in question should be varied by striking out the sum of $17,520.40 and substituting therefor the words "such sum as the Master may properly find the defendant chargeable with in respect of interest or compound interest," and that it be referred to the Master to ascertain such sum.

Judge Riddell concurred, noting at 473-4:

> While he is liable to pay some interest, the amount is not to be settled in the manner it has been by this judgment. There should be a reference to the Master to determine the amount after determining the facts. There is, so far as I know, no precedent in our Courts for compounding every 6 months. It has been considered as of course, that if compounding is to be done, it is done yearly ... I have no doubt of the power of the Court to direct half-yearly, quarter-yearly or monthly rests; the power is to be exercised according to the circumstances of the case, but there should be no direction in that regard, the Master acting according to the evidence adduced.

19 *Toronto General Trusts Co.* v. *Hogg,* [1932] 4 D.L.R. 465 (Ontario Court of Appeal) at 468-70. Judge Magee noted at 469-70:

> There is ample authority for charging a trustee in such a case with compound interest and in special cases a trustee has been charged even with such interest compounded half-yearly, and in the present case it can hardly be doubted that the trustee could have invested the moneys at even more than the half-yearly rate charged by the learned trial Judge. But on the material before this Court, there is no evidence that he did so invest them or speculate with them and no evidence that he obtained half-yearly rates for other trust moneys in his hands. The items run back from 15 to 35 years ago and under the circumstances and upon the evidence however much at fault the trustee may have been upon the findings of the Judicial Committee, I do not think he should be chargeable with interest compounded more frequently than yearly. Counsel can no doubt agree upon the proper reduction upon this basis and save the expense of a reference but if not agreed there should be a reference to make the calculation.

20 *Hogg* v. *Toronto General Trusts Corp.,* [1933] 3 D.L.R. 721 (S.C.C.). R.V. Sinclair, K.C., appeared for Hogg, and W.J. Elliott, K.C., for the trust company. The bench was composed of Chief Justice Lyman Poore Duff, and Judges John Henderson Lamont, Robert Smith, Oswald Smith Crocket, and Frank Joseph Hughes. Judge Hughes wrote the decision, delivered on 28 June 1933. He noted at 722, "There is no doubt that a Master has in Ontario frequently charged inter-

est on uninvested balances against an executor under an administration order ... The Judgment of the Judicial Committee of the Privy Council, in *Campbell* v. *Hogg, supra,* held in our opinion, that the Surrogate Court had no jurisdiction to charge interest on uninvested balances in the hands of such a trustee as was the appellant." Hughes then quoted all the passages of the Privy Council decision that spoke to the issue of interest, concluding: "We are of the opinion that the above language ... goes to the question of jurisdiction and that therefore the claim for interest is not *res judicata.*" This seems very confused. If the Surrogate Court had no authority to award interest, then the answer to whether Mrs. Campbell should receive such was clear: she should not. Why the court determined that this meant the claim was not *res judicata* is unclear. With the final sentence of the decision, the court dismissed the appeal with costs. If the Surrogate Court had no authority to award interest, why was the Supreme Court of Canada reinstating the Court of Appeal decision to send the matter back to the master to consider interest? The analysis seems haphazard and, apart from the result, the restoration of the majority decision of the Court of Appeal, it settled few of the outstanding issues.

21 Counsel for the trust company asked for interest at the prevailing rate (6 percent), with rests "made annually at least." The assistant master ruled that the "legal rate," which had been set by statute at 5 percent in Canada in 1900, was preferable to the prevailing rate, as this was more "conservative and fair." Lennox noted that the Law Lords had found Hogg liable for direct breaches of trust, failure to keep accounts, and not rendering a proper account when requested, adding: "Some of their Lordships' observations no doubt may infer more serious breaches on the part of Mr. Hogg, but they are not included as findings of fact." Lennox stated that at one time the courts would punish a trustee who had committed a direct breach of trust or who was guilty of wilful default by charging a higher rate of interest, but that such charges in the nature of penalties had been seriously challenged in later years. Noting that a trustee acting gratuitously, on such friendly terms, could hardly be expected to invest all balances with the same dispatch as a person regularly employed, he concluded that yearly — not half-yearly — rests should be awarded. The amount was calculated at $17,796.98. There appears to be no explanation as to why this amount was slightly larger than the $17,250.40 calculated earlier by Judge Jeffrey, who set the rests half-yearly. There are no surviving records setting out the calculations used by Judge Jeffrey to reach the earlier figure, so the two calculations cannot be compared. "Reasons for Judgment," O.E. Lennox, assistant master, Supreme Court of Ontario, *Toronto General Trusts Corporation* v. *Hogg,* Archives of Ontario, RG22-5800, No. 2612/30.

22 The decision of Judge Tytler of the York County Surrogate Court was unreported, but referred to in the appeal: *Re Howland,* [1934] O.W.N. 555 (Ontario High Court), a decision delivered on 29 September 1934. The trust company produced a bill of $787.10 for legal services rendered on the passing of Hogg's account before the Carleton County Surrogate Court, which was taxed by the taxing master at $492.10. The bill for legal services rendered on the appeal before Judge Masten was rendered at $346.45 and taxed at $250.00. The bill for legal services on the appeal to the Ontario Court of Appeal was rendered at

$607.70 and taxed at $466.00. The bill for legal services at the Privy Council was rendered at $1,761.00 and taxed at $1,249.00. Judge Tytler ordered the amounts paid as taxed.

John Tytler was born on 20 March 1858, and admitted as a student-at-law in 1880. He was called to the bar in 1885 and practised in Toronto. He was appointed a junior judge in York County Court in 1921, and retired in 1934. He died on 10 February 1952. Law Society of Upper Canada Archives, Past Member Record Files.

23 The argument has been extrapolated from earlier press coverage of related proceedings: "Says Trust Company Jeopardized Estate," Toronto *Star*, 24 September 1931, p. 8.

24 John Millar McEvoy was born on 28 June 1864 in Caradoc, Ontario, to A.M. McEvoy and Sarah Northcott. He obtained a B.A. from the University of Toronto in 1890 and an LL.B. in 1892. He was admitted as a student-at-law in 1890 and called to the bar in 1893. He practised in London, Ontario, with McEvoy, Wilson and Pope. For some years he taught constitutional history with the department of political science at the University of Toronto, where he published widely on municipal institutions, currency, banking, revenue tariffs, and Karl Marx. He was appointed to the Supreme Court of Ontario, High Court of Justice, in 1927. He died on 13 April 1935. Law Society of Upper Canada Archives, Past Member Record Files; Henry Morgan, ed., *Canadian Men and Women of the Times* (Toronto: Briggs, 1898), 734–5.

25 *Re Howland,* [1934] O.W.N. 555 (Ontario High Court), at 557. W.J. Elliott, K.C., represented the trust company, W.R. Wadsworth, K.C., represented Mrs. Lindsey; Annie McDougald, although served, did not appear. Mrs. Campbell appeared in person. The decision was dated 29 September 1934. "At Osgoode Hall," Toronto *Globe*, 1 October 1934, p. 16.

26 *Re Howland,* [1935] O.W.N. 340 (Ontario Court of Appeal), per Riddell, J.A., at 341–3, 345. Robert Spelman Robertson, K.C., of Fasken, Robertson, Aitchison, Pickup and Calvin, who later became chief justice of Ontario, acted for the trust company; Mrs. Campbell appeared in person. The decision was delivered by Judge Riddell on 18 June 1935, and concurred in by Judges Robert Grant Fisher and Patrick Kerwin.

27 *Re Howland,* [1935] O.W.N. 340 (Ontario Court of Appeal), per Riddell, J.A., at 342–4.

28 William Renwick Riddell was born in Cobourg, Ontario, in 1852 to Presbyterian parents who had emigrated from Dumfries, Scotland, in 1833. He obtained a bachelor of Arts and Science from Victoria College and won the gold medal at Osgoode Hall Law School in 1883. His wife, Anna Hester Kirsop Crossen, was deeply involved in the Imperial Order Daughters of the Empire, as Lady Howland had been. Riddell was named Q.C. in 1899, and served as bencher from 1891 to 1906, when he was appointed to the Ontario Supreme Court. A lifelong supporter of the Liberal Party, Riddell was also one of Canada's great publicists for the loyalist, imperialist heritage. As a judge, his reputation was that he was "a little high hat," and "always a little cocksure in all his cases," someone who was quite caught up with the prestige of his position. He was also much opposed to the admission of women to the legal profession.

Indeed, he had disrupted a meeting of the Law Society of Upper Canada in 1892 in an unsuccessful bid to prevent the admission of Clara Brett Martin, the first woman seeking entrance. In 1918 he wrote an article titled "Women As Practitioners of Law," published in the *Journal of Comparative Law* (18), in which he notes: "I do not think that the most fervent advocate of women's rights could claim that the admission of women to the practice of law has made any appreciable effect on the Bar, the practice of law, the Bench, or the people ... The admission of women is regarded with complete indifference by all but those immediately concerned" (206). In 1922 he published a manuscript titled "An Old-Time Misogynist" in *The Canadian Magazine,* March 1922, 379-80, in which he translates at length passages from ancient Latin texts describing women as "a daily injury," "perpetually complaining," "a constant liar," "fondling and caressing deceit," "a filthy bedmate," and "a piece of hell." Hilary Bates Neary, "William Renwick Riddell: A Bio-Bibliographic Study" (M.A. thesis, University of Western Ontario, 1977), 1-9, 20, 34-8; Henry James Morgan, ed., *The Canadian Men and Women of the Time,* 2nd ed. (Toronto: Briggs, 1912), 941; B.M. Green, ed., *Who's Who and Why: 1921* (Toronto: International Press, 1921), 94; W. Stewart Wallace, ed., *The Macmillan Dictionary of Canadian Biography,* 3rd ed. (Toronto: Macmillan, 1963), 623; "39 Years in Supreme Court—Mr. Justice Riddell Dies," Toronto *Daily Star,* 19 February 1945; "Justice W.R. Riddell Dies Soon after Wife," *Globe and Mail,* 19 February 1945; Law Society of Upper Canada Archives, Draft Autobiography of D'Alton Lally McCarthy, sous-fonds 1, D'Alton Lally McCarthy sous-fonds, William G.C. Howland fonds 994001SF1-1-4; Constance Backhouse, *Petticoats and Prejudice: Women and Law in Nineteenth-Century Canada* (Toronto: Women's Press, 1991), 308; Constance Backhouse, *Colour-Coded: A Legal History of Racism in Canada, 1900-1950* (Toronto: University of Toronto Press, 1999), 121-6.

29 *Re Howland,* [1935] O.W.N. 340 (Ontario Court of Appeal), per Riddell, J.A., at 345-6.

30 The amount was noted in *Re Howland,* [1935] O.W.N. 340 (Ontario Court of Appeal), per Riddell, J.A., at 341.

31 Law Society of Upper Canada Archives, Minutes of Discipline Committee, 4 January 1933 to 12 March 1937, on 15 June 1934, p. 273; Minutes of Convocation, vol. 19, 18 October 1934, p. 195. (We are indebted to Brendan O'Brien for providing a copy of these records to us.)

32 We have been unable to locate surviving archival court records, but press coverage discloses some details. "Police Court Action in Estate Dispute," Ottawa *Evening Citizen,* 16 February 1934, p. 2, reports that "Magistrate Strike initially refused to accept the informations presented by Mrs. Campbell, and his decision was upheld in Weekly Court. Mrs. Campbell then swore out informations before Alderman N.A. Bordeleau. George F. Henderson, K.C., and R.V. Sinclair, K.C., represented Hogg, and Mrs. Campbell appeared on her own behalf." "Five Charges Follow Civil Court Action," Toronto *Star,* 16 February 1934, p. 1, lists them: forgery, uttering a forged document, false pretences, theft by conversion and perjury. "W.D. Hogg Acquitted of False Pretences," Toronto *Star,* 10 March 1934, p. 1, reports that Deputy Magistrate M.J. O'Connor dismissed the charges after finding no proof of "any fraudulent intent." See also

"Chiselling Trust Co.," Toronto *Hush* 7, 41 (13 October 1934), p. 7 (copy on file with authors).

33 Interview with Brendan O'Brien, by Constance Backhouse and Nancy Backhouse, Toronto, 13 April 2001 (copy on file with authors).

34 Interview with E. Peter Newcombe, by Constance Backhouse, Ottawa, 13 August 2002 (copy on file with authors).

35 Interview with Brendan O'Brien, by Constance Backhouse and Nancy Backhouse, Toronto, 13 April 2001 (copy on file with authors).

36 Interview with E. Peter Newcombe, by Constance Backhouse, Ottawa, 13 August 2002 (copy on file with authors). Peter Newcombe added that although he thought Mrs. Campbell wrote her book "to embarrass the Hoggs," he also had the impression that his father "thought that Hogg kind of deserved what he got."

37 D'Alton Lally McCarthy notes in his draft autobiography that Mrs. Campbell's case was "the first case in my experience that such an extraordinary situation had ever occurred," and that it had been "much discussed before the different members of the Bar." See Law Society of Upper Canada Archives, Draft Autobiography of D'Alton Lally McCarthy, sous-fonds 1, D'Alton Lally McCarthy sous-fonds, William G.C. Howland fonds 994001SF1-1-4. See also interview with the Hon. Mr. Justice John Arnup, by Constance Backhouse and Nancy Backhouse, Toronto, 15 April 2001 (copy on file with authors).

38 "Woman Makes History," London *Daily Herald,* 2 May 1930, p. 4, describes her as "a tall, slim, refined-looking woman."

39 A.B. McKillop, in his brilliant account of this case, argues that Deeks's claim, although unsuccessful, was legitimate. He uncovers many other intriguing parallels: Florence Deeks was represented by many of the same lawyers who appeared in Mrs. Campbell's case. Tilley was first on the record, although he was very pessimistic about the prospects of success and eventually left the file. Deeks feared Tilley had been bribed by London solicitors to drop the case. Other lawyers working for Deeks included Gideon Grant; Percy E.F. Smiley; R.S. Robertson, K.C.; and D'Alton Lally McCarthy. H.G. Wells, who was initially represented by McCarthy and McCarthy, switched to William James Elliott. When Deeks's lawyers became uniformly critical of her desire to appeal, she took her own case before the Ontario Court of Appeal and the Privy Council, losing both times. Although Deeks was able to finance much of her case from family money, much of it obtained from a wealthy brother who was an engineer, she had none of the illustrious social and professional connections that the Bethune/Howland families had. A.B. McKillop, *The Spinster and the Prophet: Florence Deeks, H.G. Wells and the Mystery of the Purloined Past* (Toronto: Macfarlane Walter and Ross, 2000). See also "Half Million Suit against H.G. Wells: Writer of 'The Web' Claims Passages Incorporated in 'Outline of History,'" Ottawa *Evening Citizen,* 29 January 1930, p. 1, an article that appeared one day after the front-page coverage of Mrs. Campbell's Privy Council argument.

40 *Where Angels Fear to Tread,* 31.

41 For a more detailed discussion of the ways that Britishness was inscribed in Canada and Australia, see W. Wesley Pue, "Planting British Legal Culture in Colonial Soil: Legal Professionalism in the Lands of the Beaver and Kangaroo,"

in *Shaping Nations: Constitutionalism and Society in Australia and Canada*, ed. Linda Cardinal and David Headon (Ottawa: University of Ottawa Press, 2002), 91.

42 "Toronto Woman First before Privy Council," Toronto *Daily Star,* 28 January 1930, p. 1.

43 *Where Angels Fear to Tread,* 34, 58, 63,132.

44 Interview with Peter Campbell Brooks, by Constance Backhouse, San Francisco, 23 July 2002 (copy on file with authors).

45 *Where Angels Fear to Tread,* 121-3, 127-8.

46 Cecilia Morgan, "'An Embarrassingly and Severely Masculine Atmosphere': Women, Gender and the Legal Profession at Osgoode Hall, 1920s-1960s," *Canadian Journal of Law and Society* 11, 2 (1996): 19 at 42-3 notes that the term "Portia" was ubiquitous in reference to "lady lawyers" and suggests that it insinuated that women's "intrusion into the legal profession was somehow transitory and unreal, a kind of exotic play-acting." Lawyer Ruby Wigle, in her article "Sisters in Law," *Canadian Bar Review* 5 (1927): 419, objects to the use of the term, and advises that women barristers much preferred to be called "my learned friend."

47 "Canadian Portia Is Still Arguing Estate Case before Privy Council," Toronto *Star,* 13 February 1930, p. 23.

48 "Canadian Portia Is Calm in Plea to Privy Council; Is Dressed in Mauve," Toronto *Star,* 3 February 1930, p. 19.

49 "No Legal Training," Yorkshire *Evening News,* 3 February 1930.

50 Mrs. Campbell refers to the "side lights on one's make-up" as "quite amusing" in *Where Angels Fear to Tread,* 143. Presumably, she took some pride in the press coverage as well, as she quotes the Yorkshire clipping on the fly-leaf of her book.

51 N.E.S. Griffiths, *The Splendid Vision: Centennial History of the National Council of Women of Canada, 1893-1993* (Ottawa: Carleton University Press, 1993); Alison Prentice et al., *Canadian Women: A History* (Toronto: Harcourt Brace Jovanovich, 1988), 180-3.

52 *Where Angels Fear to Tread,* 137. For details regarding the case, see Book Five n. 21.

53 "Canada's Portia Is Child of Man Who Never Knew When He Was Beaten," Toronto *Evening Telegram,* 3 May 1930, p. 3; *Where Angels Fear to Tread,* 151.

54 Backhouse, *Petticoats and Prejudice,* 293-326, 334-7.

55 Cecilia Morgan, "'An Embarrassingly and Severely Masculine Atmosphere,'" 19; Moore, *Law Society of Upper Canada,* 202-3. Laura Legge would become the first woman bencher and the first woman treasurer of the Law Society of Upper Canada.

56 "Toronto Woman First before Privy Council," Toronto *Daily Star,* 28 January 1930, p. 1.

57 Rebecca Rogers, "Acquiring Polish and Manners: French Education for British Girls in the Nineteenth Century," paper delivered at the Berkshire Conference, Storrs, Connecticut, June 2002.

58 Moore, *Law Society of Upper Canada,* 116-18, 163-75, 213.

59 "Toronto Woman First before Privy Council," Toronto *Daily Star,* 28 January 1930, p. 1; "Canada's Portia Is Child of Man Who Never Knew When He Was Beaten," Toronto *Evening Telegram,* 3 May 1930, p. 3.

60 "Toronto Woman First before Privy Council," Toronto *Daily Star*, 28 January 1930, p. 1.

61 "Mrs. Campbell Talks Five Hours to Peers," Toronto *Star*, 4 February 1930, p. 1.

62 See "Lady Howland Dies after Long Illness," Toronto *Globe*, 15 August 1924, p. 9; "Avers Lady Howland Intended Destroy Will," Toronto *Star*, 27 June 1925, p. 3; "Says She Had Will Envelope, Did Not Examine Document," Toronto *Star*, 30 June 1925, p. 2.

63 For reference to the frequent depiction of Mrs. Campbell as "Lady Howland's favourite daughter," see "Lady Howland Revoked Will; Action Fails," Toronto *Evening Telegram*, 20 October 1925, p. 15.

64 Cora Ann Lindsey took Lady Howland into her home after Mr. Malcolmson of the Welland Hotel in St. Catharines advised the family that it was "quite impossible for him to retain" Lady Howland "as a guest at his hotel" any longer. William Hogg wrote to all three of Lady Howland's daughters on 7 July 1922 to tell them that the situation was urgent: "I understand that to the ordinary individual who meets your mother in the hotel there is not much appearance of trouble but the difficulty so far as I know is that she becomes violent with those about her like Miss Hick and others attending upon her, and Mr. Malcolmson finds it impossible to retain in his service people who will attend to your mother's wants." He advised the daughters that there were few sanitorium institutions that would accept Lady Howland as a patient, and those that might do so were not "a very happy place for any person to go to." He begged each of the daughters to take Lady Howland into their home, noting that his wife Agnes was not healthy, strong, or young enough to do so. Cora Ann Lindsey was the one who answered the call. Her relatively recent widowhood may have been an additional factor in the decision, as this would have presumably left Cora Ann with an absence of wifely duties and more time to attend an ailing mother. See Privy Council Archives, "Record of Proceedings," Campbell v. Hogg, No. 56 of 1929, pp. 246–7.

65 For details of the will, see Book One n. 5.

66 In his testimony before Judge Mulligan of the County of Carleton Surrogate Court in 1927, Hogg claimed that Mrs. Campbell and her husband had made "constant and insistent demands for money" upon Lady Howland, who was "very much troubled" by the requests. Lady Howland, he testified, was "overcome on several occasions and wept about it, but she said it was becoming so burdensome upon her, that she didn't know really what to do." Privy Council Archives, "Record of Proceeding," Campbell v. Hogg, No. 56 of 1929, p. 159.

67 "Says She Had Will Envelope, Did Not Examine Document," Toronto *Daily Star*, 30 June 1925, p. 2, adverts to problems but gives no details.

68 After Charles's will was probated, Lady Howland expressed concern over the exclusive disposition of assets in favour of Cora Ann. She apparently told family members that she "didn't need his money" but was upset that Charles had failed to "mention" her "in his will by name." What Mrs. Campbell thought about her own complete exclusion is unknown. "Says She Had Will Envelope, Did Not Examine Document," Toronto *Daily Star*, 30 June 1925, p. 2. Last Will and Testament of Charles James Rattray Bethune, Archives of Ontario, RG22, MS887, Reel 332, Application No. 10144, reveals that the will is dated 30

September 1920, four months after Cora Ann's husband died. The estate, composed exclusively of personalty (clothing and jewellery, household goods and furniture, moneys secured by mortgage and life insurance, bank stock, and cash), was valued at $24,229.70. Cora Ann was the sole executrix.

69 The Last Will and Testament of G.G.S. Lindsey indicates that the estate, when probated, was valued at $19,508 in personalty (composed of household goods and furniture, office furniture, book debts and promissory notes, bank stocks, and cash) and $23,800 in realty (composed of $8,800 equity in 145 Tyndall Avenue and $15,000 in a property known as "Slate Islands"). Archives of Ontario, RG22, MS584, Reel 332, Grant No. 40981. The total of $43,308 left by her husband, coupled shortly thereafter with the $24,229.70 left by Charles Bethune, suggests that Mrs. Lindsey's claims of penuriousness may have been somewhat inflated.

70 Further testimony, from a friend of Lady Howland's named Mrs. Inksater, was adduced to the effect that Lady Howland was upset about how Mr. Lindsey had left his affairs, because he had seemed to have "plenty of money" and it was "strange" that after his death her daughter was left with "so little." "Says She Had Will Envelope, Did Not Examine Document," Toronto *Daily Star,* 30 June 1925, p. 2; "Avers Lady Howland Intended Destroy Will" Toronto *Star,* 27 June 1925, p. 3.

71 Mrs. Campbell testified in 1935, under cross-examination by Robert Spelman Robertson, counsel for the trust company, that, since the litigation over the probate of the will, she had "not spoken to either of them." "Forced to Borrow for London Appeal," Toronto *Star,* 9 February 1935, p. 2.

72 Mrs. Campbell did not participate in the Jamaica Plain Tuesday Club (the local literary women's group) or in the drama club, although all the rectors' wives before and after her belonged to these. Nor did she belong to the elite Boston women's Chilton Club. Interview with David Mittell and Katharine Cipolla, by Constance Backhouse, Boston, 13 August 2001 (copy on file with authors); interview with Margaret Tyng Lawson, by Constance Backhouse, by telephone, Providence, Rhode Island, 14 August 2001 (copy on file with authors); telephone conversation with Mrs. Keenan, secretary of the Chilton Club, 3 June 2002.

73 Correspondence between David A. Mittell and Willis G. Hazard, Toledo, Ohio, 27 October 1992; interview with David Mittell and Katharine Cipolla, by Constance Backhouse, Boston, 13 August 2001 (copy on file with authors).

74 *Where Angels Fear to Tread,* 31.

75 *Where Angels Fear to Tread,* 157.

76 That such comments were made is confirmed by an interview with Margaret Tyng Lawson, by Constance Backhouse, by telephone, Providence, Rhode Island, 14 August 2001 (copy on file with authors).

77 Letter from David A. Mittell to Rev. Henry W. Sherrill, 7 April 1997 (copy on file with authors).

78 James graduated with a B.A. from Harvard University in 1931, and from Harvard Medical School in 1935. He served as a captain in the US Army medical corps in Australia and New Guinea in the Second World War, and went on to become a neurosurgeon who taught at Harvard Medical School, Columbia University, Yale University, New York University, and the University of Illinois. *Harvard*

Class of 31, 25th Anniversary Report (Cambridge, MA, 1956), 172; *Harvard College, Class of 1931, 30th Anniversary Report,* 39; *Princeton Alumni Weekly,* 3 May 1935; *The Church Militant* (May 1943): 16 (copy on file with authors); interview with Peter Campbell Brooks, by Constance Backhouse, San Francisco, 23 July 2002 (copy on file with authors).

79 Thomasine graduated from Columbia (Barnard) in 1935, continuing her studies in Vienna. After some years of fairly nomadic living, she settled into a very successful career as a librarian at Princeton University from 1953 to 1964, and then at the Harvard College Observatory. Interview with David Mittell and Katharine Cipolla, by Constance Backhouse, Boston, 13 August 2001 (copy on file with authors); interview with Peter Campbell Brooks, by Constance Backhouse, San Francisco, 23 July 2002 (copy on file with authors); *The Church Militant* (May 1943): 16; *Harvard College Class of 1931, 30th Anniversary Report; 35th Anniversary Report* (Cambridge, MA, 1956), 172; *Princeton Alumni Weekly,* 3 May 1935.

80 Interview with Peter Campbell Brooks, by Constance Backhouse, San Francisco, 23 July 2002 (copy on file with authors).

81 Interview with David Mittell and Katharine Cipolla, by Constance Backhouse, Boston, 13 August 2001 (copy on file with authors).

82 Letter of Resignation, Thomas C. Campbell to Saint John's Church, 2 November 1942; Letter to Jack A. Campbell, Ogden, Utah, 13 April 1943, dictated by Tom Campbell but written by the nurse at Baker Memorial, Massachusetts General Hospital (copy on file with authors).

83 Interview with Peter Campbell Brooks, by Constance Backhouse, San Francisco, 23 July 2002 (copy on file with authors).

84 "Canada's Portia Is Child of Man Who Never Knew When He Was Beaten," Toronto *Evening Telegram,* 3 May 1930, p. 3.

85 *Campbell* v. *Hogg,* [1930] 3 D.L.R. 673 (P.C.) at 674-6; *Where Angels Fear to Tread,* 78; Last Will and Testament of James Bethune, Archives of Ontario, RG22, GS1, Reel 998, Estate Grant 55472.

86 *Campbell* v. *Hogg,* [1930] 3 D.L.R. 673 (P.C.) at 674.

87 *Campbell* v. *Hogg,* [1930] 3 D.L.R. 673 (P.C.) at 678. By the time of Lady Howland's death in 1924, the mortgages totalled $6,600, part of an estate that amounted to $17,450. Last Will and Testament of Elizabeth Mary Howland, Archives of Ontario, RG22, MS 584, Reel 43, Estate Grant 50634, No. 1784/24, 29 September 1924.

88 *Campbell* v. *Hogg,* [1930] 3 D.L.R. 673 (P.C.) at 679-81.

89 *Campbell* v. *Hogg,* [1930] 3 D.L.R. 673 at 694-703.

90 The assessment that Hogg's accounts were "in effect accepted" comes from *Campbell* v. *Hogg,* [1930] 3 D.L.R. 673 at 686. The Carleton County Surrogate Court "made certain additions" as a result of "mutual admissions before him" but otherwise "rejected all" of Mrs. Campbell's specific objections. The Ontario High Court (in an unreported judgment of Judge Masten) struck out $1,155 in what the court believed to be an unwarranted claim by Hogg for legal fees. The Ontario Court of Appeal overturned Masten's calculation of $1,155 as being in error, and added $1,000 to Mrs. Campbell's ledger, should she be willing to accept the total sum in full settlement. *Re Howland* (1929), 35 O.W.N. 175 (C.A.).

91 *Campbell v. Hogg*, [1930] 3 D.L.R. 673 at 694-703.

92 This was the ruling of Carleton County Surrogate Court judge J.A. Mulligan (unreported but found in the Privy Council Archives, "Record of Proceedings," *Campbell v. Hogg*, No. 56 of 1929, p. 195), upheld in large measure by the Ontario High Court (unreported but found in the Privy Council Archives, "Record of Proceedings," *Campbell v. Hogg*, No. 56 of 1929, p. 203) and Ontario Court of Appeal, *Re Howland* (1929), 35 O.W.N. 175 (C.A.). For reference to these rulings, see *Campbell v. Hogg*, [1930] 3 D.L.R. 673 at 686-9.

93 *Campbell v. Hogg*, [1930] 3 D.L.R. 673 (P.C.) at 675 notes that Hogg was eighty years old at the time of the Ontario Court of Appeal hearing, in 1928.

94 *Campbell v. Hogg*, [1930] 3 D.L.R. 673 at 687-8.

95 *Campbell v. Hogg*, [1930] 3 D.L.R. 673 at 679-701.

96 This claim had "raised a conflict between the parties exceeding all the others in intensity and seriousness" see *Campbell v. Hogg*, [1930] 3 D.L.R. 673 at 697-8. *Where Angels Fear to Tread*, 70-1.

97 *Campbell v. Hogg*, [1930] 3 D.L.R. 673 at 699-700. The reference to the "joint loan" was undoubtedly to emphasize that earlier entries of Hogg's, in Exhibit 44-A, showed two loans — one for $1,100 to McAmmond in 1885, and a second for $500 to Martin the same year. The Law Lords noted that earlier levels of court had erroneously "vaguely assumed" that the transaction was "a joint loan made somewhere about 1895."

98 *Campbell v. Hogg*, [1930] 3 D.L.R. 673 at 679-701.

99 N.a., *The Toronto General Trusts Company* (Toronto, 1892), 8.

100 *Where Angels Fear to Tread*, 58.

101 Ibid., 86.

102 Some sense of the sparks that could fly between Mrs. Campbell and opposing counsel — over Mrs. Campbell's sense of her own rights and entitlement — is depicted in the press coverage on the litigation over costs. "Won Case at Privy Council, Costs Are Taxed in Toronto," Toronto *Evening Telegram,* 10 October 1930, p. 3, reads as follows:

> "I have that little piece of paper and I think when I go before a judge you will find that the Privy Council of England does command a little bit of attention." So spoke Mrs. Elizabeth Bethune Campbell, of Jamaica Plains, Boston, daughter of the late lady Howland, who appeared before Taxing Officer John MacGillivray at Osgoode Hall yesterday ... Many items were lopped off her respective bills. Her bill of costs before the Appellate Division was reduced from $500 to $234.
>
> "I win — call it any sort of victory you like," said Mrs. Campbell. "I have made a beaten path around Osgoode Hall from one judge to another. I was offered $1,000 and I said 'no.' I went to the Privy Council and won. Now you give me $234. I shall appeal. I know what a successful counsel would have tacked on his bill for expenses."
>
> W.R. Wadsworth, who appeared for W.D. Hogg, K.C., challenged items Mrs. Campbell had in her bill for trips from Boston to Toronto, saying, "You could have had an agent." Mrs. Campbell — "The British law allows me to take my own case. That is what I did and I won."

"You could have employed a solicitor for $15."

"No solicitor would take my case."

Mr. Wadsworth—"No solicitor could make the charges against Mr. Hogg that you are seeking to make."

Mrs. Campbell—"May I give the final authority of the world's court—the Privy Council. I turned a page in the annals of the Privy Council."

Mr. Wadsworth—"They do a lot of things over there that we are not quite satisfied with over here."

Mrs. Campbell—"If I had engaged counsel, Mr. Hogg would have a jolly fine bill to face." Mrs. Campbell sought $30 a week for maintenance in Toronto.

Mr. Wadsworth—"I am willing to offer $1.50 a day as a gesture of generosity."

Mrs. Campbell—"I am not asking for generosity, I am asking for my rights. You wouldn't expect any gentlewoman to live on less than $5 a day."

"What authority have you?"

"The only authority I have is the King's order, which I have always thought was a very good thing."

103 The staff of the trust company should have recognized the deficiencies in Hogg's accounts in 1922 and attempted to compile whatever missing data still existed. They wrote to Hogg in October 1922, and then sat on the unsatisfactory file for four years without further effort. When Mrs. Campbell began to demand an accounting of the discrepant records, the president, Newton Wesley Rowell, directed his staff to make further inquiries. The follow-up in the face of Hogg's partial and contradictory replies was once again deficient, casting serious doubt on "Canada's Oldest Trust Company" and its public claims of "financial responsibility." For reference to the latter claims, see John Cowan, "Canada's Oldest Trust Company," *The Canadian Magazine,* October 1922, as reprinted by the Toronto General Trusts Corporation, pp. 1 and 8.

104 When Mrs. Campbell went to court, the company appeared against her in an adversarial position that it sustained without interruption except for the 1932-3 action to enforce the Privy Council judgment. In the *coup de grâce,* the Toronto General Trusts Corporation dipped into the dwindling estate, using almost the last of the sums Mrs. Campbell had single-handedly retrieved, to recover its full legal and administrative costs.

105 The Hon. Edward Blake was a founding president, with Senator J.K. Kerr and William Mulock among the directors. Blake and Kerr had been partners with James Bethune; Sir William Mulock, as he later became, was a long-time friend of the family; he would play a central role in the adjudication of the case. Featherston Osler, another former partner of James Bethune, also served as president. Some of these, along with another of the early directors, Robert Jaffray, had been guests at Mrs. Campbell's wedding. John Cowan, "Canada's Oldest Trust Company," *The Canadian Magazine,* October 1922, as reprinted by the

Toronto General Trusts Corporation, p. 3; *The Toronto General Trusts Company*, pamphlet (Toronto: 1892), 2-3.

106 *Where Angels Fear to Tread*, 57.
107 Law Society of Upper Canada Archives, Past Member Record Files.
108 Interview with Brendan O'Brien, by Constance Backhouse and Nancy Backhouse, Toronto, 13 April 2001 (copy on file with authors).
109 See generally John D. Arnup, *Middleton: The Beloved Judge* (Toronto: McClelland and Stewart, 1988).
110 *Where Angels Fear to Tread*, 47.
111 Ibid. 46, 48. Press coverage of the unreported decision reported Judge Kelly as extremely harsh in his assessment of Mrs. Campbell:

> She has stated her mother's condition in extravagant language, describing with undue emphasis her inability to care for herself. Her demeanor and her manner of giving her evidence was so extreme, due in some degree to excitability, as to make her statements unsafe as a foundation for any reasonable conclusion even where her testimony is not contradicted. She has been contradicted in many essential particulars by the credible evidence of other witnesses. Her attitude of suspicion towards those whose opinions or actions concerning her mother's affairs have not been in accord with her wishes or plans, and her unwarranted attacks in her correspondence and in her evidence on reputable members of the legal profession, one a relative of the family, who performed useful and kindly business services for Lady Howland, were not conducive to the authenticity of her statements generally.

"Lady Howland Revoked Will; Action Fails," Toronto *Evening Telegram*, 20 October 1925, p. 15.
112 *Where Angels Fear to Tread*, 46.
113 Ibid., 84-5. "Wants Another Judge to Hear Will Appeal; Mr. Justice Masten Cites Close Friendship with Counsel in Case," Toronto *Star*, 15 December 1927, p. 3; "Trustee Got $19,000; Left About $8,415," Toronto *Evening Telegram*, 15 December 1927, p. 27.
114 Law Society of Upper Canada Archives, Draft Autobiography of D'Alton Lally McCarthy, sous-fonds 1, D'Alton McCarthy sous-fonds, William G.C. Howland fonds, 994001SF1-1-4.
115 Law Society of Upper Canada Archives, Past Member Record Files.
116 Law Society of Upper Canada Archives, Draft Autobiography of D'Alton Lally McCarthy, sous-fonds 1, D'Alton McCarthy sous-fonds, William G.C. Howland fonds, 994001SF1-1-4.
117 Privy Council Archives, "Record of Proceedings," Campbell v. Hogg, No. 56 of 1929, pp. 203-4; "Masten Gives Reasons in Dismissing Appeal," Toronto *Star*, 23 December 1927, p. 27; "Trustee Got $19,000; Left About $8,415," Toronto *Evening Telegram*, 15 December 1927, p. 27; "Judgments in Probe of Trusteeship," Toronto *Evening Telegram*, 23 December 1927, p. 21.
118 *Where Angels Fear to Tread*, 85.

119 On Chief Justice Mulock's directorship with the Toronto General Trusts Corporation, and his family's participation at Mrs. Campbell's wedding, see discussion in the Introduction. For his description of meeting Lady Howland at the hotel, see "Urge Settlement in Lady Howland Will Controversy," Toronto *Star*, 20 April 1926, p. 19.

120 *Where Angels Fear to Tread*, 49-51, 110. The reference to "pounding the table" came from the recollections of Brendan O'Brien, who remembered reading a copy of the book many years ago that contained information that was not in the 1940 version. (On the possibility of more than one printing, see the Introduction.) O'Brien states that in the version he read initially, "Mr. Justice Mulock pounded the table, but that isn't in [the 1940] version." Interview with Brendan O'Brien, by Constance Backhouse and Nancy Backhouse, Toronto, 13 April 2001 (copy on file with authors).

121 *Where Angels Fear to Tread*, 93-5.

122 Anderson, "Where Angels Fear to Tread," 19.

123 "Urge Settlement in Lady Howland Will Controversy," Toronto *Star*, 20 April 1926, p. 19.

124 *Where Angels Fear to Tread*, 102.

125 *Re Howland* (1929), 36 O.W.N. 53 (C.A.).

126 *Where Angels Fear to Tread*, 104.

127 *Re Howland* (1929), 36 O.W.N. 53 (C.A.) at 54.

128 *Where Angels Fear to Tread*, 106.

129 Difficulties first arose when Arthur Courtney Kingstone of the Ingersoll, Kingstone, and Seymour law firm in St. Catharines wrote to the trust company to state that his firm had no record in the office of any will having been drawn by Lady Howland. The young English lawyer at Kingstone's firm, Mr. Cummings, later contradicted this and showed Mrs. Campbell the firm ledger and J. Hamilton Ingersoll's personal diary that registered the drawing of the will. When the matter came before the courts, both Ingersoll and Cummings testified that the will had been duly executed by Lady Howland and placed in the law firm vaults. Yet all agreed that the firm had no copy of the will in its possession and no record of releasing it to Lady Howland or otherwise. Ibid., 40, 41-2, 45-6.

130 Strachan Johnston, a senior partner of the Tilley, Johnston law firm in Toronto, had a copy of Lady Howland's will; he wrote to tell Mrs. Campbell that there were legal precedents suggesting that a certified copy of a will could be offered to the court; and he advised her that she could "safely leave the affair in his hands." Nothing could have been farther from the truth. Johnston neither filed the will with the court, nor did he answer Mrs. Campbell's several letters or her telegraph inquiring about the estate. Remarkably, he allowed Mrs. Campbell's sisters to take out administration papers, the trust company to sign them, and the court to grant rights of administration on the basis that Lady Howland had died intestate. Ibid., 42-4.

131 Ibid., 41, 43.

132 George (Beau) Brummell was a "dandy" and "ruling spirit" in the English court in the late eighteenth century who developed a reputation for his wit, charm, insolence, audacity, and being a "connoisseur of good living." In 1924 Warner Brothers released a cinematographic depiction of his life, starring John

Barrymore and Mary Astor, titled *Beau Brummel*. See Roger Boutet de Monvel, *Beau Brummel and his Times* (London: Fawside House, 1908). For details of Slaght's career, see Introduction n. 30 and Book Two n. 32. For the "upstart" comment, see interview with Brendan O'Brien, by Constance Backhouse and Nancy Backhouse, Toronto, 13 April 2001 (copy on file with authors). O'Brien stated: "The Ontario Court of Appeal in the old days did not give Slaght the hearing that senior lawyers like McCarthy or Tilley got. Slaght was regarded as a bit of an upstart. I think Slaght had a rough time in the beginning."

133 For details of the bencher election, and Slaght's standing, see Book One n. 33.

134 *Where Angels Fear to Tread,* 62, 74.

135 "Won Case at Privy Council, Costs Are Taxed in Toronto," Toronto *Evening Telegram,* 10 October 1930, p. 3. William Ridout Wadsworth was born on 17 December 1875. Admitted as a student-at-law in 1896, he was called to the bar in 1899, and practised in Toronto. A member of the Argonaut Rowing Club, he competed in the 1904 Olympics. He died on 29 August 1971. Law Society of Upper Canada Archives, Past Member Record Files.

136 Moore, *Law Society of Upper Canada,* 174, 223-6. Lally McCarthy married Sir John Beverley Robinson's daughter, Margaret Mary Robinson (1876-1943) in 1897. Upon her death, he married a second time, to Mary Bickerton Williams. (See correspondence from Christopher Moore to Constance Backhouse, 15 July 2002, citing McCarthy Tétrault archives, Toronto, D. Lally McCarthy file (copy on file with authors). For further details about McCarthy, see the Introduction.

137 *Where Angels Fear to Tread,* 82-3.

138 Ibid., 83, 85.

139 As quoted by Moore, *Law Society of Upper Canada,* 223.

140 We are indebted to Christopher Moore for advising us of the existence of Lally McCarthy's draft autobiography.

141 Law Society of Upper Canada Archives, Draft Autobiography of D'Alton Lally McCarthy, sous-fonds 1, D'Alton McCarthy sous-fonds, William G.C. Howland fonds, 994001SF1-1-4.

142 Ibid.

143 Ibid.

144 *Where Angels Fear to Tread,* 86, 92.

145 David B. Wilkins, "Class Not Race in Legal Ethics: Or Why Hierarchy Makes Strange Bedfellows," *Law and History Review* 20, 1 (2002): 147-9; and see generally Jerald S. Auerbach, *Unequal Justice: Lawyers and Social Change in Modern America* (New York: Oxford University Press, 1976).

146 Moore, *Law Society of Upper Canada,* 149-51. The disbarment rate for African-Canadian lawyers was particularly pronounced. Ethelbert Lionel Cross, a leading anti-racist activist in the Black community of Toronto, was disbarred in 1937 for "misappropriation of funds." See Backhouse, *Colour-Coded,* 209-25, 400-1. Lance Carey Talbot, "History of Blacks in the Law Society of Upper Canada," *Law Society of Upper Canada Gazette* 24, 1 (1990): 66-8, notes that of the five Black lawyers practising in Ontario in the 1940s and 1950s, "two were disbarred, one in 1948 and the other in 1953." On the disciplinary vigilance that the Law Society showed toward Black lawyers who were accused of "touting," and "conduct unbecoming," see Oral History Transcript of Mr. Charles Roach, Osgoode

Society, interviewed by Christine J.N. Kates, November-December 1989. See also correspondence from Sheldon Taylor, 27 June 2002 (copy on file with authors). Norman Lickers, who appears to have been the first Aboriginal lawyer in Canada, was also disbarred. Born in Tuscarora Township on the Six Nations Territory, Lickers was called to the Ontario bar in 1938 and set up practice in Brantford, where he specialized in criminal law. Disbarred in 1950, Lickers moved on to a successful career as an ironworker and a leader in Aboriginal politics. See Law Society of Upper Canada Archives, Past Member Files, obituary "Canada's First Native Lawyer Dies on Six Nations Reserve," Brantford *Expositor,* 16 March 1987.

147 Moore, *Law Society of Upper Canada,* 209-10.

148 Ibid.

149 For example, Mrs. Campbell complains in her book of the departure of Mr. Cummings, a witness for the Ingersoll, Kingstone firm, whose holidays caused him to sail "very suddenly and quietly for England" during the litigation over the will. Of the delay caused by the pneumonia of her sister's lawyer, she insists that there were "quite five hundred other counsel at the Ontario Bar, many of whom might have taken Mr. Elliott's place." She expresses grave concern at seeing Arthur Slaght "almost arm in arm, evidently on most friendly terms" with McKague, counsel for the trust company. She is suspicious of George McDonnell, the Ottawa lawyer who declined to act when Slaght tried to retain an agent to represent Mrs. Campbell should he be prevented by blizzard weather from reaching court. Lawyers take holidays, they get sick, they often maintain friendly social relations with opposing counsel during litigation, and they sometimes have legitimate reasons for refusing to act as agents for out-of-town barristers. *Where Angels Fear to Tread,* 45, 48-9, 65, 73.

150 Mrs. Campbell singles out Judge William Nassau Ferguson of the Ontario Court of Appeal, a family friend who spoke frankly to her about the case when she was doing research for the Surrogate Court hearing in 1927. Ontario Court of Appeal judge William Edward Middleton, who ruled in favour of Mrs. Campbell in motions regarding the appeal to the Privy Council, offered her important advice in chambers. Ontario Court of Appeal judge James Magee, whose dissenting judgment ruled in Mrs. Campbell's favour, also gave her advice in chambers. She extols the kindness of James McGregor Young, a lawyer who practised with Blake, Lash and Cassels (a reformulation of James Bethune's old firm), who met Mrs. Campbell after she had been ejected from the McCarthy law office and offered directions about serving and filing appeal documents. Edmund Harley, the senior registrar at Osgoode Hall, was intermittently helpful. Edward Brown, K.C., the clerk in the Ontario Judgment Office, refused to allow Mrs. Campbell to pay for a copy of Judge Masten's decision, saying he "couldn't possibly take money from one of [James Bethune's] daughters." R. Reeve Wallace, chief clerk; Dudley George Lys, second clerk; and Sir Charles Neish, registrar of the Privy Council, are credited with providing substantial assistance to Mrs. Campbell, as are Enid M. Moore and Ada Wall, the secretaries at the Privy Council, and Polly and Jennings, the messengers. Ibid., 77-8, 88-9, 105, 108-9, 110-11, 116-17, 124-5, 143-4.

151 Interview with E. Peter Newcombe, by Constance Backhouse, Ottawa, 13 August 2002 (copy on file with authors).

152 *Where Angels Fear to Tread,* 77.

153 "Toronto Woman First before Privy Council," Toronto *Daily Star,* 28 January 1930, p. 1; "Woman Makes History," London *Daily Herald,* 2 May 1930, p. 4, states: "She has made legal history in London by being the first woman to plead before the highest Court in the Empire (the Judicial Committee of the Privy Council)."

154 "Woman Makes History," London *Daily Herald,* 2 May 1930, p. 4.

155 See, for example, "Will Plead Her Case at Privy Council," Toronto *Star,* 1 April 1931, p. 48, announcing that Mrs. Campbell intended to seek the intervention of the Privy Council over her failure to obtain her costs from the Ontario proceedings.

156 For reference to the "very substantial sum," see, for example, *Re Howland,* [1935] O.W.N. 340 (Ontario Court of Appeal), per Riddell, J.A., at 343. Based on statistics from the Bank of Canada's inflation calculator, a basket of goods and services that cost $7,000.00 in 1930 would cost $74,225.23 in 2002. An inflationary factor of 790 percent is suggested in A.B. McKillop, *Spinster and the Prophet,* 379, where he notes that Cdn$1,000,000 in 1920 equalled Cdn$7,958,874 in October 1996. McKillop cites Professor Campbell R. Harvey of Fuqua School of Business, Duke University, and Marianne P.F. Stevens, "Dollars and Change: The Effect of Rockefeller Foundation Funding on Canadian Medical Education at the University of Toronto, McGill University, and Dalhousie University" (Ph.D. diss., Institute for the History and Philosophy of Science and Technology, University of Toronto, 1999), 154, n. 3. The Hon. William J. Anderson suggests "a multiplier of 15" based on personal impressions, noting, "I lived through the period and have some recollection of what a dollar would buy in the 1930s." See Anderson, "Where Angels Fear to Tread," 23.

157 For details of the interest, see earlier discussion at n. 21 above.

158 In *Re Howland,* [1935] O.W.N. 340 (Ontario Court of Appeal), Judge Riddell noted at 341 that the amount was $2,201.02, supplemented by a few unrealized assets of "undetermined" value. Even this may have been reduced by a final deduction of costs awarded in that action to the Toronto General Trusts Corporation. On the latter, Judge Riddell stated at 346: "It is to be hoped that the T.G.T. will, under the peculiar circumstances, waive the claim for costs of these proceedings, but if the costs are demanded there is no principle upon which they can be withheld."

159 "Privy Council Allows Woman Her Own Appeal," Toronto *Star,* 1 May 1930, p. 2, notes: "It looks as if Mrs. Campbell and her sisters will be out of pocket as a result of the proceedings even though they have to pay only one quarter of their costs."

160 "Privy Council Allows Woman Her Own Appeal," Toronto *Star,* 1 May 1930, p. 2.

161 Interview with Peter Campbell Brooks, by Constance Backhouse, San Francisco, 23 July 2002 (copy on file with authors).

162 Law Society of Upper Canada Archives, Past Member Record Files.

163 Patricia Best and Ann Shortell, *A Matter of Trust: Power and Privilege in Canada's Trust Companies* (Toronto: Viking, 1985), 11, 61; Philip Smith, *The Trust-Builders:*

The Remarkable Rise of Canada Trust (Toronto: Macmillan, 1989), 222, 234-9; Annual Report of Toronto Dominion Canada Trust, 2001; correspondence from Shanta Ganesh, Toronto Dominion Canada Trust, 2 August 2002 (copy on file with authors).

164 Frederick Drummond Hogg was appointed to the Trial Division of the Supreme Court of Ontario on 12 August 1935, and elevated to the Court of Appeal in 1946. He retired in 1957 and died on 4 December 1961. Law Society of Upper Canada, Past Member Record Files.

165 Prime Minister William Lyon Mackenzie King notes in his diary that he was the one who had "recommended to the Crown" that "Fred Hogg" be appointed to a judicial post. See King, William Lyon Mackenzie, MG26, J13, diaries [Ottawa], NAC, Manuscript Division, Prime Ministers Archives Section, 1981, 18 September 1947, p. 895. For details of King's long-standing relationship with the Hoggs, Cora Ann Lindsey, and the Bethunes, see Introduction n. 14. Frederick Hogg's professional qualifications included a call to the bar in 1904, a K.C. in 1928, authorship of a text on parliamentary divorce, and service as the president of the Carleton Law Association. The Hon. Mr. Justice John Arnup had the following recollections of him: "He was a hardworking, sincere judge of average capabilities. He never produced any sparkling judgments, but he never made a fool of himself either. He was an ordinary lawyer and an ordinary judge. That's about the kindest thing you could say about him." Interview with Mr. Justice John Arnup, by Constance Backhouse and Nancy Backhouse, Toronto, 15 April 2001 (copy on file with authors). Peter Newcombe recalls him as a "fairly solid judge." Interview with E. Peter Newcombe, by Constance Backhouse, Ottawa, 13 August 2002 (copy on file with authors). See also William C.V. Johnson, ed., *The First Century: Essays on the History of the County of Carleton Law Association by Various Hands on the Occasion of the Association's Centenary, 1888-1988* (Ottawa: Bonanza Press, 1988), 35.

166 By 1935 William Hogg's legal firm was no longer listed in the city directory, and in 1936 he was no longer listed in the *Canadian Law List*. *Ottawa City Directory, 1935*; *Canadian Law List 1936* (Toronto: Canadian Law List, 1936); *The Canadian Who's Who, 1936-37* (Toronto: Times Publishing, 1937), 516, notes that Hogg retired in 1934.

167 Subsequent to Agnes's death, in 1934 William Hogg moved in with his son Frederick Drummond Hogg, and his daughter-in-law, Elizabeth, at 226 Argyle Avenue, in Ottawa. He lived with them until he moved into an apartment with his niece, Christine Bower, at 539 MacLaren Street around the time Frederick's new judicial responsibilities took him and his wife to Toronto. The value of his estate totalled $3,844.63, consisting of $50 in clothing, jewellery, and books; $1 in book debts; $2,850 in life insurance; $504 in bank stocks; $325.98 in cash; and $113.65 in accrued income from the estate of his deceased wife. The Toronto General Trusts Corporation was appointed the executor. The beneficiaries were William Chesley Hogg (son in Edmonton), Frederick D. Hogg (son in Toronto), Christine Bower (niece in Ottawa), Christina Bower (sister in Ottawa), Margaret Hogg (sister in Toronto), Janet Storey (sister in Newmarket), Mrs. Dorothy Ferguson (granddaughter in Toronto), and Ian Drummond Cameron (great-grandson, age one, son of Mrs. Elizabeth Cameron, deceased). Last Will and

Testament of William Drummond Hogg, Archives of Ontario, RG22, -354 Carleton, Estate File No. 19845, 12 February 1940; *Ottawa City Directory,* 1930, 1931, 1932, 1933, 1934, 1935, 1936, 1937.

168 Inquiries were made of senior Ottawa lawyers, including John Nelligan, Peter Newcombe, David Scott, Danny Maguire, Orion Low, Charles Scott, John Aylen, and Hyman Soloway, but none of them recalled William Drummond Hogg personally. Hogg had two sons. Frederick Drummond Hogg (deceased at the age of eighty-two, 4 December 1961) was married to Elizabeth Van Dusen (originally from New York City, who predeceased him by fifteen years). The couple had two daughters. Dorothy married Keith Ferguson, who was employed in the military: "permanent force hms Violet at Brit Bay" according to the 1951 and 1955 Ottawa city directories. Keith Ferguson appears to have died by 1961, as Mrs. Dorothy Ferguson was listed separately at 2-52 Frank Street, working as a stenographer for the Department of National Defence. She was no longer listed after 1965. We have been unable to discover any children born to Dorothy and Keith Ferguson. The second daughter was Elizabeth, who married Eric Cameron. Eric was in active service in 1945, and the couple lived at 361 Hinton Avenue, Ottawa. By 1951 Eric was a manager at Imperial Life Assurance and lived at 115 Lansdowne Road. There were no further listings for Eric or Elizabeth Cameron. Frederick Drummond Hogg's obituary lists only one surviving daughter, so presumably Elizabeth had predeceased him. Eric and Elizabeth Cameron appear to have had one son, Ian Drummond Cameron, for whom we have yet found no further records. See *Ottawa City Directory,* 1945-65; "Justice Hogg Dies at 82 in Ottawa," *Ottawa Journal,* 4 December 1961, p. 4; "Ex-Justice F.D. Hogg Dies at 82," *Ottawa Citizen,* 4 December 1961, p. 7.

Hogg's second son was William Chesley Hogg, who first showed up in the Edmonton city directory in 1931, residing at 9624-102nd Street, and working as a trucker for the Canadian National Railways. In 1932 he had moved to 9902-111th Street and was employed as a salesman. By 1933 he was listed as an insurance broker. By 1934 he had started his own business, W.C. Hogg and Co., a "manufacturer's agent," at 10201-104th Street. In 1935 he was listed as residing at 9936-115th Street, and in 1951 he retired. In 1952 he was no longer listed. We have found no records regarding a wife or children. See *Edmonton City Directory* 1931-52.

169 "Striking Tribute by Bench and Bar to W.D. Hogg, K.C.," Ottawa *Citizen,* 5 January 1940, p. 2; Law Society of Upper Canada Archives, Past Member Record Files.

170 James Bethune Campbell, the son, got married in 1934 while still a medical student, to a society woman ten years his senior. James met Marise Blair, from Peapack, New Jersey, who came from a wealthy railroad family, shortly after she was divorced from the nephew of J.P. Morgan. Marise had advertised at Harvard for a companion to supervise her three teenage sons at their summer home in Honolulu, James answered the ad, and the two were soon engaged. Mrs. Campbell was opposed to the match, and the hostility between the two women continued for years. The couple had no children and were divorced in 1965. James remarried Joan B. (White) Eccles in 1966. He died on 4 June 1983.

Just days before her father's death in 1943, Elizabeth Thomasine, the daughter, married an older Unitarian minister named Howard Lee Brooks, in Baltimore. Mrs. Campbell also had "a very unfavourable reaction" to this match. It was Brooks's third marriage. Although his parish was in Staten Island, Brooks spent many of the war years in Europe, doing humanitarian work with the Free World Society and becoming involved with the French Resistance. Thomasine joined him in Lisbon, Portugal, but he missed the birth there in 1944 of Peter Campbell Brooks, their only son, because he was in Casablanca helping resistance leaders escape. The couple divorced in 1947, and Thomasine took on a "Bohemian lifestyle" in which she indulged her interests in literature and the arts while holding down a series of working-class jobs throughout the northeastern United States: working in a laundry, as a chambermaid in a hotel, as a short-order cook in a beachfront sandwich stand, in a meat-packing factory. Eventually Thomasine settled into a very successful career as a librarian at Princeton University from 1953 to 1964, and at the Harvard College Observatory from 1964 to her death in 1974.

Peter Campbell Brooks and his one daughter, Erica Ivy Brooks (born in Walnut Creek, California, on 29 January 1981), are the only surviving members of the family whom we have been able to locate. Interview with Peter Campbell Brooks, by Constance Backhouse, San Francisco, 23 July 2002 (copy on file with authors); interview with Katharine Cipolla, by Constance Backhouse, Boston, 13 August 2001 (copy on file with authors); *Harvard College Class of 1931, 30th Anniversary Report; 35th Anniversary Report* (Cambridge, MA, 1956), 172; *Princeton Alumni Weekly,* 3 May 1935; *The Church Militant* (May 1943): 16.

171 Interview with Peter Campbell Brooks, by Constance Backhouse, San Francisco, 23 July 2002 (copy on file with authors); interview with Katharine Cipolla, by Constance Backhouse, Boston, 13 August 2001 (copy on file with authors).

172 Peter Campbell Brooks, whose branch of the family inherited Mrs. Campbell's books, legal records, and press clippings, regrets that they were not saved. So do we. Interview with Peter Campbell Brooks, by Constance Backhouse, San Francisco, 23 July 2002 (copy on file with authors).

INDEX

PUBLICATIONS OF
THE OSGOODE SOCIETY
FOR CANADIAN LEGAL HISTORY

1981 David H. Flaherty, ed., *Essays in the History of Canadian Law*, vol. 1

1982 Marion MacRae and Anthony Adamson, *Cornerstones of Order: Courthouses and Town Halls of Ontario, 1784-1914*

1983 David H. Flaherty, ed., *Essays in the History of Canadian Law*, vol. 2

1984 Patrick Brode, *Sir John Beverley Robinson: Bone and Sinew of the Compact*
David Williams, *Duff, A Life in the Law*

1985 James Snell and Frederick Vaughan, *The Supreme Court of Canada: History of the Institution*

1986 Paul Romney, *Mr. Attorney: The Attorney General for Ontario in Court, Cabinet and Legislature, 1791-1899*
Martin Friedland, *The Case of Valentine Shortis: A True Story of Crime and Politics in Canada*

1987 C. Ian Kyer and Jerome Bickenbach, *The Fiercest Debate: Cecil A. Wright, the Benchers and Legal Education in Ontario, 1923-1957*

1988 Robert Sharpe, *The Last Day, the Last Hour: The Currie Libel Trial*
John D. Arnup, *Middleton: The Beloved Judge*

1989 Desmond Brown, *The Genesis of the Canadian Criminal Code of 1892*
Patrick Brode, *The Odyssey of John Anderson*

1990 Jim Phillips and Philip Girard, eds., *Essays in the History of Canadian Law*, vol. 3, *Nova Scotia*
Carol Wilton, ed., *Essays in the History of Canadian Law*, vol. 4, *Beyond the Law: Lawyers and Business in Canada 1830-1930*

1991 Constance Backhouse, *Petticoats and Prejudice: Women and Law in Nineteenth Century Canada*

1992 Brendan O'Brien, *Speedy Justice, The Tragic Last Voyage of His Majesty's Vessel* Speedy
Robert Fraser, ed., *Provincial Justice: Upper Canadian Legal Portraits from the Dictionary of Canadian Biography*

1993 Greg Marquis, *Policing Canada's Century: A History of the Canadian Association of Chiefs of Police*
Murray Greenwood, *Legacies of Fear, Law and Politics in Quebec in the Era of the French Revolution*

1994 Patrick Boyer, *A Passion for Justice: The Legacy of James Chalmers McRuer*

Charles Pullen, *The Life and Times of Arthur Maloney: The Last of the Tribunes*

Jim Phillips, Tina Loo, Susan Lewthwaite, eds., *Essays in the History of Canadian Law*, vol. 5, *Crime and Criminal Justice*

Brian Young, *The Politics of Codification: The Lower Canadian Civil Code of 1866*

1995 David Williams, *Just Lawyers — Seven Portraits*

Hamar Foster and John McLaren, eds., *Essays in the History of Canadian Law*, vol. 6, *British Columbia and the Yukon*

W.H. Morrow, ed., *Northern Justice, the Memoirs of Mr. Justice William G. Morrow*

Beverley Boissery, *A Deep Sense of Wrong: The Treason, Trials and Transportation to New South Wales of Lower Canadian Rebels after the 1838 Rebellion*

1996 Carol Wilton, ed., *Essays in the History of Canadian Law*, vol. 7, *Inside the Law: Canadian Law Firms in Historical Perspective*

William Kaplan, *Bad Judgment: The Case of Mr. Justice Leo A. Landreville*

Murray Greenwood and Barry Wright, eds., *Canadian State Trials*, vol. 1, *Law, Politics and Security Measures, 1608-1837*

1997 James W. St. G. Walker, *"Race," Rights and the Law in the Supreme Court of Canada: Historical Case Studies*

Lori Chambers, *Married Women and Property Law in Victorian Ontario*

Patrick Brode, *Casual Slaughters and Accidental Judgments, Canadian War Crimes and Prosecutions, 1944-1948*

Ian Bushnell, *The Federal Court of Canada: A History, 1875-1992*

1998 Sidney Harring, *White Man's Law: Native People in Nineteenth-Century Canadian Jurisprudence*

Peter Oliver, *"Terror to Evil-Doers": Prisons and Punishments in Nineteenth-Century Ontario*

1999 Constance Backhouse, *Colour-Coded: A Legal History of Racism in Canada, 1900-1950*

G. Blaine Baker and Jim Phillips, eds., *Essays in the History of Canadian Law*, vol. 8, *In Honour of R.C.B. Risk*

Richard W. Pound, *Chief Justice W.R. Jackett, by the Law of the Land*

David Vanek, *Fulfilment, Memoirs of a Criminal Court Judge*

2000 Barry Cahill, *"The Thousandth Man": A Biography of James McGregor Stewart*

A.B. McKillop, *The Spinster and the Prophet: Florence Deeks, H.G. Wells, and the Mystery of the Purloined Past*

Beverley Boissery and F. Murray Greenwood, *Uncertain Justice: Canadian Women and Capital Punishment*

Bruce Ziff, *Unforeseen Legacies: Reuben Wells Leonard and the Leonard Foundation Trust*

2001 Ellen Anderson, *Judging Bertha Wilson: Law As Large As Life*

Judy Fudge and Eric Tucker, *Labour before the Law: Collective Action in Canada, 1900-1948*

Laurel Sefton MacDowell, *Renegade Lawyer: The Life of J.L. Cohen*

2002 John T. Saywell, *The Law Makers: Judicial Power and the Shaping of Canadian Federalism*

David Murray, *Colonial Justice: Justice, Morality and Crime in the Niagara District, 1791-1849*

F. Murray Greenwood and Barry Wright, eds., *Canadian State Trials*, vol. 2, *Rebellion and Invasion in the Canadas, 1837-8*

Patrick Brode, *Courted and Abandoned: Seduction in Canadian Law*

2003 Robert Sharpe and Kent Roach, *Brian Dickson: A Judge's Journey*

George Finlayson, *John J. Robinette, Peerless Mentor*

Peter Oliver, *The Conventional Man: The Diaries of Ontario Chief Justice Robert A. Harrison, 1856-1878*

Jerry Bannister, *The Rule of the Admirals: Law, Custom and Naval Government in Newfoundland, 1699-1832*

2004 John D. Honsberger, *Osgoode Hall: An Illustrated History*

Frederick Vaughan, *Aggressive in Pursuit: The Life of Justice Emmett Hall*

Constance Backhouse and Nancy L. Backhouse, *The Heiress versus the Establishment: Mrs. Campbell's Campaign for Legal Justice*

Philip Girard, Jim Phillips, and Barry Cahill, *The Supreme Court of Nova Scotia, 1754-2004: From Imperial Bastion to Provincial Oracle*

LAW AND SOCIETY SERIES

W. Wesley Pue, General Editor

Gender in the Legal Profession: Fitting or Breaking the Mould
Joan Brockman

Regulating Lives:
Historical Essays on the State, Society, the Individual, and the Law
Edited by John McLaren, Robert Menzies,
and Dorothy E. Chunn

Taxing Choices:
The Intersection of Class, Gender, Parenthood, and the Law
Rebecca Johnson

Collective Insecurity:
The Liberian Crisis, Unilateralism, and Global Order
Ikechi Mgbeoji

Unnatural Law:
Rethinking Canadian Environmental Law and Policy
David R. Boyd

Murdering Holiness:
The Trials of Franz Creffield and George Mitchell
Jim Phillips and Rosemary Gartner

People and Place: Historical Influences on Legal Culture
Edited by Jonathan Swainger and Constance Backhouse

Compulsory Compassion:
A Critique of Restorative Justice
Annalise Acorn

Feminist Activism in the Supreme Court:
Legal Mobilization and the Women's Legal Education and Action Fund
Christopher P. Manfredi

LAW AND
SOCIETY